Climate Change Adaptation for Transportation Systems

Michael A. P. Taylor
Emeritus Professor of Transport Planning
University of South Australia, Adelaide,
SA, Australia

ELSEVIER

Elsevier
Radarweg 29, PO Box 211, 1000 AE Amsterdam, Netherlands
The Boulevard, Langford Lane, Kidlington, Oxford OX5 1GB, United Kingdom
50 Hampshire Street, 5th Floor, Cambridge, MA 02139, United States

Library of Congress Cataloging-in-Publication Data
A catalog record for this book is available from the Library of Congress

British Library Cataloguing-in-Publication Data
A catalogue record for this book is available from the British Library

ISBN: 978-0-12-816638-3

For information on all Elsevier publications visit our website at https://www.elsevier.com/books-and-journals

Publisher: Joe Hayton
Acquisitions Editor: Brian Romer
Editorial Project Manager: Andrae Akeh
Production Project Manager: Omer Mukthar
Cover Designer: Greg Harris

Typeset by TNQ Technologies

Climate Change Adaptation for Transportation Systems

To Amye,
who believes

Contents

Preface

I finished writing this book at the end of March 2020, after a labour of love spanning the previous 18 months, a little longer than the original proposed time line. Yet that extra time was actually most useful, for a large amount of relevant new material from both academic research and professional practice on climate change adaptation became available, throughout 2019 and in to 2020. The book is much enriched because of that. 2019 also saw a tremendous global buildup of interest, concern and calls for action on climate change. In my country, Australia, this then reached a crescendo in early 2020 as a brutal summer wreaked havoc in the form of heat waves leading to wildfires across large swathes of the nation. Fires starting at times of year never before experienced, taking hold in areas seldom experiencing wild fire in the past, of intensities never before recorded, and occurring simultaneously in so many places. Firefighting and emergency services were stretched: the modern cooperation between the services in the different states – sharing equipment, sending replacement fire crews for relief – could not occur because all were needed everywhere. In the words of one state fire chief, 'nature started these fires, only nature can put them out'. The realisation hit home, with politicians who had previously been at least 'climate change sceptics' openly stating that things were different, we had to change what we had been doing and how could we do that?

And then the COVID-19 pandemic took over and took all the world's attention. All else seems forgotten. Nations and states have mobilised quickly, introducing health, economic and social initiatives and actions to mitigate and hopefully, eventually, remove the threat. Some of these actions such as social isolation seem unprecedented, at least in modern times in modern democracies. Perhaps, this is understandable. There is a fire in the kitchen, so put the fire out. After that worry about the creeping erosion that may soon imperil the foundations of the house itself. That latter problem has not gone away, but time is of the essence for the former, and that requires all immediately available resources.

In the 21st century, climate change is that latter problem. Can the problem be solved, or at least mitigated? The 2016 Paris Agreement[1] suggests a possible pathway to this end:

1. See https://unfccc.int/process-and-meetings/the-paris-agreement/the-paris-agreement (accessed 30/03/2020).

(a) Holding the increase in the global average temperature to well below 2°C above preindustrial levels and to pursue efforts to limit the temperature increase to 1.5°C above preindustrial levels, recognising that this would significantly reduce the risks and impacts of climate change
(b) Increasing the ability to adapt to the adverse impacts of climate change and foster climate resilience and low greenhouse gas emissions development, in a manner that does not threaten food production
(c) Making finance flows consistent with a pathway towards low greenhouse gas emission and climate-resilient development.

The reality is that climate change is already with us: the Paris Agreement recognised that 'in the first half of 2016 average temperatures were about 1.3°C above the average in 1880, when global record-keeping began'. Indeed, 2019 was the second warmest year on record according to the US National Oceanic and Atmospheric Administration (NOAA).[2] The warmest year on record was 2016. The trend seems to continue; NOAA indicates that the Northern Hemisphere had its hottest January–February (2020) period since global records began in 1880, while the Southern Hemisphere had its second warmest such period, behind 2016. The five warmest years on record have all occurred in the period since 2015 and 9 of the 10 warmest years have occurred since 2005. Globally, the only 20th century year among the 10 warmest years on record is 1998, which ranks as the 10th warmest. All of the United Kingdom's 10 warmest years have occurred since 2002.[3] At the end of 2018, Europe's five hottest summers in 500 years had all occurred in the period 2004–2018,[4] and then 2019 was the hottest year on record for the continent.[5] The Australian Bureau of Meteorology states that 2019 was Australia's warmest year on record,[6] with the annual national mean temperature 1.52°C above average. It was also Australia's driest year on record, and there was widespread severe fire weather throughout 2019, with the national annual accumulated Forest Fire Danger Index at its highest level since 1950, when national records began. 9 of the 10 recorded hottest years in Australia have occurred in the 21st century (to 2019), with 8 of the 10 years in the decade 2010–19 being in that top ten (the exceptions are 2011 and 2012). This nation has left the 20th century well behind.

Statistically speaking, to continually observe new values in the extreme upper tail of the distribution of a random variable is a clear indication that something about that distribution has changed. This is the basis of quality control theory.

---

2. See https://www.noaa.gov/news/2019-was-2nd-hottest-year-on-record-for-earth-say-noaa-nasa (accessed 20/03/2020).
3. See https://www.bbc.com/news/science-environment-49167797 (accessed 20/03/2020)
4. See https://www.nationalgeographic.com/environment/2019/europe-has-had-five-500-year-summers-in-15-years/ (accessed 20/03/2020)
5. See https://www.euractiv.com/section/climate-environment/news/last-year-was-europes-hottest-ever-eu-data-shows/ (accessed 20/03/2020)
6. See http://www.bom.gov.au/climate/current/annual/aus/ (accessed 20/03/2020).

Statistical distributions of temperature and the effects of climate change are discussed in Chapter 2 of this book. Thus, while climate change mitigation is wholly laudable and should be pursued vigorously, the reality is that climate change is already with us and so we must adapt to the new and emerging climate situation. This is the topic pursued in this book, with the focus on the transportation systems, modes, networks and infrastructure that facilitate economic and social activity. Transportation is a major contributor to greenhouse gas emissions – Chapter 9 indicates that some 25%–30% of global emissions come from transportation, and that this sector is one where emissions continue to increase. As is discussed throughout this book, global warming, which can be attributed to the increases in greenhouse gas emissions, is a major factor in affecting the operational and engineering performance of transportation systems and infrastructure. The changes that are occurring are thus challenges that policymakers and the managers and planners of transportation systems must address. Whatever efforts we make in mitigation, climate change cannot be turned off. It is the reality for the foreseeable future. Climate and environment have always been factors considered in planning and designing transportation infrastructure, but in the past, we have been able to use current and historical knowledge for this. This is no longer possible, and indeed, the further we look into the future, the less certain we can be about the climate in which our infrastructure is situated. Climate change adaptation has thus to consider climate uncertainties, probably by utilising a set of alternative scenarios for future climate.

Climate change is a long-term trend, so we need to look some way into the future. The end of this century might be taken as a convenient way station, at least for the present. Considerations of physical infrastructure assets and their design and effective lives must influence our decisions on appropriate planning horizons. Transportation infrastructure such as road pavements and rail tracks are actually designed to wear out and so need refurbishment or replacement at some time in the future. Other assets such as bridges also have finite useful lives. A sweeping generalisation might suggest lives of 25 years for pavements, 50 years for tracks and 100 years for bridges. What this means is that much of the new infrastructure installed in the present will be operating during the time spans envisaged for concern over climate change. The new infrastructure therefore requires to be designed and constructed with climate change in mind. The maintenance regimes for this infrastructure will also need attention to meet the changing environment. In addition, existing infrastructure assets must also be accounted for, and perhaps the considerations here are more important – or perhaps more stressful – because that infrastructure was designed and constructed in the past using the design parameters of the time. How to maintain, rehabilitate and retrofit that infrastructure becomes the important question. The uncertainties of climate change must also be considered amongst with other uncertainties, such as technological change and social change, which may place new demands (e.g., higher axle loads on bridges and pavements or new travel demands) on the existing infrastructure and on new infrastructure. Planning under uncertainty requires particular attention to risk management: what are the risk events that may be foreseen, how likely is any particular event to occur and what is the likely impact of that event on affected assets? Conceptually, risk in this situation is the product of the probability of an event and its expected impact. Managing risks involves both this analysis of potential outcomes and decisions about how to anticipate and cope with these outcomes. The decisions may require us to justify our existing practices and approaches to the management of transportation infrastructure, consider the extent to which existing practices can be modified or refined to cope with the changing situation and whether there is need and opportunity to look at alternative practices that may be better suited to the emerging situation. We will also need to study carefully the physical phenomena that will be the manifestation of climate change and which will impact on our infrastructure assets.

This book attempts to provide an overall account of the needs for climate change adaptation for transportation infrastructure and the potential methods for that adaptation that will be of use to transportation agencies and their managers. Three underlying themes provide the basis for its content. The first theme is that while adaptation can include the improvement or refinement of existing practices – extending and honing the skills and expertise and corporate knowledge inherent in an agency – adaptation options must also include considerations of changing practices as well, i.e., not just doing things better but doing different things. Alternative practices may be found in a variety of ways, for example, through innovations using new technologies or by studying the practices of those in other regions, where the present climate of those regions may provide some kind of analogue to the future climate of the home region. The second theme is the importance of adopting best practice risk management techniques and the development of adaptation frameworks and pathways, accompanied by the introduction, development, implementation and use of decision support tools that account for uncertainty and the mix of short- and long-term impacts on transportation system performance. The decision support tools may be based on or similar to those already in use but must be able to properly consider these factors. These two themes may be considered as general requirements in adaptation planning for any infrastructure system. The third theme may be more specific to transportation. This theme concerns the climate factor perhaps of most importance to the performance of transportation infrastructure. Climate change at the global scale means global warming, as the discussion earlier in this piece has outlined. Temperature is the obvious climate factor in this regard. While temperature rise will play its part in affecting the performance of transportation infrastructure (e.g., in the case of rail track buckling, see Chapter 8), in terms of the natural phenomena affecting transportation systems and themselves affected by climate change, it is water, in its many guises, that will play the major role in the degradation and limitation of the performance of transportation facilities, assets and systems. Sea level rise, storm surges, groundwater rise, changing patterns of precipitation, rain storm intensity, flooding and inundation and freezing and thawing cycles all are manifestations of water and all stand to be affected by a changing climate.

The future task for transportation agencies is to keep their infrastructure and systems climate resilient, able to serve the communities, societies and economies in their jurisdictions. This is essential in maintaining efficient and safe transportation operations and should reduce – or help prevent excessive increases in – future costs such as congestion, delays, service disruption, supply chain disruption and severance. On the demand side, ensuring resilience will require transportation policies, plans and incentives for travel behaviour changes by the community, as part of wider climate change mitigation initiatives. On the supply side, climate change adaptation is the essential concern for transportation agencies. Existing infrastructure may require rehabilitation, refurbishment or retrofitting to make it more adaptable, along with new methods for the management and maintenance of the infrastructure. Planning and design methods will require review, evaluation and revision. New infrastructure will need to be planned, designed, constructed, maintained and operated to accommodate the shifts in climate that may occur over the operational lives of the infrastructure assets. Monitoring and review are key considerations in the adaptation learning process that transportation agencies will have to adopt. Climate-resilient infrastructure should then offer improved service reliability, increased asset life and protection for asset returns. Given the uncertainties that still surround potential climate change at the local or regional level, flexible and adaptive approaches are required in the provision and operation of infrastructure. The uncertainties – which in the long term include social and technological change as well as climate change – need to be recognised and accepted, even if they cannot be adequately described. This will provide the means to ensure resilience across a range of future climate scenarios. Policy analysts and decision-makers require access to high-quality information, comprehensive data collection, consistent and expanding databases, increasing knowledge and deepening understanding of the impacts of climate change and suitable analytical techniques to ensure informed planning and decision-making. This access to information needs to be complemented by the development of technical and institutional capacities to manage climate-related risks. This book is intended to provide guidance towards this achievement.

There are many people whom I must thank for their support, guidance and advice, which helped me learn about the subject and gather the information for this book. My friends and colleagues in ACCARNSI (the Australian Climate Change Adaptation Research Network for Settlements and Infrastructure), especially Ron Cox, Tamara Rouse and Rodger Tomlinson, were an invaluable source of knowledge and support, through mutual learning. To Rodger in particular, I offer a special vote of thanks for enlightening me about coastal engineering and for providing me with the core information that I drew on in writing Chapter 6. In the International Transport Forum of OECD, Philippe Crist and my colleagues in the International Working Group on Infrastructure Adaptation to Extreme Weather and Climate Change deserve special recognition and thanks. My research assistant Michelle Philp worked tirelessly in our projects on road pavement performance and was always able to find the information that we needed. Likewise, my PhD student Ivan Iankov contributed strongly in the area of mathematical modelling of road pavement performance. Raluca Raicu, Peter Pudney and Phil Howlett stimulated my interest in rail transportation and the modelling of rail systems. My interactions with Pongrid Klungboonkrong and Hussein Dia on land use transport integration and sustainable transportation stood me in good stead for Chapter 9, as did the opportunity to work again with Peter Newton, my close colleague from the early days of our research careers and now again in the latter years too, on urban design and low carbon precincts. Working with Andrew Beer on the South Australian Transect project for climate change adaptation was both invaluable and rewarding and provided important insights used in this book. Nicholas Holyoak and Rocco Zito helped me learn about greenhouse gas emission from transportation sources, and our joint work pointed the way to the formulation of a methodology for including climate factors in performance modelling for transportation infrastructure. Brian Romer and Andrae Akeh at Elsevier deserve my sincere thanks: to Brian for the opportunity to write this book and to Andrae for his patience, perseverance, advice and guidance as the writing progressed, sometimes faster than other times. Thanks to both of them for their constant support and encouragement during the authoring process and thanks also to the always efficient yet understanding production staff at Elsevier. Finally to my wife Marg, my inspiration and guiding light always, for her encouragement and support throughout this endeavour.

This book aims to assist in defining and meeting the challenges faced by those whose responsibility is in planning and managing our transportation systems, adapting them to meet our changing climate. We will depend on these people in the coming years, and I hope that this work proves useful to them.

Michael A. P. Taylor
Hindmarsh Island
March 2020

Chapter 1

Introduction

Transportation systems face many challenges. Some of these are ongoing, such as the need to provide efficient and reliable services to meet growing demands. Others are new. Climate change is an example, providing a new raft of challenges for transportation network and infrastructure owners, managers and operators. The reality and potential global impacts of climate change have been discussed widely, and the ongoing studies by the UN International Panel on Climate Change (IPCC) continue to provide indications of the implications of climate change on natural and manmade systems. The latest report by the IPCC (IPCC 2018) discussed the current trends in global warming and the likely relative impacts of increases in global mean surface temperature of 1.5 and 2°C. It concludes that mean temperatures in most land and sea regions will increase, with extreme high temperatures increasing more than the mean values. Numbers of hot days will increase in most land regions, with the highest increases in the tropics. Risks from droughts and rainfall deficits will be higher in some regions, although risks from extreme rainfall events will also increase, especially in East Asia and eastern North America. Tropical cyclones (hurricanes and typhoons) will bring more heavy rainfall. Flood hazards are likely to affect more areas. Sea level rise will continue beyond 2100 even if global warming is limited to 1.5°C.

Why are these forecasts of concern for transportation systems? The simple answer is that transportation infrastructure and the services that use it are strongly affected by high temperatures, high rainfall, extreme weather events, floods, droughts and sea level rise. This is well known – climate has impacts on transportation. The point of concern is a changing climate. Whereas past and existing practices have been cognisant of climate impacts, a changing climate changes the circumstances affecting a given region and its ambient environment. Thus, the old rules and practices for transportation systems operation may no longer be appropriate, and alternatives will be needed. Perhaps these alternatives can be found by considering other regions where hotter, drier or wetter conditions have been experienced before, but perhaps

Climate Change Adaptation for Transportation Systems. https://doi.org/10.1016/B978-0-12-816638-3.00001-5

this is not always possible, or relevant, or even valid. A theme throughout this book is the idiom 'not doing the same but better, but doing differently'. The primary challenge for transportation systems is the determination of what will change and how the changes can be managed in terms of ongoing service provision.

In a wider sense, climate change has other relationships with transportation, for transportation is a major source of carbon emissions, for example, through the combustion of the liquid fossil fuels that still provide the bulk of the energy required for transportation. Here is the question of climate change mitigation: urban planners and transportation engineers work steadily on new policies and plans that can integrate land use and transportation, change transport technologies and modify travel behaviour (by providing closer destinations and alternative transport modes) with the aim of reducing carbon emissions. Mitigation is not the subject of this book, although Chapter 9 is concerned with active transport – walking and cycling – and urban design which can contribute to mitigating the carbon emissions from transport. Climate change mitigation for transportation is dealt with by others, see, for instance, Sperling and Cannon (2006), Givoni and Banister (2013), Nakamura and Hayashi (2013), Philp and Taylor (2017) and Dia (2017). Rather, the subject here is adaptation, exploring the needs and opportunities for transportation system managers to adapt their strategies, plans and practices to meet the challenges of a different operating environment driven by changes in climate, both presently apparent and future forecast.

Risk management is a crucial concern for system managers. This is especially true when contemplating future developments such as climate change, where the actual level of change and the likely impacts of the change involve high degrees of uncertainty. The prudent manager cannot ignore the possibilities, yet the levels of resources and activity required to account for the potential developments may be so significant as to require wholesale reorganisation and repositioning of the agencies involved in the system management, with major implications for policy determination and governance. Planning for adaptation is not easy. Risk management is thus a second theme for this book.

A proper understanding of current risks and of likely future risks is absolutely essential for infrastructure management. Risk management further raises the need for evaluation frameworks under which systematic consideration of transportation systems operations and infrastructure planning can be conducted. Evaluation leads further into economic analysis of infrastructure performance, suitability of and priorities for new projects and optimum effectiveness of maintenance systems. Existing economic analysis tools, such as benefit–cost analysis (BCA), may need adaptation or supplementation under climate change regimes. This is because the time scales involved with climate change phenomena may stretch beyond the typical periods in which BCA is 'sensitive' to time streams of discounted cash flows (e.g., 5–15 years) but are still commensurate with the engineering/economic life of infrastructure components (e.g., road pavement 15–30 years, bridges 80–100 years). Including environmental effects into economic analysis is also challenging, although great progress has been made in recent times (e.g., see OECD (2018)). In addition, the question of uncertainty in the estimation of the future values of parameters for use in economic analysis is important, and seen by some as a stumbling block. The use of multicriteria analysis (MCA) as an alternative approach is suggested in some quarters, but strongly resisted in others. Some researchers and analysts propose alternative methods such as robust decision-making (RDM), e.g., Kwakkel et al. (2016), or real options analysis (ROA), e.g., Skourtos et al. (2016). The issues of risk management, evaluation frameworks and pathways and evaluation methods are considered throughout the following chapters of this book, and especially in Chapters 3–5.

Another recurrent theme under the umbrella of climate change is the impact of water on the condition and performance of transportation infrastructure. Whether in penetration into pavement structures, corrosion of steel components, scour at bridges, flooding of roadways, sea level rise or other factors, water is an ongoing concern for network managers. Changing climatic conditions will change the extent and intensity of water-related phenomena in a region and on its transportation systems.

What is climate change adaptation?

There are many different definitions of adaptation, depending on the area of application (e.g., from theory to practice) and on the geographical region of the origin of the definition. The definitions also range from the general to quite specific. For instance, VCCCAR (2018) provided the following set of definitions:

- 'Actions taken to help communities and ecosystems cope with changing climate conditions' (UNFCCC–UN Framework Convention on Climate Change)
- 'Adjustment in natural or human systems in response to actual or expected climatic stimuli or their effects, which moderates harm or exploits beneficial opportunities' (IPCC)
- 'A process by which strategies to moderate, cope with and take advantage of the consequences of climatic events are enhanced, developed and implemented' (UN Development Program)
- 'The process or outcome of a process that leads to a reduction in harm or risk of harm, or realisation of benefits associated with climate variability and climate change' (UK Climate Impacts program)

- 'Actions undertaken to reduce the adverse consequences of climate change, as well as to harness any beneficial opportunities' (NCCARF, the Australian National Climate Change Adaptation Research Facility)
- 'Taking deliberate and considered actions to avoid, manage or reduce the consequences of a hotter, drier and more extreme climate and to take advantage of the opportunities that such changes may generate' (State Government of Victoria).

These definitions not only show a range of scopes for application but they also portray a number of common features. They suggest the need for a systematic and considered approach to adjustments in plans and methods, designed to minimise any potential harmful effects on human-based systems from changes in climatic conditions. They also indicate that there may be beneficial impacts from a changing climate, and that these should be exploited where possible.

For the European Union (EU 2018), adaptation is defined as anticipation of the adverse effects of climate change and implementation of appropriate plans and actions to prevent or minimise the damage that may result, or that take advantage of opportunities that may arise from climate change. The EU asserts that well-planned early adaptation action saves money and lives in the future. As a supranational organisation, the EU has implemented an adaptation strategy to complement the activities of its member states and encourages coordination and information sharing between those states. It recognises that adaptation plans are needed at all levels of government, from the local, regional, national and international levels. In the case of Europe, climate impacts stand to be of varying severity and nature across the continent, so that adaptation initiatives will need to be taken at the regional or local levels, supported by resources made available from the higher levels. There is also the situation that the ability of different regions to cope and adapt differs across populations, economic sectors and geographical regions. The direct role of an organisation such as the EU is of most importance when climate change impacts transcend the borders of individual states, such as in the case of river basins.

Schmidt-Thomé (2017) provided further consideration of the nature of adaptation, drawing on the work of the IPCC. On the basis that adaptation may be seen as a process of adjustment to actual or expected climate change and the ensuing effects from that change, adaptation in manmade systems seeks to moderate or avoid harm and exploit beneficial opportunities. In some natural systems, human intervention may also facilitate adjustment to expected climate and its effects. This then leads to consideration of two types of adaptation:

1. *Incremental adaptation*, in which the main aim of the adaptation action is to maintain system nature and integrity at a given scale
2. *Transformational adaptation*, in which the fundamental attributes of the system are changed in response to climate effects.

For the purposes of the discussion presented in this book, climate change adaptation is taken to be the anticipation of the potential adverse effect of climate change and the formulation of strategies, policies and action plans to prevent or ameliorate the impact of those adverse effects, or take advantage of opportunities that may arise, to ensure the safe, efficient and equitable provision and operations of a transportation system.

Critical infrastructure

Functioning infrastructure systems are essential for modern societies. These systems provide us with energy, water, telecommunications and transportation, and they remove solid and liquid wastes. Our economic, financial and social activities all depend on infrastructure systems, networks and the services they offer. Transportation and communications infrastructure systems are also vital in dealing with emergencies and disaster relief, including considerations of population evacuation, the ability of emergency services to reach an affected area and individual locations within it and to ensure the necessary coordination of rescue and humanitarian resources required. The provision, management, upkeep and maintenance of infrastructure is a major task for governments and the private sector alike, and society expects these systems to be fit for purpose, adequately provided and provisioned, and available as required, if not 'on demand'. Failure or service degradation in an infrastructure system can have significant impacts on economic and social activities. Flows of information, personal mobility and the physical movement of goods all require infrastructure systems, and indeed there are interdependencies between systems that are of concern. Failures can be localised, regional or global – affecting an entire system – but even localised failures are significant for the individuals and enterprises affected.

Some infrastructure systems are deemed to be 'critical', which in broad terms means that they are so important to a community or society that they need to be designed, managed and protected to minimise the opportunity that they will fail or become unavailable. Transportation systems certainly fall into this category, as do energy, water and telecommunications systems. The chance of failure or significant degradation can never be completely eliminated, and so the resilience of a system – its ability to be reinstated, to recover or to 'bounce back' in a short period of time – is of interest. Infrastructure system failure, resilience and criticality are all issues that can be addressed using vulnerability analysis (Taylor, 2017). In particular, the identification of specific elements, locations and facilities most at risk in a particular infrastructure system is a key task providing vital inputs into system planning, design and management.

From the perspective of the managers of transportation systems, the definition of critical infrastructure provided by the American Society of Civil Engineers (ASCE) provides a firm basis for determination of needs, priorities and responsibilities. For the ASCE, the focus is on specific infrastructure systems, and how they should be planned, designed and operated. Thus, ASCE (2009) defines critical infrastructure as

> *Critical infrastructure includes systems, facilities, and assets so vital that their destruction or incapacitation would have a debilitating impact on national security, the economy, or public safety, health, or welfare. Critical infrastructure may cross political boundaries and may be built, natural, or virtual. Built critical infrastructure includes energy; water and wastewater treatment, distribution, and collection; transportation; and communications systems. Natural critical infrastructure systems include lakes, rivers, and streams that are used for navigation, water supply, or flood water storage, as well as coastal wetlands that provide a buffer for storm surges. Virtual critical infrastructure includes cyber, electronic, and information systems.*

To use this definition in practice, the ASCE developed a set of interrelated guiding principles for the protection of public safety, health and welfare to be used in the management of critical infrastructure:

1. *Quantify, communicate and manage risk*, where risk management is the application of a systematic process for identifying, analysing, planning, monitoring and responding to risk so that critical infrastructure will meet service expectations. For the purposes of the guiding principles, risk is defined as product of the probability that an event may occur and the magnitude of consequences that would result from that event
2. *Employ an integrated systems approach.* Critical infrastructure requires planning, funding, design, construction and operation as a system, appropriately integrated with all other interdependent systems. Critical infrastructure systems must also be resilient and sustainable throughout the system's life cycle. The systems must be properly maintained, operated and modified as necessary to perform effectively under changing conditions
3. *Exercise sound leadership, management and stewardship in decision-making processes*, given that the long-term viability of any critical infrastructure system, irrespective of its resilience and sustainability, will ultimately rely on the human and organisational stewardship applied to the system. Effective organisations can control program outcomes through technical oversight, coordination with related projects and activities, appropriate control and change management and effective communication with project stakeholders. In the absence of sound leadership and management of critical infrastructure, the safety, health and welfare of the public are placed at risk
4. *Adapt critical infrastructure in response to dynamic conditions and practice.* Critical infrastructure systems generally have long life cycles, spanning decades. These projects are normally designed to meet expected performance levels deemed appropriate at the time of design. However,

conditions continually evolve and change, and system managers must adopt change management systems that can effectively address new conditions. Change management systems need to be flexible and robust, and must establish discipline in the way critical infrastructure systems are operated, reviewed, maintained and upgraded throughout their life cycle.

The guiding principles provide the high-level advice on how those responsible for infrastructure systems should fulfil their duties. A clear example of the recognition of those requirements and their application is shown by the US Federal Highways Administration (FHWA) in its framework for assessing the vulnerability of road systems to climate change and extreme weather (FHWA 2018). This framework and its application are discussed in Chapter 4.

Consideration of risk is an important feature, with risk being taken to represent to overall product of the probability of a failure in a system, at a specific location, and the consequences of such a failure. Management of risk is a key part of climate change adaptation for transportation. The topic is a major theme running through this book. Risk management in an infrastructure system requires consideration of vulnerability and resilience.

A more detailed treatment of critical transportation infrastructure and the identification of critical components of that infrastructure is given in Taylor (2017). Evaluation methods and frameworks for identifying transportation facilities and locations at risk from a changing climate are addressed in Chapter 4.

Transportation and society

Functioning infrastructure systems are essential for modern societies. These systems provide us with energy, water, telecommunications and transportation, and they remove solid and liquid wastes. Our economic, financial and social activities all depend on infrastructure systems, networks and the services they offer. The previous section on critical infrastructure indicated some of the specific requirements of transportation systems in serving society, notably their role in responses to emergencies and disaster relief.

The provision, management, upkeep and maintenance of infrastructure is a major task for governments and the private sector alike, and society expects these systems to be fit for purpose, adequately provided and provisioned, and available as required, if not 'on demand'. Failure or service degradation in a transportation system can have significant impacts on economic and social activities in a region. Societal expectations are that transportation systems are always available for use and kept in acceptably good states of serviceability. Modern societies demand high levels of mobility independent of environmental conditions, in all but the most severe weather conditions. Transportation system managers are charged with meeting these expectations, both in the present and in the future. Flows of information, personal mobility and the physical movement of goods all require infrastructure systems, and indeed there are interdependencies between systems that are of concern.

The concept of 'level of service' is a key factor in setting the operational expectations for transportation networks and systems. Level of service is a designation of what are considered to be reasonable travelling and operating conditions to be experienced by system users. For instance, highway engineers have long used the level of service concept to set design values for traffic volumes, which may be much less than the physical capacity of the road but ensure smooth traffic operations under normal conditions (TRB 2016). Here the main concerns for road design are to provide a given minimum average travel speed that can be maintained by vehicles in a traffic stream and avoid flow breakdowns and consequent 'stop–start' traffic congestion. In broader terms, this implies a demand–supply equilibrium between the provision of transport capacity and the travel demand seeking to use that capacity. Level of service parameters (such as a design traffic volume per lane for a road) is used to establish the minimum level of operating conditions for the infrastructure component that should apply over a reasonable spectrum of the demand to use the component (i.e., for all but the most extreme cases of demand). Level of service is a realisation that it is not possible to cater for all levels of demand, but that reasonable operating conditions should occur for most of the time. For instance, the notion of the 'highest hourly volume' has been part of traffic design (TRB, 2016). This condition would identify a design traffic volume on the basis that this was the volume only exceeded in n hours of the year – with n typically taken as 80 in urban areas and 30 in rural areas. This would mean a design traffic volume for an urban road would be one only exceeded in 80 separate hours during a year, i.e., roughly three times a fortnight.

Travel speed and travel time would be the factors generally determining a level of service state. Speed and travel time can be affected by many factors besides traffic volume, with infrastructure-related factors such as pavement condition, road and track roughness, pavement and lane width, gradients and exposure to cross winds being prominent. All of these factors may be impacted by climate change.

Transportation infrastructure owners and managers are responsible for maintaining transportation systems in good operating condition, suitable for the designed levels of service for which the system was planned, given an assumed level of demand for usage to be met at some time (planning horizon) in the future. The planning, design and maintenance of the infrastructure has to take account of the environmental and climatic conditions pertaining to the locations of the various assets that form part of the infrastructure system. Climate change can pose a significant risk to the infrastructure and its owners, managers and long-term operators because the changes may affect both the structural integrity of assets and their ability to provide the required or planned level of service. All assets have a limited useful lifespan. For road pavements, this may be 2–3 decades, for bridges it may be several decades (if not centuries). These lifespans are such that climate change may have real impacts on both existing and proposed future assets.

A number of likely impacts of climate change on transportation infrastructure may be identified. These include

- Increased ground movement and changes in groundwater (and water tables) may lead to accelerated degradation of materials, foundations and structures
- Increased temperature and solar radiation could reduce the life of asphaltic road surfaces and airport tarmacs, as well as increased or new stresses on steel components of bridges and rail track, due to increases in expansion and contraction
- Increased temperature may also cause expansion of concrete joints, protective cladding, coatings and sealants on bridges, and port and airport infrastructure
- Increased frequency and intensity of extreme rainfall events may lead to significant flood damage to transportation infrastructure. In addition, rails, bridges, ports and airports may be susceptible to extreme wind events, while coastal infrastructure and ports face additional risks when storm surges combine with sea level rise.

These factors are all indications of the need for systems managers to pay particular heed to climate change in the planning and design of new infrastructure, in consideration of asset maintenance programs, and in assessment of the needs for rehabilitation, replacement or relocation of existing infrastructure assets.

Governance arrangements for transportation infrastructure systems may also need adaptation for climate change. The impacts and risks highlighted above represent a significant governance challenge for infrastructure owners, managers and decision makers. Decision-making challenges arise for the design, construction and management of infrastructure. The challenges are further compounded by the long lifespans for infrastructure components and assets, and the restricted capability to modify or amend fundamental design parameters once the infrastructure has been constructed. Infrastructure owners and managers must ensure that any infrastructure component must ensure that it is designed to operate effectively at the designated level of service throughout its design life. That is not to say that others involved in the design, financing, construction and regulation of infrastructure do not share in the responsibility for ensuring that level of operation, consistent with their area of expertise and any statutory obligations they face.

Risk and uncertainty

For transportation system managers, climate change adaptation can be seen through the prism of risk management, as indicated previously. A changing climate may lead to changes of the physical environment in which a given transportation system exists and operates. The assets of the system may become more or less susceptible to environmental damage or degradation, or suffer a change in capability to offer transport service at the specified or required level of service. System managers thus need to assess the risks associated with these changes in their planning for the ongoing operation and maintenance of the system.

Risk can be defined in many different ways, but most definitions focus on two factors: the probability that an event with negative impacts will occur, and the extent and severity of the resultant consequences of that event. Commonly, the product of probability and a measure of consequence (impact) is used as an index of risk. This may be shown schematically as a 'risk matrix', as in Fig. 1.1.

In concept the expected value (risk) of an event A with probability of occurrence $\Pr\{A\}$ of magnitude (consequence) $X(A)$ can be written as

$$E(A) = \Pr\{A\}X(A) \tag{1.1}$$

This value may be used in comparisons of different events possible in a given environment. Commonly, the consequence $X(A)$ is expressed in monetary terms, involving first an estimation of the physical size of the impact (e.g., the area of land inundated in a flood of a given magnitude) and then an estimation of the cost borne because of that level of flooding (e.g., size of crop destroyed or the number of houses inundated). In addition, a third factor may be brought into the risk equation. This is 'risk proximity', at what point in time

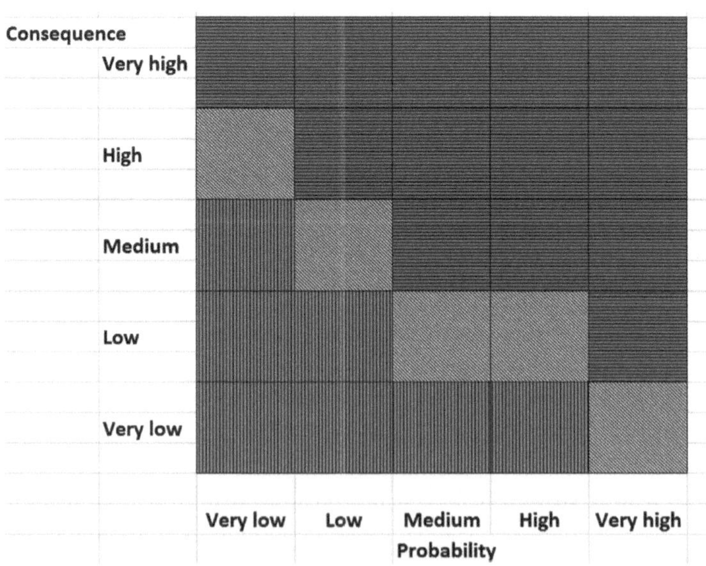

FIGURE 1.1 Conceptual risk matrix.

will the risk be manifest? For instance, if the risk (e.g., sea level rise above a certain height) will occur after the end of the engineering life of an asset (e.g., a road along a beach front), then this risk could be disregarded with respect to the existing asset – it might have an impact on the replacement for the asset. Under a changing scenario when that sea level rise is brought forward, as could occur under climate change, then a different assessment of the risk to the asset would be called for.

A general definition of risk can be expressed as follows: risk refers to a future event, or set of events, with a probability of occurrence and the potential for consequences from that event (set). This also provides for a distinction between risk and uncertainty: risk is for cases where we can estimate the probability of the event (e.g., we have a statistical distribution or a mathematical model that defines the probability), whereas uncertainty applies when the probability of the event is unknown (and there is no known distribution or model describing that probability). Another way of looking at the somewhat subtle difference between risk and uncertainty is to muse over the famous quotation from former US Defense Secretary Donald Rumsfeld: 'There are known knows; that is to say there are things we know that we know. There are known unknowns; that is to say there are things that we know we don't know. But there are also unknown unknowns, i.e., things we do not know that we don't know'.

Risk management is a part of management practice involved with the exploration of potential risks and the assessment of those risks to ascertain what plans of action are appropriate to deal with the contingency that the risk will occur. Attitudes to risk also feature in risk management. This is because emotion and subjectivity will often feature in the formulation of plans. In essence, we could picture individuals and organisations as lying somewhere on a spectrum from risk-averse to risk-seeking. Risk-aversion perceives risk as something to be avoided, while risk-seeking looks for opportunities that may arise from a high-risk situation. A generalisation would be that risk aversion is perhaps more common, but the risk spectrum would suggest that the (potential adverse) consequences of the risk have an important part to play in acceptance of a risk. If the consequence can be borne without catastrophic loss, then the risk may be worth taking. Risk management does not always mean avoidance of risk. Rather it is a process for assessing the level of risk and planning to mitigate against the bad consequences of the risk. Adaptation to climate change fits well into an umbrella of risk management.

Risk analysis is mostly concerned with the top-right quadrant of the matrix in Fig. 1.1, where increasing probability and increasing consequences combine. Risks with low probability but high impact are often viewed as far more severe than those with a high probability and low impact. Nicholson and Dalziell (2003) applied this framework to the risk assessment of transport networks in New Zealand. They measured risk as simply the sum of the products of the event probabilities and the economic costs of the event (e.g., the expected annual economic cost of a given event). Their risk evaluation process involved the following steps:

1. Establish the context (i.e., the technical, financial, legal, social and other criteria for assessing the acceptability of risk)
2. Identify the hazards (i.e., the potential causes of closure)
3. Analyse the risks (i.e., identify the probabilities, consequences and expectations)
4. Assess the risks (i.e., decide which risks are acceptable and which are unacceptable).

If any risk is found unacceptable, it needs to be managed. This generally involves either (a) treating the unacceptable risks, using the most cost-effective treatment options, or (b) monitoring and reviewing the risks (i.e., evaluating and revising treatments).

A more general view of risk management as a systematic process for identifying, analysing and responding to risks is given by the following fice-step risk management model:

1. Risk identification
2. Qualitative risk analysis
3. Quantitative risk assessment
4. Risk response planning
5. Risk monitoring and control.

Risk identification is concerned with explicit definition of the range and scope of the risk environment in which a system is operating. This includes identification of the various sources of risk for the system and the factors that give arise to a risk.

Qualitative risk analysis is the process of prioritising the identified risks in terms of their seriousness and timeliness. This process helps to determine where the systems manager should focus attention and resources. This includes indications of the capability of the system (or organisation) to cope with a given risk event of a given magnitude.

Quantitative risk assessment is the next stage in the process, involving estimation of the probability of a particular risk event, at a given point in time, and the likely magnitude of the event (i.e., its consequence). Whenever possible the scale of the consequence would be assessed in financial terms. This allows for trade offs in resource allocation to meet the risk, using established economic appraisal techniques such as BCA.

Given the results from the quantitative assessment, the prioritisation of the risks can be refined and a response for dealing with the risk developed. Response may include (1) risk avoidance, in which the circumstances that would lead to the risk occurring are prevented (if possible), (2) risk mitigation, in which attempts are made to reduce the probability or impact of the risk, (3) risk transference, in which the consequence of the risk is moved to a third party (presumably better equipped to deal with it), (4) risk deferral, when the circumstances leading to the risk can be manipulated so that the risk is put off to a time when its consequences will be smaller, or the probability of the risk is reduced, and (5) risk acceptance, when the risk is dealt with by contingency measures (prepared in advance) when it occurs.

Not all of these five responses are always available, especially when the risk eventuates from external sources, such as the environment, extreme weather or world politics!

Risk monitoring and control is involved with keeping track of the identified risks, monitoring the effectiveness of the measures put in place as risk responses, and looking out for new or changed risks. Hence, the process of risk management is an ongoing one.

Vulnerability analysis as described in Taylor (2017) refined this risk assessment framework in several important ways pertinent to transportation systems. Firstly, it extended the region of interest to areas of high consequences and low or unquantifiable (but nonzero) probability of occurrence – on the basis that measurement of occurrence probability and consequences (human and economic) is imprecise for many types of incidents, and society may well consider some consequences to be unacceptable and worthy of safeguarding against, despite uncertainty about their probability of occurrence. Secondly, vulnerability analysis provides a framework for targeting risk assessment. One of the key conclusions of the Nicholson–Dalziell risk assessment of the New Zealand highway network was that it is impractical and financially infeasible to conduct detailed geophysical and other risk assessment across an entire transport network (Nicholson and Dalziell, 2003). The costs of deriving accurate location-specific risk probabilities across a range of risk factors are too high to make it viable – what is needed is a way of targeting risk assessment resources to get best value from them. Vulnerability analysis provides another way of approaching this problem. It can be used to find component weaknesses in the transportation network that render the network vulnerable to consequences of failure or degradation. Resources can then be targeted at assessing these 'weak links'. Thirdly, vulnerability auditing admits a more proactive and targeted approach to the issue of transport network risk assessment and remediation. This is particularly important in networks liable to damage or degradation through climate change, and hence is a key concern in adaptation for the network.

Adaptation planning principles

What guidance can be suggested for managers seeking to implement adaptation programs? There are several attempts to provide guidelines and planning principles that may be applied to this issue, e.g., Environment Australia (2015), FHWA (2018), NCCARF (2012) and PIARC (2015), amongst others. Common elements in all of the principle sets tend to include (1) recognition of shared responsibilities for adaptation plans and actions, (2) the include of climate change risks in decision-making, (3) requirements for evidence-based risk management and (4) ongoing monitoring and evaluation of adaptation programs, including awareness of changing circumstances and new, arising issues. Integration is also a major issue in understanding needs for adaptation and the implementation of adaptation plans.

A useful espousal of principles for adaptation planning was provided by Prutsch et al. (2010). In particular, their list of ten guiding principles for adaptation indicated the major linkages between some of the principles, and thus how the principles could operate as an integrated set. The ten principles are

1. Initiate adaptation, ensure commitment and management
2. Build knowledge and awareness
3. Identify and cooperate with relevant stakeholders
4. Work with uncertainties
5. Explore potential climate change impacts and vulnerabilities and identify priority concerns
6. Explore a wide spectrum of adaptation options
7. Prioritise adaptation options
8. Modify existing policies, structures and processes
9. Avoid maladaptation
10. Monitor and evaluate systematically.

These principles may be seen in the context of three broad stages within the adaptation process: planning, implementation and evaluation. Fig. 1.2 maps the ten principles into these stages.

The first four principles span each stage of the adaptation process. Principle no 5 (exploring climate change impacts) applies in the planning stage only, while monitoring and evaluation (Principle 10) applies once implementation has begun.

A rationale can be provided for each principle. This also indicates the direct connections between some of the principles. Fig. 1.3 provides a graphical representation of the connections between specific guiding principles.

Initiate adaptation, ensure commitment and management

In general, climate change adaptation processes begin with the activities of motivated individuals. Many organisations, regions and sectors may start with low priorities for implementing adaptation, so that the motivated individuals need to act as drivers of the processes and as orchestrators of a growing movement for adaptation. Given that climate change has wide-ranging effects across society, the adaptation process requires a governance dimension involving cooperation between individuals, sections and organisations (i.e., stakeholders), and hence this first principle links to Principle no 3. A clear

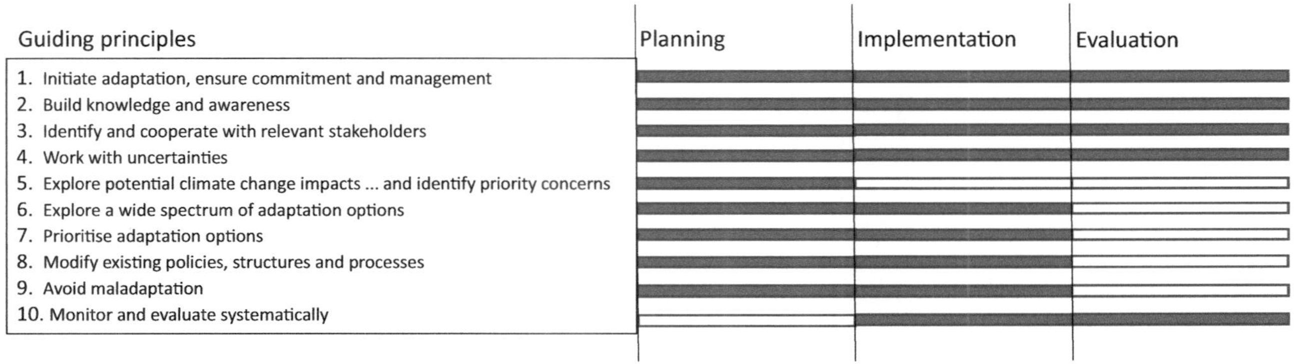

FIGURE 1.2 Guiding principles for climate change adaptation as applying to each stage of the adaptation process. *Derived from Prutsch, A, Grothmann, T, Schauser, I, Otto, S, and McCallum, S (2010).Guiding principles for adaptation to climate change in Europe. ETC/ACC Technical Paper 2010/6, The European Topic Centre on Air and Climate Change (ETC/ACC), Bilthoven, The Netherlands. http://air-climate.eionet.europa.eu/*

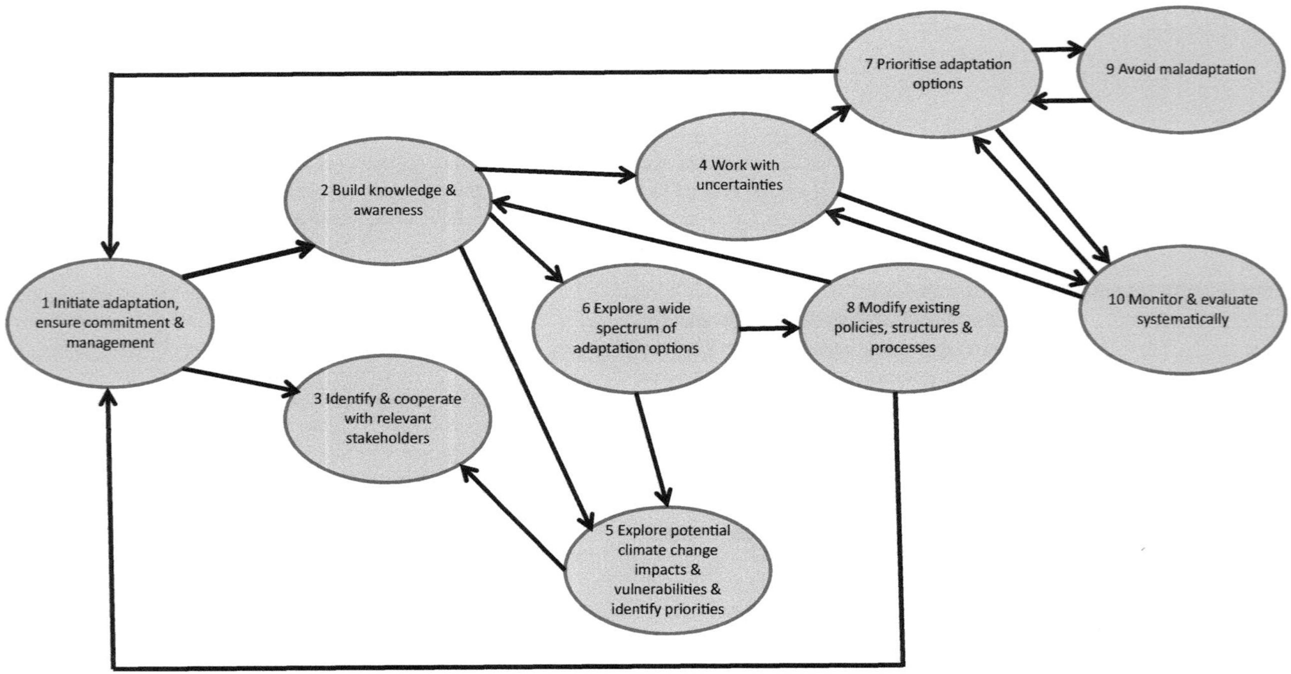

FIGURE 1.3 Linkage between the guiding principles. *Derived from Prutsch, A, Grothmann, T, Schauser, I, Otto, S, and McCallum, S (2010).Guiding principles for adaptation to climate change in Europe. ETC/ACC Technical Paper 2010/6, The European Topic Centre on Air and Climate Change (ETC/ACC), Bilthoven, The Netherlands. http://air-climate.eionet.europa.eu/*

commitment from decision makers is required, which may itself require awareness raising amongst those decision makers. Hence, there is a linkage to Principle no 2.

For an adaptation process to be sustainable – noting that climate change impacts are expected to occur over the long term – a clear mandate is required for the management of the process. This management is best handled by a managing unit which seeks to (1) facilitate the process by motivating stakeholders to participate in it and (2) promoting discussion, coordination and understanding between the different stakeholders.

Build knowledge and awareness

Knowledge transfer and awareness raising are key components in the climate change adaptation process, given the complexities associated with climate change and its potential impacts. Thus, an adaptation strategy needs to include provisions for learning and communication.

An adaptation strategy should include provisions for communication (and education), which

- Differentiate between different stakeholder groups that need different information and communication instruments
- Build a common knowledge base and a common language among stakeholders to support stakeholder cooperation
- Incorporate considerations for raising awareness in the general public
- Formulate information as simply and comprehensible as possible without losing insights into, or respect for, the complexities
- Explicitly include ways to communicate gaps and uncertainties of climate change (impact) information – this requires a linkage with principle no 4
- Conceptualise communication as mutual dialogue and learning between technical, scientific and stakeholder knowledge.

The adaptation management unit should provide access to understandable and useful information on potential impacts and adaptation plans through targeted assessments – thus, linking this principle to Principle nos 5 and 6.

Identify and cooperate with relevant stakeholders

Adaptation is likely to require coordination between sections, organisations, sectors and perhaps different levels of government and different jurisdictions. This coordination is necessary to ensure that stakeholder knowledge is widely disseminated, conflicts can be avoided or solved, and synergies and compromises identified. This cooperative process needs to have a clear vision or goal, and be integrated into the wider decision-making context to ensure policy relevance – a linkage to Principle no 1.

Work with uncertainties

Uncertainties are integral in all projections of climate change and its impacts. Organisations such as IPCC have attempted to handle uncertainties by providing climate impacts scenarios offering plausible descriptions of the ranges of possible future impacts. It is not realistic to disregard the need for adaptive actions on the basis of these uncertainties. The risk management approach mandates consideration of adaptation on the basis of the potential for serious or irreversible harm from the identified potential impacts. Adaptation management requires a flexible process of planning, implementation and revision through research, monitoring and evaluation (a linkage to Principle no 10).

Explore potential climate change impacts and vulnerabilities and identify priority concerns

Analysis of both short-term and long-term, direct and indirect impacts of climate change is essential, as must extend across the whole of the region of interest. Prutsch et al (2010) considered that a useful way to ensure the full extent of the analysis meets these requirements would be to adopt the following procedure:

1. Identify key components (e.g., critical infrastructure elements, relevant economic sectors and vulnerable population groups)
2. Analyse the known impacts of past weather events and recent climate trends on these key components
3. Assess likely future climate and socioeconomic scenarios for the study region
4. Identify potential impacts of climate change including cost, magnitude, timing, persistence, likelihood and distribution
5. Assess the vulnerability of the key components to current and potential future impacts
6. Rank the potential impacts on the basis of the vulnerability analysis
7. Set priorities for staging of adaptation measures on the basis of the rankings.

The assessment of potential impacts should also consider relevant nonclimatic factors and future developments, such as demographic and socioeconomic changes and habitat destruction through land use change, as these will also influence climate change impacts. Stakeholder agreement on the criteria for estimating the importance of the impacts is also a key consideration in setting priorities, and thus this principle is connected to Principle no 3.

Explore a wide spectrum of adaptation options

A wide-ranging exploration of adaptation options is required to ensure that the final selection of options is effective, equitable, cost efficient and fit for purpose. Thus, this principle is strongly connected to Principle no 5. Each possible option should be described in as much detail as possible, perhaps using a pro forma of the following type:

- Objectives
- Direct and indirect effects, emphasising potential benefits
- Duration and spatial coverage
- Socioeconomic and environmental contexts
- Interactions with other options
- Previous experiences with the use of this option (when available)
- Financial resource requirements
- Responsible actors, stakeholders and likely opponents.

In this way, the best interconnections between the proposed adaptation actions and existing structures and processes can be determined – a link to Principle no 8.

Prioritise adaptation options

Adaptation has to be meshed to the prevailing spatial and temporal circumstances. Thus, the selected options need to be based on the overall adaptation objectives and criteria. Rarely will there be a single best option, so different sets of actions will need to be combined with the learning assessments stemming from Principle no 10. In addition, transparency in decision-making is necessary, and this requires ongoing discussion and consensus with stakeholders – a link to Principle no 1. MCA may be employed in this process, which should include BCA (including indirect costs and benefits) as one facet of MCA. Care is needed to avoid maladaptation – a link to Principle no 9.

Modify existing policies, structures and processes

Adaptation cannot be attempted independently of the existing regime of established policies, management structures and decision-making processes. The relevant policy instruments already in use should be reviewed and adapted so that they can be used to tackle the current and future negative impacts of climate change. This should be done in such ways as to make the adaptation fully visible. Integrated climate change adaptation into existing structure and processes links strongly to Principles nos 1 and 2.

Avoid maladaptation

Maladaptation covers adaptation measures that are ill suited or work against overall plans for climate change adaptation and mitigation. Often they arise as short-term measures realising some early benefits, but lead to harmful future consequences. Types of maladaptation include

- Measures that conflict with mitigation
- Actions that use resources in an unsustainable fashion
- Actions that fail to distribute benefits equitably across society.

Maladaptation can be avoided by detailed assessment of adaptation actions over the long term – a link to Principle no 7.

Monitor and evaluate systematically

Adaptation is an ongoing process. As such it requires systematic monitoring of performance with periodic evaluation of that performance, so that the adaptation process stays focussed on the prioritised impacts of climate change and that adaptation actions continue to respond, without delay, to new knowledge and changes in the evidence base. Monitoring and evaluation is thus linked to Principle no 7 and provide the basis for adjustments of decisions when needed. While monitoring and evaluation do not start until the implementation phase of the adaptation process, the processes for them need to be established during the design of adaptation options, i.e., before implementation, and must be directed at meeting set objectives and criteria for the adaptation action program. The inclusion of new knowledge is an explicit requirement in monitoring and evaluation, as an important component of the adaptive management approach. This approach enables decision makers to continuously fine tune decisions and actions based on experiences gained and new scientific information. This includes the ongoing consideration of uncertainties, and hence a link to Principle no 4.

Structure of the book

This book is intended as an introductory guide to climate change adaptation for transportation systems, for systems managers and operators, researchers, and students. The expectation is that these people will have backgrounds in engineering, planning, economics, project management and similar disciplines, but are unlikely to be climate scientists. Thus, Chapter 2 of this book is intended as a primer on climate change basics. It provides a brief overview of climate system dynamics together with some discussion of observed changes in climate as reported, e.g., by the IPCC. The chapter then examines weather events (e.g., rainfall, storms, hurricanes, droughts, blizzards and heat waves). These form one part of climate, and their intensity and frequency are of interest, leading to consideration of what may be considered as extreme weather events, which can lead to disruptions in transport operations (e.g., through weather induced events such as floods and storm surges). The possible contributions of human activity over time to climate change and to the potential impacts of weather on transportation infrastructure are then introduced. Sea level rise is also considered, as a major factor affecting coastal and estuarine infrastructure. The importance of these phenomena for transportation network operations is also reviewed.

Chapter 3 builds on the basic understanding of climatic impacts to look at the performance of transportation infrastructure in different environments. It does so by considering transportation networks and their components, and the transport services that use these networks. This chapter describes the basic components of a transportation system and their characteristics, including rights-of-way, terminals and depots, roadway and trackway, ports, harbours and airports. Critical infrastructure components are highlighted. This chapter further describes the physical characteristics of transportation networks, including earthworks and built structures such as pavements, bridges, tunnels, viaducts and culverts. Weather and climatic impacts on specific components are introduced, as well as the considerations of traffic loads on the design parameters for the components.

Chapter 4 is specifically concerned with adaptation planning. This chapter describes the concepts of risk and uncertainty, and vulnerability and resilience as these apply to transportation systems. Requirements for decision-making are introduced, along with the available tools for decision-making, with details on the latter provided in subsequent chapters. The distinction between mitigation and adaptation is reinforced, as a requirement for understanding the issues related to risk management – in this case dealing with a situation that exists or is evolving, rather than looking for an alternative condition. A range of adaptation frameworks is described, including those provided by FHWA and the International Road Federation (PIARC), as these provide good case study applications in the real world. The management of risk and uncertainty in the planning and management of transportation systems is a major feature of the chapter, with an overview of the costs of extreme weather and related events. Climate stressors and their effects on infrastructure are described, leading to an examination of how climatic factors can be represented in performance assessment.

Risk management proceeds into Chapter 5 as well, with the focus on asset management, including asset life and maintenance regimes. The role of performance measures and performance indicators in assessment and evaluation follows, with the consideration of climate and environmental influences and impacts. This includes failure types for different components and limits on service operations under different weather conditions. The weather-related impacts on transportation operations are reviewed, including aviation. Uncertainty and risk management is a key consideration, leading to a review of BCA and alternatives, with an emphasis in decision-making under uncertainty and the approaches and tools available for this.

Coastal regions stand out as a primary area of concern for the impacts of climate change and the needs for adaptation of transportation assets and infrastructure. Thus, Chapter 6 focuses on these regions. Sea level rise and its implications are the underlying issues, manifest in the effects of storms, surges and flooding, and resultant coastal damage. Damage includes specific threats to network components located in close proximity to the coast. Thus, the transport facilities and structures in these areas, and their components and the materials they are constructed from, are of interest. Susceptibility to corrosion and water damage for these structures is well known, but a changing climate may lead to new requirements to guard against these, both in intensity and in coverage. Ports and harbours are of necessity located in coastal areas, as are many airports, so the infrastructure requirements and potential climate impacts on these are examined, including citation of some recent case studies.

Chapters 7 and 8 consider road and rail transportation systems, respectively. These systems share many common elements, such as structural components such as bridges, tunnels and culverts, but they have their differences too. Thus, the two chapters consider each system separately. Road pavement structures and design methods are considered in Chapter 7, including consideration of temperature impacts and water penetration. Mathematical modelling of road pavement performance is described, and used to indicate how climate change factors could be incorporated in performance evaluation and therefore influence both design methods and maintenance regimes for road systems. Temperature and rainfall are the main factors included in the performance models, but other factors related to extreme weather events (e.g., storms, flooding and washouts) also have to be considered. These weather events may also lead to limits on traffic operations, for periods of hours to weeks, depending on the level and extent of damage. Road agencies and operators then have to have plans and procedures to deal with these disruptions. Similar situations exist for rail track managers and train operators, and rail maintenance systems and railway performance assessment are therefore discussed in Chapter 8. Case studies for both road and rail are provided as illustrations of good practice.

Active transport is discussed in Chapter 9. As indicated previously, the encouragement of increased usage of active transport modes is a fundamental part of transportation policies for climate change mitigation. The adaptation perspective for active transport is on the provision and maintenance of infrastructure specifically provided for active travel. This infrastructure is most likely to be found in urban areas, and so issues of urban design that encourage — or remove impediments to — active transport are important. The chapter begins by discussing land use—transport integration as a planning philosophy that encourages active travel, by reorganising urban land use distribution to bring destinations closer and thus reduce travel distances. The ASSI —'avoid, shift, share, improve'— paradigm is described, as an approach to policy development for active travel and the provision and operation of suitable infrastructure, including access to public transport. The chapter concludes by examining the emerging principles for low carbon design of urban precincts and neighbourhoods, and the implications for transportation infrastructure provision that result.

The final chapter of the book looks at the future directions in research and practice for climate change adaptation in transportation systems. It highlights the need for and use of decision-making tools that can incorporate uncertainty and that are valid for the time periods over which transportation asset life and climate change impacts impinge. Further, the evaluation processes in which these tools are applied need to explicitly account for environmental and climate factors. While conventional BCA can remain as the bedrock of analysis in evaluation, other methods such as MCA and risk-based policy analysis tools such as RDM and ROA should be considered as complements or extensions, in line with the principles for evaluation discussed by the OECD (OECD, 2018).

Overall this book presents and discusses three major themes for climate change adaptation for consideration by transportation system managers:

1. The options for changing practice, not merely refining or improving current practice
2. Risk management and the development of adaptation frameworks and pathways, accompanied by the introduction, development and use of decision support tools that account for uncertainty and the mix of short and long-term impacts on system performance
3. In terms of the natural phenomena affecting transportation systems and themselves affected by climate change, the central role of water, in its many guises, in the degradation and limitation of the performance of transportation facilities, assets and systems.

This book is intended as a consolidated introduction to these aspects of climate change adaptation for transportation, and is aimed at a wide but interested audience: practitioners, policy analysts and policy makers, researchers and above all the students, from whom the generations of professionals whose careers will be deeply involved in climate change adaptation will come.

To set the scene, we first need to look at an overview of the science on climate change, albeit briefly, before considering the potential impacts on transportation.

References

ASCE, 2009. Guiding Principles for the Nation's Critical Infrastructure. American Society of Civil Engineers, Reston, VA. http://www.pubs.asce.org.

Dia, H., 2017. Low Carbon Mobility for Future Cities. The Institution of Engineering and Technology, London.

Environment Australia, 2015. National climate resilience and adaptation strategy 2015. Department of Environment and Energy, Canberra. http://www.environment.gov.au/climate-change/adaptation/strategy. (Accessed 29 October 2018).

EU, 2018. Adaptation to climate change. Policies, Information and Services. European Union. https://ec.europa.eu/clima/policies/adaptation_en. (Accessed 29 October 2018).

FHWA, 2018. Vulnerability Assessment and Adaptation Framework, 3rd edition. Federal Highways Administration, Washington DC. https://www.fhwa.dot.gov/environment/sustainability/resilience/adaptation_framework/chap00.cfm.

Givoni, M., Banister, D., 2013. Moving towards Low Carbon Mobility. Edward Elgar Publishing, Cheltenham.

IPCC, 2018. Global warming of 1.5°C. Special Report 15, UN International Committee on Climate Change. www.ipcc.ch/report/sr15/.

Kwakkel, J.H., Haasnoot, M., Walker, W.E., 2016. Comparing Robust Decision-Making and Dynamic Adaptive Policy Pathways for model-based decision support under deep uncertainty. Environmental Modelling and Software 86, 168–183. https://doi.org/10.1016/j.envsoft.2016.09.017.

Nakamura, K., Hayashi, Y., 2013. Strategies and instruments for low-carbon urban transport: an international review on trends and effects. Transport Policy 29, 264–274. https://doi.org/10.1016/j.tranpol.2012.07.003.

NCCARF, 2012. Eight principles of adaptation planning. AdaptNote, National Climate Change Adaptation Research Facility, Brisbane. https://www.nccarf.edu.au/sites/default/files/attached_files_publications/AdaptNote.pdf. (Accessed 28 October 2018).

Nicholson, A.J., Dalziell, E., 2003. Risk evaluation and management: a road network reliability study. In: Bell, M.G.H., Iida, Y. (Eds.), The Network Reliability of Transport. Elsevier, Oxford, pp. 45–59.

OECD, 2018. Cost-benefit analysis and the environment: further developments and policy use. OECD Publishing, Paris. https://doi.org/10.1787/9789264085169-en.

Philp, M., Taylor, M.A.P., 2017. Research agenda for low-carbon mobility: issues for New World cities. International Journal of Sustainable Transportation 11 (1), 49–58. https://doi.org/10.1080/15568318.2015.1106261.

PIARC, 2015. International climate change adaptation framework for road infrastructure. Report 2015R03EN. World Road Association, Paris. www.piarc.org.

Prutsch, A., Grothmann, T., Schauser, I., Otto, S., McCallum, S., 2010. Guiding principles for adaptation to climate change in Europe. In: ETC/ACC Technical Paper 2010/6, The European Topic Centre on Air and Climate Change (ETC/ACC), Bilthoven, The Netherlands. http://air-climate.eionet.europa.eu/.

Schmidt-Thomé, P., 2017. Climate change adaptation. Oxford Research Encyclopedia of Climate Science – Risk Management and Adaptation. https://doi.org/10.1093/acrefore/9780190228620.013.635. http://climatescience.oxfordre.com/view/10.1093/acrefore/9780190228620.001.0001/acrefore-9780190228620-e-635. (Accessed 29 October 2018).

Skourtos, M., Damigos, D., Kontogianni, A., Tourkolias, C., Markandya, A., Abadie, L.M., Sainz de Murieta, E., Galarraga, I., Wellman, J., Hunt, A., 2016. Future values for adaptation assessment. Deliverable 2.2. ECONADAPT FP7 Research Project, European Union. www.econadapt.eu.

Sperling, D., Cannon, J., 2006. Driving Climate Change: Cutting Carbon from Transportation. Academic press, New York.

Taylor, M.A.P., 2017. Vulnerability Analysis for Transportation Networks. Elsevier, Oxford.

TRB, 2016. Highway Capacity Manual, 6th ed. Transportation Research Board, Washington DC.

VCCCAR, 2018. Climate change adaptation definitions. Victorian Centre for Climate Change Adaptation Research. http://www.vcccar.org.au/climate-change-adaptation-definitions. (Accessed 29 October 2018).

Chapter 2

Climate change basics

Weather and climate are important factors in transportation engineering, both in the design of transportation infrastructure and in the operational management of transportation systems. According to the US National Weather Service (NWS, 2020), weather is 'the state of the atmosphere with respect to wind, temperature, cloudiness, moisture, pressure, etc', whereas climate is 'the composite or generally prevailing weather conditions of a region, throughout the year, averaged over a series of years'. Weather thus refers to these conditions at a given point in time (e.g., today's maximum temperature), while climate refers to the average weather conditions for an area over a long period of time (e.g., the average maximum temperature for today's date). More precisely, IPCC (2007) defined climate as 'the statistical description in terms of the mean and variability of relevant (weather) quantities over a period of time ranging from months to thousands or millions of years'.

The climate in a particular region depends on the flows of energy through the global climate system, and these flows are influenced by many factors, including the concentrations of greenhouse gases in the atmosphere. The primary driver of climate on Earth is the energy received from the Sun, and the solar energy received by the planet at large depends on how much energy the Sun emits and the distance between the Sun and the Earth. The amount of solar energy received at a given location on the Earth's surface depends on the number of hours of daylight experienced at that point over a day, which itself varies over the seasons of a year and with the tilt of the Earth's axis of rotation, and hence with latitude. Part of the solar energy falling on the Earth is reflected directly back into space by the atmosphere, clouds, land masses, water surfaces and ice. Tiny particles in the atmosphere (aerosols) also increase the reflection of solar energy. The solar energy actually absorbed by the Earth is eventually returned to space as infrared (heat) radiation. This return process involves interactions with the global climate system and including the atmosphere, oceans, land masses and ice sheets (AAS, 2015). These flows of radiation in the atmosphere are major determinants of climate. Nitrogen and oxygen, the main gases in the atmosphere, do not interact with infrared radiation, but some of the other gases present in the atmosphere – albeit at very small concentrations – do. These gases, including carbon dioxide (CO_2), methane (CH_4) and water vapour (H_2O), absorb infrared radiation flowing up from the surface of the Earth and redirect it in all directions, including back down to the surface. In this way,

Climate Change Adaptation for Transportation Systems. https://doi.org/10.1016/B978-0-12-816638-3.00002-7

they impede the outward flow of infrared energy from the planet into space. This is the 'greenhouse effect'. The gases that cause the impedance and redirection of the infrared energy flows are termed the 'greenhouse gases'.[1] Without the greenhouse effect, the Earth's surface would be considerably cooler, perhaps 33°C cooler (AAS, 2015), and life as we know it would not exist.

A disturbance to the Earth's climate system can initiate further changes that may dampen or amplify the impacts of the initial disturbance through feedback processes, as there are strong connections between temperature, atmospheric water vapour, the polar ice sheets and the concentrations of the longer-lived greenhouse gases (notably carbon dioxide). The feedback processes can occur over a set of time scales. Atmospheric processes tend to be rapid, such as the role of water vapour in the atmosphere. Processes involving oceans and ice sheets are much, much slower. For instance, the ice age cycles experienced by the Earth over the last million years or so were triggered by fluctuations in the Earth's rotation and its orbit around the Sun. The consequence of these fluctuations was to change the distribution of solar radiation over the Earth's surface, leading to temperature changes which in turn led to changes in the polar ice sheets and carbon cycling. The combination of these two factors then amplified the temperature response (AAS, 2015).

The Earth's climate has changed and continues to change naturally over time, including geological time. Natural changes are due to internal fluctuations that exchange energy, water and carbon between the atmosphere, oceans, land masses and ice sheets and from external effects, including variations in solar energy received from the Sun and from volcanic eruptions. Human activities may also influence climate (IPCC, 2007; AAS, 2015). Changes in the concentrations of greenhouse gases in the atmosphere, alterations of the reflectivity of the Earth's surface due to changes in the built environment and land cover and changes in the concentrations of aerosols in the atmosphere can all influence the climate.

Climate change

Climate change may be defined as 'a change in the pattern of weather, and related changes in oceans, land surfaces and ice sheets, occurring over time scales of decades or longer' (AAS, 2015, p.6). As an addition, this change should be seen to be statistically significant. For instance, Olsen (2015) stated that:

> *Changes in the statistical character of climate-related observations can be driven by natural variability on a variety of spatial and temporal scales ... Shorter-term variability (at the seasonal-to-interannual scale out to the decadal*

1. The greenhouse effect has been known for a long time, since the mid-19th century. See, for example, Arrhenius (1896).

scale) is associated with cyclic variability within atmospheric and oceanic systems, and typically occurs at the continental or subcontinental level. By definition, global climate change produces a signal that is detectable at the global scale and persists over multiple decades (generally considered to persist for at least 30 years). Anthropogenic global climate change would produce a globally persistent signal that could not be attributed to natural variability (for example, due to internal variability of the ocean-atmospheric system or external variability due to changes in solar input or orbital mechanics).

Olsen (2015, p. 3)

Fig. 2.1 shows some representations of the consequences of climate change for distributions of daily temperature in the present and in the future. The effects on temperature extremes are of most interest. First the figure shows the effect of an increase in the mean temperature, but no change in variability – that is the temperature distribution is shifted to the right by an amount equal to the change in the mean temperature. Second is the case where there is an increase in the variability of the temperature distribution as well as an increase in the mean temperature. In the latter case, the variability is represented by the standard deviation of the distribution.[2]

The general effect of an increase in mean temperature is that the amount of hot weather, which is the right-hand tail of the distribution, increases – the area under the distribution curve to the right of any temperature (*T*) gives the proportion of days with temperatures exceeding *T*. This also means that new extreme temperatures can occur, 'breaking previous temperature records'. In the case where only the mean temperature increases, then there is also a clear reduction in the amount of cold weather – the area under the curve to the left of *T* is the proportion of days with temperatures less than *T*. This is the case shown in Fig. 2.1A. When there is increased variability in the distribution (as in Fig. 2.1B), then the same phenomenon is seen for hotter weather, but the situation with colder weather is less clear and will depend on the actual shape of the distribution and the relative difference between the change in mean temperature and the change in the standard deviation of temperature.

The reality of climate change in recent decades is also apparent. Olsen (2015) cites the following quotations, first from IPCC (2014a):

Warming of the climate system is unequivocal, and since the 1950s, many of the observed changes are unprecedented over decades to millennia. The atmosphere and ocean have warmed, the amounts of snow and ice have diminished, sea level has risen, and the concentrations of greenhouse gases have increased

2. Or, more properly in statistical terms, the variance of the distribution. The standard deviation is the square root of the variance.

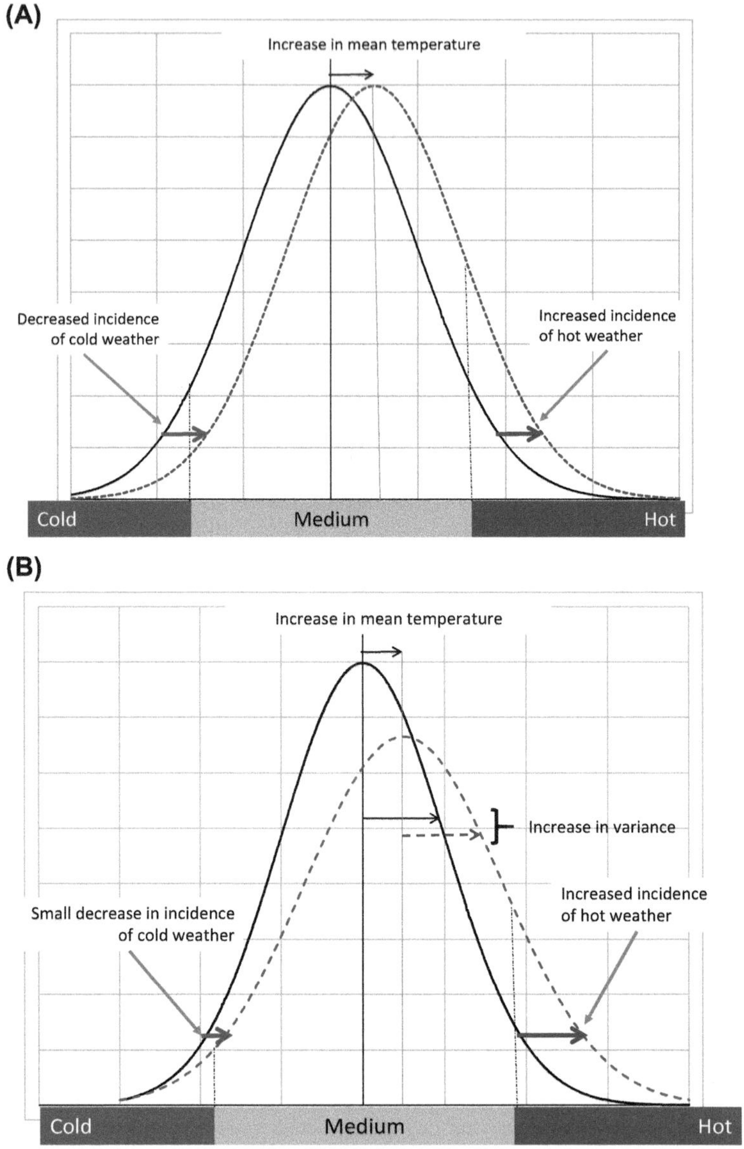

FIGURE 2.1 The effects of changes in the distribution of daily maximum temperatures with special focus on the extremes of cold and hot temperatures: (A) increase in mean temperature, (B) increases in mean and variance.

and then from the US National Climate Assessment (NCA):

Evidence for climate change abounds, from the top of the atmosphere to the depths of the oceans. Scientists and engineers from around the world have meticulously collected this evidence, using satellites and networks of weather balloons, thermometers, buoys, and other observing systems. Evidence of climate change is also visible in the observed and measured changes in location and behavior of species and functioning of ecosystems. Taken together, this evidence tells an unambiguous story: the planet is warming, and over the last half century, this warming has been driven primarily by human activity.

Melillo et al. (2014).

Donat and Alexander (2012) studied the statistical distributions of minimum and maximum daily temperatures. They found that the distributions of both daily maximum and minimum temperatures have significantly shifted towards higher values in the period 1981–2010 compared to the period 1951–80 in almost all regions of the Earth, whereas changes in variance were spatially heterogeneous and mostly less significant. Changes were greater for daily minimum (nighttime) temperatures than for daily maximum (daytime) temperatures. These changes had the greatest impact on the extremes of the distribution, and Donat and Alexander (2012) concluded that the distribution of global daily temperatures had become 'more extreme' since the middle of the 20th century. Data published by the Australian Bureau of Meteorology (BOM, 2020a) give further weight to the occurrence of a warming climate. Fig. 2.2 shows the mean annual daily temperature anomaly across the continent over the 100 years from 1919 to 2018. The mean annual daily temperature anomaly is the difference between the mean average daily temperature in each year and the mean calculated over the standard reference period 1961–90 (the mean annual daily temperature for this reference period is 21.8°C). The increase in temperature over the 100 years from 1919 is clear, and indeed 9 of the 10 recorded hottest years in Australia have occurred in the 21st century (to 2019), with 8 of the 10 years in the decade 2010–19 being in that top 10 (the exceptions are 2011 and 2012) (BOM, 2020b).

Fig. 2.2 also shows a linear trend line for the temperature anomaly. The R^2 value for this line is $R^2 = 0.5845$ and this value is statistically significant at $P < .001$. Statistically speaking, the trend is real.

Mean (atmospheric) temperature is a fundamental climate variable for transportation infrastructure. The mean temperature and temperature extremes (i.e., statistical distributions of temperature) are basic inputs in infrastructure planning and design and in transportation operations and management. In addition, temperature is a key factor influencing other climate parameters. A warmer atmosphere will hold more moisture and when coupled with differences in temperature between the atmosphere and sea affects cloud cover, the propensity for storms, and precipitation. Atmospheric temperature affects the formation or melting of ice on land (including permafrost) and on

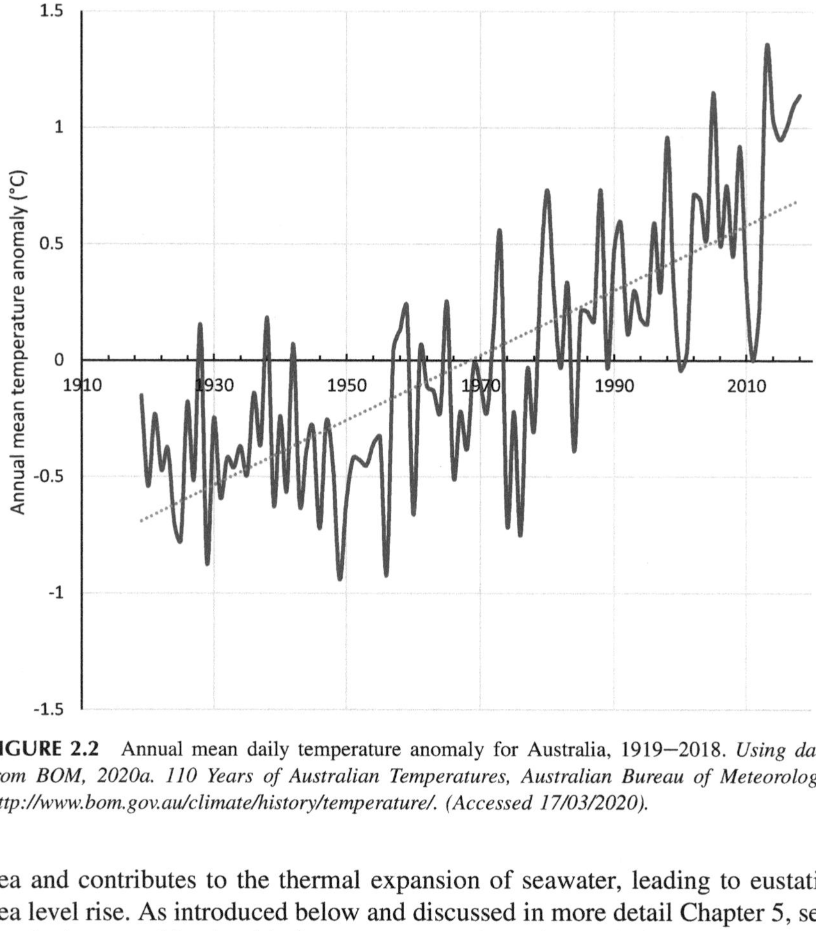

FIGURE 2.2 Annual mean daily temperature anomaly for Australia, 1919–2018. *Using data from BOM, 2020a. 110 Years of Australian Temperatures, Australian Bureau of Meteorology. http://www.bom.gov.au/climate/history/temperature/. (Accessed 17/03/2020).*

sea and contributes to the thermal expansion of seawater, leading to eustatic sea level rise. As introduced below and discussed in more detail Chapter 5, sea level rise, combined with increase storm intensity and frequency, places coastal infrastructure at greater risk through the damaging effects of storm surges. Sea level rise itself puts low-lying infrastructure and assets at risk of temporary or permanent inundation, requiring significant cost expenditures for asset protection, rehabilitation or relocation. Increased atmospheric temperatures together with high concentrations of carbon dioxide in the atmosphere generate accelerated rates of carbonation in concrete materials and structures, leading to the earlier degradation if not failure of the concrete.

Olsen (2015, p. 5) provided the following key messages on the impacts of climate change globally and in the United States:

1. Global climate is changing and this change is apparent across a wide range of observations. The global warming of the past 50 years is primarily due to human activities

2. Global climate is projected to continue to change over this century and beyond. The magnitude of climate change beyond the next few decades depends primarily on the amount of heat-trapping gases emitted globally, and how sensitive the Earth's climate is to those emissions
3. Average temperatures in the USA have increased by 0.7–1.1°C (1.3–1.9°F) since record keeping began in 1895 and most of this increase has occurred since 1970. The most recent decade was the nation's warmest on record. Temperatures in the USA are expected to continue to rise. Because human-induced warming is superimposed on a naturally varying climate, the temperature rise has not been, and will not be, uniform or smooth across the nation or over time
4. The length of the frost-free season (and the corresponding growing season) has been increasing nationally since the 1980s, with the largest increases occurring in the western US, affecting ecosystems and agriculture. The growing season is projected to continue to lengthen across the USA
5. Average US precipitation has increased since 1900, but some areas have had increases greater than the national average, and some areas have had decreases. Over the 21st century more winter and spring precipitation is projected for the northern US, and less for the Southwest
6. Heavy downpours are increasing nationally, especially over the last three to five decades. Largest increases are in the Midwest and Northeast. Increases in the frequency and intensity of extreme precipitation events are projected for all US regions
7. There have been changes in some types of extreme weather events over the last several decades. Heat waves have become more frequent and intense, especially in the West. Cold waves have become less frequent and less intense across the nation. There have been regional trends in floods and droughts. Droughts in the Southwest and heat waves everywhere are projected to become more intense, and cold waves less intense, everywhere
8. The intensity, frequency and duration of North Atlantic hurricanes, as well as the frequency of the strongest (Category 4 and 5) hurricanes, have all increased since the early 1980s. The relative contributions of human and natural causes to these increases are still uncertain. Hurricane-associated storm intensity and rainfall rates are projected to increase as the climate continues to warm
9. Winter storms have increased in frequency and intensity since the 1950s, and their tracks have shifted northward over the USA. Other trends in severe storms, including the intensity and frequency of tornadoes, hail, and damaging thunderstorm winds, are uncertain and are being studied intensively

10. Global sea level has risen by about 0.2 m (8 in) since reliable record keeping began in 1880. It is projected to rise another 0.3−1.22 m (1−4 ft) by 2100
11. Rising temperatures are reducing ice volume and surface extent on land, lakes and sea. This loss of ice is expected to continue. The Arctic Ocean is expected to become essentially ice free in summer before mid-century
12. The oceans are currently absorbing about a quarter of the carbon dioxide emitted to the atmosphere annually and are becoming more acidic as a result, leading to concerns about intensifying impacts on marine ecosystems.

The impact of human activity on climate change has been contentious, and is discussed in the next section. This book, however, is concerned with climate change adaptation as its main thrust. The evidence for climate change, a snippet of which was presented above, is clear. Climate change is occurring and transportation agencies, their managers and planners need to be aware of this and to be making and implementing plans for adaptation directed at ensuring the ongoing safe, efficient and equitable operations of our transportation systems. Climate change mitigation may also be required, and transportation can play a leading role in that, especially in view of the significant contributions of transportation to global greenhouse gas emissions — nearly one-quarter of these emissions, according to IPCC (2014b).

Human activity and contribution to climate change

IPC (2014a).

Despite the contention, there is strong evidence that human-made emissions — anthropogenic emissions — have made a major contribution to global warming (e.g., see IPCC, 2014a,b, Olsen, 2015; AAS, 2015 and ITF, 2016). There is, however, much uncertainty about the exact scope, scale and regional impact of climate change, so that policy formulation is difficult. This is particularly so for transportation, where there is a definite need for synergy between transportation and climate policy goals. Any trade-offs between the (sometimes) competing objectives from these policies must be considered in an informed and transparent way.

Fossil fuel consumption has been closely related to global growth in energy use and economic activity (AAS, 2015). The increases in greenhouse gas concentrations since 1800, and most pronounced since 1950, may be credited to the burning of fossil fuels in human activities, of which transportation is a prime example. The global contributions of human-made emissions appear clear. Precise identification of the impact of anthropogenic emissions at the spatial resolutions and temporal scales relevant to transportation systems management is much, much more difficult. Anthropogenic impacts on climate are necessarily superimposed on natural variations in climate so that short-term — year by year — variations in greenhouse gas emissions and global warming are inevitable. Weather variability affects vegetation, and sporadic volcanic activity – major volcanic eruptions – can have significant indirect impacts on greenhouse gas concentrations in the atmosphere (AAS, 2015). This combination of natural variability and long-term anthropogenic changes is an important consideration for transportation infrastructure design and management, where, for example, changes in precipitation levels and patterns may require substantial changes in previously established practices. According to Melillo et al. (2014), 'while significant trends in average precipitation have been detected, the fraction of these trends attributable to human activity is difficult to quantify at regional scales because the range of natural variability in precipitation is large'. Nevertheless, transportation system planners and managers must develop understanding of weather and climate changes and incorporate these in the planning and design of new infrastructure and in the maintenance and refurbishment of existing infrastructure assets. How to do this is the subject of this book and is developed in the succeeding chapters. The best available approach is based on the principles of risk management, which is an already understood concept in current transportation systems management.

Extreme weather events

Transportation engineering design is based on considerations of extremes – the 'design load'. Extreme weather events can affect both the structural integrity of infrastructure assets and the operational capability of transportation systems. Extreme weather events include droughts, heat waves and high temperatures, storms, cyclones and hurricanes, cold freezes and blizzards. Stemming from extreme weather events come related phenomena (and possibly disasters) such as floods, wild fires, storm surges, avalanches and landslides. All of these can have severe impacts on transportation systems and infrastructure. As indicated earlier in this chapter – see Fig. 2.1 – a warming climate will lead to more extremes, e.g., high temperatures and heat waves. Depending on the variability inherent in the particular weather factor, extremes may occur at either end of the distribution of that event (see Fig. 2.1).

The following points should be borne in mind for extreme weather events when considering transportation systems:

- *Temperature extremes*, either hot or cold, have detrimental impacts on the physical properties of the materials used in the construction of infrastructure assets and on the geotechnical works associated with those assets. They can also affect travel demand and on the operational and maintenance activities of transportation agencies. Extreme temperatures can lead to significant problems of rail buckling with disruptions to rail services (see Chapter 7). Extreme heat is also associated with increased fire risk, and fires affect network performance, asset integrity and user safety

- *Extreme precipitation* events cause heightened stream and river flows, increased runoff from soils, scouring, flooding and possibly erosion. Extreme rainfall (in either intensity or duration) can lead to reduced soil cohesion, resulting in landslides and mudslides. Such hydraulic hazards are perhaps the most damaging hazards afflicting major transportation infrastructure assets (e.g., bridges and tunnels), with the potential for significant asset damage and sudden failures leading to major interruptions of transportation services and network connectivity
- *Extreme storms* (hurricanes, typhoons and cyclones) include high winds, extreme precipitation, lightning, coastal storm surges and increased wave energy and wave amplitude. While these storm phenomena are particular damaging to affected coastal areas, local thunderstorms anywhere can produce significant asset damage, network disruption and flash flooding. Hail and lightning can also inflict significant damage and disruption

While extreme events in climate science are often defined as being those events 'as rare or rarer than the 10th or 90th percentile of the observed probability density function' (IPCC, 2007; Olsen, 2015), for transportation engineering an extreme (design) event is generally defined in terms of an acceptable frequency of failure probably well outside that definition: e.g., flood risk management is typically concerned with events which have mean recurrence intervals of 100 to perhaps 500 years, while stormwater design may be concerned with events occurring more frequently, say 30–50 years. The latter recurrence intervals may be closer to those inferred from the IPCC definition – the likely extent of damage and disruption from an extreme event exceeding the design level is the key determinant in the selection of that design level. A major issue for transportation systems is the likelihood that extreme events at the current design levels may become more frequent under climate change, thereby reducing the recurrence interval – and requiring a new assessment of what the design level should be in the future.

The potential impacts of extreme weather on transportation network operations are also of concern. For example, Amin et al. (2014) and Jaroszweski and McNamara (2014) considered the impacts of weather on road crashes, while Bollinger and Dijkema (2016) explored the impacts of weather on the resilience of infrastructure systems under extreme weather events. The road safety studies suggest that weather events do affect crash frequency, but not in simple ways. While crash numbers could increase as a response to some weather events, they tended to decrease under the most extreme events – perhaps because of the suppression of travel demand under those conditions. The study of crash rates (i.e. the inclusion of a measure of traffic exposure as well as crash numbers) would be seem more appropriate. The broader impacts of weather on transportation operations and travel demand are considered in more detail in Chapter 9.

Sea level rise

Sea level rise is a vital concern for coastal areas, and the management of the transportation networks and infrastructure in those regions. Increased sea levels will place low-lying infrastructure at increased risk of temporary or permanent inundation, requiring significant expenditures on asset protection, rehabilitation or relocation. Storm surges are an ever-present concern for coastal infrastructure, and sea level rise will exacerbate this situation. Coupled then with more intense and more frequent storms, storm surges will increase in size and energy, leading to more frequent overtopping and potential damage to assets on the landward side of coastal defences. Asset failures and network discontinuities are then likely.

In addition, mean sea levels are a vital parameter in the planning of port infrastructure and for bridge clearances over navigable waterways.

Sea level rise may have several components. The basic driver is an increase in the volume of water in the oceans, from expansion due to thermal warming (as sea temperatures increase) and from melting of the polar ice sheets. This is global or eustatic sea level rise. In addition to any climate-driven sea level rise, local factors may also be present and may dominate at some locations. These include ocean currents and local climate peculiarities, tectonic land movements and geological compression of land masses, subsidence stemming from the extraction of groundwater or hydrocarbons close to the coast and sediment loading and compaction. Sea level rise is expected to continue for some centuries to come due to climate change effects that are already in place (AAS, 2015).

The design parameters for coastal infrastructure are based on potential storm surge and wave action expected at a given location. Rising sea levels and potentially more intense storms, compounded by regional subsidence, might increase the inundation of transportation infrastructure in coastal areas (FHWA, 2014). Many of these facilities are also designated as regional evacuation routes, and so these could be compromised during extreme weather. Storm surge and wave action can cause bridge scour and increase erosion of roads and supporting structures (FHWA, 2014). Sea level rise and saltwater intrusion could also accelerate infrastructure corrosion in coastal areas, reducing life expectancy, increasing maintenance costs and increasing the potential for structural failure during extreme events (FHWA, 2014).

Siebentritt (2016) offered the following summary on sea level rise and the commensurate need for adaptation planning is response:

> *Global sea levels have risen by approximately 21 cm since 1880. Thermal expansion and melting glaciers explain about 75 per cent of the observed rise in sea levels over the past four decades. This has been driven by increasing temperatures in the atmosphere and absorption of heat by the oceans. The observed rates of rise for Australia are consistent with global average values. There is*

very high confidence that sea levels will continue to rise over the coming century. Compared to the period 1986–2005, global mean sea levels are projected to increase by the end of the century by:

- 0.26–0.55 m under a low emissions scenario
- 0.33–0.63 m under an intermediate scenario, where emissions stabilise late-century
- 0.45–0.82 m under a high emissions scenario.

It is virtually certain that sea levels will continue to rise after 2100, with sea-level rise due to thermal expansion to continue for many centuries due to the slow response of the oceans to the accumulating greenhouse gases in the atmosphere. Regional sea-level rise projections have been prepared for Australia and show that the extent of rise is likely to be similar around the nation, with only small differences existing between locations for different time frames and emissions scenarios. Extreme sea levels are expected to change in the future because of increases in regional sea level and changes in climate events. This means that when planning for climate change, consideration needs to be given to the combined effects of tides, storm surges and wind waves.

Chapter 5 of this book is devoted to considerations of coastal issues and climate change. Sea level rise, its direct consequences and its effects when combined with extreme weather events, tides, inundation and flooding are discussed at length in that chapter. Available methods for adaptation planning in transportation management for coastal infrastructure are also discussed in Chapter 5.

Climate trends

Historical climate records date from the latter part of the 19th century, when suitable gauges and recording devices began to become available. While historical climate records offer some opportunity to study trends in the climate, these records are not sufficient in duration or coverage to provide more than localised information. They are certainly not suitable for providing guidance on the likely future climatic conditions, especially in the second half of the 21st century or at a global scale. Modern weather forecasting systems are quite accurate up to a week or so ahead and can provide useful if not accurate advice for perhaps up to 3 months into the future. The prediction of future climate trends, years and decades ahead, is challenging and uncertain – yet such information is sought for infrastructure design and asset maintenance requirements.

One approach to this issue is perhaps to look at existing climate conditions in other regions, which are assumed to represent the expectations of future climate at a given location. ITF (2016) discussed this approach, using the example of Barcelona, Spain and Casablanca, Morocco under the assumption that the climate of the former may become more like that of the latter.[3] Perhaps for regions facing future warmer temperatures, this seems a reasonable initial supposition, but there would be concern about other climate factors such as humidity and precipitation (and indeed hours of sunlight). Two difficulties arise in this search for climate analogues:

1. There is little if any certainty that an evolving climate match can be found through an analogue ('which analogue?') and
2. As large transportation assets such as bridges have long engineering lives, a given asset may be subject to a series of climate analogues over its life. Constructing and maintaining infrastructure suitable for operating in a series of different climates is a challenging design task and likely to be an expensive option.

A second approach, that also offers potential to examine a number of different climate scenarios, is to use climate models. The outputs of these models can be used to inform infrastructure planning, investment and design decisions. These models exist in two major classes: Global Climate Models (GCMs) and Earth System Models (ESMs) (Olsen, 2015). The latter are more recent developments and offer a wider range of features, such as simulation of the carbon cycle, but the GCMs are still finding widespread applications in estimating future climate impacts. The GCMs typically comprise four main components: atmosphere, ocean, land surface and sea ice. The ESMs explicitly add the components plant ecology and land use and ocean ecology and biogeochemistry to the modelling system and are thus able to complete the carbon cycle, i.e., an ESM explicitly models the flows of carbon through the Earth system. The primary variables describing the state of the atmosphere are temperature, air pressure, humidity, winds, currents and water and ice condensate (in clouds). Both GCM and ESM solve thermodynamics and fluid mechanics equations for a set of climate variables defined on a spatial grid, in spherical coordinates.[4] Fig. 2.3 provides a schematic diagram that compares GCM and ESM. SOCCOM (2020) and CSIRO (2020) provide examples of operational ESM.

The models simulate future climate parameters such as temperature, humidity and precipitation in each cell of the grid using iterative procedures

3. The two cities are about 1530 km apart, roughly north-south. A similar example for the United States might be Portland, Oregon and Los Angeles, California, which are a similar north-south distance (approximately 1580 km) apart.
4. Thus, latitude and longitude are used to fix a location on the Earth's surface. Grid resolutions vary, from perhaps 0.5–4.0 degrees, for the atmospheric component and from 0.2 to 2.0 degrees for the ocean component (Olsen, 2015). The calculations for the Representative Concentration Pathways (RCPs) – to be discussed in the next section – used a grid resolution of 0.5 degrees for all components (Van Vuuren et al., 2011). One degree of latitude represents a distance of about 110 km on the surface of the Earth.

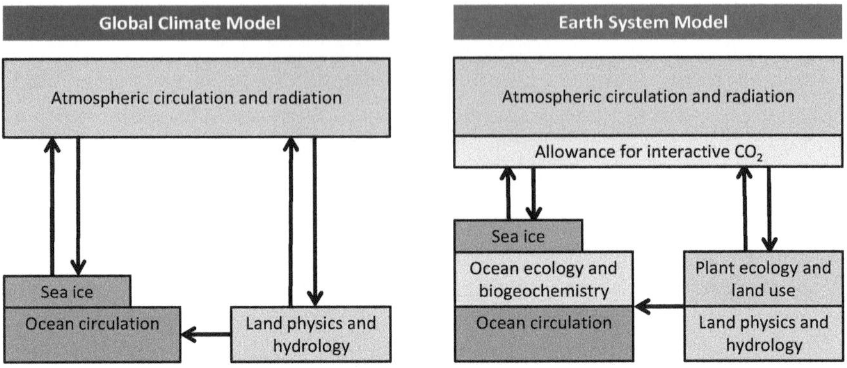

FIGURE 2.3 Schematic diagram of Global Climate Models (GCMs) and Earth System Models (ESMs) showing the similarities and differences between the two model types. *Derived from SOCCOM, 2020. What Is an Earth System Model (ESM)? https://soccom.princeton.edu/content/what-earth-system-model-esm. (Accessed 21/03/2020).*

that capture interactions between neighbouring cells. At the common levels of resolution used for them, which equate to hundreds to tens of km across, the GCM and ESM may not be able to represent topographical features very well, nor the impacts of these features on regional weather and climate. This is certainly an issue for transportation policy formulation and systems planning, for even a 20 km × 20 km cell size (corresponding approximately to a 0.2 degrees grid cell size), is too coarse for assessing risks posed to transportation infrastructure by weather phenomena such as thunderstorms, flash floods and extreme precipitation events. Downscaling modelling procedures exist to help overcome this issue, and are described below.

An imperative for the models is to approximate the natural variability of climate systems so that those climate variables evolving away from historical norms can be identified. The general procedure for this process is to undertake repeated runs of a given model, with different starting conditions, and compare and average the model results. The global models are complex and computationally demanding but also are subject to some inherent limitations and uncertainties. For example, IPCC (2013) indicated that the global models are sensitive to a number of factors including

- Inaccurate specifications of climate mechanisms, due to uncertainty in process representation or incomplete scientific understanding of the processes
- Inherent randomness, especially in the area of cloud physics
- Error propagation
- Uncertainties in observed data
- Sensitivity to model resolution
- Uncertainty surrounding human activities that impact climate, such as activities leading to greenhouse gas emissions, or impacts on carbon sinks.

The models therefore need to be used with care and with the best available expert advice on suitability for a given application. Further, the use of temperature, humidity and precipitation outputs in absolute terms is not recommended (ITF, 2016). A better approach is to consider the relative changes in the climate variables and apply these to observed climate data to create climate change scenarios.

Downscaling methods and models are available to provide more specific climate data and forecasts for regions (e.g., Brekke et al., 2013; Olsen, 2015; CSIRO, 2020). Downscaling can be attempted in two ways:

1. Statistical downscaling assumes a relationship between large-scale changes and local climate changes. It then adjusts regional climate projections by matching global, historical, simulated and observed climate variables. It requires a small amount of computation and therefore lends itself to the generation of climate change scenario ensembles spanning decades or even centuries. Common practice is to adjust for any biases in the climate models using the historical data and then assume that the statistical relationships developed for the historical period will also apply in the future
2. Dynamic downscaling uses regional climate models that are similar to the GCMs/ESMs but are cast at a regional or local scale. These models can include relevant topographical, land use and vegetation features. Thus, they are often more computationally demanding than the statistical methods. Dynamic downscaling provides better resolution for regional applications and may better represent important local climate processes such as convection and sea breezes, but may still be subject to any large-scale errors in the global model simulations used to set the boundary conditions for the regional model. For this reason, a statistical correction similar to that used in statistical downscaling is often applied.

Downscaled information for regions is useful input for policy making and planning purposes, although it must be realised that downscaled data may still inherit some of the limitations of the global models. While climate data from global, regional or downscaled models may seem analogous to historical climate data, they are not the same and model projections should not be used to replace the historical data in asset planning and management. The best use of the modelled data is to help establish a set of plausible future climate scenarios that can then inform transportation agency planning for the future. Care is needed in the consideration of climate scenarios in that these should not be used as predictions of future conditions. Rather climate scenarios provide a framework to examine the plausible spread of potential climate future and, perhaps, the conditions that might lead to those futures. As stated by IPCC (2014a), the intention for the use of scenarios 'is not to predict the future but to better understand uncertainties and alternative futures, in order to consider how robust different decisions or options may be under a wide range of possible futures'. To assist in this process, the global models have been used to model a set of pathways which link human activities, greenhouse gas emissions, atmospheric concentrations, radiative forcing[5] and climate impacts. These pathways are termed the 'Representative Concentration Pathways' (RCPs).

Representative Concentration Pathways

Transportation systems planning and management require socioeconomic scenarios for use in travel demand forecasting and in planning for the provision of transportation networks with levels of service suitable to meet present and future travel demands. Emissions scenarios are then needed as inputs to the adaptation planning that is a necessary part of the planning process in an era of climate change. While it is possible to set out potential socioeconomic scenarios for climate change studies, these scenarios are not really suitable for examination of potential climate change or as input into the climate models described above. Socioeconomic scenarios do not allow for flexibility or alternative options in for socioeconomic change. At the instigation of the IPCC (2007), a worldwide consortium of climate scientists took an alternative approach; the development of the RCPs. The RCPs consider the scenario problem in a different way, by fixing an emissions trajectory for each RCP and accompanying global warming. Then the socioeconomic options become flexible and can be altered to meet aspects such as technological change and changes in community aspirations and goals. The RCPs were first described by Van Vuuren et al. (2011).

Four RCPs have been proposed to represent different levels – or targets – for radiative forcing. Each RCP is associated with a specific level of radiative forcing and an indicative atmospheric concentration of greenhouse gases matching the radiative forcing. There are multiple potential socioeconomic scenarios that can lead to each RCP 'end-point' (year 2100). This flexibility is important for adaptation planning as it allows the RCP to be included in the more general transportation planning scenario development and provides future climate conditions for that purpose.

---

5. Radiative forcing is the difference between the solar energy absorbed by the Earth and energy radiated back into space. Positive radiative forcing means that the Earth is receiving more incoming energy from the Sun than it radiates back to space. This net gain of energy will cause warming. On the other hand, negative radiative forcing means that Earth loses more energy to space than it receives from the Sun, which produces cooling. A system in thermal equilibrium has zero radiative forcing. Radiative forcing is cited in units of Watts per square metre (W/m^2) of the Earth's surface. Radiative forcing varies with the amount of solar energy received, and the atmospheric concentrations of greenhouse gases and aerosols.

Four design criteria were used in developing the RCPs (Van Vuuren et al., 2011):

1. The RCPs should be based on scenarios published in the existing literature, developed independently by different modelling groups and, as a set, be 'representative' of the total literature, in terms of emissions and concentrations. At the same time, each of the RCPs should provide a plausible and internally consistent description of the future
2. The RCPs should provide information on all components of radiative forcing that are needed as input for climate modelling and atmospheric chemistry modelling (emissions of greenhouse gases, air pollutants and land use). Moreover, they should make such information available in a geographically explicit way
3. The RCPs should have harmonised base year assumptions for emissions and land use and allow for a smooth transition between analyses of historical and future periods
4. The RCPs should cover the time period up to 2100, but information also needs to be made available for the centuries thereafter.

Van Vuuren et al. (2011) also described the selection process used to designate the four RCPs. The four pathways cover radiative forcing levels of 2.6, 4.5, 6.0 and 8.5 W/m^2, respectively, and have been designated as RCP2.6, RCP4.5, RCP6.0 and RCP8.5 as a result. The RCPs cover the range of climate scenarios suggested in the climate science literature. The term 'concentration' is used because atmospheric greenhouse gas concentrations are a primary input used in the climate models, rather than the emission of the greenhouse gases.

Fig. 2.4, based on data in Van Vuuren et al. (2011), plots the carbon dioxide emissions under each of the RCPs, while Table 2.1 shows a set of indicators (greenhouse gas concentrations, temperature increases and sea level rise) for each RCP.

Pathway RCP8.5 represents a high emissions pathway, implying little effective mitigation of emissions, while RCP2.6 presents a pathway in which significant mitigation does take place. In the latter case, the need for climate change adaptation is small, whereas significant adaption is required under RCP8.5. The intermediate pathways RCP4.5 and RCP6.0 represent stabilisation of radiative forcing at 4.5 and 6.0 W/m^2, respectively, before 2100. All of the scenarios include time paths for emissions and concentrations of the full range of greenhouse gases and aerosols, as well as for land use and vegetation.

The fourth criterion cited by Van Vuuren et al. (2011) defined the year 2100 as an endpoint for the RCPs, but indicated that scope to provide information for periods after that year was also essential. This was done by developing a single 'Extended Pathway Concentration (ECP)' for each RCP, to extend the scenarios up to 2300. However, the ECP were developed using simple rules for future radiative forcing on the basis that socioeconomic factors cannot be predicted with any reliability so far into the future.

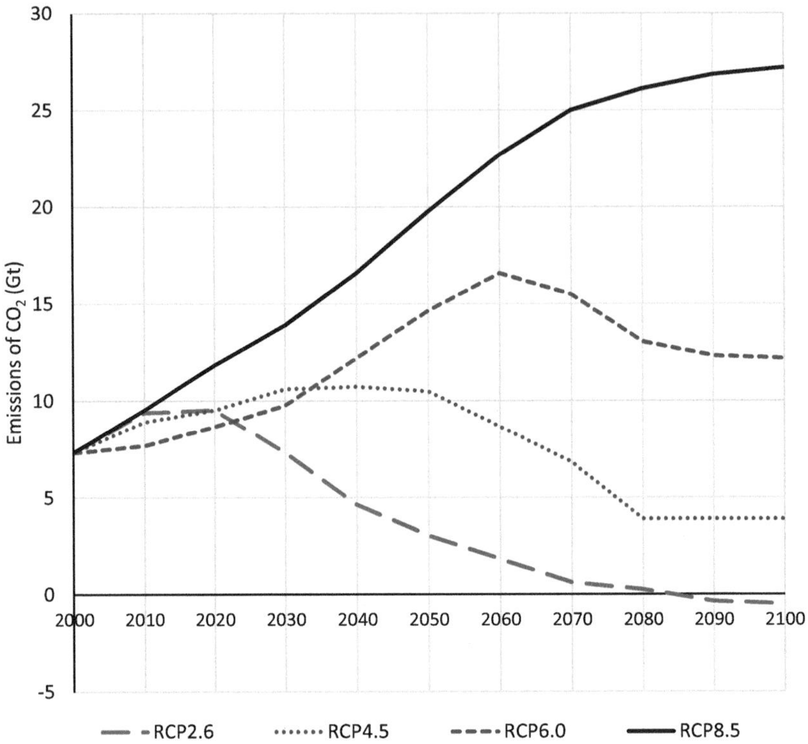

FIGURE 2.4 Estimated emissions of carbon dioxide 2000–2100 under the four Representative Concentration Pathways, *Based on data in Van Vuuren, D.P., Edmonds, J., Kainuma, M., Riahi, K., Thomson, A., Hibbard, K., Hurtt, G.C., Kram, T., Krey, V., Lamarque, J.F., Masui, T., Meinshausen, M., Nakicenovic, N., Smith, S.J., Rose, S.K., 2011. The representative concentration pathways: an overview. Climatic Change 109, 5–31.*

The RCPs provide a strong foundation for further research and assessment in emissions mitigation, climate change impact analysis and climate change adaptation planning. A downloadable database of information for the RCPs, for use in modelling and analysis studies connected with climate change adaptation planning, is available from IIASA (2020). Case study examples of the use of RCPs in adaptation planning for transportation systems are provided in Chapter 6 (concerning the impacts of groundwater rise on road pavements in coastal zones, see Knott et al. (2017)) and in Chapter 7 (concerning rail buckling in the US railway network, see Chinowsky et al. (2019)).

In addition to the RCP, some other climate scenarios have also been suggested recently. In particular, the 'H++' scenarios representing the foreseeable extreme climate change scenarios, i.e., outside the 10th and 90th percentile ranges. The H++ scenarios are seen as assisting in the full exploration of the potential consequences of climate change and in the

TABLE 2.1 Some characteristics of the four Representative Concentration Pathways.

Scenario	Atmospheric concentration of greenhouse gases (CO_2e ppm)	Radiative forcing in 2100 compared to preindustrial levels (W/m^2)	Average increase in temperature 2081–2100 compared to 1986–2005 (°C)	Average sea level rise 2081–2100 compared to 1986–2005 (m)	Remarks
Situation in 2011	390.5				From ITF (2016)
Situation in 2019	411.8				From NOOA (2020)
RCP2.6 in 2100	453	+2.6	+1.0	+0.40	Strong mitigation measures in place, less need for adaptation
RCP4.5 in 2100	586	+4.5	+1.8	+0.47	
RCP6.0 in 2100	779	+6.0	+2.3	+0.48	
RCP8.5 in 2100	1396	+8.5	+3.7	+0.63	Low levels of mitigation mean high need for significant adaptation. Current emissions are tracking close to this pathway

Based on data from IPCC, 2013. Summary for policymakers. In: Climate Change 2013: The Physical Science Basis. Stocker, T.F., Qin, D., Plattner, G.K., Tignor, M., Allen, S.K., Boschung, J., Nauels, A., Xia, Y., Bex, V., Midgley, P.M. (Eds.), Contribution of Working Group I to the Fifth Assessment Report of the Intergovernmental Panel on Climate Change. Cambridge University Press, Cambridge, UK and New York, NY; ITF, 2016. Adapting transport to climate change and extreme weather: implications for infrastructure owners and network managers. ITF Research Reports, OECD Publishing, Paris. https://doi.org/10.1787/9789282108079-en; CoastAdapt, 2020. www.coastadapt.com.au/infographics. (Accessed 22/03/2020) and NOOA, 2020. National Oceanic and Atmospheric Administration, Earth System Research Laboratory, Boulder, CO. https://www.esrl.noaa.gov/gmd/ccgg/trends/full.html.

flexibility provided by current and future adaptation plans (Met Office, 2015). The H++ scenarios represent low probability, high impact risks and thus provide valuable input in risk management studies. For instance, they may be used in sensitivity testing of different adaptation options against an extreme level of risk, which may be particularly useful for longer-terms adaptation planning. Risk analysis and planning for climate change adaptation in transportation systems are discussed in detail in Chapters 3 and 4 of this book, and adaptation planning for particular circumstances — coastal infrastructure, road networks and rail networks — is discussed in Chapters 5, 6 and 7, respectively. Sea level rise predictions under pathways RCP2.6, RCP8.5 and an H++ scenario are described in Chapter 5, using the work of Lincke and Hinkel (2018).

Summary

This chapter provides a primer on climate change basics. It includes a brief overview of climate system dynamics together with some discussion of observed changes in climate as reported, for example, by the IPCC (2007, 2013, 2014a,b). This chapter then examines weather events (e.g., rainfall, storms, hurricanes, droughts, blizzards and heat waves) and their potential impacts for transportation. These events form one part of climate, and their intensity and frequency are of interest, leading to consideration of what may be considered as extreme weather events, which can lead to disruptions in transport operations (e.g., through weather-induced events such as floods, wild fires, landslides and storm surges). The possible contributions of human activity over time to climate change and to the potential impacts of weather on transportation infrastructure are then introduced. Sea level rise is also considered, as a major factor affecting coastal and estuarine infrastructure. The importance of these phenomena for transportation network operations is also reviewed. GCMs are outlined, as an information source for use as inputs in adaptation planning for future climate change affecting transportation. Given the climate models and the capability to downscale from global to regional studies, the RCP approach is introduced to conclude this chapter. The RCP approach offers climate input data for use in adaptation planning on the basis of climate change scenarios.

This book now turns to considerations on transportation infrastructure and the possible impacts of climate change on that infrastructure. General methods for adaptation planning in transportation, based on risk management analysis, are described in Chapter 3, with detailed methods for analysis and assessment discussed in Chapter 4. This chapter also deals with adaptation planning for airports. Chapters 5–8 of this book consider specific parts of transportation infrastructure considerations, including issues for coastal areas, ports and harbours, road networks, rail networks and multimodal transportation (including provision for walking and cycling).

References

AAS, 2015. The Science of Climate Change: Questions and Answers. Australian Academy of Science, Canberra ACT. www.science.org.au/climatechange.

Amin, M.S.R., Zareie, A., Amador-Jiménez, L.E., 2014. Climate change modeling and the weather-related road accidents in Canada. Transport. Res. Part D 32, 171–183.

Arrhenius, S., 1896. On the influence of carbonic acid in the air upon the temperature of the ground. Phil. Mag. J. Sci. 41, 239–276.

Bollinger, L.A., Dijkema, G.P.J., 2016. Evaluating infrastructure resilience to extreme weather – the case of the Dutch electricity transmission network. Eur. J. Transport Infrastruct. Res. 16 (1), 214–239.

BOM, 2020a. 110 Years of Australian Temperatures. Australian Bureau of Meteorology. http://www.bom.gov.au/climate/history/temperature/. (Accessed 17 March 2020).

BOM, 2020b. Annual Rainfall, Temperature and Sea Surface Temperature Anomalies and Ranks. Australian Bureau of Meteorology. http://www.bom.gov.au/climate/current/annual/aus/2019/annual-summary-table.shtml. (Accessed 17 March 2020).

Brekke, L., Thrasher, B.L., Maurer, E.P., Pruitt, T., 2013. Downscaled CMIP3 and CMIP5 Climate Projections: Release Of Downscaled Cmip5 Climate Projections, Comparison With Preceding Information, and Summary of User Needs. http://gdo-dcp.ucllnl.org/downscaled_cmip_projections/. (Accessed 27 January 2020).

Chinowsky, P., Helman, J., Gulati, S., Neumann, J., Martinich, J., 2019. Impacts of climate change on operation of the US rail network. Transport Pol. 75, 183–191.

CoastAdapt, 2020. www.coastadapt.com.au/infographics. (Accessed 22/03/2020).

CSIRO, 2020. https://www.csiro.au/en/Research/OandA/Areas/Assessing-our-climate/ACCESS. (Accessed 21/03/2020).

Donat, M G, Alexander, L V, 2012. The shifting probability distribution of global daytime and night-time temperatures. Geophysical Research Letters 39 (L14707).

FHWA, 2014. Highways in the Coastal Environment: Assessing Extreme Events. Hydraulic Engineering Circular No 25 – Volume 2. Federal Highways Administration, Washington DC report FHWA-NHI-14-006. https://www.fhwa.dot.gov/engineering/hydraulics/pubs/nhi14006/nhi14006.pdf.

IIASA, 2020. RCP Database 2.0. International Institute for Applied Systems Analysis, Vienna. http://tntcat.iiasa.ac.at:8787/RcpDb/dsd?Action=htmlpage&page=welcome. (Accessed 15 March 2020).

IPCC, 2007. In: Solomon, S., Qin, D., Manning, M., Chen, Z., Marquis, M., Averyt, K.B., Tignor, M., Miller, H.L. (Eds.), Climate Change 2007: The Physical Science Basis. Contribution of Working Group I to the Fourth Assessment Report of the Intergovernmental Panel on Climate Change. Cambridge University Press, Cambridge, UK and New York, NY).

IPCC, 2013. Summary for policymakers. In: Stocker, T.F., Qin, D., Plattner, G.-K., Tignor, M., Allen, S.K., Boschung, J., Nauels, A., Xia, Y., Bex, V., Midgley, P.M. (Eds.), Climate Change 2013: The Physical Science Basis. Contribution of Working Group I to the Fifth Assessment Report of the Intergovernmental Panel on Climate Change. Cambridge University Press, Cambridge, UK and New York, NY).

IPCC, 2014a. In: Field, C.B., Barros, V.R., Dokken, D.J., Mach, K.J., Mastrandrea, M.D., Bilir, T.E., Chatterjee, M., Ebi, K.L., Estrada, Y.O., Genova, R.C., Girma, B., Kissel, E.S., Levy, A.N., MacCracken, S., Mastrandrea, P.R., White, L.L. (Eds.), Climate Change 2014: Impacts, Adaptation, and Vulnerability. Part A: Global and Sectoral Aspects. Contribution of Working Group II to the Fifth Assessment Report of the Intergovernmental Panel on Climate Change. Cambridge University Press, Cambridge, UK and New York, NY).

IPCC, 2014b. In: Edenhofer, O., Pichs-Madruga, R., Sokona, Y., Farahani, E., Kadner, S., Seyboth, K., Adler, A., Baum, I., Brunner, S., Eickemeier, P., Kriemann, B., Savolainen, J., Schlömer, S., Von Stechow, C., Zwickel, T., Minx, J.C. (Eds.), Climate Change 2014: Mitigation of Climate Change. Contribution of Working Group III to the Fifth Assessment Report of the Intergovernmental Panel on Climate Change. Cambridge University Press, Cambridge, UK and New York, NY).

ITF, 2016. Adapting transport to climate change and extreme weather: implications for infrastructure owners and network managers. In: ITF Research Reports. OECD Publishing, Paris. https://doi.org/10.1787/9789282108079-en.

Jaroszweski, D., McNamara, T., 2014. The influence of rainfall on road accidents in urban areas: a weather radar approach. Trav. Behav. Soc. 1, 15−21.

Knott, J.F., Elshaer, M., Danieal, J.S., Jacobs, J.M., Kirshen, P., 2017. Assessing the effects of rising groundwater from sea level rise on the service life of pavements in coastal road infrastructure. Transport. Res. Rec. 2639, 1−10.

Lincke, D., Hinkel, J., 2018. Economically robust protection against 21st century sea-level rise. Global Environ. Change 51, 67−73.

Melillo, J.M., Richmond, T.C., Yohe, G.W. (Eds.), 2014. Climate Change Impacts in the United States: The Third National Climate Assessment. US Global Change Research Program, p. 841. https://doi.org/10.7930/J0Z31WJ2.

Met Office, 2015. Developing H++ Climate Change Scenarios for Heat Waves, Droughts, Floods, Windstorms and Cold Snaps. Met Office, University of Reading and Centre for Environmental Hydrology (CEH), Exeter. https://www.theccc.org.uk/publication/met-office-for-the-asc-developing-h-climate-change-scenarios/. (Accessed 20 March 2020).

NOOA, 2020. National Oceanic and Atmospheric Administration. Earth System Research Laboratory, Boulder, CO. https://www.esrl.noaa.gov/gmd/ccgg/trends/full.html.

NWS, 2020. National Weather Service Glossary. US National Weather Service, National Oceanic and Atmospheric Administration, Silver Spring MD. https://w1.weather.gov/glossary/. (Accessed 15 March 2020).

Olsen, J.R. (Ed.), 2015. Adapting Infrastructure and Civil Engineering Practice to a Changing Climate. American Society of Civil Engineers, Reston, VA. www.asce.org/publications.

Siebentritt, M., 2016. Understanding Sea-Level Rise and Climate Change, and Associated Impacts on the Coastal Zone. CoastAdapt Information Manual 2,. National Climate Change Adaptation Research Facility, Gold Coast. www.coastadapt.com.au.

SOCCOM, 2020. What Is an Earth System Model (ESM)? https://soccom.princeton.edu/content/what-earth-system-model-esm. (Accessed 21 March 2020).

Van Vuuren, D.P., Edmonds, J., Kainuma, M., Riahi, K., Thomson, A., Hibbard, K., Hurtt, G.C., Kram, T., Krey, V., Lamarque, J.-F., Masui, T., Meinshausen, M., Nakicenovic, N., Smith, S.J., Rose, S.K., 2011. The representative concentration pathways: an overview. Climatic Change 109, 5−31.

Chapter 3

Transportation infrastructure

Introduction

Transport infrastructure is ubiquitous and is critical for the economic and social well-being of a modern society, by providing for personal mobility, accessibility to services and the movement of goods and facilitating economic activity and social interaction. The infrastructure includes ports, harbours and airports, road, rail and pipeline networks, the depots and facilities associated with these networks and the public and private transport services that operate on them. The physical components on transport infrastructure include bridges, tunnels, pavements, rail tracks, culverts, wharfs, aprons and pipes. These elements are located on the ground or above or below ground level – but always associated with or attached to the ground. They may exist in cuttings or embankments or on the natural surface. Thus, transport infrastructure is directly affected by local environmental and climate conditions.

Transport infrastructure is a valuable asset. For instance, the road network of Australia and New Zealand comprises over 900,000 km of roads valued at more than $200 billion, the single largest community asset in Australasia (Austroads, 2019). Road assets are owned and managed by all levels of government, but local government is directly responsible for the lion's share of this asset. Balston et al. (2017) outlined the responsibilities of local government and the implications of climate change for local government. Transport assets have engineering and economic life spans ranging from a decade (for road signage) to 2–3 decades for road pavements and rail tracks and to several decades (or longer) for bridges and tunnels. This means that most road assets will be subject to the impacts of climate change over their usable lives, and thus adaptation to changing climatic conditions is necessary in the design, management and maintenance or the assets. Transport systems are recognised as one of the major critical infrastructure systems in any economy (ASCE, 2009), while being subject to adverse impacts from extreme weather, climate change, natural disasters and man-made incidents

Climate Change Adaptation for Transportation Systems. https://doi.org/10.1016/B978-0-12-816638-3.00003-9

and disasters. Furthermore, transport networks, and especially the road network, are vital enablers of regional economy and indeed life, as described in Beer et al. (2015).

Transportation systems belong to the set of distributed infrastructure systems, in that their infrastructure components are connected and spread across a region. The physical components of the system exist in a connected network spanning that region allows the movements of people, vehicles and goods across the region. The physical elements are thus subject to the prevailing environmental and climatic conditions of the area. Land-based transportation systems — road and rail — require connected physical assets for their operations. Water-based transportation requires some fixed assets besides ports and harbours for operations (e.g., locks and canals). Aviation systems require airport facilities, but otherwise no fixed connective assets except for service and supply by the land-based systems, and thus are also reliant on them. Intermodal interchanges are required whenever people and/or goods move from one transportation mode to another.

The multimodal and hence multinetwork nature of transportation systems is also a pointer to a further feature of those systems. Transportation is inextricably linked to other infrastructure systems (e.g., energy and communications systems). These linkages need to be considered along with transportation systems, and this is best done by considering the interdependencies that can exist between infrastructure systems.

Infrastructure networks and systems

Infrastructure exists in the form of systems and networks, with the following applications prominent (Rinaldi et al., 2001):

- transportation
- water supply and wastewater removal and treatment
- telecommunications
- electrical power
- oil and gas
- banking and finance
- government services
- emergency services
- medical and health care
- food and agriculture
- goods movement and supply chains.

A general characteristic of these infrastructure systems is that they tend to be spread geographically and thus are represented by networks, with nodes of activity and/or connection and links between the nodes. Each system will have both physical and virtual facets. The physical facets include the structures, assets and facilities and connections between them. The virtual facets include the operating rules and systems under which the infrastructure operates, and the policy, governance and regulatory environment in which the infrastructure is placed. For a transportation system, the physical facets include roads or rail lines, intersections and interchanges, stops, stations and pick-up points, and the depots, parking, storage facilities and refuelling stations. The virtual facets include the traffic operating rules and control systems applied to the infrastructure. The latter indicates a further point, which is that an infrastructure system may depend on other infrastructure systems for its operations. For example, modern traffic control systems use telecommunications systems for the flows of information that are required for the system operation. Thus, a failure in one system may lead to degraded performance in another. Physical proximity is also an issue affecting the performance of different infrastructure systems. For instance, a road bridge in a transportation network may be used to carry pipes and cables for other infrastructure systems (e.g., water and telecommunications) across a waterway. Damage to the bridge may then affect the operation of these other systems as well. In many cities, water, sewerage and gas pipelines and underground power cables are located in a road reserve or indeed under the road pavement. Maintenance and repair work on these facilities – which constitute a large part of the activity generally known as 'roadworks' – may thus lead to capacity reduction and disruptions in the operation of a road traffic system.

An overall picture of the system conditions and interrelating factors is shown in Fig. 3.1 which presents six separate dimensions for consideration of infrastructure systems and the relationships between different systems. These dimensions cover the characteristics of a given infrastructure, its possible states of operation, types of interrelations with other systems, the economic, technological, security and governance environment in which it exists, the degree of linkage or coupling with other systems and the types of failure that can be experienced. Thus, the level of independence, dependence or interdependence between infrastructure systems has to be considered. According to Rinaldi et al. (2001), one infrastructure system is dependent on another if there is a unidirectional relationship between the pair, i.e., one system depends on the other, but the second one does not depend directly upon the first. Thus, an electric passenger rail system such as a subway system is dependent on the electrical power system. Infrastructure dependency then exists when the state of one infrastructure system influences or is correlated with the state of another. Two infrastructure systems are interdependent when there is a bidirectional relationship between them, that is, the operating state of each system affects or is influenced by the state of the other. An electric rail system used to haul coal to a power station would be an example of two interdependent infrastructure systems. The rail system requires the electrical energy from the power system to operate, and the power generating infrastructure requires the fuel brought to it by the rail system. In general, if we wish to take an holistic view of the operation of a set of infrastructure systems, it is perhaps best to consider interdependency as the overriding perspective.

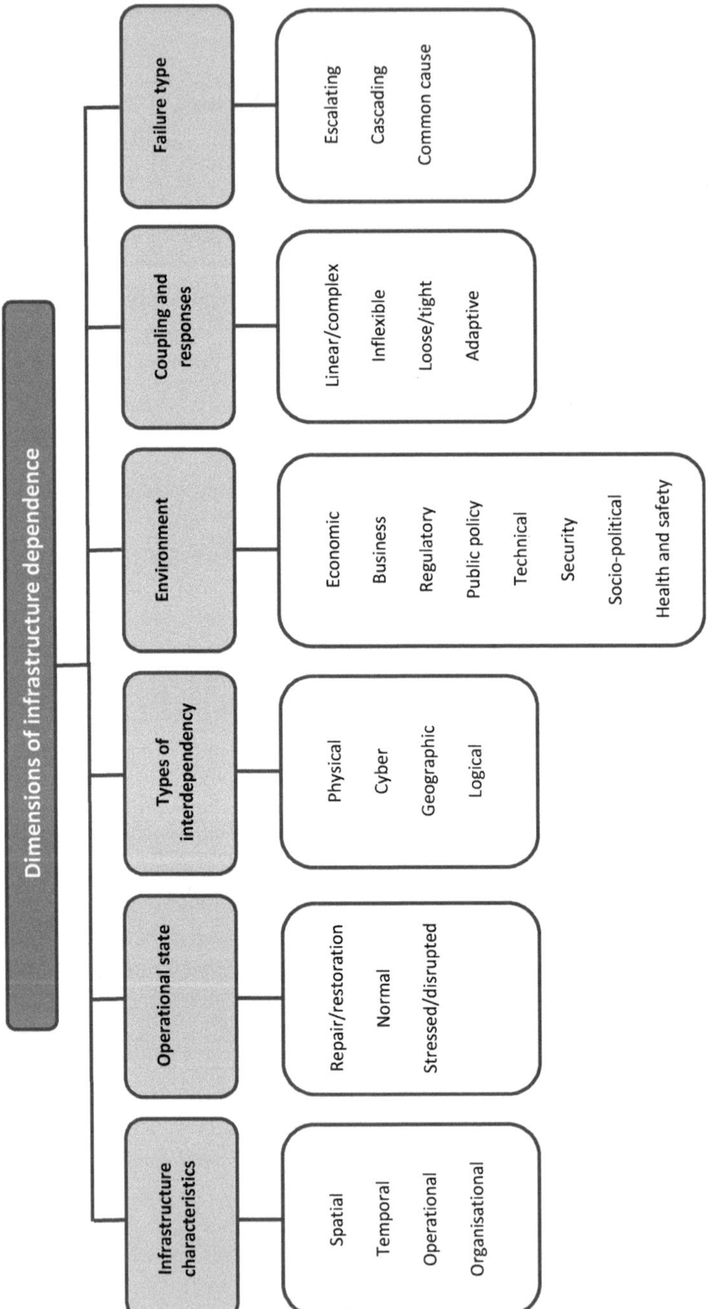

FIGURE 3.1 Dimensions of infrastructure interdependencies. *Adapted from Rinaldi, S.M., Peerenboom, J.P., Kelly, T.K., December 2001. Identifying, Understanding and Analysing Critical Infrastructure Interdependencies. IEEE Control Syst. Mag. pp.11–25.*

Interdependencies exist in a number of forms, as illustrated in Fig. 3.1. Four types of interdependencies are shown in the figure:

- *physical interdependency*, which occurs when there is a physical linkage between the inputs and outputs of two systems, i.e., some commodity produced or treated by one infrastructure (its output) is used by another infrastructure in its operations (thus an input to that system). If, as in the case of the coal train delivering supplies to the power station (as above), the output of the second infrastructure system (electrical energy generation) is itself an input to the first, then a degradation in the performance of one system can lead to a degraded performance of the other. Positive feedback may occur, with changes in the operating state of one system having effects on the other, to its further detriment.
- *cyber interdependency* is found when the operating state of an infrastructure system depends on the transmission of information through an information infrastructure such as a telecommunications system. As modern infrastructure systems have become more and more dependent on information gathered across the system (such as traffic volumes at different intersections in a road system) or taken from other systems (such as GPS satellites for location and vehicle tracking) and base their optimal operating states on the ready availability of reliable and accurate information, so transportation infrastructure has become more and more cyber-dependent.
- *geographic interdependency* is found when a local environmental event, such as a traffic accident, roadworks, road closure for a special event, an extreme weather event, flooding, wild fire or an earthquake, leads to changes in the operating states of a set of infrastructure systems. Such interdependency generally reflects close proximity of the systems, such as colocation or sharing of common facilities (e.g., power, water and telecommunications systems using a road bridge to span a river). While the performance of one system and the change in its operating state may not directly affect the other systems, their performances may be correlated because of their proximity to or involvement in the environmental event. Multiple infrastructure systems can be affected simultaneously under geographic interdependence.
- *logical interdependency* between two infrastructure systems occurs when the state of each depends on the state of the other through a connection or mechanism that is not a physical, cyber or geographic connection. Logical dependency is thus a 'catch all' for other forms of dependency, such as those resulting from public policy decisions, public sector service provision or private sector investment decisions. For instance, the contraction of health and education services from small rural communities to larger urban centres may have an effect on the operation of the road transport system as residents of outlying areas have to travel further to access these services.

Infrastructure characteristics, as also indicated in Fig. 3.1, influence system operations and interdependency. The principal characteristics of an infrastructure system include spatial or geographic scales, temporal scales, operational factors and organisational characteristics. These scales are particularly important for transportation infrastructure, which is characterised by its distribution over geographical regions and the requirement that it can operate at all times under a wide range of environmental and weather conditions.

In terms of geographic (or spatial) scale, transportation infrastructure operates at the local (precinct) level, the metropolitan level, the regional level, the state/provincial level, the national level, the international level and the intercontinental level. The composition of the infrastructure may be described in hierarchical terms, following the taxonomies described by Perrow (1984) and Rinaldi et al. (2001), as follows:

- item (or part), the smallest component of a system that can be identified in an analysis. A traffic light standard would be one item in a road transport system
- unit, which is a functionally related collection of parts, such as a road intersection, which would include the parts such as traffic lights, traffic islands, designated traffic lanes and pedestrian crossing facilities
- subsystem, an array of units, such as the set of intersections along an arterial road
- system, a grouping of subsystems, such as the set of arterial roads, highways and local streets that comprise the traffic network in a city or region
- infrastructure, a complete collection of like systems, such as the road network in a state or province
- interdependent infrastructures, which (as described above) form the interconnected web of infrastructures and environment. Road and rail transportation systems often operate in the same locations and can interact with each other in different ways, e.g., delays to road traffic at level crossings, or the connections between urban passenger rail services and feeder buses at suburban train stations.

A useful way to consider climate change impacts on transportation infrastructure, and associated interdependent infrastructure systems was suggested by Tavasszy et al. (2016). This is summarised by the conceptual framework shown in Fig. 3.2, based on a similar framework proposed by Bollinger et al., (2014). The framework places the transportation system within the milieu of the society and physical environment in which it exists. It also links transportation to other related or interdependent infrastructure systems. Within the milieu of society, policies and plans are formulated and promulgated. These result in projects and actions to support, manage and extend the infrastructure systems. The framework allows for the impacts of climate change in general and climate-related episodes and events that impinge on the provision and operation of transportation systems. The figure

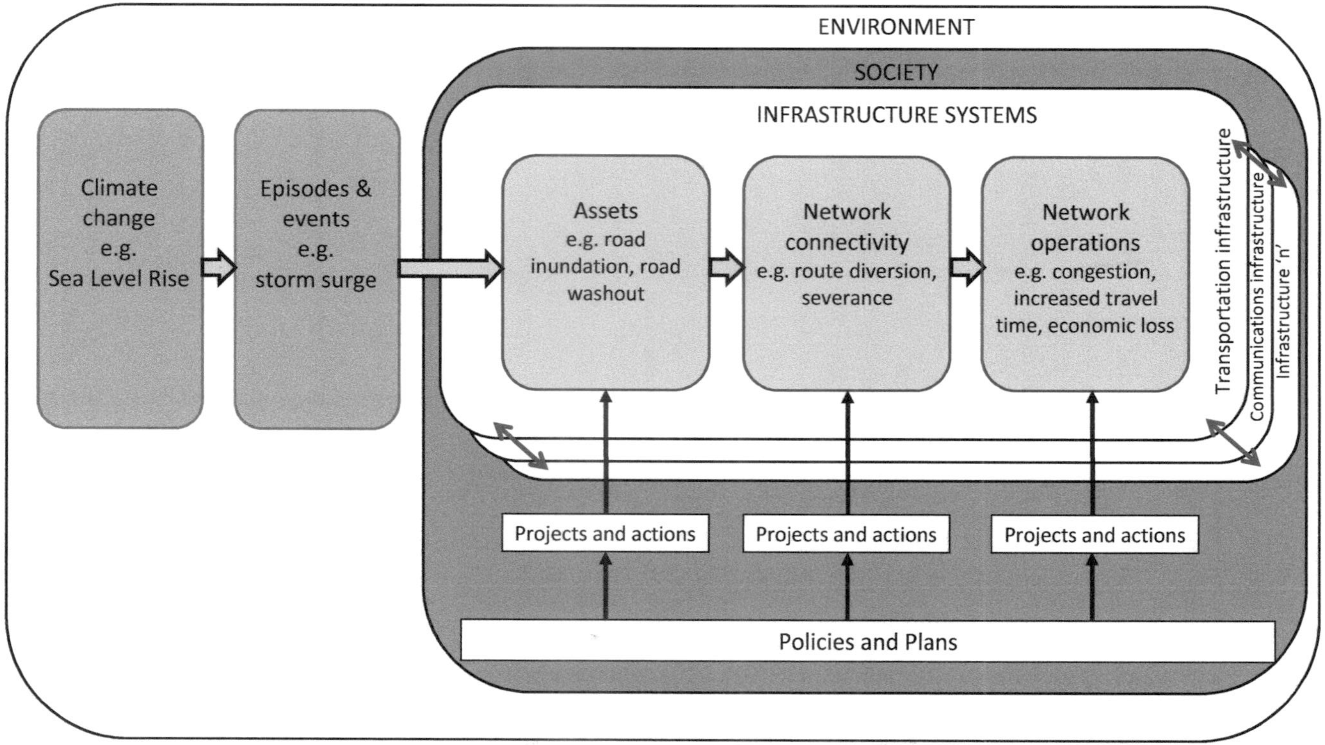

FIGURE 3.2 Conceptual framework for climate change impacts on transportation infrastructure and associated interdependent infrastructure systems. *Adapted from Tavasszy, L., Bollinger, A., Dijkema, G.P.J. 2016. Editorial: special issue on climate adaptation of infrastructure networks. Eur. J. Transport Infrastruct. Res. 16 (1), 95–97, www.tlo.tbm.tudelft.nl/ejtir.*

uses the example of sea level rise as a climate change impact, with impacts through storm surge events then affecting transportation. In terms of transportation assets, the storm surge may lead to road inundation or road washout in an affected coastal region. This leads to reduction in network connectivity as affected roads are impassable for some time period, leading to route diversions and possible severance for some communities. Network operations are thus impacted through increased travel times and perhaps increased traffic congestion in parts of the degraded network. In the longer term, economic losses may accrue through the reduced network performance and severance. Society, government and responsible agencies need to have policies and plans in place which lead to actions and projects (e.g., increased coastal protection such as higher sea walls) to protect the transportation assets.

This book is not only primarily concerned with land transportation systems —road and public transport systems — but also considers water-based transportation and aviation insofar as these share common elements with the land-based systems. These elements are the land-based components of the systems, such as ports and harbours, and airports and terminal facilities.

Road traffic systems

The road traffic system can also be seen as comprising three interrelated systems: the road infrastructure itself, the users of the road system (vehicles, drivers, cyclists, pedestrians and public transport) and the environment (topography, light conditions, climate and weather). This designation has been widely employed in studies of road safety (Ogden, 1996). This consideration leads to a further concern: the factors (internal and external) affecting the performance of an infrastructure system. We can identify three broad groupings of such factors:

1. *supply factors*, relating to the coverage (in time and space) and capacity of the different components (items, units and subsystems) of a transport system. Urban road networks tend to be dense, with many alternatives available between separated locations in the network; whereas, rural road networks may be sparse, with few alternative routes available. Even when there are alternative routes, some of these may be inadequate or inconvenient. Public transport networks, especially suburban networks and intercity networks, tend to be directional in nature, e.g., providing good access to a city centre but poor if any access between adjacent suburbs, while high-speed rail networks may provide good connections between some towns and cities but bypass others. Road link and intersection capacities can also be limited, or subject to degradation because of vehicle breakdowns, crashes, road works and weather events (e.g., floods)

2. *demand factors*, which relate to the mobility requirements of a community and the travel intentions and behaviour of individuals, in terms of their needs to travel and where, when and how they wish to travel
3. *external factors*, such as weather conditions and (transport) energy supply, population growth that affects the utilisation and provision of system capacity, environmental factors and climate change, which may lead to changes in environment and population distribution.

Road networks constitute a major public asset in most jurisdictions. For instance, the road network of Australia and New Zealand comprises over 900,000 km of roads valued at more than $200 billion, the single largest community asset in Australasia (Austroads, 2015). The road asset includes kilometres of road pavement (often expressed as lane-km to account for multilane roads), as well as other components (units) such as bridges, tunnels, culverts, car parking stations and fuelling stations. Road networks provide for both through movements across a region and for access to properties and facilities within it. The network is often split into (interconnected) subnetworks in terms of the jurisdictional and legal responsibility for ownership and maintenance of road facilities, with national highway systems the responsibility of national or federal governments, main road systems the responsibility of state or provincial transportation agencies, and local roads and streets the responsibility of local government. Increasingly, in many parts of the world, there are now significant toll road facilities, largely urban highways and intercity routes in private hands. One outcome of these ownership arrangements is that different design standards and maintenance regimes may be applied on different parts of the road network in the same region, which can have consequences if a major road is blocked or unavailable, and heavy volumes of traffic have to detour by other roads. The primary considerations for road network managers are the provision, operation and maintenance of the infrastructure components that is collectively for the road transportation network; which places a focus on asset management.

Different components in a road system will have different design lives, so that a road sign may last for 10–15 years, a road pavement be designed for satisfactory performance over 20–25 years and a road bridge designed to provide good performance for 80 years. Lifecycle analysis for individual transport assets and the set of assets comprising a given road is important, especially when concerned about environmental changes over time, such as ongoing urban development or climate change, are pertinent. Urban development issues are well-understood and planning agencies have established methods to address these, but climate change is relatively new. Methods for including climate change in the ongoing transportation planning and systems management process are still evolving. Subsequent chapters of this book consider some of these methods.

Road networks also cater for two dimensional flows and indeed for two-way flows on individual links, a point of difference between them and some other infrastructure networks such as water supply and conventional electrical power generation[1] They are also populated by myriad decision makers – individual travellers – whose travel decisions can have significant impacts on the operation of the transport system. Electrons, water and gas molecules do not have that capability. The human influences on travel behaviour thus have to be accounted for in any consideration of transportation network performance. A large range of vehicle types, from bicycles to heavy goods vehicles, may have to be accommodated on a road network and on the individual road links in it.

One subtle point of differentiation between road networks and public transport networks is that the former are ubiquitous, intended to provide for access widely across a region, and available for use at any time by a variety of vehicles and users. This is often not the case for transit services. Indeed, transit may be more severely impacted by climate and weather events because of the formal restrictions from the basic operating rules of system. A rail track blockage is not easily bypassed.

Public transport systems

Public transport (transit) networks possess similar characteristics to road networks, but add some additional features and perhaps operate under more restrictive control systems. The additional features include the necessary presence of stops and stations, where passengers can access or alight from the transit services, a necessary part of the system operation. Catering for passenger movements thus imposes particular tasks in system operation and perhaps for differentiation of services, especially but not uniquely for rail systems, where a mixture of local (frequently stopping) and express services may exist. Transit systems operate with fewer (but often larger) vehicles, often quite homogenous in performance characteristics, and with more restrictive operational rules, especially in guided path system such as railways, where overtaking opportunities are few and limited to places where sections of parallel tracks, sidings or spur lines can be provided. The flows of public transport vehicles may best be described as granular in nature, as they consist of a few large vehicles with relatively long headways separating them. This is particularly the case for railway systems.

1. Similar issues are now arising in the consideration of microgrids and distributed power generation systems

According to Vuchic (2007), a public transport system can be defined in terms of three dimensions:

1. its right-of-way (ROW) class
2. the system technology employed, which is made up of four basic elements: support, guidance, propulsion and control
3. the type of service provided.

The ROW for a transit line is the spatial area on which the transit vehicles operate. There are three basic classes of ROW:

- the lowest class (Vuchic's classification 'Category C') comprises surface streets with mixed traffic, typified by urban bus operations and sometimes streetcars. The transit vehicles may have special priority treatments such as exclusive bus lanes, but these are only nominally separated from other traffic, e.g., by painted lane markings, and so other road users can – and sometimes must – encroach on that space. Transit services operating in this environment are subject to the general traffic congestion found on the road
- the second ROW class is longitudinal separation, where some form of kerbing, physical barrier or grade separation exists to keep other traffic clear of the transit services, which can then proceed largely unimpeded – although there may be strong interactions between transit and other traffic at crossing points and road intersections. Light-rail transit (LRT) often operates in this environment
- the highest class of ROW is fully controlled access, where the transit service operates on an exclusive track completed separated from other transport modes, with grade separation between the track and intersecting transport. A metro (or subway) system is a good example. Fully controlled access transit may operate above ground, below ground or at ground level. Regional rail systems with widely spaced at-grade crossings (protected by signals and boom or gate barriers) can also be regarded as belonging to this ROW class, at least for the transit mode, as the crossings have little practical effect on transit line performance (as long as the crossing facilities are functioning properly).

Transit system technology relates to the mechanical features of the transit vehicles and trackways in terms of support, guidance, propulsion and control:

- support is the vertical contact between the vehicle and the riding surface, for instance as rubber tyre on road pavement or steel wheel on steel rail, with other support types such air cushions or magnetic levitation also possible
- guidance relates to the means of steering or lateral guidance of the vehicle, with rail vehicles guided by rail flanges and the shape of the wheel surfaces. Note that a rail system and its wheel-rail assembly integrate support and guidance

- propulsion is defined by the type of propulsion unit (engine or motor) and energy source (e.g., diesel fuel or electricity) and the method of traction
- control is the means employed to regulate and separate the movements of the vehicles in a system, with longitudinal separation the key, especially in rail-based systems. Control systems can be manual or automatic.

One further characteristic of public transport that contrasts with road transport is the general 'lumpiness' of transit services from the granular flow characteristics of transit services. While the ROW – the transit network – is in place at all times,[2] the ability to access and use the system depends on the availability of a transit vehicle to the potential traveller. Thus, service frequency by destination is an important consideration. If no vehicle is present, the system cannot be used. Additionally, a vehicle breakdown or component failure at one location in a transit network may lead to cascading impacts across the system. This is dealt with in detail in Taylor (2017).

Support and guidance for rail-based modes are provided by fixed rail tracks. Compacted crushed stone ballast is widely used as the base for rail tracks. The rails are mounted on sleepers which are fastened to the ballast layer by ties. The ties between the sleepers and the rails hold the rails in place, vertically and horizontally, and are designed to ensure precise and stable gauge width. The ballast serves to transfer the vehicle loads to the underlying wider roadbed. For at-grade and embankment alignments, the roadbed is generally of earth, but in elevated sections, it will consist of other structural materials, such as concrete. Modern practice for elevated sections is to use tracks without ballast, and the rails are fastened to the (concrete) structure using spring-loaded ties. In modern railway systems, sleepers are generally made of concrete, but timber sleepers were widely used in the past and many countries sections of regional rail lines may still utilise wooden sleepers.

Airports, ports and harbours

Airports, ports and harbours are major terminal points (hubs) in transportation systems, at which intermodal transfers occur and which attract significant volumes of passengers and freight. They are important hubs for economic activity in a region and are likely to be major traffic generators. The airport is a regional focus for air transportation, served by one or more land modes (e.g., road and rail) and providing air link connections to airports in other regions.

2. For the case of rail-based transport and perhaps bus rapid transit (BRT) systems, the transit ROW is visually obvious at all times, even when no transit vehicles are present. This is not the case with buses using the road system, and this observation is sometimes considered as a limitation on the public perception of the availability of bus public transport in an area.

Ports provide an interface between waterborne transportation and land transport. They may be found on sea coasts, in river estuaries and along major rivers themselves.

The basic requirement for ports and airports is therefore land space, and this space is generally flat and sometimes not readily available. Such terrain is commonly found at or near coasts, or indeed on flood plains. This will certainly be the case for shipping ports, and is often the case for airports. Thus, there are likely to be bodies of moving water close to the port or airport. The port or harbour will be immediately adjacent to the body of water. Some airports are constructed on artificial islands in the water.

By location, if nothing else ports and airports are thus exposed to water movements, whether tides, river flows, floods, storm surges or sea level rise. If any of these movements are to be affected by climate change, as they may well be, then the transportation assets and their connections to the surrounding transportation networks and systems are vulnerable to the potential changes. Consequently, particular care is needed in the management of these vital transportation assets in the face of climate change.

Generic infrastructure components

There are a number of physical infrastructure components that are common to different transportation systems. These components include bridges, viaducts, tunnels, culverts, pavements, track, cuttings and embankments. To see where and why these components are used, consider a road or rail route. This can be seen as a continuous ribbon through three-dimensional space (the surrounding terrain). For much of the time, the ribbon will sit on the natural surface of the land, but occasionally it will be above or below that surface. When the ribbon does not lie on the natural surface, then construction work is necessary either to support the route or to allow it to lie beneath the surface. Fig. 3.3 shows a schematic elevation for a road or rail route traversing a landscape. In this elevation, on the left hand side, the route lies beneath the natural surface. This is in a cutting, where the natural surface has been excavated to allow the route to proceed along the designed alignment. Further to the right, the route is above the natural surface and is situated on an embankment created to provide the physical support for the infrastructure. At the right hand end of the elevation, the route is located on the natural surface. Section A-A in Fig. 3.3 shows a cross section in the cutting, indicating the original level of the natural surface and the slopes of the excavation required. Section B-B is a cross section through the fill, showing the embankment created to support the route.

In situations where cuttings and embankments cannot be created to support the routes, e.g., where insufficient lateral space is available, in mountainous terrain or when crossing waterways or chasms, then other physical structures need to be constructed. These structures include bridges, viaducts and tunnels.

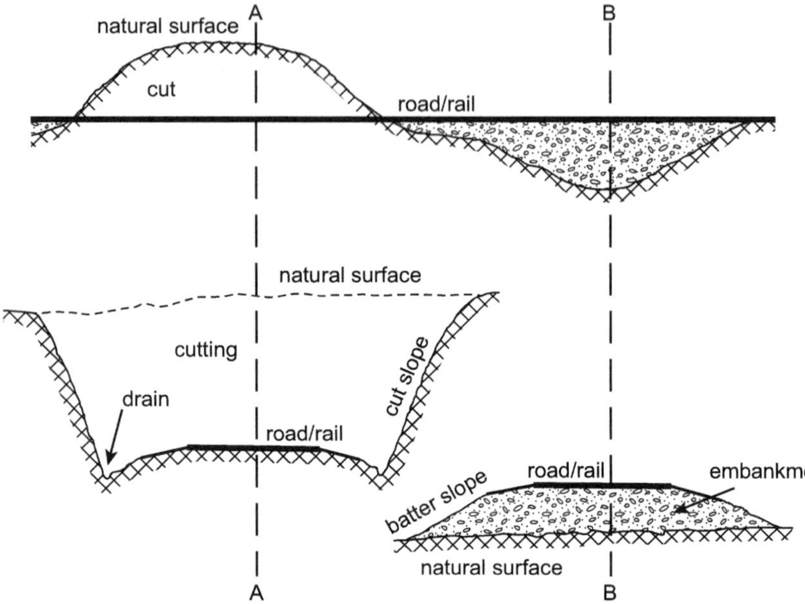

FIGURE 3.3 Schematic of a road or rail track alignment through a natural terrain.

Fig. 3.4 provides a schematic representation of a route alignment requiring a bridge or viaduct to cross a river valley and a tunnel through a mountainside. It also indicates some potential natural hazards that may be found in this environment, such as scouring of bridge piers located in the river and potential landslides at a tunnel entrance.

Bridges are physical structures that carry a roadway or railway over a physical gap or obstruction, such as a river, waterway or other roads

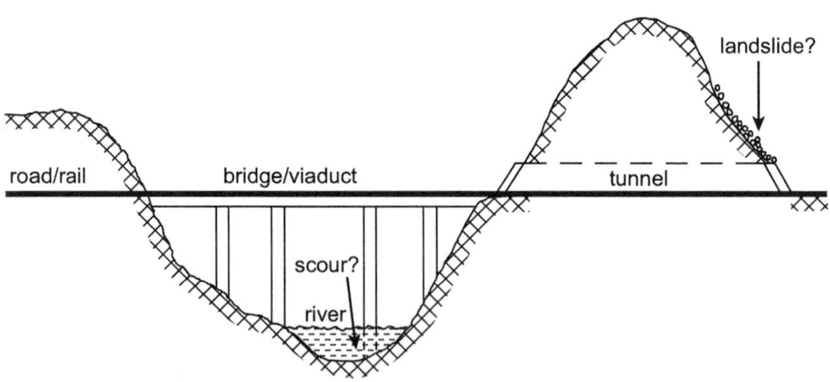

FIGURE 3.4 Schematic of usage of bridges and tunnels along a transport route.

and railways. A bridge consists of two basic components: (1) the substructure comprising abutments and piers which supports and (2) the superstructure (bridge deck) on which the roadway/railway is located. Important geometric features of a bridge are its span (the distance between supporting piers) and its elevation (the height above the feature – river, ground or trackway – to be bridged).

A *viaduct* is a bridge comprising several short spans, generally crossing a wide valley, wetland or flood plain. It would be used when there is no requirement for a long span bridge and where construction of an embankment is not suitable for the transport infrastructure. For instance, on soft ground an embankment may not be physically capable of bearing the traffic loads from the vehicles using the crossing. This has often been the case with railway structures and so viaducts are more commonly associated with railways.

A *tunnel* is an underground passageway dug through the surrounding earth or rock and enclosed except for its entrance and exit points. It is used when the cost of excavating a cutting is too high. Tunnels are commonly found in steep or mountainous terrain. While a tunnel can provide an efficient crossing connection in that terrain, the limited access and egress possible for the tunnel adds a level of vulnerability for its use in some circumstances. Tunnel blockages can have catastrophic effects.

Culverts are tunnel-like structures that allow running water to pass under a roadway or railway. Minor rivers and streams passing under the route are likely to be put into culverts. They are generally of short span and are generally simple structures embedded in to soil.

Road *pavements* and rail *tracks* provide the basic structures on which transport vehicles operate. They also form the largest components of transportation systems assets. Pavement design is discussed in Chapter 7, and rail track design in Chapter 8.

Climate and weather impacts

Climate change can be expected to have transport-specific implications related to design, material selection, operations and management; economic costs; planning systems; liability and insurance; user behaviour; and emergency evacuation, transport network and vehicle efficiencies (Taylor and Philp, 2011).

Water in its many manifestations – e.g., sea level rise, tidal surge, flooding, rain storms and wash outs, ponding, seepage, freezing, thawing, corrosion and drying – is the major natural element that degrades the performance and integrity of transport assets. While natural disasters such as earthquakes can have immediate and serious local impacts on the assets, the insidious impacts of water in inappropriate locations over time is an ongoing universal threat to transport infrastructure. This is of particular concern for road pavements, which form the majority part of the transport infrastructure asset. Water penetration into and under road pavements has serious impacts on the structural integrity (and hence usability) of pavements and can significantly decrease the engineering life of the asset. Thus the impacts of climate change on the water cycle in a given environment may have significant impacts on the condition and performance of the transportation assets in that situation, possibly outside the design conditions assumed in the initial planning and installation of the assets, and there ongoing maintenance.

Road pavement design methods have always included an environmental component, albeit implicitly, relating to the location of individual road sections by geographic area. Austroads (2010) described a method for explicit inclusion of local environment and climate in its pavement design model, using the Thornthwaite Moisture Index (TMI) as a composite index of climate (Thornthwaite, 1948). TMI includes data on patterns of rainfall and temperature variations over the months of the year, and the model developed by Austroads (2010) included nation-wide modelling of the expected changes in TMI until 2100 under a range of climate change scenarios. Taylor and Philp (2015, 2016) used the Austroads model to examine potential impacts of climate change on sealed road pavements over time, from which policy implications for the design and maintenance of road assets in the face of expected climate change could be determined. In addition, TMI has applications for climate change adaptation studies involving other physical infrastructure assets that are located on or just below ground level (such as pipelines, slabs and foundations), as described in Taylor and Philp (2016). Balston et al (2017) developed a financial simulation model and supporting decision tools to provide a clear, comparative analysis of the financial impacts of climate change on three major road asset classes of importance to Australian Local Government – sealed roads (hot mix and spray sealed) and unsealed roads.

Seaports are critical components of the national infrastructure portfolio that are considered vital to the functioning of nations such as Australia and their ability to trade with the rest of the world. Extreme weather events are important factors in determining port performance. Both the seaward-side of operations and the supply chain hinterland are affected by current climate variability, vulnerabilities which will intensify under a changing climate (McEvoy and Mullett, 2013). Resilience to current day climate variability appears evident within the immediate port environment. This can be attributed to autonomous adaptation primarily as a result of a combination of regulatory and operational mechanisms such as OH&S requirements, risk management strategies, and incremental changes to practice brought about by the ports experience of weather-related events; rather than as part of a conscious adaptation strategy (McEvoy and Mullett, 2013).

It should also be noted that climate change may bring some benefits for individual ports – e.g., sea level rise may allow the passage of ships with deeper draught; hence reducing the need for channel dredging in some ports.

Systematic assessments of potential vulnerability of transport infrastructure elements to climate impacts, including climate change and extreme weather, is essential in transport infrastructure asset management. These assessments need to follow a set framework but be sensitive to local environmental conditions. An exemplar in this regard is the climate resilience program initiated by the Federal Highways Administration (FHWA) of the US Department of Transportation (DOT). FHWA developed a vulnerability assessment framework for identifying, assessing and prioritising transport infrastructure assets at risk from climate change and extreme weather events (FHWA, 2016). This framework is being applied by state DOTs across the United States, cognisant of their own environmental circumstances. In addition, FHWA (2015) provided an international review of climate change adaptation policies and procedures. It highlights the state of the practice of how transportation agencies are addressing climate adaptation through the following: adaptation frameworks/strategies; climate change risk assessments; selecting adaptation measures and strategies; long range planning and land use; changes in design standards; maintenance and operations; asset management; and research. It is relevant to transportation planners, asset managers, design engineers, and policy-makers.

The issues raised above are considered in the subsequent chapters of this book.

References

ASCE, 2009. Guiding Principles for the Nation's Critical Infrastructure. American Society of Civil Engineers, Reston VA. www.pubs.asce.org.

Austroads, 2010. Impact of Climate Change on Road Performance: Updating Climate Information for Australia. Report AP-R358/10. Austroads Incorporated, Sydney.

Austroads, 2015. Repositiong for a Sustainable Future: Austroads Strategic Plan 2016-2020. Austroads Incorporated, Sydney. www.austroads.com.au.

Austroads, 2019. Austroads Incorporated, Sydney. www.austroads.com.au.

Balston, J.M., Li, S., Iankov, I., Kellett, J., Wells, G., 2017. Quantifying the Financial Impact of Climate Change on Australian Local Government Roads, pp. 1–16. https://doi.org/10.3390/infrastructures2010002 (Infrastructures 2 92).

Beer, A., Tually, S., Kroehn, M., Martin, J., Gerritsen, R., Taylor, M., Graymore, M., Law, J., 2015. Climate change and the future of Australia's country towns. In: Palutikof, J.P., Boulter, S.L., Barnett, J., Rissik, D. (Eds.), Applied Studies in Climate Adaptation. John Wiley and Sons, Chichester, pp. 332–341.

Bollinger, L.A., Bogmans, C.W.J., Chappin, E.J.L., Dijkema, G.P.J., Huibregtse, J.N., Maas, N., Schenk, T., Snelder, M., Van Thienen, P., De Wit, S., Wols, B., Tavasszy, L.A., 2014. Climate adaptation of interconnected infrastructures: a framework for supporting governance. Reg. Environ. Change 14, 919–931. https://doi.org/10.1007/s10113-013-0428-4.

FHWA, 2015. International Practices on Climate Adaptation in Transportation. Report FHWA-HEP-15-012. Federal Highways Administration, US Department of Transportation, Washington DC. Available at: http://www.fhwa.dot.gov/environment/climate_change/adaptation/publications_and_tools/.

FHWA, 2016. FHWA Climate Resilience Pilot Program. Federal Highways Administration, US Department of Transportation, Washington DC. http://www.fhwa.dot.gov/environment/climate_change/adaptation/.

McEvoy, D., Mullett, J., 2013. Enhancing the Resilience of Seaports to a Changing Climate: Research Synthesis and Implications for Policy and Practice. Work Package 4 of Enhancing the Resilience of Seaports to a Changing Climate Report Series, National Climate Change Adaptation Research Facility, Gold Coast, p. 49.

Ogden, K.W., 1996. Safer Roads: A Guide to Road Safety Engineering. Avebury Technical Books, Aldershot.

Perrow, C., 1984. Normal Accidents: Living with High-Risk Technologies. Basic Books, New York.

Rinaldi, S.M., Peerenboom, J.P., Kelly, T.K., 2001. Identifying, Understanding and Analysing Critical Infrastructure Interdependencies. IEEE Control Systems Magazine, December, pp. 11–25.

Tavasszy, L., Bollinger, A., Dijkema, G.P.J., 2016. Editorial: special issue on climate adaptation of infrastructure networks. Eur. J. Transport Infrastruct. Res. 16 (1), 95–97. www.tlo.tbm.tudelft.nl/ejtir.

Taylor, M.A.P., 2017. Vulnerability Analysis for Transportation Networks. Elsevier, Oxford.

Taylor, M.A.P., Philp, M.L., 2011. Adapting to climate change – implications for transport infrastructure, transport systems and travel behaviour. Road Transp. Res. 19 (4), 69–82.

Taylor, M.A.P., Philp, M.L., 2015. Investigating the impact of maintenance regimes on the design life of road pavements in a changing climate and the implications for transport policy. Transport Pol. 41, 117–135.

Taylor, M.A.P., Philp, M.L., 2016. Beyond agriculture: a review of the Thornthwaite moisture index with respect to road pavements and other infrastructure applications. Int. J. Sustain. Transp. 10 (6), 528–540.

Thornthwaite, C.W., 1948. An approach toward a rational classification of climate. Geogr. Rev. 38, 55–94.

Vuchic, V.R., 2007. Urban Transit: Systems and Technology. John Wiley and Sons, Hoboken NJ.

Chapter 4

Adaptation planning

This chapter turns attention to the basic principles of planning and decision-making for transportation agencies with a focus on the inclusion of climate change adaptation in agency planning processes. To do this, it first revisits the concepts of risk and uncertainty, and vulnerability and resilience, as discussed earlier in Chapter 1. These concepts are applied to the management of transportation assets and the potential susceptibility of those assets to changes in climatic conditions. This in turn may affect the management and operational practices of the transportation agency. Risk and uncertainty are inherent in any systems planning process (SPP) – such as in transportation – where external factors (e.g., the state of the economy) may affect the demands to use the system and the operating characteristics of that system. Climate change is then just another, albeit novel, external factor to be included in the risk analysis. Uncertainty is exacerbated because the predictions of future climate must necessarily be made on a scenario basis, and as such there are many potential variations possible. The potential impacts of climate change on transportation systems can best be dealt with by considering 'climate stressors', which are the different natural phenomena potentially linked to climate variables that affect the engineering service life, physical condition, and operational characteristics of transportation assets. These stressors already exist (e.g., the effects of blizzards and hurricanes on transportation system operations), but the potential change in the nature, intensity and severity of the stressors under a changing climate becomes a major concern for transportation agencies.

The key message of the chapter is that planning for climate change adaptation can be readily included in established 'best practice' processes available in transportation planning, with some small additions tailored to the particular circumstances relating to climate change.

Risk and uncertainty

For a transportation agency considering the potential impacts of climate change, risk is the potential for unwanted outcomes from events, i.e., changes

Climate Change Adaptation for Transportation Systems. https://doi.org/10.1016/B978-0-12-816638-3.00004-0

in the level, intensity and frequency of climatic conditions and extreme weather events – the climate stressors. The overall measure of risk is given by the product of the likelihood (probability) of an event and its estimated consequence (impact), which is then related to the vulnerability of an asset to that event. In general terms, the assessment of risk for a given event requires the following steps:

- Review assets in terms of their vulnerability to projected climate change
- Assess the likelihood of a particular impact on a given asset arising from a predicted set of climate stressors
- Assess the consequences of the impact (and most properly include not only the immediate transportation consequences but also the wider socioeconomic consequences for the study region)
- Make an integrated assessment of the risk to the asset.

To undertake this assessment, the agency needs to consider both the historical performance of its assets during specific weather events and whether or not future climate change may introduce greater climate vulnerability. The historical records can indicate the following:

- Repair and rehabilitation costs because of previous weather events
- Ongoing maintenance and service costs incurred in response to weather events (e.g., snow clearance)
- The effects of past events on the level of service offered by an asset and the travel demand to use it (e.g., changes in vehicle kilometres (VKT) of travel and travel times and delays)
- The required role of the asset in terms of emergency responses (e.g., evacuation or emergency service access)

The agency should then have a good understanding of the performance of its assets in the face of the climate stressors to which the region is subjected. Future climatic conditions may, however, introduce new stressors or alter the frequency and/or magnitudes of the existing stressors. Extreme temperatures not previously experienced may occur in the future, or the frequency of the extremes may increase. The frequency and incidence of flooding may change. Cumulative effects of repeated occurrence of stressors (such as floods) may be important, so that if frequency increased so will the risk of asset damage or failure. The agency will thus need to seek out climate projections as part of the evaluation of likely future impacts, and this may require the assembly of a number of future climate change scenarios (e.g., 'best', 'worst' and 'average') for the study region.

An integrated assessment for those assets seen as vulnerable to climate change can then be undertaken. The 'risk matrix' introduced in Chapter 1 provides a useful approach for this assessment. Note that those assets deemed as not vulnerable should not be entirely ignored. The assessment process may need to be repeated at intervals in the future, as new data, new experiences and new circumstances arise. As discussed later in this chapter, monitoring and learning are an important and inherent part of systems planning for climate change adaptation.

The integrated risk assessment considers both the likelihood that an asset will undergo a particular impact and the consequence of that impact on the asset and the communities and region that use the asset. This analysis will yield an overall risk assessment for each asset considered, e.g., in terms of a classification such as the following:

- Low – minimal impact on the asset, with minimal oversight required to ensure that the risk remains low.
- Moderate – the asset may face some disruption and may require alternative management approaches, possibly including additional management surveillance.
- High – the asset faces an unacceptable level of risk and major disruption is likely. This will entail adoption of alternative management practices and the asset requires priority management surveillance.

Fig. 4.1 shows a schematic interpretation of the risk classification for an asset in terms of its level of likelihood and consequence for a defined weather event.

Vulnerability and resilience

The previous section used the notion of vulnerability of an asset in the face of climate stressors. Vulnerability concepts may be applied to individual assets and to the transportation network or system of which the asset is part. In broad terms, network vulnerability deals with the socioeconomic impacts and transport systems performance of degraded transport networks. Thus, network vulnerability is not just an interesting topic for research by transport network modellers; it is also of great importance to modern society. Degraded network performance from system failures, disaster situations, or even traffic congestion can have significant social and economic impacts. Network failures, whether full or partial or whether because of natural or man-made events, are of great significance. These failures can range from disasters such as earthquakes and bridge collapses, whose effects may persist for long periods of time, to incident-based congestion episodes of relatively short duration but still with large social and economic impacts. Transportation agencies need well-defined concepts, validated models and verified tools to test networks for their robustness and resilience to failure at different locations, as an integral part of network design and incident management planning, and indeed planning for emergencies. These notions and models come to the fore in estimating the potential impacts of climate change and in identifying specific assets and areas most at risk.

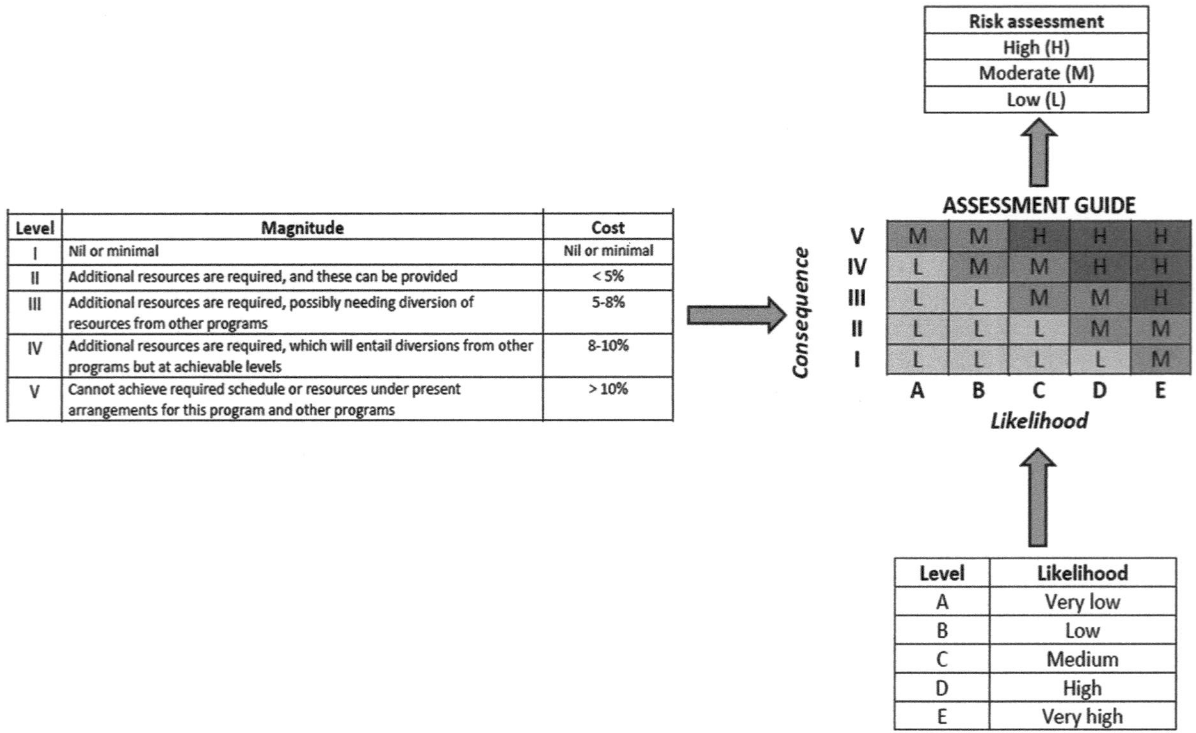

Level	Magnitude	Cost
I	Nil or minimal	Nil or minimal
II	Additional resources are required, and these can be provided	< 5%
III	Additional resources are required, possibly needing diversion of resources from other programs	5-8%
IV	Additional resources are required, which will entail diversions from other programs but at achievable levels	8-10%
V	Cannot achieve required schedule or resources under present arrangements for this program and other programs	> 10%

Consequence	A	B	C	D	E
V	M	M	H	H	H
IV	L	M	M	H	H
III	L	L	M	M	H
II	L	L	L	M	M
I	L	L	L	L	M

Level	Likelihood
A	Very low
B	Low
C	Medium
D	High
E	Very high

FIGURE 4.1 Use of the risk matrix approach in classifying the levels of risk to transportation assets.

A general definition of vulnerability for a transportation system concerns the functional serviceability of the system when placed under stress, such as an extreme weather event (or a road crash, flood, wildfire, earthquake, even major roadworks). For climate change, this means the sensitivity of a given asset or network to climate effects and extreme weather events, present or future exposure to those effects and events and the adaptive capacity of the system (e.g., availability of alternative routes in the event of a network blockage). As discussed in Taylor (2017), functionality relates to the following:

- The capability of an individual asset to continue to operate – safely and efficiently – when in a degraded state (e.g., a damaged road, following a flood) and when its engineering life may have been reduced.
- The ability of an asset and surrounding network to continue to provide for safe and efficient regional traffic movement when degraded (such as an available detour around a flooded road section).
- The potential for social and economic loss in a region as a result of the degradation of an asset (e.g., a bridge collapse leading to a cut in a network, with consequent inability for full movement in that network).

These considerations lead to three main objectives for vulnerability analysis:

- Asset management and the protection of networks and their component assets, which may be best represented by an asset inventory which includes the susceptibility of the assets to expected climate change effects and extreme weather.
- Traffic planning and management, in which the ability of the network to continue to meet travel demands under a range of climate, environmental and operating conditions needs to be assessed.
- Regional economic planning and service provision, which takes a broader and longer term view of system performance, focussing on the capability of the network to facilitate the movements of people and goods in efficient and timely fashion so that economic and social activities can take place at expected levels of service provision.

Taylor (2017) provides a comprehensive account of the methods for vulnerability analysis in transportation systems and the applications of those methods in practice, including consideration of climate change effects and extreme weather events. He identifies four main approaches to vulnerability analysis, discusses the relationships, differences and commonalities between them and recommends an integrated approach to vulnerability analysis that permits the analyst to select the most appropriate approach for a particular application. The four main methods are the following:

1. Inventory-based risk assessment, concerned with the state of operation of the system assets (including physical components and operating systems) and the likely impacts of internal and external factors on the ability of the assets to continue functioning

2. Topologically based methods, which consider the structure and interconnections in a network and seek to identify those network locations where failure would have the widest or deepest impact on network operations
3. Serviceability-based methods, which consider the transport-related features of the network, such as link and node capacity, link length and travel time characteristics, along with topological structure of the network, to gauge the likely impacts of network failures on traffic operations and travel demand satisfaction
4. Accessibility-based methods, which consider travel demand in its widest context and which are concerned with the ability of the population of a region (and individual sections within that region) to continue their normal economic and social activities when the transportation system undergoes some level of degradation.

These methods and their applications are each described in detail in Taylor (2017), for both private and public transportation modes. As indicated later in this chapter, consideration of vulnerability of assets and networks is a key component of the risk assessment to climate effects, covering all three of the stated objectives for vulnerability assessment. Further consideration is also required of the resilience of a transportation system to cope with unusual or extreme events.

The resilience of a system is its ability to be reinstated, to recover or to 'bounce back' in a short period of time following a partial or full failure of the system. Resilience includes the ability to withstand and recover from deliberate attacks, accidents or naturally occurring threats or incidents. Reggiani (2013) concluded that, in terms of the assessment of the level of resilience in a transportation system, resilience may be described through four key dimensions:

- robustness – avoidance of direct and indirect economic losses
- redundancy – untapped excess economic capacity (e.g., inventories and suppliers)
- resourcefulness – stabilising measures (e.g., capacity enhancement and demand modification, external assistance and optimising recovery strategies)
- recovery – optimising time to return to preevent functionality

She also indicated that three measures of the level of resilience of a system should be considered, through reductions in the following:

1. probability of failures,
2. consequences from failures and
3. time to recovery.

Taylor (2017) provided a detailed account of the methods for vulnerability analysis in transportation systems and the use of those methods to a wide range of applications, including but not limited to climate change impacts. The concepts of vulnerability and resilience are important in considerations of policies and plans for climate change adaptation in transportation systems.

Decision-making for transportation

Decision-making is an inherent part of transportation system planning and management. Planning involves the formulation of alternative proposals and the collation of supporting information on these, which is then presented to the decision-makers – the best decisions are most likely to come from a process of *informed* decision-making. The decision-makers have to consider the consequences (e.g., risks, with the embedded probabilities and levels of severity) of the alternatives and then select an alternative for implementation and perhaps prioritise between a set of different projects (project scheduling).

The role of information in planning – evidence-based decision-making – is reflected in the following propositions:

1. history is made as a result of decisions, not as a result of plans
2. planning is only effective if it is based on information of direct relevance to those who make decisions. Good decisions require proper understanding of the short- and long-term consequences of the alternatives under consideration – noting that this may not always be appreciated by the decision-makers themselves
3. all decisions involve the 'evaluation' of alternative scenarios of the future and the selection of the most highly valued feasible alternative. This evaluation may be quite cursory or may involve sophisticated analysis, but, even where the evaluation is cursory, decision-making requires an agenda (outlining the alternative scenarios and some analysis of their likely implications) and a valuation scheme (outlining the preferences for the characteristics of the likely outcomes of any one decision)
4. the degree of uncertainty associated with items on the agenda affects the evaluation and decision strategies and the quality of the decisions themselves. Decisions concerning future actions are based on assumptions about the likely consequences of choosing alternatives and the future state of the system in which the decision will be implemented. Thus, the greater the degree of uncertainty associated with these assumptions, the higher the value that should be placed on decisions that leave future options open
5. the products of the planning process should be designed to increase the probability of making better decisions. Thus, the planning process needs to examine a wide range of agendas and to consider alternative goals and objectives. Much can be learned by examining past decisions that were not successful and from watching out for the early warning signs of emerging problems, each of which will benefit from monitoring system performance before and after implementation of supposed solutions

6. the outcomes of the planning process are but a small part of the information required by decision-makers. The usefulness of planning information will be increased if attempts are made to adapt the products of the planning and analysis process to fit the substantive and interpretative requirements of the decision-makers. To want to use the planning information, the decision-makers will need to be convinced of its accuracy and relevance. This can only be accomplished by presenting the information in forms acceptable to and easily understood by them.

A systematic way to consider the overall planning and decision-making process is the 'SPP' model, presented in Fig. 4.2. This process has been widely applied in transportation planning, especially for the data analysis and information assembly tasks involved in evidence-based decision-making (see Richardson et al., 1995; Taylor et al., 2000 for examples).

Fig. 4.2 is a process diagram of the decision-making process. It shows a central chain of actions, with multiple feedback loops. Indeed, the first observation from Fig. 4.2 is that there is no obvious starting or finishing points in the process. Planning and decision-making are ongoing activities, and the outcomes of earlier decisions provide important lessons for future ones.

Perhaps the likely place to enter the process is 'problem definition', i.e., the realisation that there is some deficiency, current or impending, in an existing system or state. This means some perceived difference between the actual state, now or in the future, and the desired state. Problem definition depends on

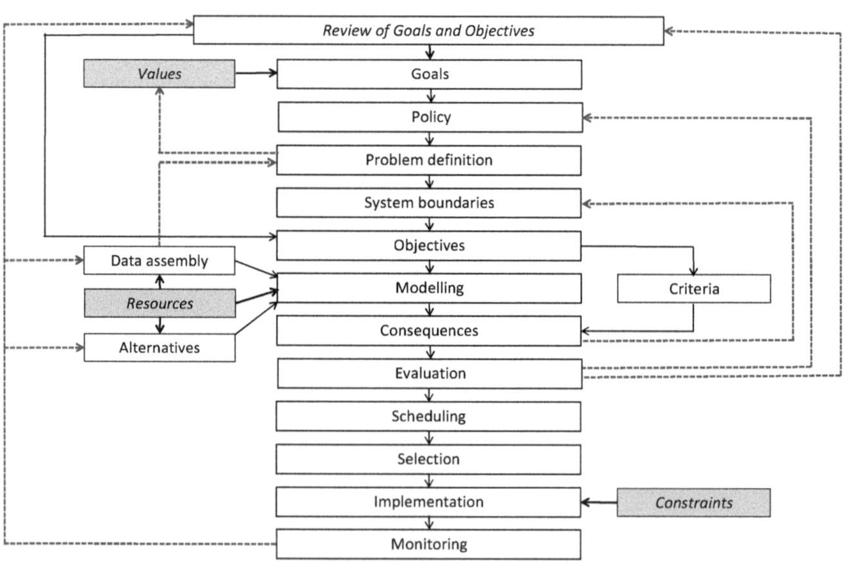

FIGURE 4.2 The system planning process model of decision-making in the planning and management of transportation systems.

the values and aspirations of the affected community, which are manifest in a set of goals (sometimes conflicting) that the community will establish, wittingly or otherwise. The careful definition of the problem will greatly assist in suggesting possible solutions. Indeed, the proper enunciation of the problem may well be a crucial step in its solution.

Following the realisation of the existence of a problem, there is the investigation of the extent of that problem, i.e., the 'system boundaries'. Who, where and what does the problem affect? Given the community's goals and the system boundaries for the problem, specific goals may be refined into particular objectives, and criteria may be established to indicate the success in solving a problem. For instance, a municipality in a coastal region may be concerned about sea level rise under climate change and the potential impacts on communities, economic activity and supporting infrastructure along the coast. The objective might then be to provide sufficient protection along the coast. The criterion for determining success in this objective might be specified precisely, for example, 'provision of a seawall able to withstand a 1 in 50 year storm surge under a projected sea level rise of 0.7 m by 2100'.

Solution of a problem requires the allocation of (often scarce) resources such as time, money and people. The levels of these resources that can be made available will determine the following:

- the type, scale and number of alternative solutions to be investigated,
- the types and quantities of data that can be collected or assembled and
- the amount of modelling and data analysis that can be undertaken.

The next input into the process is the formulation of a number of alternative approaches to solving the perceived problem or reaching the desired standard. Analytical techniques are then employed to forecast or estimate the likely consequences of each of the proposed solutions. In drawing up the list of candidate solutions, the planner needs to account for externally imposed constraints such as financial limits, political acceptability and institutional practicality.

The planning process is an ongoing one with many linkages between its components. Evaluation involves comparing predicted consequences of possible 'solutions' with previously established criteria and constraints. If none of the proposed solutions meet the criteria and constraints, it may be necessary to define and assess alternative options. Failing this, it may become necessary to amend the criteria to attempt to overcome the constraints or even reconsider the underlying goals and objectives.

The planning process does not properly finish with the implementation phase. Monitoring the performance of the selected alternative will indicate whether the chosen alternative really provides the predicted level of performance. The results of such monitoring will also provide information with which to improve the forecasting techniques and more accurately specify the system boundaries and so contribute to more accurate predictions in the future.

An ongoing monitoring process will also alert the planner to the emergence of new problems and will reveal any shift in community goals and values, possibly occurring as a result of their experiences with the selected policy option.

A further consideration highlighted in Fig. 4.2 is that influences external to the planning process system can have strong impacts in its operations. Three such broad influences are indicated in the figure, by means of the shaded boxes: for 'values', 'resources' and 'constraints'. The values reflect the overall situation in the community or society that the transportation system is servicing. Processes of stakeholder discussion and public consultation are undertaken to indicate the relevant value set influencing the transportation agency in its deliberations. Values can change over time, either evolutionarily or abruptly, and the agency must be in tune with these developments. Available resources dictate the nature and scope of the alternatives that can be considered and the level of activity that can be undertaken in evaluation. External constraints, e.g., from other levels of government, can limit the ability of an agency to schedule and implement its plans. Realisation of such limitations is a fundamental aspect of the decision-making process.

Modelling and analytic support for decision-making

Modelling and quantitative analysis tools play an important role in transport systems decision-making. Risk analysis and indeed informed decision-making require some level of estimation of the likely impacts of alternatives and options, commensurate with the quantity and quality of the available data and resources. Transportation systems are generally modelled on the basis of a supply—demand equilibrium: the operating state of the transportation system affects the travel demand to use the system (e.g., through the travel times and costs between different locations in a network), and the travel demand affects the operating state of the system (e.g., through the development of traffic congestion). The basic inputs that affect the system operating state are the system characteristics (the available transportation technologies and modes and the physical characteristics of the infrastructure assets). The inputs behind travel demand are the distribution of land uses across the region, the characteristics of the population (including socioeconomic factors) and the types, distribution and intensities of industry in the region. Fig. 4.3 provides a schematic view of the demand—supply equilibrium modelling framework. The figure also indicates that the outputs of the demand—supply models can be used to estimate the potential impacts (e.g., economic, social and environmental) of alternative transport policies and plans, which then provide substantial information for decision-making. There is also potential, outside the system displayed in this figure, for study of the possible interactions between the transportation system and the land use system that it supports. This land use—transport interaction is beyond the scope of this book, as indeed is the

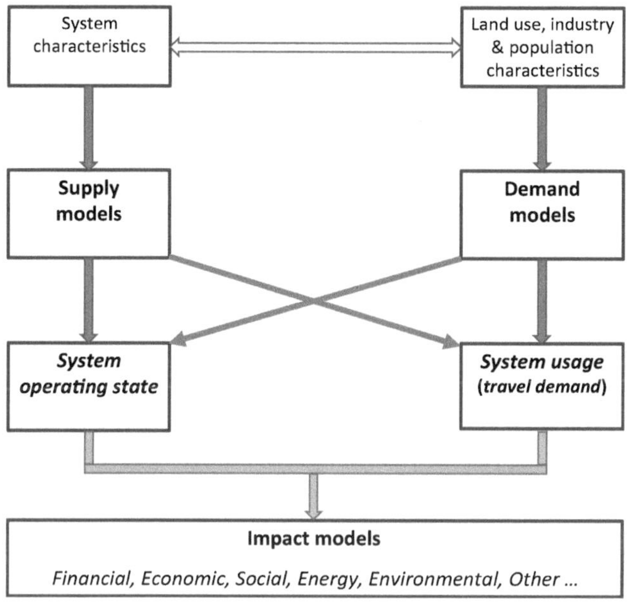

FIGURE 4.3 Supply-demand and impact models.

detailed study of the types of models actually employed for the demand-supply modelling system. Interested readers can further improve their knowledge of these topics by considering other works, such as Ortuzar and Willumsen (2011), which provides a comprehensive account of transportation systems models.

Decision support tools

The evaluation phase of the SPP uses the information assembled for each option under consideration to compare, evaluate and rank the options for selection. A number of decision support methods and tools are available for use in this stage. Two methods often used or proposed in transportation planning are the following:

- Benefit–cost analysis (BCA) and
- Multicriteria analysis (MCA).

BCA attempts to determine the economic efficiency of alternative proposals, by comparing the economic costs of a proposal with its economic benefits. It can indicate whether or not a given alternative is worthwhile (i.e., its economic benefit exceeds its economic cost) and may be used to compare alternatives to determine the best one of a set or a best subset of the alternatives The strength of BCA is that it compares all alternatives on a common basis (unit of measurement) by requiring all costs and benefits to be expressed as amounts of money. This may also be the weakness of the method when applied in an environment fraught with risk and uncertainty – as is the case in climate change adaptation – for small variations in the estimated costs and benefits may lead to different results. MCA is sometimes offered as an alternative approach. It seeks to broaden the approach beyond economic efficiency alone by explicitly including range of other criteria (e.g., environmental impact or social equity), applying weights to each criterion to provide an overall score on which an option can be judged. This explicit recognition and identification of different objectives is seen as a strength of MCA, providing transparency in decision-making. The main weakness with the approach is how to allocate appropriate (if not objective) weights to the criteria. MCA may become a subjective and biased process if arbitrary weights are used. The other weakness of the approach is that it is seen to lack as proper theoretical basis – although it may also be seen as mirroring the process of political decision-making.

BCA consists of seven stages:

1. The identification of the relevant benefits and costs for the proposed option or project.
2. The quantification (in physical terms) of each of the benefits and costs, including the determination of where over time these benefits and costs will occur.
3. The valuation of the streams (over time) of the benefits and costs in monetary terms.
4. The reduction of all future costs and benefits to equivalent present-day values.
5. The comparison of the costs and benefits using an explicit decision criterion.
6. Sensitivity testing of the results to see if small variations in the amounts of the costs and benefits may lead to different findings under the decision criterion (this is especially important where values are uncertain or risks are high).
7. Presentation of the results to allow comparisons of the performance of the alternatives under consideration.

Identification of the full sets of costs and benefits is a fundamental task to ensure a proper analysis of each option under consideration. The magnitude, in physical terms, of each benefit and cost then requires estimation, and the application of unit values (i.e., how much per physical unit) then converts the physical amounts into money values. The time when each benefit and cost is realised is another major concern, for cash amounts gained or spent in the future are worth less than equivalent amounts today. Under many options (and projects), the major costs (e.g., capital costs such as construction) occur up front, and the benefits occur as a stream of (annual) amounts over time. Replacement and refurbishment costs will also occur in future times, and there will probably be annual maintenance and management charges for any asset. Common practice in transportation systems management has been to see the upfront capital costs as the main costs, with future maintenance and refurbishment costs deducted from the annual benefits to give a stream of net benefits over the life of a project. This often reflects the nature of the budgets that are part and parcel of transportation agency management practices.

The process of reducing future costs and benefits to their present-day values is known as discounted cash flow analysis. This is accomplished by assuming a discount rate (i per cent p.a.), so that an amount S (\$) n years in the future has a present value P (\$) given by

$$P = \frac{S}{(1+i)^n} \tag{4.1}$$

In similar vein, the present worth P of a stream of annual sums R (\$) over n years is given by

$$P = R\frac{(1+i)^n - 1}{i(1+i)^n} \tag{4.2}$$

These two formulae may be applied to provide the total present values of the benefits and costs associated with the option.

Choice of discount rate is crucial and also controversial. In public sector practice, the controversy has been diminished by the use of explicit values of discount rates, usually set by government treasuries to provide a common basis for decision-making across a wide range of subject areas (e.g., health, education and transportation). The appraisal period (n) is also of concern, and most transportation applications of BCA have tended to consider relatively short periods, perhaps 5–6 years for minor projects and up to 20 years for major construction projects. This situation is not well suited to the case of climate change because much longer time frames, perhaps 80–100 years, may be needed in proper consideration of the impacts of climate change. Benefits and costs occurring a long time in the future tend to have very small present values because of discounting. Uncertainties may also increase about the actual value if not existence of benefits and costs in the distant future. Approaches to deal with these considerations are discussed in the next chapter.

Given the present value of the costs ($PVC_x(n, i)$) and benefits ($PVB_x(n, i)$) of each alternative option x over an n year period and with discount rate i, various decision criteria may be applied in the evaluation of the option(s). The option is worthwhile if the present value of the benefits exceeds that of the costs, i.e., $PVC_x(n, i) > PVB_x(n, i)$.

Three commonly used decision criteria are the following:

- Net present value (*NPV*)
- Benefit–cost ratio (*BCR*)
- Internal rate of return (*IRR*).

In the simplest case where a single option is being considered on the basis of its merit alone, the different criteria will provide the same result. However, this may not be the case when several options are being considered and ranked.

Net present value is the difference between the present value of the benefits and the present value of the costs,

$$NPV_x(n,i) = PVB_x(n,i) - PVC_x(n,i) \tag{4.3}$$

The option is worthwhile if $NPV_x(n,i) > 0$.

BCR is given by the resent value of the benefits divided by the present value of the costs,

$$BCR_x(n,i) = \frac{PVB_x(n,i)}{PVC_x(n,i)} \tag{4.4}$$

The option is worthwhile if $BCR_x(n,i) > 1$. This is equivalent to the result for net present value – for a single option. Comparison of alternative options is, however, not so straightforward. A large project may have a large NPV, but a relatively small BCR compared to a small project, so a comparison between the two on a single criterion may be ambiguous. Such comparisons are best done with like-size options.

IRR requires computation of that discount rate (r per cent) for which the total net present value is zero, i.e., $IRR_x(n,r) = PVB_x(n,r) - PVC_x(n,r) = 0$. If $r > i$, then the option is worthwhile. The advantage of *IRR* is that decision-makers can compare it to potential yields from investments, and this may make its significance easier to comprehend. However, it has a number of disadvantages. It is difficult to use in comparing and ranking alternatives and may give more weight to short-term effects. This latter issue is a particular problem for its application in climate change adaptation studies.

The major problem with the use of conventional BCA for climate change matters is future uncertainty and risk, especially when considering factors and impacts expected a long way into the future (e.g., more than 15 years hence). The issue of risk and uncertainty is covered in conventional BCA through the use of sensitivity tests: how robust is a BCA result to changes in the assumptions used in calculating it, especially with respect to the estimated sizes and unit values of the benefits and costs? To perform sensitivity tests involves systematic changes to the values used, treating each as coming from an assumed statistical distribution, and applying 'Monte Carlo' simulation methods in repeated recalculation of the BCA values. This can be done for climate change effects, e.g., see Balston et al., (2017). The basic premise to be tested under this regime is under what conditions would a different decision be made from that determined under the initial analysis?

The full results of the analysis can then be presented to the decision-makers for a final determination.

BCA has been widely used in transportation evaluations and is well understood. It is a likely tool for use in climate change studies, but there are issues with it in those circumstances that need to be addressed.

A longstanding concern in some areas with BCA is its lack of transparency as to how the analytical results emerge, e.g., what trade-offs occur in determining the final BCA value or who are the 'winners' and 'losers'. In particular, when there are multiple objectives – and possibly some objectives are conflicting – then there will be concerns about the degree to which each objective is satisfied. In addition, while BCA provides good evidence for economic efficiency, care is needed that this efficiency is actually contributing to the achievement of the set goals and objectives. Economic efficiency is not necessarily an end in itself. This has led some researchers and agencies to consider MCA. The basic premises of MCA are the following:

- few decisions are made in isolation.
- often many stakeholders and decision makers will be involved in the process.
- different decision-makers may have different weights for different objectives.
- decisions often require compromise if not consensus.

MCA seeks to provide a rating system that can compare the performance of alternative options across a set of objectives and indicate how each option satisfies the criteria set for those objectives. The dilemma for the decision-makers is whether to choose the very best overall alternative, or one that performs satisfactorily on all of the objectives and their criteria, without necessarily being the 'best' in any one of them. The former suggests optimisation and may require trade-offs between the criteria. BCA enables this result. The latter may be more equitable, but the decision rules to be applied may be vaguer. The approach generally adopted in the satisfying case is to assign weights to the different criteria and make an overall assessment using those weights. The overall assessment process under MCA is then the following:

1. Assign weights to the criteria.
2. Apply the weights to the impact assessments of the alternative options[1]
3. Sum the weighted assessments.
4. Produce a final score for each alternative.
5. Use the scores to rank the alternatives.
6. Select the best performing alternative(s).
7. Present the results.

1. Note that the impact assessments are often normalised to make comparisons easier (e.g., set the assessment score for criterion k to a value x_k, where $0 \leq x_k \leq 1$). This may be done by selection of minimum and maximum values of the original assessment values.

One form of MCA applied as an adjunct to BCA is to make an assessment of the alternatives in terms of the degree to which each meets the objectives and their criteria and thus contributes to the strategic goals of the agency. This assists in ensuring that solutions are being found to the 'right' problems, rather than just a good solution to the 'wrong' problem. This approach is exemplified by the 'strategic merit test' approach used by TIC (2018).

The basic MCA methods use 'simple additive weights', although there are more rigorous methods, such as the analytic hierarchy process (Saaty, 1980). The issues of determining criteria weights and applying these to transportation problem are widely discussed elsewhere (e.g., Klungboonkrong and Taylor, 1997; Tsamboulas et al., 1999; Quinet, 2000; Sayers et al., 2003; Aldian and Taylor, 2005; Marcharis and Bernardini, 2015; Barbosa et al., 2017). Given a set of criteria k, $k = 1, \ldots, n$ with weights w_k and (normalised) merit scores x_{jk} for alternative j, then the overall merit score of alternative j is

$$S_j = \sum_{k=1}^{n} w_k x_{jk} \tag{4.5}$$

where $k = 1, \ldots, n$.

$$\sum_{k=1}^{n} w_k = 1 \tag{4.6}$$

and $0 \leq w_k \leq 1$ for all k. The computed values of S_j may be used to compare and rank the alternatives, and examination of the individual criteria scores x_{jk} may be undertaken to assess the degree to which each alternative contributes to meeting the objective criteria.

Chapter 5 provides a more detailed account of the BCA and MCA methods and their related tools for application to climate change adaptation initiatives, policies and plans. It also introduces some alternative methods intended for use in situations involving risk and uncertainty.

Adaptation and mitigation

As discussed in Chapter 2, climate change is a complex issue involving many dimensions, including science, economics, environment, society, politics, morality and ethics. It is a global problem realised at local levels that will be part of our future for many, many years to come. Even if it were possible to cease the emission of all greenhouse gases, global warming and climate change will continue to affect us well into the future. This highlights the need for climate change adaptation: to meet the new and evolving norms. The extent to which climate change will occur does depend on the future levels of greenhouse gas emissions, and there is scope for some degree of reduction in emissions through mitigation. This is especially the case in the transportation sector, which is a significant contributor to greenhouse gases – through the combustion of liquid fossil fuels – and rates as second only to electrical power generation as an emissions source. Thus, adaptation and mitigation have to be complementary measures.

Mitigation involves the reduction of the degeneration and flow of greenhouse gases into the atmosphere. This can be done by reducing the sources of these gases (e.g., using alternative fuels for transportation, including electrical power generated from renewable sources) or by the increased use of sinks that can accumulate and store these gases (e.g., reforestation). The overall goal of climate change mitigation stated by IPCC (2014) is to avoid significant human interference with the climate system, i.e., to stabilise greenhouse gas levels in a timeframe sufficient to allow ecosystems to adapt naturally to climate change, to ensure that food production is not threatened and to enable economic development to proceed is a sustainable manner (IPCC, 2014).

Climate change adaptation concerns adjusting human activity to actual or expected future climate conditions. The goal then is to reduce vulnerability to harmful impacts of climate change, including sea level rise and more severe and more frequent extreme weather events. It can also include harnessing any potential beneficial opportunities arising from climate change, such as longer crop growing seasons in some regions. Adaptation measures are most likely to be applied at local and regional levels because of the different trajectories that climate change and its impacts may take in different areas of the world.

For a transportation agency, adaptation is likely to focus on the protection and preservation of transportation infrastructure to enable ongoing economic and social activity in the region of interest to the agency. The next section of this chapter considers suitable frameworks for those agencies to use in policy setting and planning for climate change adaptation.

Adaptation frameworks

Given the worldwide, national and local importance of transport networks, a systematic approach to transport infrastructure management is required in all circumstances, including consideration of climate change adaptation. A number of frameworks have been proposed to enable proper consideration of climate change adaptation in the planning, design and management of transport networks and systems. Some prominent examples of these frameworks in transportation are the following:

- ROADADAPT (Bles et al., 2016)
- World Road Association (PIARC, 2015)
- US Federal Highways Administration (FHWA, 2012, 2018, 2019).

ROADADAPT

A useful starting point to consider adaptation frameworks is to look at recent applied research where a general adaptation framework (ROADADAPT) has been specifically tailored to transportation. The framework is described in detail in Bles et al., (2016). ROADAPT provides guidelines for

- the use of climate data for current and future climate,
- the application of scanning tools for climate change risks in transportation systems,
- methods for performing vulnerability assessments,
- methods for undertaking socioeconomic impact assessment and
- the selection of a suitable adaptation strategy.

Its starting point is a seven-step framework for climate change risk assessment, as shown in Fig. 4.4. These steps assist transportation agencies to identify, analyse, prioritise, evaluate and mitigate climate change risks. The seven steps are

1. context analysis
2. risk identification
3. risk analysis
4. risk evaluation
5. risk mitigation
6. implementation of adaptation plans
7. monitoring and review.

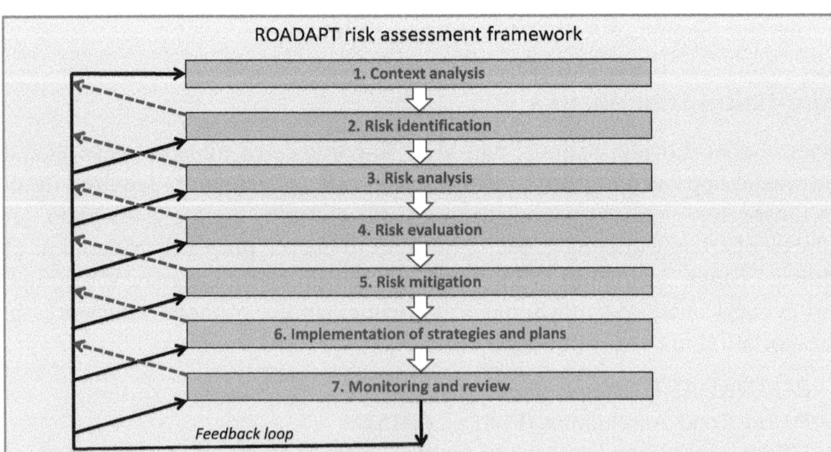

FIGURE 4.4 The basic framework for climate change adaptation in ROADAPT. *Derived from Bles, T., Bessembinder, J., Chevreuil, M., Danielsson, P., falemo, S., Venmans, A., Ennesser, Y., Lofroth, H., 2016. Climate change risk assessments and adaptation for roads – results of the ROADADAPT project. Transp. Res. Procedia 14, pp. 58–67.*

As indicated in Fig. 4.4, there are feedback loops between the stages and for the overall purpose of monitoring and review to improve future planning.

The use of the framework is facilitated by the accompanying guidelines, which cover cause (climate change), effect (vulnerability assessment of transportation assets) and consequence (socioeconomic impacts), as indicated in Fig. 4.5.

Application of the method provides an overview of available adaptation measures and assistance in choosing a suitable adaptation strategy. This latter task is facilitated through the use of an adaptation policy matrix, which sets out the different stages at which policies and plans need to be directed and their underlying objectives. These are related to the different activities that the transportation agency undertakes, so that the contents of the policy matrix indicate broad adaptation measures suitable for application in each stage. The matrix in Fig. 4.6 is based on the policy and planning requirements needed to cope with a given extreme (weather) event. The stages start with anticipatory planning in advance of a possible event, through preventive measures to ameliorate the potential impacts of the event, to prepare for an impending event (e.g., a hurricane) and the responses (during the event and in its immediate aftermath), to the recovery stage after the event has passed.

Note that the activities of capacity building in the agency, monitoring and research are ongoing throughout the whole process. These enable the agency to develop its knowledge and expertise and learn from previous events in planning for future adaptations.

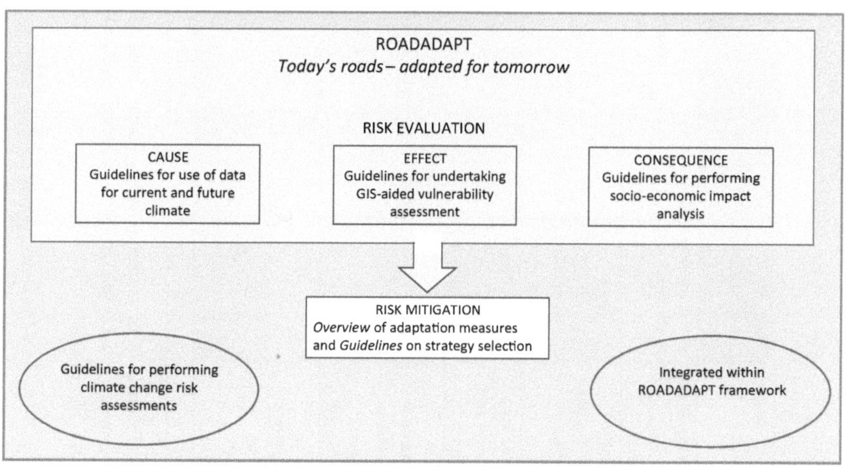

FIGURE 4.5 Structure for the ROADADAPT guidelines supporting the adaptation framework. *Derived from Bles, T., Bessembinder, J., Chevreuil, M., Danielsson, P., falemo, S., Venmans, A., Ennesser, Y., Lofroth, H., 2016. Climate change risk assessments and adaptation for roads – results of the ROADADAPT project. Transp. Res. Procedia 14, pp. 58–67.*

Stages	ANTICIPATION	PREVENTION	PREPARATION		RESPONSE		RECOVERY
			Advance planning for extreme events	Lead up to an extreme event	During the extreme event	Aftermath of the extreme event	After an extreme event
Objectives **Activities**	*Enable smooth, efficient and safe traffic flows*		*Support reductions in disaster consequences*	*Evacuation routes, emergency service access, life support*	*Minimise loss of function*	*Supply routes for repairs and humanitarian aid*	*Supply routes for recovery of affected area*
Planning for climate change and extreme events	Pro-active attitude and initiatives			Extreme event management			
Construction		Prevention					
Legislation and regulation							
Resilient construction		Upgrade, rehabilitate, retrofit and renew					
Maintenance and asset management			Preventive maintenance and refurbishment				Corrective maintenance & replacement
Traffic management		Traffic control and management					
Capacity building	Capacity building and knowledge transfer						
Monitoring	Monitoring and prediction						
Research	Research development and innovation						

FIGURE 4.6 Example of an adaptation policy matrix using ROADADAPT. *Derived from Bles, T., Bessembinder, J., Chevreuil, M., Danielsson, P., falemo, S., Venmans, A., Ennesser, Y., Lofroth, H., 2016. Climate change risk assessments and adaptation for roads – results of the ROADADAPT project. Transp. Res. Procedia 14, pp. 58–-67.*

PIARC framework

Cognisant of the climate change risks and opportunities facing road transportation systems, the World Road Association (PIARC) developed a broad framework to guide road authorities in

- identifying relevant assets and climatic variables for assessment,
- defining and prioritising risks,
- developing a robust adaptation response and
- integrating assessment findings into decision-making processes.

The framework provides a life cycle and iterative approach to climate change adaptation. It was developed through an international program of research and consultation, resulting in a synthesis of international knowledge and best practice. Given the direct inputs from road authorities across the globe, it provides a useful tool for any road authority, irrespective of geographical, climatic, economic or environmental condition. While there are acknowledged barriers to taking action to understand and adapt to climate change, this framework is designed to ensure that any road authority (even those with limited resources and knowledge) can commence effective steps to increase the resilience of their roads to climate change.

The framework facilitates the identification and replication of lessons learned from many countries, accounting for differing levels of preparedness and adaptive capacity and knowledge regionally and internationally. It may also be applied at different scales (e.g., national, regional, local or asset specific). The PIARC framework is summarised in Fig. 4.7. This framework is intended to guide road authorities through the process of identifying relevant

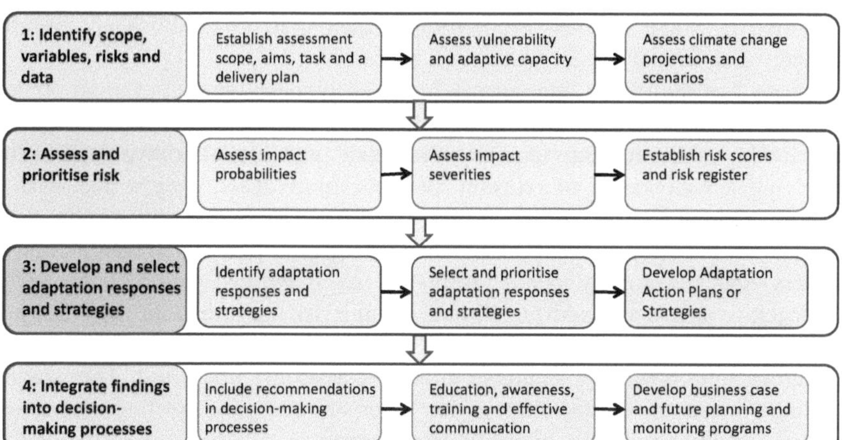

FIGURE 4.7 Representation of the PIARC (2015) framework for incorporation of climate change adaptation in transport infrastructure planning.

assets and the risks they face from climate change to the incorporation of adaptation responses and assessment findings in decision-making. It has four stages:

1. Identification of the scope, variables, risks and data requirements.
2. Assessment and prioritisation of risks.
3. Development and selection of adaptation responses and strategies.
4. Integration of findings into decision-making processes.

PIARC (2015) stresses that climate change risks and impacts cannot be considered in isolation, as they are linked to other risk types (both natural and man-made) and other forms of environmental, social and economic impact. Indeed, the impacts of climate change may see the emergence of new risks or the exacerbation of other existing risks and impacts or possibly both of these. Stage 1 in the PIARC framework is thus intended to provide a sound footing for the planning and design of adaptation initiatives. The first consideration in this stage is to establish the relevant scope and aims, from which the structure of a delivery plan for risk mitigation can be defined. The assessment of relevant vulnerabilities in the transportation system can then be undertaken. This needs to be done with the inclusion of climate change projections and scenarios for the region in question.

In Stage 2, the identifiable risks are assessed, and the priorities are set. The processes for identifying, understanding and assessing climate change risks should not be different from those used to assess any other types of risk. Thus, the risk assessment processes and approaches already employed by a transportation agency to understand and manage risks should generally be applicable for considering climate change risks. In other words, climate change risks form part of the overall risk set that an agency has to address. Impact probabilities and likely severities need to be estimated using the scenarios identified in Stage 1. This information is then used to establish an overall register of risks and the estimated risk scores.

Stage 3 of the PIARC framework involves the development of appropriate responses and strategies that deal with the identified risks. This is most effectively achieved through an integrated and collaborative approach involving a wide range of relevant interests, individuals, groups and stakeholders. This would include engineers, scientists, environmental experts, risk modellers, businesses and investment managers, operational staff, policy makers and the supply chain. Applying an integrated and collaborative approach to assess and address climate change risks ensures that the interests of these different players are accounted for, information is shared and the resources and knowledge available to address risks are optimised. The output of Stage 3 is a set of adaptation action plans or strategies, meeting the scope and responsibilities of the transportation agency.

Stage 4 of the framework brings together the outcomes and outputs of the earlier stages so that they can be incorporated in the established decision-making processes used by the agency. Climate change risks are then part of the overall situation considered by the agency in its regular activities. Recommendations on risk mitigation are key outputs at this stage, but there is also a need to ensure that these recommendations take effect, through education and awareness training in the organisation. The detailed outputs from this stage will include the development of business cases along with future planning and monitoring programs.

Monitoring of performance is essential, for assessments need to be considered dynamically and updated or refined as more information becomes available, as priorities and evidence change, and if resource levels change. As a result of the interdependencies and interconnectivities between road infrastructure and other sectors (see Chapter 3), as well as between climate risks and other risk types (such as other natural hazards and security risks), investing in climate change adaptation responses is part of the investment in the wider economy and the increased resilience of wider infrastructure systems and, indeed, society in general. Climate change risks are not to be considered in isolation but form part of a wider holistic approach to risk management.

Given its origins at the supranational level, the PIARC framework is by its nature a practical but broad-brush approach, aimed at providing a sound basis for climate change adaptation responses across its wide international membership. The framework needs to be adapted to the particular circumstances for a given transportation agency responsible for a specific region, with the issues and resources available to that agency. It is now time to consider a specific framework that has been developed and applied to specific situations. A prime example of such a framework is described in the next subsection of this chapter.

Federal Highways Administration framework

Over the last decade, the Federal Highways Administration (FHWA) of the US Department of Transportation has developed and tested a vulnerability assessment and adaptation framework (FHWA, 2019). The framework and its supporting resources form an adaptation planning package that has been applied by several transportation agencies in the United States as part of a process of learning and ongoing improvement in adaptation policy. The framework aids agencies in assessing the vulnerability of their transportation infrastructure and systems to climate change and extreme weather. It also provides assistance for the integration of climate adaptation measures in transportation decision-making.

The framework includes seven major steps:

1. Articulate objectives and define study scope.
2. Obtain asset data.
3. Obtain climate data.

4. Assess vulnerability.
5. Identify, analyse and prioritise adaptation options.
6. Integrate assessment results into decision-making.
7. Monitor and review assessments and implementations.

Fig. 4.8 shows this framework. In this diagram, steps 2 and 3 above are considered together in a generalised data collection task. The framework provides a closed system because of the emphasis on monitoring and review. The diagram also indicates potential alternatives for assessment and analysis.

The FHWA framework may be seen as a particular application of the SPP described earlier in this chapter.

The first step in the vulnerability assessment process is to set objectives and determine the scope of the assessment. Then a clear focus is set for the study, which can minimise the data collection and analysis activities by excluding extraneous or irrelevant data. Given that resource constraints (e.g., time, people and money) are likely to restrict an agency from considering every asset in its transportation system, the sharpening of the focus for a specific study provides for the efficient use of the available resources. In addition, not all projected changes in future climate will be significant for a local or regional transportation network. The FHWA framework package provides guidance and information on how to select the assets and climate variables to be examined as part of the vulnerability assessment.

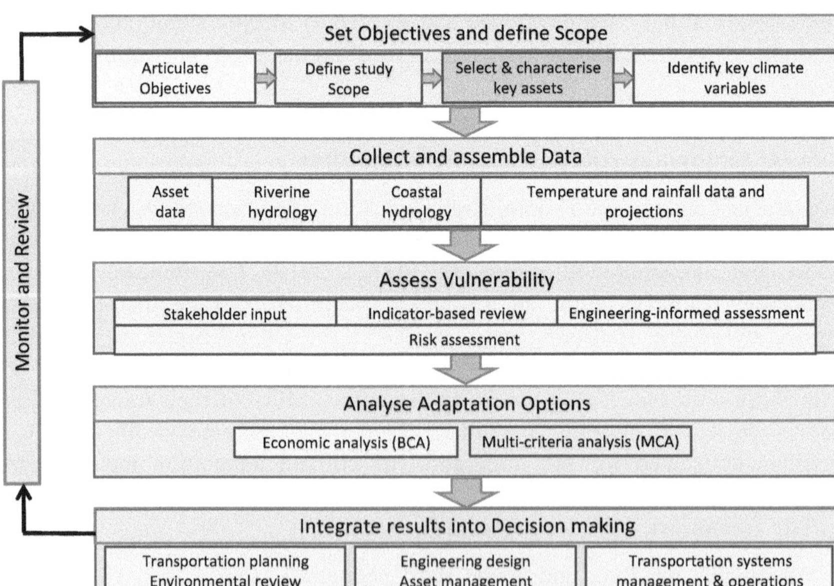

FIGURE 4.8 The vulnerability assessment and adaptation framework developed by the US Federal Highways Administration. *As derived from FHWA, 2019. Vulnerability Assessment and Adaptation Framework, third ed. Federal Highways Administration, Washington DC https://www.fhwa.dot.gov/environment/sustainability/resilience/adaptation_framework/chap00.cfm.*

The next stage, comprising steps 2 and 3 above, is the collection and assembly of the required data for analysis. The study scope and objectives will determine the asset data to be considered. Most modern transportation agencies use asset management systems which provide ready data on major assets, such as bridges, tunnels and highways. These assets are likely to be in the core information requirements. However, there may not be as much data readily available on smaller assets (e.g., local roads) and supporting structures (e.g., culverts, floodways, road furniture and signage). Liaison with other stakeholders such as municipalities, professional societies and (even) universities can provide additional data that will fill the gaps and perhaps reduce needs for the collection of new data. One useful feature of the FHWA framework package is that it includes descriptions of the types of assets and the characteristics of those assets that can assist in defining data needs and data collections strategies. The package also indicates best practices for different data collection. Data on present climate and future projections of climate for the study region are key considerations in the assessment. The FHWA framework indicates a number of ways that agencies can obtain data on temperature, rainfall, hydrology, floodplains, sea level rise and storm surges. While the methods discussed in the framework are specifically for use in the United States, the approaches involved are relevant elsewhere as well.

As discussed previously in this chapter – and in detail elsewhere, see Taylor (2017) – vulnerability in broad terms is concerned with the transport and socioeconomic impacts of degraded transportation networks and infrastructure. For the FHWA framework, as also in ROADADAPT, vulnerability is seen in the context of a transportation asset's sensitivity to climate induced effects, its exposure to extreme weather events and climate effects and its adaptive capacity. This is the inventory-based vulnerability assessment approach. Step 4 in the framework uses this approach. Exposure is determined by the location of an asset (or assets) in an area experiencing direct climate change effects (e.g., sea level rise), sensitivity concerns how the asset(s) perform when facing a given climate variable and adaptive capacity is given by the ability of the asset(s) to cope with existing climate variability or anticipated future climate change. The analyst uses the climate and weather variables defined in Step 3 to determine asset vulnerability and assign a level of risk to each asset under consideration. Three specific approaches to the assessment are included in the step:

1. Stakeholder input, which allows for the direct use of local knowledge for the study region.
2. Indicate-based desk review, which utilises the available general knowledge on asset sensitivity and performance from a range of sources, then applied to the study area.
3. Engineering-informed assessment, which focuses on specific assets and uses detailed knowledge of asset performance.

These approaches are not mutually exclusive and may be used together, depending on the available resources and the set objectives for the study.

With the results of the vulnerability assessment in hand, Step 5 aims to determine those assets with the highest priority for action and the appropriate adaptation options to employ. This is done using the established procedures for analysis and prioritisation employed in the evaluation of transportation projects – with suitable modifications to include climate effects. Economic analysis – largely based on BCA – is the most widely used approach for such evaluation; MCA is also available and can include qualitative criteria that may not be accounted for in the quantitative methods of BCA. Step 5 then produces a ranked list of adaptation options for the study area assets seem to be at risk from climate change and extreme weather.

Step 6 in the framework seeks the incorporation of the assessment results into the agency's decision-making processes. This is an essential step to ensure that the results of the analysis will actually be applied in practice, as part of the work programs of the agency. The FHWA framework sets out a series of strategies to achieve this outcome for the following:

- Transportation planning.
- Project development and environmental review.
- Engineering project design.
- Asset management and maintenance programs.
- Transportation systems management and operations, including emergency management.

The process of the framework is ongoing; Step 7, involving monitoring and review, is essential in the dynamic situations of climate change and extreme weather. Our understanding of climate-based risks is still evolving, and experiences gained from new implementations of climate change options provide essential input into the ongoing process of transportation systems and asset adaptation. This is the way that we can build resilience into our transportation systems. The monitoring and review step stands to influence all of the earlier steps in the framework, including setting objectives and defining the scope for a study as well as the technical and analytical steps in the middle of the framework.

As reported by FHWA (2019), the framework has been employed extensively across the United States, in 22 reported studies from 19 states. It provides a prime example of an adaptation framework specifically designed for use in transportation.

Adaptation pathways

Climate change involves uncertainty about future conditions. The adaptation planning frameworks discussed above provide a firm basis for agency-wide adaptation policy and planning, but planning for specific problems and projects may require flexibility in the design and implementation of action plans. The inherent uncertainty in climate change predictions, especially at the local level, as well as changes in social and economic systems over time need to be accounted for in the plans. One approach to project planning that allows for flexibility is the 'adaptation pathway'. This approach maps the possible futures for a given situation and allows for consideration of the robustness and flexibility of the alternative options spanning these futures. Robustness is included because the alternatives need to be examined against the likely future scenarios while flexibility is important to allow for potential changes of plans and switches to other alternatives if circumstances change (Moss and Martin, 2012; Yohe and Leichenko, 2010).

The pathways approach includes five connected stages that fit within the SPP and reinforces the need for reflection through feedback between the stages (Bosomworth et al., 2015). The five stages are the following:

1. Define objectives for the pathways.
2. Study and understand the existing situation.
3. Analyse possible futures.
4. Develop adaptation pathways.
5. Implement, monitor and evaluate, leading to improvement and learning.

Fig. 4.9 shows the five stages and their linkages for adaptation pathways planning. The approach is a closed system, with primary feedback connecting each stage to its successor and secondary feedback between stages 3 (analyse possible futures) and 4 (develop adaptation pathways). Stages 3 and 4 represent major extensions to the SPP specifically intended to address climate change issues. Stage 3 involves the exploration of different potential future scenarios and the development of a range of management responses – cognisant of the likely social values, economic circumstances and agency policies that may be in play over the durations of the scenarios. Uncertainty about the future is a key concern, and the development of a set of scenarios means that a range of alternative options may be tested and assessed, including the robustness and flexibility levels associated with each option. Stage 4 is perhaps the main component of the pathways approach. This stage includes the identification of potential adaptation options and their robustness and flexibility. It also identifies potential:

- Tipping points (terminals), which are physical thresholds where the magnitude of change is such that the current plan will no longer be able to meet the objectives.
- Turning points (transfer nodes), where alternative pathways (plans) can be implemented.
- Trigger points (decision nodes), which set the required lead time for action before reaching a turning point.

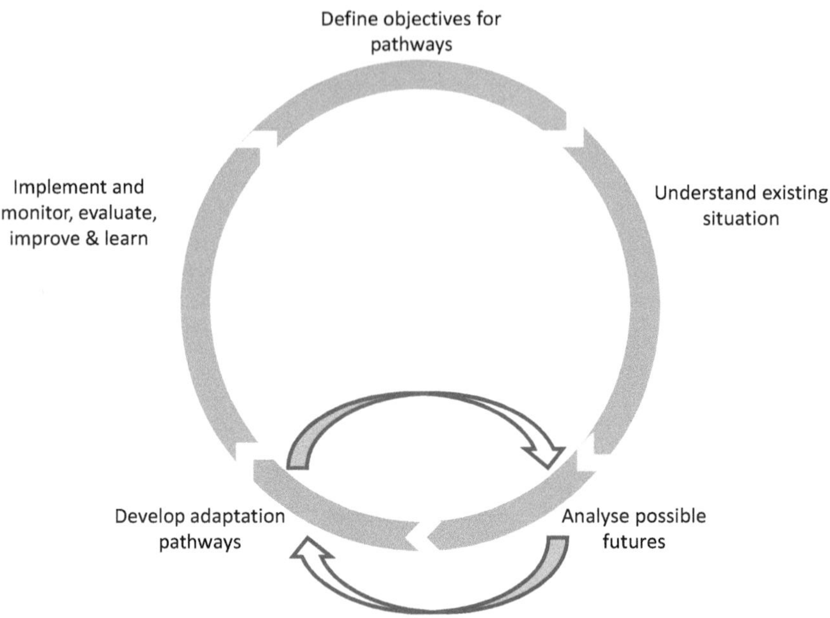

FIGURE 4.9 The five stages in adaptation pathways planning. *As derived from Bosomworth, K., Harwood, A., Leith, P., Wallis, P., 2015. Adaptation Pathways: A Playbook for Developing Options for Climate Change Adaptation in Natural Resource Management. Southern Slopes Climate Change Adaptation Research Partnership (SCARP): RMIT University, University of Tasmania, and Monash University. RMIT University: Melbourne.*

The aim of the pathways approach is to devise a set of policies which includes the timing and sequencing of the different response options given one or more drivers of future change, including climate change. The output of the approach is an adaption pathways map, which shows the feasible alternative options and their possible staging over time and includes the trigger points, turning points and tipping points identified in Stage 4. The pathways map then shows how and when each option could be implemented and when there are opportunities (or necessities) for switches between policies. It can also allow for the introduction of new alternatives if the initial set is found wanting in the face of unforeseen changes in the future. Fig. 4.10 provides an example pathways map. It is based on a hypothetical situation: a road in a coastal zone undergoing substantial erosion of the beachfront and abutting land (e.g., sand dunes). The erosion may be exacerbated in the future by sea level rise and increases in storm surge severity and frequency as a result of climate change. Five options are identified as possible, over an 80-year period:

1. Do nothing, i.e., continue with the existing situation.
2. Undertake minor extensions to existing sea walls and coastal protection measures, and do so over time as needed or feasible.

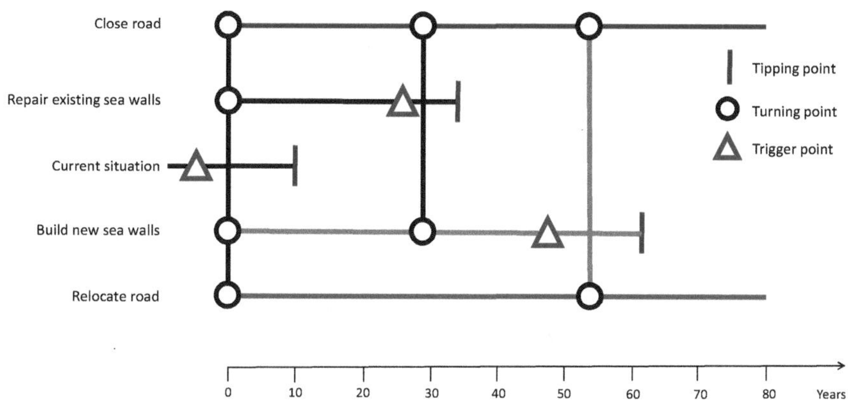

FIGURE 4.10 Example of adaptive pathway for the case of a road in a coastal zone subject to erosion.

3. Construct new sea walls, replace existing walls by higher structures and install new coastal protection measures.
4. Close the road – removing it from the network.
5. Relocate the road to some distance inland from the existing alignment.

Of these, option 5 (relocation) is the most expensive option, while option 4 is the most disruptive for the local community.

The pathways map in Fig. 4.10 shows that the 'do nothing' option will become infeasible after about 10 years. Repairing the existing coastal protection should be effective for a couple of decades after that, but a decision will then have to be made, with options then being to build new sea walls or close the road. Building new walls also has a restricted serviceability under the climate change scenarios, after about 50–60 years. The options to close the road or relocate it offer feasible alternatives – subject of course to the assessments of their respective socioeconomic impacts – over the longer term.

The pathways approach offers planners, managers and decision-makers a visual appreciation of the likely impacts and utilities of the alternative adaptation actions available under different change scenarios. Zandvoort et al., (2017) provide a more detailed discussion of the use of adaptation pathways in practice, through a number of European case studies.

Climate stressors for transportation infrastructure

This chapter has been concerned with the methodologies for policy and planning in transportation and how climate change adaptation can be included in the methods. To complete the chapter requires consideration of the climate factors and variables – the 'climate stressors' – that can affect the location, design, construction, operation and maintenance of transportations systems and infrastructure. Climate stressors may be manifest through both extreme weather events or through gradual changes in climate. ITF (2016) provides a detailed description of transportation climate stressors, and the following discussions summarise that description.

The starting point is to remember, from Chapter 2, that climate change will change both average climate variables and the magnitude, frequency and severity of natural phenomena (the extreme events). The climate stressors for transportation systems include the following:

- Temperature – average, extremes (magnitude and duration) and amplitude (daily and seasonal).
- Humidity – for both air and soil.
- Precipitation, including rainfall and snowfall – total annual, seasonal (or monthly) variations and extreme intensities.
- Wind – prevailing direction, average speed, incidence of gusts and gates and incidence of hurricanes
- Sea level rise.

All of these climate factors stand to be impacted by climate change, probably in the medium to long term. In addition, changes in the incidence and severity of weather-related natural phenomena such as storms and related storm surges, flooding, blizzards, dust storm, wildfires and hurricanes could have severe of not catastrophic effects on transportation infrastructure at any time.

Table 4.1, derived from FHWA (2019), provides a list of major transportation assets that can be affected by climatic conditions and weather events. Table 4.2 expands on this list in terms of asset components, mainly for road transportation, potentially affected by climate. This table shows the generally accepted engineering life of each component, indicating that components with lives exceeding 25 years are likely to be affected by climate change impacts, possibly detrimentally. The components in this grouping include major individual assets such as earthworks, drainage networks, bridges, tunnels and culverts.

Table 4.3, derived from ITF (2016), provides a cross-classification of changes in average (climatic) conditions and extreme weather-related events with the climate stressors.

Climate stress experienced by an infrastructure asset depends to a large degree on the design and construction materials of the asset and the intensity of a given climate variable. For instance, a culvert designed to cope with 200 mm of rain over a day should not be affected by 100 mm of rain falling in a 24 h period, but should that rain fall in 1 h the culvert may fail. Two observations may be made:

- Climate stressors will affect different assets and their components in different ways. Any one asset may be affected by a number of different

TABLE 4.1 Major transportation assets and their primary characteristics, as identified by FHWA (2019).

Asset type	Primary characteristics
Airports	Location (e.g., GIS shapefiles and runway lengths)
	Condition (e.g., materials, service life and historical asset failure)
Bridges	Location
	Condition
	Design thresholds and parameters (e.g., scour, inundation, velocity/capacity and design loads)
Bus routes	Location
	Service frequencies
	Vehicle type
	Average daily ridership
Culverts and flood control structures	Location
	Condition and functionality
	Design thresholds and capacity
Evacuation routes	Location
	Detour length
Floodplain	Location
	Extent (e.g., estimated 100 and 500 year floodplains, historical flood records)
Freight rail	Location
	Track type (e.g., dual or single track)
	Condition
	Goods movement data
Passenger rail	Location
	Track type
	Condition
	Service frequency
	Average daily ridership
Ports	Location
	Type (e.g., inland, coastal, container)
	Condition
	Goods movement data

Continued

TABLE 4.1 Major transportation assets and their primary characteristics, as identified by FHWA (2019).—cont'd

Asset type	Primary characteristics
Roadways	Location
	Condition
	Geotechnical data (e.g., soil plasticity)
	Function (e.g., interstate highway, arterial road, local road, evacuation route)
	Annual average daily traffic volume
	Truck traffic volume
Signals, switches and track	Location
	Condition and functionality
Tunnels	Location
	Length
	Condition
	Design thresholds and parameters
Wetlands	Location
	Condition and functionality (e.g., inundation velocity/capacity, water level)

climatic factors, with each factor contributing to the degradation of one or more components. Complex assets with many components, e.g., pavements and bridges, may thus be a greater risk of overall degradation.

- Climate stressors can operate simultaneously or cumulatively, so that the individual impacts on an asset may be amplified.

A summary overview of climate stressor impacts on transportation systems is given in Table 4.4. It identifies a number of key assets for which vulnerability to climate chnage may exist.

Summary

This chapter has reviewed the concepts of risk and uncertainty and of vulnerability and resilience as these apply to transportation systems, with a focus on the application of these concepts in the consideration of climate

TABLE 4.2 Lifespans of road asset components.

Time span (years)	Pavements	Technology	Geotechnics	Central reserve	Property	Structures	Plant and equipment
5		Lamp					Leased vehicles
8					Leased buildings		Winter maintenance vehicles
10		Lantern					
15	Surface layer flexible pavement	Signs and signals Emergency roadside phone CCTV cameras and fibre network					
25	Base/subbase of road pavement			Steel safety barrier			
30		**Steel lighting columns**				**Sign and signal gantries** **Masts**	
40	**Concrete pavement**						
50				**Concrete safety barrier**			

Continued

TABLE 4.2 Lifespans of road asset components.—cont'd

Time span (years)	Pavements	Technology	Geotechnics	Central reserve	Property	Structures	Plant and equipment
60			**Embankments Roadside cuttings**		**Owned buildings**	**Drainage**	
80		**Aluminium lighting columns**					
100						**Retaining walls Tunnels Bridges Culverts**	
110							
120+							

Shaded area indicates component lives in climate-relevant timescale.
Derived from ITF, 2016. Adapting Transport to Climate Change and Extreme Weather: Implications for Infrastructure Owners and Network Managers, ITF Research Reports, OECD Publishing, Paris https://doi.org/10.1787/9789282108079-en.

TABLE 4.3 Gradual and sudden changes and climate-related stressors.

Category of change	Climate-related stressors
Changes in average values	Change in average temperature
	Change in precipitation (rain, snow)
	Change in humidity
	Sea level rise
	Permafrost melt
Changes in intensity, frequency and severity of weather-related phenomena	Storms
	Storm surge
	Extreme precipitation
	Flooding
	Drought
	Wildfire
	Heat wave
	Hurricane

Derived from ITF, 2016. Adapting Transport to Climate Change and Extreme Weather: Implications for Infrastructure Owners and Network Managers, ITF Research Reports, OECD Publishing, Paris https://doi.org/10.1787/9789282108079-en.

TABLE 4.4 Summary overview of climate stressor impacts on transportation systems.

Climate stressor	Potential impacts on transportation systems
Warmer summers	Heat-related deterioration of materials asphalt rutting rail buckling
	Longer airport runway requirement for aircraft movements
	Loss of inland navigation capacity through lower water levels
	Thermal expansion of bridges and joints
	Heat damage to ITS and traffic control systems hardware
	Wildfire and smoke risk
	Reduced construction and maintenance work opportunities and hours
	Accelerated heave and/or loss of cohesion in permafrost soils

Continued

TABLE 4.4 Summary overview of climate stressor impacts on transportation systems.—cont'd

Climate stressor	Potential impacts on transportation systems
Warmer winters	Reduced ice and snow removal costs
	More opportunities for winter-time maintenance and construction
	Potential increases in incidence, coverage and severity of fogs
	Asset deterioration resulting from more frequent freeze-thaw cycling
	More accessible inland waterways
	Increase in permafrost heave
	Increased flooding because of increases in winter rainfall
Changes in soil and air humidity	Decreased soil humidity: subsidence of geotechnical substrata
	Increased soil humidity: increased runoff from saturation
	Loss of soil cohesion: instability of bridges, subbases, cut slopes and embankments (or increased landslide risk)
	Increased risk of corrosion in steel and concrete structures
	Increased air humidity (with increased temperatures) leading to reduced working hours for maintenance and construction
Increased precipitation (average and extremes)	Increases in weather-related crashes, traffic disruptions and delays
	Flooding and inundation of transportation infrastructure
	Hydraulic damage to bridges, abutments, footings and culverts
	Road and rail washouts
	Collapse of embankments, mudslides, landslides and slope failures
	Flooding of subways and public transit facilities
Stronger and more frequent extreme winds	Damage to technical superstructure of roads, railways, ports and airports
	Damage to lighting, power and communications networks
	Traffic disruption and closures because of fallen trees
	Temporary closures of airports and ports and consequent delays to services
	Clearance of storm debris

TABLE 4.4 Summary overview of climate stressor impacts on transportation systems.—cont'd

Climate stressor	Potential impacts on transportation systems
Sea level rise and storm surges	Erosion of coastal and estuarine roads and railways
	Disruption for transportation networks and activities located in low-lying areas
	Higher tides for port facilities and potential loss of road and rail access to ports
	Increased flooding because of inadequate drainage facilities
	Exposure of low-lying coastal airports to storm-surge damage and flooding
	Higher frequency (or permanent inundation) of transportation facilities (e.g., depots) in low-lying areas
	Corrosion of steel and concrete materials
	Increased scour of bridges and coastal defences
Change in frequency of winter storms	Less or more snow or ice for all transportation modes

Derived from ITF, 2016. reportAdapting Transport to Climate Change and Extreme Weather: Implications for Infrastructure Owners and Network Managers, ITF Research Reports, OECD Publishing, Paris https://doi.org/10.1787/9789282108079-en.

change adaptation by a transportation agency. This assessment requires the understanding and use of systematic decision-making processes, along with the introduction of the available tools for decision-making. More detailed descriptions of the nature and use of these tools are in the next chapter.

The distinction between mitigation and adaptation was reinforced, as a requirement for understanding the issues related to risk management – in this case dealing with a situation that exists or is evolving, rather than looking for an alternative condition. A range of adaptation frameworks was described, including those provided by FHWA and the International Road Federation (PIARC), as these provide good case study applications in the real world. The management of risk and uncertainty in the planning and management of transportation systems is a major feature of the chapter, with an overview of the costs of extreme weather and related events.

The final part of the chapter discussed climate stressors and their effects on infrastructure, leading to an examination of how climatic factors can be represented in performance assessment. The next chapters of the book pick up this topic and describe a range of the methods that can be applied to different transportation systems, networks and modes.

References

Balston, J., Li, S., Iankov, I., Kellett, J., Wells, G., 2017. Quantifying the financial impact of climate change on Australian local government roads. Infrastructures 2 (2), 1–16.

Barbosa, S.B., Ferreira, M.G.G., Nickel, E.M., Cruz, J.A., Forcellini, F.A., Garcia, J., Osório de Andrade Guerra, J.B.S., 2017. Multi-criteria analysis model to evaluate transport systems: an application in Florianópolis, Brazil. Transport. Res. Pol. Pract. 96, 1–13.

Bles, T., Bessembinder, J., Chevreuil, M., Danielsson, P., Falemo, S., Venmans, A., Ennesser, Y., Lofroth, H., 2016. Climate change risk assessments and adaptation for roads – results of the ROADADAPT project. Transp. Res. Procedia 14, 58–67.

Bosomworth, K., Harwood, A., Leith, P., Wallis, P., 2015. Adaptation Pathways: A Playbook for Developing Options for Climate Change Adaptation in Natural Resource Management. Southern Slopes Climate Change Adaptation Research Partnership (SCARP). RMIT University, University of Tasmania, and Monash University. RMIT University, Melbourne.

FHWA, 2012. Climate Change and Extreme Weather Vulnerability Assessment Framework. Report FHWA-HEP-13-005. US Federal Highways Administration, Washington DC.

FHWA, 2018. Climate Change and Extreme Weather Vulnerability Assessment Framework. Report FHWA-HEP- 18-020, third ed. US Federal Highways Administration, Washington DC.

FHWA, 2019. Vulnerability Assessment and Adaptation Framework, third ed. Federal Highways Administration, Washington DC https://www.fhwa.dot.gov/environment/sustainability/resilience/adaptation_framework/chap00.cfm.

IPCC, 2014. Climate Change 2014: Mitigation of Climate Change. Working Group III Contribution to the Fifth Assessment Report of the Intergovernmental Panel on Climate Change. Cambridge University Press, New York. https://www.ipcc.ch/report/ar5/wg3/.

ITF, 2016. Adapting Transport to Climate Change and Extreme Weather: Implications for Infrastructure Owners and Network Managers, ITF Research Reports. OECD Publishing, Paris. https://doi.org/10.1787/9789282108079-en.

Maracharis, C., Bernardini, A., 2015. Reviewing the use of Multi-Criteria Decision Analysis for the evaluation of transport projects: time for a multi-actor approach. Transport Pol. 37, 177–186.

Moss, A., Martin, S., 2012. Flexible adaptation pathways. Clim. X Change Scotl. http://www.climatexchange.org.uk/adapting?to?climate?change/flexible?adaptation?pathways/.

Ortuzar, J. de D., Willumsen, L.G., 2011. Modelling Transport, fourth ed. John Wiley and Sons, Chichester.

PIARC, 2015. International climate change adaptation framework for road infrastructure. In: Report 2015RO3EN, World Road Association/Association Mondiale de la Route (PIARC). www.piarc.org.

Quinet, E., 2000. Evaluation methodologies of transportation projects in France. Transport Pol. 7, 27–34.

Reggiani, A., 2013. Network resilience for transport security: some methodological considerations. Transport Pol. 28, 63–68.

Richardson, A.J., Ampt, E.S., Meyburg, A.N., 1995. Survey Methods for Transport Planning. Eucalyptus Press, Melbourne.

Saaty, T.L., 1980. The Analytic Hierarchy Process: Planning, Priority Setting, Resource Allocation. McGraw-Hill, New York.

Sayers, A.M., Jessop, A.T., Hills, P.J., 2003. Multi-criteria evaluation of transport options – flexible, transparent and user-friendly? Transport Pol. 10, 95–105.

Taylor, M.A.P., 2017. Vulnerability Analysis for Transportation Networks. Elsevier, Oxford.

Taylor, M.A.P., Bonsall, P.W., Young, W., 2000. Understanding Traffic Systems: Data, Analysis and Presentation, second ed. Ashgate Publishing, Aldershot.

TIC, 2018. Australian Transport Assessment and Planning Guidelines: F3 Options Generation and Assessment. Commonwealth Department of Infrastructure and Regional Development, Canberra. http://atap.gov.au/. (Accessed 11 November 2019).

Tsamboulas, D., Yiotis, G.S., Panou, K.D., 1999. Use of multicriteria methods for assessment of transport projects. J. Transport. Eng. 125 (5), 407–414.

Yohe, G., Leichenko, R., 2010. Adapting a risk-based approach. In: Rosenzweig, C., Solecki, W. (Eds.), Climate Change Adaptation in New York City: Building a Risk Management Response. Annals of the New York Academy of Sciences, New York, 1191–1354.

Zandvoort, M., Campos, I.S., Vizinho, A., Penha-Lopes, G., Lorencova, E.K., Van Der Brugge, R., Van Der Vlist, M.J., Van Den Brink, A., Jeuken, A.B.M., 2017. Adaptation pathways in planning for uncertain climate change: applications in Portugal, the Czech Republic and The Netherlands. Environ. Sci. Pol. 78, 18–26.

Chapter 5

Managing transportation infrastructure and assets

Chapter 3 included an introduction to systematic decision-making processes as applied in transportation systems planning and management. It outlined two of the important decision-making tools commonly used in transportation, namely benefit–cost analysis (BCA) and multicriteria analysis (MCA). This chapter builds on the previous discussion by considering the decision-making requirements inherent in the planning and management process, and in particular in transportation asset management. It includes more detailed descriptions of BCA and MCA and discusses their relevance in climate change adaptation planning. The need for other tools when deep uncertainties exist—as in the case for climate change in the longer term, i.e., more than two decades hence – is explored, and some other tools are introduced, including real options analysis (ROA) and robust decision-making (RDM).

This chapter also continues the discussion on the likely impacts of climate change on different transportation assets. While subsequent chapters (e.g., Chapters 6–8) look at mode-specific impacts (for ports and harbours, roads and railways, respectively), the discussion in this chapter is on infrastructure assets such as bridges and culverts that are common across the range of transportation modes. This chapter also includes an introduction to climate change impacts likely to affect airports, given that the airport is a hub where several modes often meet.

The starting point for the discussions is the systematic management of transportation assets.

Transportation asset management

Earlier discussions in this book, especially in Chapters 2 and 3 (note in particular the FHWA climate adaptation framework as a good example), have included the utility of an asset management database as a core resource in the assessment of potential climate change impacts on transportation infrastructure and on the usage of transportation systems. The asset management system provides a systematic approach to knowledge of the types of assets in the transportation system, the locations of those assets, their current condition and their projected service lives. At this stage, it is therefore useful to consider the

Climate Change Adaptation for Transportation Systems. https://doi.org/10.1016/B978-0-12-816638-3.00005-2

nature of asset management systems, the principles on which they are based, their role in overall planning and management of the transportation system, the data that they hold and how that data are applied.

The implementation of asset management systems in transportation dates from about the turn of the 21st century, at least as far as their systematic application is concerned. For the developed Western economies, this coincides roughly with the realisation that transportation asset maintenance—meaning the stewardship of well-established transportation infrastructure assets—had become the primary responsibility of transportation agencies, certainly in terms of the allocation of available resources. The construction of new assets had become a secondary function, given the extent of the existing transportation system. If in previous eras existing assets could be discounted—because the installation and construction of new assets took precedence—this was no longer the case. Managing the existing assets and their operating capacity was the primary responsibility undertaken by the transportation agency. Further was the realisation that resources were finite and the time for ever increasing annual budgets was over. Available resources needed to be marshalled to achieve optimal performance of the transportation system.

The underlying goal of asset management is to facilitate a broad approach to resource allocation, agency productivity and program planning that will enhance the transportation system and provide greater satisfaction for users through improved program effectiveness and enhanced system performance. Key to realising this wide-ranging goal is the availability of comprehensive, quality data on the state of the system and its components and the ability to extrapolate the likely state of the system into the future. FHWA (2007) identified five core principles for asset management systems in the transportation sector:

1. Policy-driven, in which resource allocation decisions are based on a well-defined set of policy goals and objectives
2. Performance-based, where the policy objectives are translated into system performance measures capable of use for both day-to-day and strategic management
3. Analysis of options and trade-offs, by which decisions on the allocations of funds and resources within a particular type of investment (e.g., preventive maintenance as opposed to rehabilitation) or between different investment types (e.g., pavements versus bridges) are based on analysis of how alternative levels of allocation will affect the achievement of relevant policy objectives
4. Decisions based on quality information, requiring that the merits of different alternatives relevant to the agency's policy goals are evaluated using current and credible data
5. Monitoring to provide clear accountability and feedback, by which performance results are monitored and reported for both impacts and effectiveness.

FHWA (2007, p.4) offered a broad definition of transportation asset management, as 'a strategic and systematic process of operating, maintaining, upgrading and expanding physical assets effectively through their lifecycle. It focuses on business and engineering practices for resource allocation and utilization, with the objective of better decision making based upon quality information and well defined objectives'.

On the basis of this definition and the five principles enunciated above, a schematic framework for an asset management system can be set down, as in Fig. 5.1.

This figure is something of a simplification of the Systems Planning Process diagram (Fig. 5.2 in Chapter 3). The framework has two basic input points: goals and policies and budget allocations. An asset inventory (the asset database) is utilised to provide assessments of the condition (state) of the component assets, subject to performance modelling. This modelling considers the existing state of an asset, the physical environment (including climatic conditions) in which it is located and the traffic load to which the asset is subject, to provide an estimate of the likely state of the asset into the future. Assessment of the current and future estimated states against the (level of service (LoS)) criteria for the asset class then provides an indication of the oncoming needs for maintenance, refurbishment or replacement of the asset in future years. On the basis of this systematic assessment of the states of the transportation assets, alternative works programs (including maintenance of existing assets and the provision of new assets to meet future demands) can be considered, within the constraints imposed by the available budget allocations. This process includes the prioritisation of projects and the selection of sets of projects to be undertaken in the next and forthcoming budgetary periods. The implementation of the works program for the next period then follows. Experiences gained in this implementation feed back into considerations of future program optimisation and the evaluation of alternative options. Performance monitoring is essential in the framework, to provide information on the level of realisation of the goals and objectives on which the works program is based. Two separate approaches are sometimes recognised for the use of an asset management system (FHWA, 2007):

1. Policy-based asset management, which tends towards a long term, life-cycle approach to the evaluation of program and project benefits and costs
2. Performance-based asset management, where the preservation of existing transportation assets is sought through the use of identified key performance indicators (KPIs) and targets (often expressed in terms of minimum acceptable LoS criteria).

The former may be more easily related to considerations of climate change adaptation strategies, but the latter is a key factor in the wider social performance assessment for transportation systems. A hybrid of both approaches may thus be needed for climate change adaptation.

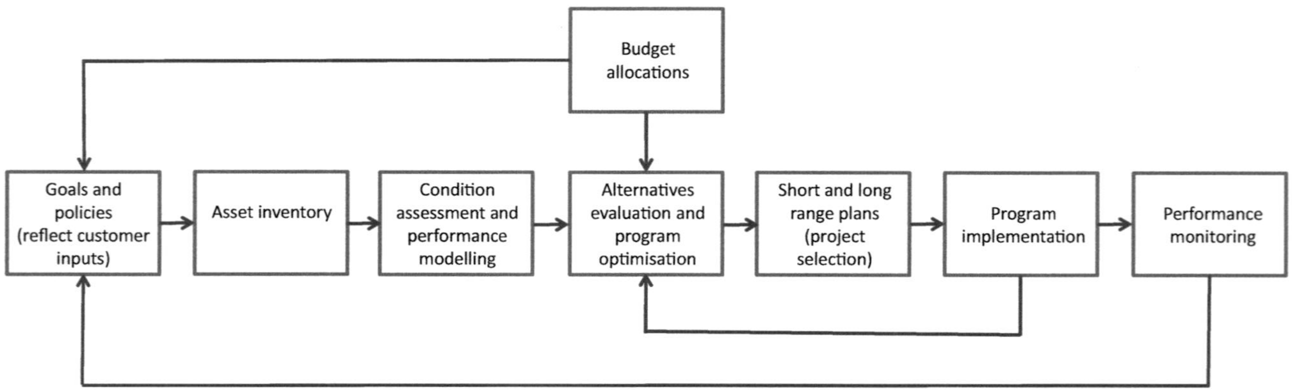

FIGURE 5.1 Schematic representation of a generic asset management system. *As derived from FHWA, 2007. Asset Management Overview. Report FHWA-IF-08-008. Federal Highways Administration, Department of Transportation, Washington DC. https://www.fhwa.dot.gov/asset/if08008/amo_02.cfm. (Accessed 18 November 2019).*

The asset management system may thus be seen to seek the attainment of set performance goals and objectives, which then cover an extended time horizon, account for both engineering and economics and consider a broad range of assets. Indeed decision-making in an asset management environment commonly involves considerations of multiple asset types. The decisions therefore tend to be wider in scope and require more economic analysis, than decisions made in less focused management systems. That said, the early adoptions of asset management systems in transportation tended to concentrate on short-term operations and the financial aspects of maintenance (Bhamidipati, 2015) rather than be directed to strategic planning in the long term. The latter is clearly the area of interest for the impacts of climate change on transportation systems and the concomitant development of adaptation strategies. In addition, the early focus on budgeting and infrastructure maintenance programs often narrowed the scope of asset management to engineering, economic and fiscal considerations, with social aspects possibly ignored (Trojanova, 2014). Given that the social aspects include the usage of the transportation system by individuals, communities, businesses and society at large, the low priority accorded to societal concerns was a deficiency in the early implementation of asset management strategies. A further consideration is the impact of interconnected infrastructure systems, as discussed in Chapter 2. Transportation infrastructure is often located close to if not sharing space with other infrastructure systems (e.g., water supply, communications, energy supply, drainage and sewerage) and these systems may utilise transportation assets (e.g., bridges, where conduits, cables and pipes are often incorporated into the structure).

Framework for an asset management system

The most recent descriptions of asset management (e.g., ISO, 2014; Austroads, 2018a,b,c) recognise these multiple factors and also seek to place transportation asset management systems into the wider context of the obligations of a transportation agency to the society that it serves. Austroads (2018a) thus defines asset management as

> *'A systematic process of effectively maintaining, upgrading and operating assets, combining engineering principles with sound business practice and economic rationale, and providing the tools to facilitate a more organised and flexible approach to making decisions necessary to deliver optimal community benefits' (Austroads, 2018a, p.7).*

This definition includes consideration of both the technical aspects of asset management and the need for a wider institutional approach. The integration of an asset management system into the governance and risk management framework of an agency can then contribute wider benefits and facilitate the connection of the agency's operations to its broader policy goals and objectives. Using a risk management approach—as discussed in earlier chapters of this book—asset management can then relate the agency's objectives to asset-related decisions, plans and activities. This provides a valuable approach for the incorporation of climate change adaptation goals into the agency's normal activities. Three levels of asset management then emerge, and—as discussed subsequently in this chapter—data needs and information requirements can be formulated to suit these three levels, which are

1. The strategic level, where policies, objectives, strategies and plans are established, to respond to the current and future service expectations of the agency
2. The tactical level, in which prioritised work programs are developed to address the service expectations and challenges
3. The operational level, which is the implementation of the programs.

Under this approach Austroads (2018a) indicates that asset management provides an integrated approach to the creation and management of assets which deliver the services sought by the transportation agency's customers in the most cost-effective and efficient manner. It then follows that the purpose of asset management is 'to provide the required levels of service at the lowest life-cycle cost to present and future road (sic) users and customers, using a "whole of agency" approach to the acquisition and management of physical assets' (Austroads, 2018a, p.8). An integrated framework for transportation asset management may then be proposed, which includes explicit recognition of climate change and the adoption of climate change adaption strategies by transportation agencies. Fig. 5.2 shows this framework.

The top half of framework in Fig. 5.1 shows the three levels of asset management—strategic, tactical and operational—at the top. In broad terms the strategic level involves the definition of objectives and the determination of asset strategies, after which come the tactical tasks of developing an asset investment program and identifying asset needs. The developed work program is then put in place under operations. In addition, a performance review is undertaken: this involves monitoring and evaluation of the projects and asset in the works program and the preparation of review reports. The information gathered in this process provides vital feedback to direct future strategy, tactics and operations, for the framework describes an ongoing process. More detail on the framework is given in the bottom half. This actually involves two processes running in parallel: the systems planning process (as discussed in Chapter 3) and an information and communications process. The former presents the flow of activities inherent in the asset management system. The latter indicates the vital needs for information dissemination within the agency and with the community and stakeholders that the agency serves. Both processes are vital for the successful running of the asset management system.

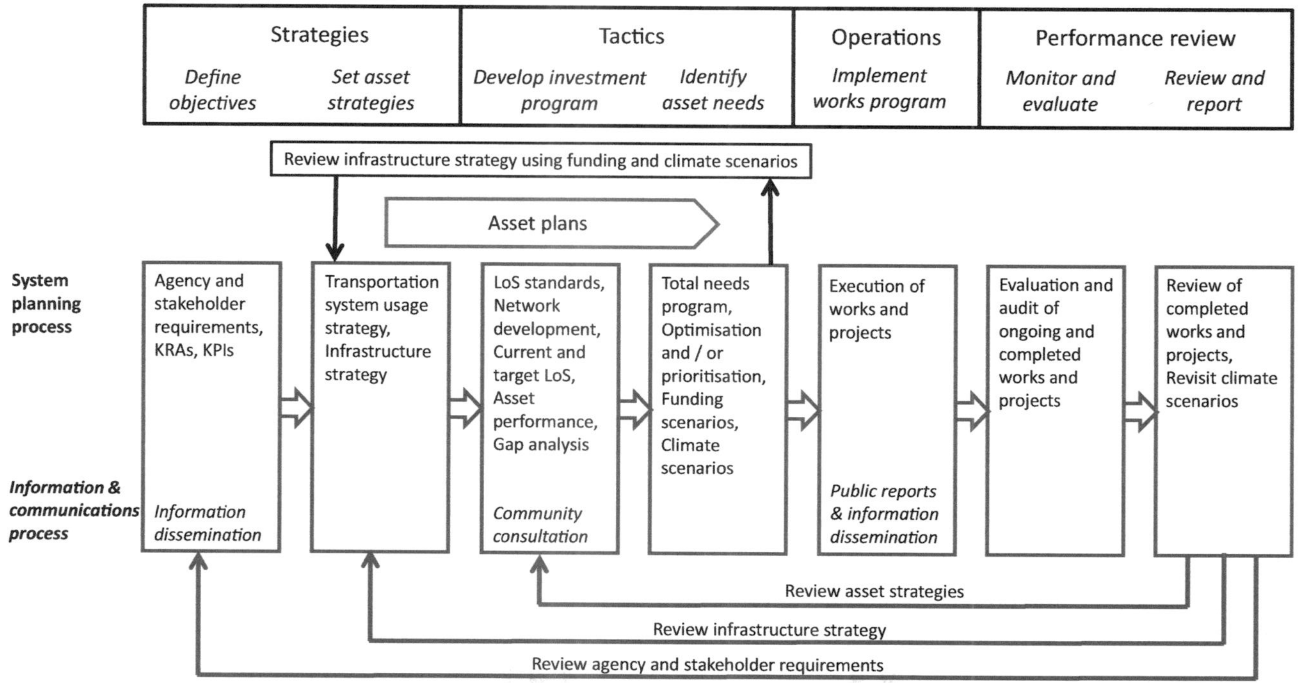

FIGURE 5.2 An integrated asset management framework with explicit recognition of climate change adaptation in transportation asset management.

The planning process first involves the determination of the transportation requirements for the agency and its stakeholders, and the definition of key resource areas (which identify the resources, including labour, equipment and funding, available to the agency over time) and the KPIs (which set the criteria on which the success of the agency's works programs can be gauged). The main consequence of this activity is the definition of the objectives to be achieved by the agency. Then the strategies for the usage of the transportation system (the travel demands it is intended to meet) and for the provision of infrastructure assets (the form, layout and locations of the transportation facilities) can be determined. LoS standards (e.g., expected travel speeds, acceptable travel times and delays, vehicle operating costs) provide the basic criteria on which system and asset performance can be judged. These standards may be different between present day and future years. The performance of existing assets and the estimated needs for upgrades or new assets to enable attainment of desired LoS standards can then be made. Community consultation is an important part of this stage. Works programs to deliver the identified needs may then be devised and compared, subject to the scenarios for available funding over time and considering available climate scenarios relevant to that period (and beyond). This may lead to possible review of the infrastructure strategy—a first feedback loop in the framework.

Once the tactics and strategy have been determined, then operations can be invoked, with the implementation of the optimised works program and its prioritised projects. Reporting and information dissemination on project implementation and asset availability are also undertaken at this stage. The success of the works program and the needs for potential fine tuning of the program and the modification when necessary of the asset strategies is then assessed through the evaluation and auditing of the ongoing and completed projects, leading to a review of completed works. The opportunity also exists to revisit the climate scenarios adopted in the earlier stages of the framework, in the light of the observations being made as the works program proceeds. Feedback opportunities to review the asset strategies, the more general infrastructure strategy and the agency and stakeholder requirements can be undertaken using the outcomes of the evaluations and program review.

Transportation agencies face evolving external challenges. Besides changing user and stakeholder expectations and global environmental concerns (viz. climate change), risk, economics and funding issues require consideration. While transportation user service expectations are likely to increase and new technologies may offer different service options (e.g., autonomous vehicles, and smart infrastructure through the 'internet of things'), there are likely to be fiscal pressures to spend less (and get more from existing infrastructure assets) along with greater focus on risk and resilience. Increasing traffic volumes and competition for space may increase traffic congestion. A sound asset management system of the type described above is then a necessity. Effective long-term asset management, especially for climate change considerations, is essential. The following characteristics for effective asset management in the long term were identified by Austroads (2018a):

- *Make fair long-term decisions*, i.e., decisions made today should not compromise the ability of future generations to experience similar or better transportation services as those of the present (and not expecting future technologies alone to provide that ability)
- *Set fair and equitable pricing*, which ensures that transportation system users of today and tomorrow continue to pay fair and equitable prices for similar (or equivalent) LoS and access to transportation networks
- *Manage life-cycle costs effectively*, by avoiding cheap short-term measures which lead to higher future costs or increased risks for system users
- *Remember that transportation assets* (e.g., bridges) *are long life assets*, so that future agency managers and personnel will inherit the legacy of asset management decisions made today while future users will require to use the assets
- *Risk and resilience are of growing importance*, and transportation systems need the capability to both serve normal community expectations and provide for emergency and other essential services in dealing with major events, disasters (e.g., hurricanes, fires and floods) and service disruptions (from storms, blizzards, blackouts, etc.)
- *Transportation corridors often serve as utility corridors*, especially for road transportation, interdependency between transportation and other infrastructure systems is a key feature and these other infrastructure systems (e.g., electricity, gas, water, telecommunications and wastewater) are also vital community assets.

Data requirements for asset management

The asset management process described above is based on the premise that timely, up to date, reliable and accurate data are available on the existence, location and state of the assets. Data are required first to underpin the decision-making and prioritisation process in the development of works programs, and to support the monitoring, evaluation and audit processes involved in performance review (see Fig. 5.2). Data collected for the latter requirement also inform future decision-making processes. The asset management database is an ongoing system. The effective use of the data assists in the present day decision-making and in scenario generation and risk management for future decisions. The data provide sound evidence to support decisions about the performance, risks, maintenance requirements and optimal funding for the refurbishment or replacement of assets. The functions for which data are collected include

- Monitoring of performance over time to test whether or ensure that LoS and agency objectives are being satisfied
- Monitoring and benchmarking of asset condition

- Monitoring life-cycle costs for significant assets (e.g., bridges)
- Assistance in establishing future maintenance and asset replacement funding requirements
- Monitoring of construction quality and maintenance standards
- Maintenance of an asset inventory including current (and projected) asset condition
- Monitoring the usage of the assets (e.g., traffic volumes, passenger volumes, freight volumes)
- Research and development for modelling of asset deterioration (e.g., riding quality of pavement surfaces).

In broad terms, the data collected on asset condition are used to provide statistical information for monitoring purposes and to provide quantitative information for management and optimal decision-making. While the data may be collected at a fine grained, elemental level, aggregation of the data may be required for some management purposes and for system reviews and reporting. The choice of the specific data to collect and the level of detail required for the data depend on multiple factors, and may be specific to the needs of a particular agency. Two broad classes of data are relevant: operational data, which considers the condition of the assets and the performance and usage of those assets, and supporting data, which indicates design standards and operating rules and procedures used in the development and use of the assets, as well as definitions of the various data items. There is also an important question about the frequency with which different data items need to be collected and updated. For an asset database, five data types relating to frequency of observation and collection can be defined:

- Dynamic data, being data items (e.g., traffic volume and travel speed), that are in continual flux and may need ongoing collection over very short time intervals, if not in 'real time'
- Periodic data, which require ongoing observation with data recording at frequent intervals (hours, days or weeks)
- Static data, which may be recorded 'one-off' (e.g., installation of a new asset), with only infrequent updating (months or years)
- Standing data, which include the design parameters and standards used in the construction, usage and maintenance of assets which are essential for systems operation but are likely to change infrequently
- Meta data, which are data describing data, e.g., a data dictionary.

Table 5.1 lists and compares these data types.

The question of the required level of detail in the data can best be answered by considering the 'data triangle' for the asset database. This triangle, as depicted in Fig. 5.3, shows the level of detail in the data, the areas

TABLE 5.1 Data types commonly found in transportation asset management systems.

Data type	Rate of change of data values	Data category	Description	Examples	Audit requirements
Operational data	High	Dynamic data	Data continually subject to update, e.g., operational records, traffic usage	Near-real time traffic data such as travel times; road surface ice and temperature; roadside pollution measurements	Frequent calibration and checking of measuring instruments
	Medium	Periodic data	Data requiring regular collection and updating	Routine inspections; pavement condition surveys; maintenance reviews; traffic counts; air temperature and precipitation	On-site validation; load validation including referencing to network location; data codes; value ranges
	Low	Static data	Data requiring one-off collection and validation, with infrequent updates as needed	Network asset inventory; construction records; climate change scenarios	Initial load validation; procedures to record changes as they occur (e.g., asset refurbishment or new construction)
Supporting data		Standing data	Data including constants, rules, and design parameters essential to the operation of the asset but which change infrequently—includes climatic factors and climate change scenarios	Look-up tables for coded database fields design standards; valid data ranges	Confirmation of consistency with agency or national standards
		Meta data	Data that describe data	Data dictionary	

Derived from Austroads, 2018c. Guide to Asset Management – Overview Part 9: Asset Management Information System and Data. Austroads, Sydney.

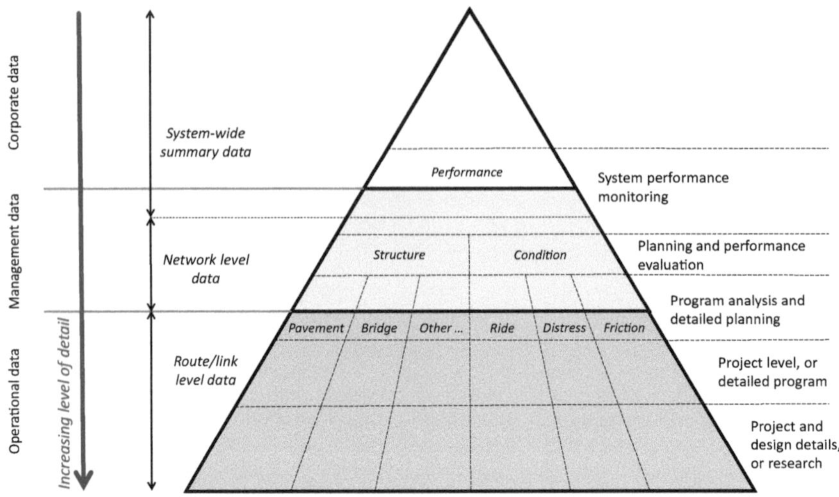

FIGURE 5.3 The data triangle, showing level of data detail, and areas of application and data aggregation.

of application of the data and the process of data aggregation from the most detailed, at the individual project level, to the least detailed, at the corporate reporting level.

Data are needed at the operational, management and corporate levels, and while these data are obviously related, the general trend is for aggregation and hence less detail at the higher levels. The usage of the data covers

1. Project and design details, and research data on the usage and performance of individual asset components
2. Project level data, including design parameters and detailed program data
3. Program analysis and detailed planning data
4. Planning and performance evaluation
5. System performance monitoring.

In terms of the transportation network managed by the agency, usages 1–3 are generally concerned with link and route level studies and are largely operational in nature. Usages 3 and 4 apply to management at the network level, i.e., there is some overlap for program analysis and detailed planning between operations and management. Likewise, system performance monitoring (usage 5) applies to both management and corporate data applications, with the latter primarily but not exclusively concerned with system-wide performance. The structure and condition of each asset item is included at the network level, with the data for these factors aggregated from the more detailed data on the state, performance and use of each asset from the route/link level. Most data are collected at the more detailed, lower end of the data triangle, with appropriate aggregation mechanisms and rules required so that relevant but less detailed data are provided at the higher levels.

The basic data items required for each component asset in the system are (1) an asset reference code, which provides the identification, type and location of each component asset in the asset management database, and (2) an asset register, which holds the state and condition information for the asset, such as inventory condition, traffic usage data, historical records of construction, refurbishment and routine maintenance and periodic maintenance and rehabilitation. The register may also include information on incidents affecting the asset, such as flooding and road crashes. Additional information would also be sought and held for each asset, including

- Key operational and performance data
- Detailed maintenance data (e.g., available treatments, dates of application, and their costs and benefits)
- Unit costs for maintenance, rehabilitation and refurbishment
- Technical design standards applying to the asset
- Works management, including contract documentation, tracking and inspection of completed works, records of work history and as-built details (which may vary from the as-designed details).

The next section of this chapter deals with the potential climate and environmental impacts on transportation assets, including the possible impacts of extreme weather events. For this purpose, and indeed as a unifying thread for this book, it is worth noting that different transportation modes/systems actually include many of the same asset components, such as bridges, tunnels, pavements and drainage. The four main transportation systems considered in this volume are road, rail, airports and ports and harbours. Table 5.2 lists a number of the asset components and indicates the transportation systems to which they apply. The list is not exhaustive, but provides a useful indication of the usage of the components and their importance to transportation in general. The discussion in the next section focuses on the components rather than necessarily the transportation modes.

Climate and environmental influences

Climate and environmental factors can affect the performance and condition of transportation infrastructure in many ways, and the design, operations and maintenance activities of transportation agencies have long been geared to recognising and dealing with these factors as they affect a given agency and the region that it serves. However, changes to climate and environment can upset the established situation, and this is why adaptation to climate change is important in the present era. Consider the following five climate trends often associated with climate change:

- Drier summers
- Increases in temperature

TABLE 5.2 **Broad list of transportation asset types and the transportation systems they apply to.**

Asset type	Asset component	Transportation system			
		Road (including bus)	Rail	Airport	Ports and harbours
Road/track ('Right-of-way')	Pavement	✓		✓	✓
	Apron			✓	✓
	Surfacing	✓		✓	✓
	Earthworks	✓	✓	✓	✓
	Rail track		✓		✓
	Traffic management devices	✓		✓	
Structure	Bridges	✓	✓		
	Tunnels	✓	✓		
	Major culverts	✓	✓	✓	
	Retaining walls	✓	✓	✓	✓
	Terminals		✓	✓	✓
	Stations		✓		
	Stops	✓			
	Depots	✓	✓	✓	✓
	Wharves				✓
	Other structures	✓	✓	✓	✓
Drainage	Open drains	✓	✓	✓	✓
	Kerb and channel	✓			
	Pits	✓	✓	✓	✓
	Minor culverts	✓	✓	✓	✓
	Pipes	✓	✓	✓	✓

TABLE 5.2 Broad list of transportation asset types and the transportation systems they apply to.—cont'd

		Transportation system			
Asset type	Asset component	Road (including bus)	Rail	Airport	Ports and harbours
Roadside/ trackside environment	Signs	✓	✓	✓	✓
	Slopes	✓	✓		
	Embankments	✓	✓		
	Noise barriers	✓	✓	✓	
	Lighting	✓		✓	✓
	Fences	✓	✓	✓	✓
	Pathways	✓			
	Safety barriers	✓		✓	

- Increases in extreme precipitation (i.e., rainfall and snowfall)
- More powerful storms
- Increases in winter rain.

Each of these climatic phenomena can have significant impacts on infrastructure. Fig. 5.4 provides a summary view of the likely climate impacts of the above climate trends and the types of adverse impacts on road infrastructure that may result from the climate impacts. This figure, derived and extended from ITF (2016), links the climate trends to specific types of road damage through the climate impacts.

The connections in Fig. 5.4 show the opportunities for multiple climate impacts on different aspects of road damage. Increases in temperature can affect road surface and base courses in several ways, including rutting, bleeding, swelling and cracking. Thermal fatigue is another damage type, and noting—as discussed in Chapter 6—that the general failure for road pavements is fatigue failure after exposure to multiple heavy axle loads—that thermal fatigue due to excessive temperature variations will only add to the earlier potential for pavement failure. Increases in extreme precipitation and the frequency of more powerful storms are also climate factors of concern, especially for cut slopes and embankments.

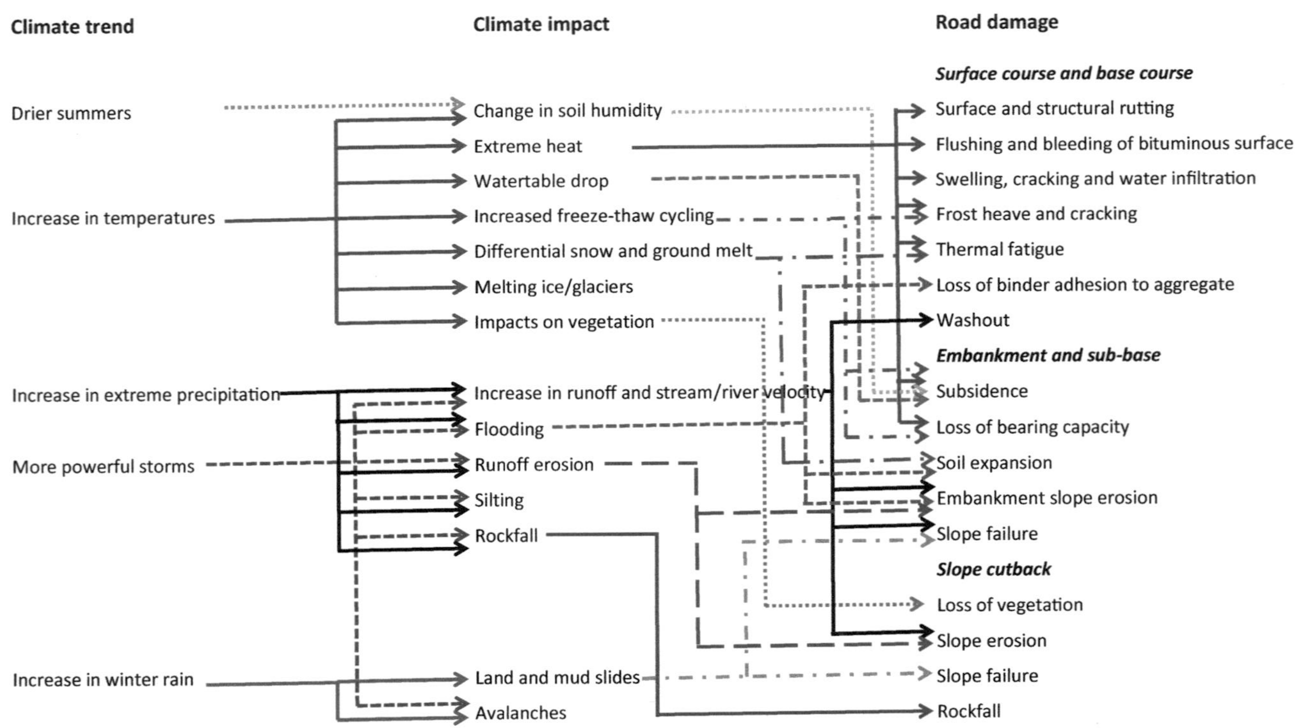

FIGURE 5.4 Indications of climate trends and their impacts on climate and potential damage to road infrastructure. *Adapted from ITF, 2016. Adapting Transport to Climate Change and Extreme Weather: Implications for Infrastructure Owners and Network Managers. ITF Research Reports. OECD Publishing, Paris. https://doi.org/10.1787/9789282108079-en.*

Infrastructure components

The following infrastructure components are of general interest and are found in different transportation infrastructure systems (e.g. road, rail and airports):

Earthworks
Bridges
Culverts
Tunnels

Extreme weather events may significantly affect the functioning of these infrastructure components and the transportation service operations that use them.

Earthworks

Earthworks are common to both road and rail foundations, as embankments created to support road/rail foundations above the natural surface level and as cut slopes where the alignment falls beneath that surface (see Figures 2.3 and 2.4). Earthworks are susceptible to inundation and hydraulic damage, as well as slope erosion and slope failure. ITF (2016) indicates that changes in precipitation intensity and frequency are more likely to affect earthworks than road pavement and rail track. Changes in water table levels may also have adverse effects on both earthworks and pavements. Changes in the frequency of freeze–thaw cycles are also likely to affect earthworks. Similarly increases in extreme weather events, such as storms, also stand to affect road/rail foundations and the earthworks that support them. Drainage failures, e.g., due to inadequate culvert capacity, can have significant impacts on road pavements and rail tracks, by weakening embankment slopes and ultimately by washouts that puncture the road pavement or rail track. In addition, climate impacts on other earthworks and geotechnical structures outside the domain of the transportation agency, e.g., river levee banks and seawalls when breached, may also have detrimental impacts on pavements and tracks, through inundation, storm surges and flooding.

While road pavements and rail track structures have relatively short design lives, of the order of 20–30 years, so that climate change impacts on them may be accounted for under normal asset management operations, earthworks and their associated structures have design lives two or three times greater, so that climate change impacts may be more severe and need to be explicitly accounted for. This is especially valid for valley, flood plain and coastal areas prone to storm damage and flooding.

Bridges

Bridges are in many ways the most vital infrastructure elements in a (land) transportation system. They have a strategic role in connecting otherwise physically separated regions and the closure or failure of a bridge may have serious consequences—beyond long detours and increases in travel times, failure can devastate the economy and social fabric of a now-isolated community (Lock and Gelling, 1976). Bridges can also become major cultural icons for a region or city (e.g., the Brooklyn Bridge in New York, Tower Bridge London, Sydney Harbour Bridge, Mostar Bridge, Bosnia and Herzegovina, and the Golden Gate Bridge, San Francisco)—see Salamak and Fross (2016). Fig. 5.5 shows a less well-known but locally important bridge: the Hindmarsh Island Bridge at Goolwa, South Australia. Bridges are often major and strategic infrastructure investments, with design lives in excess of 60 years and actual useful lives well in excess of that figure. They are thus infrastructure assets expected to be exposed to future climate change. In addition, and as discussed in previous chapters, interdependency between infrastructure systems is an important consideration, well exemplified by road bridges. Bridges often provide the physical support for pipelines and cables to cross a waterway or other gap between land masses. Fig. 5.6 shows the underside of the Hindmarsh Island Bridge at its abutment on the mainland, clearly showing the water mains, power cables and telecommunications cables attached to it, to carry those infrastructure services to the island.

A further issue with many bridges in the developed world is their age and perhaps decreasing capability to provide desired LoS, and capacity to accommodate climate change impacts. For instance, in 2016 there were

FIGURE 5.5 The Hindmarsh Island road bridge, Goolwa, South Australia.

FIGURE 5.6 Underside of the Hindmarsh Island road bridge, showing the western abutment and the water, power and telecommunications connections supported by the bridge.

614,387 bridges in the United States, of which about 40% were 50 years of age or older. Just over 9% of the bridges were assessed as structurally deficient[1] (FHWA, 2016; ASCE, 2017). Many of the existing bridges were constructed on the basis of engineering standards inferior to those now in use (e.g., in terms of the traffic loads, especially heavy goods vehicle mass) and which used climate, meteorological and environmental conditions less representative of current and likely future conditions (ITF, 2016). Bridge construction materials include concrete, steel and timber and as these have different performance properties with respect to climate-related variables

1. ASCE (2017) defines a structurally deficient bridge as one requiring significant maintenance, rehabilitation or replacement. A bridge designated as structurally deficient request inspection at least on an annual basis as it includes critical load-carrying elements known to be in poor condition due to deterioration or damage.

such as temperature and water so that steel and concrete bridge components may need to be considered separately.

Fig. 5.7 is a composite schematic drawing showing the basic components of a bridge, as well as three major types of bridge (arch, suspension and cable-stayed). In general terms, a bridge may be seen to comprise two major components: superstructure and substructure. The substructure includes all elements below the bearings—these support the superstructure (including the bridge deck) and distribute loads (dead weight and live weight) into the ground and include abutments, piers, foundations and possibly piles. The superstructure comprises all elements above the bearings, including the deck (although, given its particular importance, the deck is sometimes regarded as a third major component). Bridge superstructure includes the bridge spans, which support the deck loads and connect the substructure components. Superstructure may be constructed using steel, concrete or timber beams, steel trusses, and cables or other load-bearing/load-distributing elements. The typical service lives for bridge components are of the order of 60–80 years (or more) for substructure and superstructure elements except for bridge decks, for which service life is perhaps 30–50+ years (ITF, 2016). The deck is the roadway, railway or pedestrian path surface of the bridge. Decks are constructed from concrete slabs or (stiffened) steel plates, with a surface layer of asphalt or concrete.

Changes in average and extreme temperatures will affect both concrete and steel components of a bridge:

- Thermal expansion of steel components and thermal mismatch between cement and aggregates in concrete elements can lead to material deterioration, weakening the structural strength of the elements
- Thermal strains induced by increased temperatures can also affect component performance, especially when tensile stresses are increased.

In these cases, adaptation measures aimed at reducing heat absorption by structures are appropriate.

Increased water infiltration and air humidity along with increased temperatures can accelerate chemical deterioration of steel and concrete components:

- Rusting of steel due to moisture
- Chloride or carbonation corrosion of concrete (which may also be affected by increased atmospheric carbon dioxide concentrations).

Concrete corrosion can lead to greater exposure of steel reinforcing, adding to the likelihood of rusting of the steel (see Stewart et al., 2011, 2012). Chloride-induced corrosion presents a particular threat to submerged or partially submerged reinforced concrete structures, through sea level rise and perhaps salt water intrusion into coastal fresh water bodies.

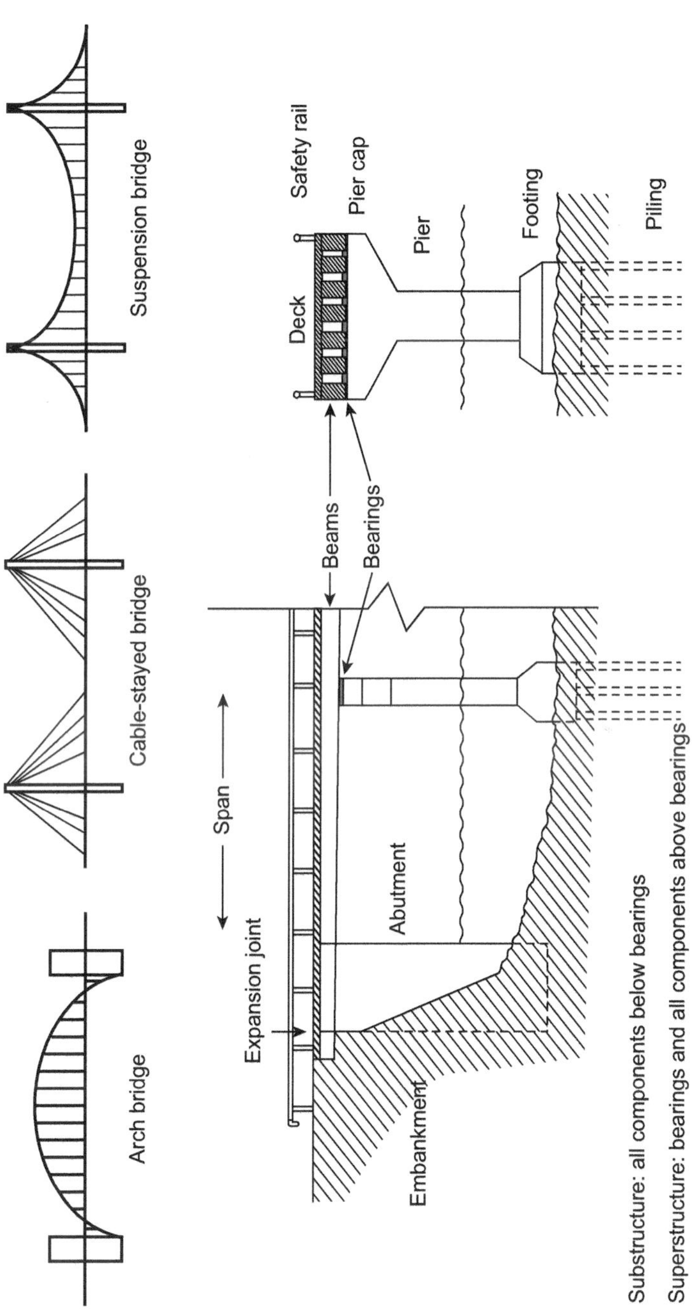

FIGURE 5.7 Schematic of typical bridge components and types of bridges.

Increased rainfall can also affect bridge components:

- Decks and superstructure may be damaged by water intrusion, leading to corrosion and deterioration, especially if the drainage system is not designed to cope with increased rainfall
- Substructure may be affected by increased water levels and flow volumes under a bridge due to increased rainfall and frequency of heavy storms.

ITF (2016) indicates that more than 60% of over-water bridge failures result from hydraulic damage. This damage includes scouring of piers and foundations and increased lateral dynamic loads.

Table 5.3 summarises these potential impacts of climate change on bridges.

Culverts

The culvert is a ubiquitous piece of infrastructure, largely forgotten and often unseen, but it plays a vital role in the successful operation of transportation networks. Indeed the structural integrity of transportation infrastructure can be severely compromised by culvert failure—see Fig. 5.8.

TABLE 5.3 Potential climate change impacts on bridges.

	Type of bridge component	
Climate change variable	Concrete	Steel
Temperature increases	Deterioration of upper deck surfaces	
Precipitation increases	Damage from temperature differential between cement and aggregate	Damage from thermal expansion of steel components
Increased moisture	Chloride or carbonation-induced corrosion Scouring of substructure Foundation failure from soil saturation	Corrosion due to rusting
Increase in atmospheric CO_2	Carbonation-induced corrosion	
Sea level rise	Scouring of substructure Foundation failure from soil saturation	Corrosion due to rusting
Extreme weather events	Inundation and flood damage leading to reduced serviceability and possible collapse of structure	

Derived from ITF, 2016. Adapting Transport to Climate Change and Extreme Weather: Implications for Infrastructure Owners and Network Managers. ITF Research Reports. OECD Publishing, Paris. https://doi.org/10.1787/9789282108079-en.

FIGURE 5.8 Washout due to failure of culvert on R M Williams Way, at Yanyarrie Creek north of Carrieton, mid-North region of South Australia, following flash flood on 20 January 2007. *Attribution: Creative Commons Attribution 4.0 International (CC BY 4.0), Government of South Australia, January 2007 flood images, sourced on 8 May 2007, www.transport.sa.gov.au/quicklinks/jan_2007_flood_images/3.jpg.*

The basic function of a culvert is to pass water—usually rainfall runoff—under a right-of-way. In this way water can be prevented from ponding on the upstream side where it could potentially damage earthworks or passing over and therefore damaging road pavements, rail tracks and airport runways. Minor culverts may be little more than a PVC pipe, while more important culverts are structures (concrete or corrugated sheet metal) designed to accommodate a given level of stream flow—this is the case for the culvert shown in Fig. 5.8. Thus, the culvert is designed to withstand a specific rainfall event occurring over a designated time period. Under climate change, if the frequency of rain storms of a given magnitude increases, or the magnitude of rainfall events increases, then the culvert may become inadequate for purpose. The design life of culvert structures is comparable to that of the infrastructure that they protect, perhaps 50–100 years for concrete culverts and 30–50 years for corrugated steel culverts. Thus, existing culverts are likely to experience future climate conditions for which they were not designed. New culverts need to be designed to accommodate projected climate change impacts over their design life. Besides increasing the capacity of culverts to handle larger water volumes, other design measures to protect them include

- Installing headwalls, side wings and endwalls to protect embankments from scour (on both upstream and downstream ends)
- Providing ‘trash racks’ to prevent debris from clogging the culvert entrance.

Adequate maintenance to ensure that culverts do not silt up and to remove piled up debris is also an important consideration for the ongoing efficient operation of a culvert. Culvert maintenance has often been a forgotten aspect of road maintenance, a situation that should not be allowed to continue.

Tunnels

Tunnels are another major infrastructure asset in transportation. While weather events may not in the main affect the tunnel and its operations, some weather hazards, such as flooding which penetrates into the tunnel, may result in temporary closure (until the water can be removed) or damage to the tunnel structure and its equipment (lighting, ventilation, etc.). Given that tunnels may play a role akin to bridges in connecting different parts of a network, tunnel closure may have sever effects on traffic movement and economic and social activities.

Extreme weather and operations

In addition to climate impacts on infrastructure assets, there is another impact of great significance. This is the impact on traffic operations of extreme weather events. Storms, blizzards and smoke from wild fires curtail transport operations if not bring them to a standstill, at least temporarily. Hurricanes may lead to mass evacuations and closure of network links. Floods may sever networks, preventing movement across a region and reducing mobility. These disruptions to service may continue well after the weather event has passed, as maintenance crews attempt to restore serviceability in the network.

These effects are well known. The concerns from the perspective of climate change adaptation are the possibilities that

- Extreme weather events may occur more frequently in the future
- The severity of these events may increase in a given region
- The geographical spread of extreme events may change, e.g., areas not previously susceptible to hurricanes or wild fires may begin to experience these events.

Extreme weather imposes large costs on society. There are direct costs in the form of the resource requirements needed to repair or reconstruct damaged infrastructure. There are also significant indirect costs, from the disruptions to networks and services due to extreme weather events. These costs include excess travel times and delays, losses from toll roads, interruptions to freight supply and service cancellations (ITF, 2016). Planning for climate change adaptation requires consideration of these costs and how they may change under different climate change scenarios. For example, a roadway may be subject to minor flooding under present conditions so that it is unusable a few times a year; an inconvenience. If the frequency of flooding increased so that the road were subject to flooding on a more regular basis, say once a month, then the road may need reconstruction to a higher level above ground. This leads to the analytical study of network vulnerability for the assessment of the likely costs of occasional or recurrent network and service degradation, which is discussed in depth in Taylor (2017). Vulnerability studies for transportation systems have been undertaken using one of three approaches, each of which has its particular applications. The first approach is the asset inventory analysis, as exemplified by FHWA (2018) and described earlier in this book—see Chapter 3. This method is designed for direct application in climate change adaptation studies. The second approach to vulnerability analysis is the serviceability approach. This method examines the performance of a transportation network in different operating states under which degradation of the network is expected, such as road closures due to flooding or traffic jams and congestion caused by incidents. It compares the operational performance of the degraded network against some presupposed acceptable LoS. The method was introduced by Berdica (2002), who defined serviceability vulnerability as 'the susceptibility to incidents that can result in considerable reductions in (road) network serviceability', where 'the serviceability of a link/route/network describes the possibility to use that link/route/network during a given time period'. This definition is concerned with traffic performance and emphasises the importance of risk—the product of probability and consequence—through its statement of *considerable reductions* in performance, and on capacity, through its notion of a *specified time interval* applied to the incident. The use of this approach is exemplified by the work of Jenelius et al. (2006) and Jenelius and Mattsson (2012). Its primary use is the identification of critical infrastructure components—links and nodes—in a transportation network.

The third approach is accessibility-based vulnerability analysis, which seeks to widen the scope of vulnerability analysis by explicitly including the potential economic and social impacts of network disruptions. Accessibility analysis is often used in transportation systems modelling where it measures the ability of people to reach facilities and services, thus 'accessibility is the ease with which desired destinations may be reached' (Niemeier, 1997), or 'the ease for people to participate in activities from specific locations to a destination using a mode of transport at a specific time' (Primerano and Taylor, 2005). Accessibility-based vulnerability analysis looks at the changes in accessibility suffered by people at different locations when a network is degraded. It too can be used to identify critical locations and infrastructure components in a network. In this approach, network vulnerability is defined as follows (D'Este and Taylor, 2003):

- A network node is vulnerable if loss (or substantial degradation) of a small number of links significantly diminishes the accessibility of the node, as measured by a standard index of accessibility
- A network link is critical if loss (or substantial degradation) of the link significantly diminishes the accessibility of the network or of particular nodes, as measured by a standard index of accessibility.

Applications of the method are given in Taylor et al. (2006), Taylor (2008) and Taylor and Susilawati (2012).

Each of the three methods can be applied in network analysis studies for climate change adaptation, because they offer distinct approaches to the identification of critical locations and infrastructure elements. Use of the three methods in concert thus provides a means for definitive, multidimensional identification of such elements. An integrated approach to using the methods is given in Taylor (2017).

Infrastructure summary

This section has considered some transportation infrastructure assets that are common to multiple transportation modes. Specific issues relating to airports are considered in the next section, while the following chapter, on coastal infrastructure, includes ports and harbours. Chapters 6 and 7 are devoted to road infrastructure and railway infrastructure, respectively.

Airports

Airports are major multimode transportation terminals which include multiple infrastructure components, such as buildings (terminals, hangars, maintenance facilities, control towers and emergency service depots), pavement infrastructure (runways, aprons, taxiways and access roads), public transport termini and lines (taxi, rail and bus), outdoor navigation facilities and telecommunications equipment. This infrastructure is exposed to the same hazards and impacts as other transportation networks. Indeed, given the requirement for airports to be located on flat ground to accommodate runways, they are often located in valleys, estuarine and coastal locations—and sometimes on reclaimed land and purpose-built offshore islands—so that they may be more prone to those climate change impacts that affect water volumes and levels (e.g., sea level rise, inundation and flooding. Extreme weather events can disrupt airline operations and services, and disruption at one airport can throw airline schedules into chaos, affecting operations at other airports. Strong winds, storms and extreme precipitation (both rain and snow) are important factors in this regard. Given that extreme weather events of these kinds are expected to become more frequent under many climate change scenarios so service delays and schedules may be more and more prone to adverse impacts in the future. Localised changes in weather patterns, such as changes to prevailing wind direction and convective weather, may also affect flight operations and lead to reduced capacity and greater delays. ITF (2016) lists the following possible impacts to airport infrastructure from climate change:

- Changes in temperatures and precipitation will have similar impacts on airport pavements as on roadway infrastructure, and increased salt and chemical usage for de-icing as a result of more frequent lower temperatures would exacerbate these impacts

- Sea level rise will lead to increased inundation of coastal airports
- Phenomena associated with extreme weather events, such as storm surges and strong winds, may damage outdoor airport equipment and buildings.

Airports are complex infrastructure systems. An examination of climate change risks for airports is thus best addressed by a dissection of the main elements of an airport system. The vulnerability of these elements to different climate change impacts may then be assessed, and this can lead to a better understanding of the level of resilience of the airport to climate change. Lopez (2016) provided a structured list of major elements in an airport, classified by the three groupings of infrastructure, buildings and operations. Table 5.4 shows this list.

The infrastructure elements include the physical assets at the airport for both aviation (apron, taxiways and runways) and ground transportation (road and rail, plus car parks). All of the elements are distinct and necessary, and all may be vulnerable to different impacts from climate change. Table 5.5, derived from EUROCONTROL (2014), considers five major likely climate change risks: changes in precipitation, changes in temperature, sea level rise, changes in wind and extreme weather events. For each of these risks, there are a number of potential impacts, and these impacts may act on different aspects of airport systems operation. Table 5.5 indicates how each impacts may affect the airport, by considering four broad groupings of players: aircraft operators, airport operators, air navigation service providers and external agencies (e.g., utility providers). Many of the listed risks, e.g., changes in precipitation, extreme weather and (especially) sea level rise), may affect multiple aspects of airport operations. In addition, disruptions to operations at one airport may have significant flow on effects at other airports due to flight delays and cancellations. Airports present significant vulnerabilities to climate change.

TABLE 5.4 Ordered listing of airport system elements.

Infrastructure	Buildings	Operations
Ground transportation access (road, rail) Car parks Interterminal connections (tunnels, walkways, etc.) Telecommunications Utilities Fuel distribution system Runways Taxiways Apron	Terminals Offices Hangars Emergency services stations Aero bridges Control tower	Emergency service and fire fighting Vehicles (buses, tugs, fuel tankers, etc.) Navigation aids and equipment Human resources (personnel)

Derived from Lopez, A, 2016. Vulnerability of airports on climate change: an assessment methodology. Transp. Res. Proced. 14, 24–31.

TABLE 5.5 Climate risks and likely impacts for airports.

Climate risk	Impact	Players			
		Aircraft operators and airlines	Airport operators and managers	Air navigation and air traffic control providers	External
Changes in precipitation	Disruption to operations (e.g., airfield flooding, ground subsidence)	✓	✓	✓	
	Reduction in airport throughput	✓	✓	✓	
	Inundation of underground infrastructure (e.g., electrical, telecomms)		✓	✓	
	Inundation of ground transportations access (passengers and personnel)	✓	✓	✓	✓
	Loss of service provision by local utilities (e.g., power)	✓	✓	✓	✓
Changes in temperature	Changes in aircraft performance	✓		✓	
	Changes in noise impact due to changes in aircraft performance		✓		
	Heat damage to airport surfaces (runway, taxiway, apron)		✓		
	Increased heating and cooling requirements		✓		
	Increased pressure on local utilities (e.g., water and power for cooling)				✓

Sea level rise	Loss of airport capacity	✓	✓	✓	
	Impacts on en-route capacity due to lack of ground capacity	✓		✓	
	Loss of airport infrastructure		✓		
	Loss of ground transportation access	✓	✓		✓
Changes in wind	Convective weather disruption to operations (e.g., thunderstorms)	✓	✓	✓	
	Convective weather: route extensions and flight diversions	✓		✓	
	Jet stream: potential increases in en-route turbulence	✓			
	Local wind patterns: potential disruption to operations and changes to distribution of noise impacts		✓		
Extreme weather events and consequences	Disruptions to operations, route extensions and flight diversions	✓	✓	✓	
	Disruptions to ground transportation access	✓	✓	✓	✓
	Disruptions to supply of utilities	✓	✓	✓	✓

Derived from EUROCONTROL, 2014. Adapting Aviation to a Changing Climate: Key Climate Change Risks for Aviation. European Organisation for the Safety of Air Navigation (EUROCONTROL), Brussels. www.eurocontrol.int/resilience.

Evaluation methods

Decisions on project selection and prioritisation and on program design in transportation have long been supported by quantitative analysis using evaluation tools. Foremost amongst these tools is BCA, while MCA has also achieved popular usage. These tools were introduced in Chapter 3, and they certainly have their applications when considering climate change adaptation. However, as indicated in Chapter 3, there are issues regarding their usage which must be considered. There may also be advantage in considering other decision support tools, especially in long-term strategic planning.

The main issue at stake is the consideration of risk in the long-term planning required for climate change adaptation. The existing, conventional tools such as BCA (and indeed also MCA) were not really designed to account for long-term risks when there is a high level of uncertainty about future conditions and situations. This is the situation with climate change. The established methods for handling climate change involve the consideration of a set of alternative scenarios about the likelihood and impact of future climate change. These scenarios are largely developed by mathematical models (ITF, 2016) and direct observations of the uncertainties regarding the future effects are not possible. ITF (2016) provides a list of relevant climate-related uncertainties that cannot be resolved. This list in fact represents a set of cascading uncertainties:

- The actual volumes of greenhouse gases to be emitted over time
- The sequestration rates for these gases and the resulting atmospheric concentrations
- The response rate of global temperatures to the evolving atmospheric concentrations
- The impacts of changes in temperature on hydrometeorological phenomena at finer levels of spatial resolution
- The impact of the changes in hydrometeorological cycles and sea level rise on ecosystems and the built environment
- The ways in which humans will react and adapt to these impacts.

The following conclusion may then be drawn: a changing climate leads to two basic challenges for infrastructure managers:

1. The need to ensure continued infrastructure asset performance under possible significantly altered climatic conditions. These new conditions may result in significant degradation in value of the existing assets and/or increase maintenance and refurbishment cost
2. Agencies will need to design and construct new or replacement assets cognisant of the changes in climate including largely uncertain climate variables. This uncertainty may lead to overspecification of infrastructure

design standards which could lead to wasted resources in nonproductive assets. It could also lead to underspecification, which would lead to asset failure and degradation of network LoS.

In these circumstances, the decision support tools employed by asset managers must be well chosen and well understood.

Benefit–cost analysis

BCA has been widely applied in transportation systems planning. It places monetary values on the relevant benefits and costs of considered options and computes a new present value of these, accounting for the life of the option investment and an assumed discount rate. The computation method is summarised by Eqs (3.1)–(3.4) in Chapter 3. The decision maker selects the time horizon for the discounting and the time sequence of costs and benefits to be considered. Transportation system options generally use the technical life span of the asset as the time horizon. Most transportation infrastructure assets, such as roads and railways, have time horizons of between 20 and 50 years. Intelligent transportation systems and traffic control systems may have much shorter life spans, perhaps no more than 10 years, because of the rapid changes in the technologies employed in these systems. Some transportation assets, such as bridges and tunnels, may however have much longer life spans, 80–100 years, as discussed earlier in this chapter. Assets with longer life spans are clearly likely to be more heavily impacted by changes in climate.

Costs and benefits may be internal to the transportation system, such as travel time and delays or maintenance costs, or external to it (e.g., the costs of road crashes and environmental concerns such as noise and air quality pollution). Externalities are costs (and benefits) not borne within the transportation system but by third parties or society at large. Extreme weather and climate change risks can be considered as externalities in this regard. Here then is the dilemma. The usual approach to handling risk in BCA is to increase the discount rate, but this has the effect of greatly diminishing the present value of medium- to long-term benefits and costs—and these represent the impacts of climate change. ITF (2015) discusses the use of risk-adjusted discount rates and the provision of explicit assessments of climate-related uncertainties as approaches to improve the utility of BCA for longer time horizons. Given that many climate change impacts are subject to the cascading uncertainties described above, it may be difficult to provide objective or subjective probabilities and so make explicit assessments of the uncertainties. Likewise, the choice of different discount rates for different periods within the time horizon, as suggested by ITF (2015) and OECD (2018) may not be feasible, because it requires consensus between stakeholders on the actual values to be used and the time spans to which they apply.[2] These issues constrain the utility of BCA as an authoritative tool for evaluating long-lived infrastructure assets under climate change. In a risk management situation, conventional BCA calculations involve discounting future cash flows for benefits and costs either by adjusting the discount rate or by estimating expected costs and benefits using probabilities. The first of these approaches, risk-adjustment of discount rates, requires care. Arguably any risk may be a valid reason for adjusting the discount rate, but not all risks should be included in BCA: uncertainty may exist with the extent and value of any future cost or benefit, technologies change, levels of demand for services may change. The one common factor for all such risks is time—these risks increase with time. The longer the time period considered, the more uncertain the operating states and conditions that provide the basis for future projections.

ITF (2015) discussed specific strategies for improving BCA to deal with uncertainty regarding climate change and extreme weather. Uncertainty assessments should be made first in terms of the likely range of scientific uncertainty pertaining to hazards, then on socioeconomic uncertainty for impacts and exposure. While these assessments cannot be included as quantitative inputs in BCA, they can provide qualification on the results of CBA that may be used to formulate levels of confidence in the BCA results. Discount rates under uncertainty may be treated either by adding a risk premium to the discount rate or applying a (subjective) probability distribution to the discount rate, and so simulate the uncertainty ranges. Balston et al. (2017) provide a useful example of the latter approach.

In summary, BCA is a well-known technique for economic evaluation that can be a useful technique for assessing adaptation options when

- Climate probabilities are known
- Sensitivity to climate change impacts may be assumed to be small compared to the overall costs and benefits of a project
- High quality data exist for the major cost and benefit items
- There is strong agreement on the valuation scales adopted for the benefits, costs and discount rates.

These conditions (can) apply in the short- to medium-term, but are unlikely to apply for longer-term analyses.

---

2. This consensus is actually an implicit requirement for all inputs to BCA. The basic tenet of BCA is the acceptance of trade-offs between the sequences of costs and benefits and the factors employed in the analysis. The result of a BCA analysis is a net present value in which all present and future costs and benefits are lumped together. The consensus required to allow this is generally acceptable in a technical setting, but may not be possible in a political situation where competing ideas and beliefs may not allow consensus to develop. This is one of the reasons for the advent of MCA.

Cost-effectiveness analysis

Another technique wide used alongside BCA is cost-effectiveness analysis (CEA). This technique also uses monetary values and discounted cash flow analysis. It has been applied in situations where the benefits of an option cannot be estimated in monetary terms, if at all. Rather, it would be assumed that the costs of design, construction, operation and maintenance of different option can be estimated—that after all is a basic part of asset management systems. Then the net value of the costs of each option can be estimated, and the options ranked along a given single, comparable metric, e.g., cost per unit of desired outcome. The method would then suggest the least-cost option for achieving a desired outcome, e.g., cost to reduce a potentially flooded area or cost to limit the extent of flooding to some set threshold. However, as for BCA, CEA cannot properly account for the basic uncertainties of many climate change impacts.

CEA may be used in the same situations as BCA. It may be helpful in assessing adaptation options when

- A high level of agreement on social objectives exists (such as the broad acceptance of risk thresholds)
- A reduced set of impacts is being considered
- For short- to medium-term time periods when impacts are not subject to strong uncertainty.

CEA is thus potentially applicable to short-term adaptation assessments. It does not deal with uncertainty and can only optimise option selection in terms of a single objective, and probably only under one climate scenario (PIARC, 2019).

Multicriteria analysis

As discussed in Chapter 3, MCA offers a decision-making approach suited to multiobjective planning. It can include both quantitative and qualitative information, and can indicate the degrees to which different, possibly competing, objectives would be realised under different options. It can include other assessment methods, such as BCA, under its overall umbrella of assessment. MCA may be seen as a systematic method for assessing and ranking options over a set of criteria, some of which may be expressed in monetary terms, some of which in physical terms, and some in qualitative–subjective terms (e.g., 'feelings of safety' or 'environmental amenity'). The method also encourages consultation with stakeholders. The main drawback to the MCA approach is perhaps a lack of firm theoretical basis.[3] On the other hand, it is a pragmatic approach suited to application in a political environment, due to its

3. As opposed to BCA, which comes from an established theoretical base in welfare economics.

explicit, separate treatment of individual criteria—before generation of an overall result or 'score' (see Eq. 3.5). It may be seen as suitable for the assessment of climate change impacts that cannot be valued in monetary terms, such as political sensitivity, public acceptance and some environmental impacts (PIARC, 2019).

Application of MCA involves the scoring of each option on several scales, each of which represents a particular criterion (or objective). These elemental scores are then weighted and summed, to produce an overall score (see Chapter 3, especially equations (3.5) and (3.6)). While there are techniques, such as the analytic hierarchy process (AHP, see Saaty (1980) for objective determination of criterion weights), there is always some concern about the possible subjectivity of the approach despite its transparency. In particular, MCA may not be able to capture uncertainty in anything but a subjective manner.

Appendix A provides a discussion on the use of SAW (simple additive weights) MCA methods, including the use of AHP to determine criterion weights. Velasquez and Hester (2013) provide a wide-ranging review of the use of MCA in infrastructure planning, while Tsamboulas et al. (1999), Morisugi (2000), Nellthorpe and Mackie (2000) and Sayers et al. (2003) provide an international view of the use of MCA in transportation planning.

Decision-making under uncertainty

The three decision support tools discussed above—BCA, CEA and MCA—are not generally well suited to handling the deep and possibly cascading uncertainty that may be involved in climate change adaptation decision-making. They may find applications for short- to medium-term planning decisions, but are perhaps poorly suited for longer-term decisions. Other decision support tools better suited to considerations of uncertainty have been proposed. Marchau et al. (2019) describe a number of such tools. Two of these—ROA and RDM – are described below.

Real options analysis

ROA is an evaluation method originally used in financial markets. It seeks to quantify the investment risk associated with uncertain future outcomes and can be used to consider the likely value and flexibility of investments. A real option is one that, taken today, makes it possible to take a particular action in the future. Under this option an investor would have the right, but not the obligation, to acquire some particular asset in the future. The investor can then use this opportunity as a buffer against market volatility and uncertainty of the value of assets over time.

Indeed, over time decision makers will obtain better knowledge about the scale and scope of climate change impacts in a given region, so that ROA provides flexibility in decision-making that may provide some guidance in climate change adaption planning. The flexibility relates to both the timing of an investment decision, such as when to construct a new asset and the ability for infrastructure assets to be adjusted to meet changing conditions over time. Employing this flexibility may lead to different investment decisions than those indicated by the conventional economic appraisal techniques. Under ROA, an option may be to delay a specific investment until better information on climate change is available, or that there is merit in undertaking the initial stages of a project despite a weak conventional economic analysis result so that the option of future development or completion of the project is kept open.

The value of delaying an investment is greater when the time for acquiring relevant new information is shorter and the degree of uncertainty of outcomes is higher. There are a number of alternative outcomes relating to costs and benefits from the staging of options, e.g.,

- Costs due to delayed delivery of services or other benefits when an investment is scheduled for some time in the future rather than now
- Opportunity cost from overinvestment in the initial phase of a project, to be weighed against the benefit of reduced future investment should an uncertain option become infeasible.

The trade-offs implied by these possible outcomes can be analysed and compared using decision-tree techniques using probabilistic expected values, as outlined in ITF (2016). Projects should proceed if the ROA analysis indicates that the overall lost value from benefits forgone in the waiting time exceeds the value of waiting, or if the option value computed from a series of optimal choices at decision points over each phase in a multiphase project exceeds the conventional appraised value of average returns over the life of a project (ITF, 2016).

ROA is best suited to large, capital-intensive and irreversible investments. Given that the use of ROA requires specification of probabilities regarding climate impacts, it may be less well suited to situations involving deep uncertainty. Bowman and Moskowitz (2001) provided a detailed introduction to ROA. The adaptation pathways approach outlined in Chapter 3 may provide a useful platform for the use of ROA in climate change adaptation planning.

Robust decision-making

A peculiar feature of decision-making is that, although many of the decision support tools offer a fine grained score or merit value for each option under consideration, the actual decision mechanism is quite coarse—there are only a limited number of options available. By way of example, the decisions are of the types (1) whether or not 'option A' is useful, worth pursuing, or (2) that 'option B' is preferable to 'option C'. The issue with the use of a decision support tool when some inputs are stochastic or uncertain is thus whether or not it can indicate when a particular decision would change, e.g., when 'option A' would not be acceptable, or when 'option C' should take precedence over 'option B'. RDM is based on this premise that the actual decision to be made is a relatively simple choice.

The method seeks to find those strategies and decisions that are robust—i.e., stable—over a wide range of feasible outcomes and impacts. It does not require probabilistic information regarding the outcomes or impacts. It is thus well suited to situations involving deep uncertainty. It may point to outcomes that are never optimal in any particular case but which are satisfactory ('good enough') in most circumstances. Considerable computations may be required as multiple scenarios each involving complex decision outcomes may need to be modelled, e.g., using the following steps:

1. Characterise the problem to be solved (e.g., climate change impact on a given infrastructure asset type)
2. Select several alternative adaptation options for this problem
3. Generate a wide range of potential future scenarios
4. Assess the performance of each option under each of the scenarios
5. Summarise the key trade-offs found amongst the options and select the option that is most robust to the alternative futures.

RDM thus provides a 'stress test' which may help to determine the combination of uncertainty factors and parameters that are most important in the choice between the options. Then one or more options best able to deliver the desired outcomes over the widest range of possible futures can be selected.

RDM is perhaps best suited for those situations where specific climate impacts are highly uncertain, such as precipitation. Lempert (2019) and Kwakkel et al. (2016) provide more details and case study applications for RDM.

Summary overview on decision-making methods

Table 5.6 provides a summary view of the economic decision-making techniques reviewed in this chapter, including their usefulness for planning and management for climate change adaptation in transportation. The table uses information supplied in ITF (2016) and PIARC (2019).

There are new decision support tools emerging that are specifically designed for climate change adaptation. Schweikert et al. (2014) provides one example; the infrastructure planning support system. The development and use of these new tools is explored further in the final chapter of this book.

Summary

This chapter considered asset management systems for transportation, including asset life, maintenance regimes, performance measures and

TABLE 5.6 Summary set of economic decision-making techniques useful for climate change adaptation.

	Conventional economic decision support			Economic decision-making under uncertainty	
	Benefit–cost analysis	**Cost-effectiveness analysis**	**Multicriteria analysis**	**Real options analysis**	**Robust decision-making**
Summary	Values all benefits and costs of all options, and estimates the net present values in monetary terms—trade-offs between costs and benefits.	Compares costs of options against their effectiveness (monetary or nonmonetary) to rank the options, then uses cost curves for targets and resources.	Allows consideration of qualitative data as well as quantitative, for ranking alternative options. The impacts on individual criteria can also be seen.	Allows economic analysis of future options, accounting for value and economic benefit of waiting, gathering further information over time, and maintaining flexibility in planning.	Identifies strategies that are robust, rather than optimal, by 'stress testing' a large number of plausible scenarios.
Strengths	The method is well known and widely applied, and has a strong theoretical basis in social welfare economics. It provides direct analysis of economic costs and benefits, and optimal solutions.	Benefits are expressed in physical terms rather than monetary terms and thus apply to nonmarket sectors. Relatively simple to understand and can resonate with policy makers.	Combines quantitative and qualitative data, and monetary and nonmonetary units, and is thus applicable when quantification is difficult. Can use expert judgement and local stakeholder knowledge together.	Assesses the value of flexibility and learning in quantitative and economic terms. The decision trees used in its working provide visualisations of adaptive management.	Assesses robustness rather than optimisation. Can be applied when probabilistic information is scarce, or climate uncertainty is high. It can be sued with physical and economic metrics, applied across all sectors.

Continued

TABLE 5.6 Summary set of economic decision-making techniques useful for climate change adaptation.—cont'd

	Conventional economic decision support			Economic decision-making under uncertainty	
	Benefit–cost analysis	**Cost-effectiveness analysis**	**Multicriteria analysis**	**Real options analysis**	**Robust decision-making**
Weaknesses	Difficult to set monetary values for nonmarket sectors and nontechnical options.	Benefits can be difficult to identify and a single metric may not cover all costs and benefits. The method does not allow consideration of uncertainty, as it works with central tendency measures.	MCA results may need further interpretation and elaboration in more detailed studies. The method often deals with uncertainty in qualitative and subjective terms only.	Data and resource intensive, with high complexity and requiring expert input. Data requirements are substantial and perhaps difficult (e.g., probabilistic climate data).	Lack of quantitative probabilities can make more subjective, influenced by stakeholders. Requires considerable resources for its formal application.
Potential use in climate change adaptation	To identify low- and no-regret options in the near future. Use as a decision support tool in iterative climate risk management. It is most useful when (1) climate probabilities are known, (2) climate sensitivity is small compared to overall costs and benefits and (3) good data exist for the major cost and benefit components.	As for benefit–cost analysis, but for applications where benefits are not expressed in monetary terms.	As for benefit–cost analysis. Best used for scoping options to indicate potential poor performance on individual criteria. Can complement other tools and capture qualitative effects.	Economic analysis of major asset investment decisions over the medium term. Allows analysis of flexibility within staging of major projects.	Identification of combination of strategic (i.e., long-term, scenario-independent) and operational (short-term, scenario-dependent) decisions.

Based on ITF, 2016. Adapting Transport to Climate Change and Extreme Weather: Implications for Infrastructure Owners and Network Managers. ITF Research Reports. OECD Publishing, Paris. https://doi.org/10.1787/9789282108079-en and PIARC, 2019. Adaptation Methodologies and Strategies to Increase the Resilience of Roads to Climate Change: A Case Study Approach. Report 2019R25EN. World Road Association, Paris. www.piarc.org.

performance assessment. It continued the discussion of climate and environmental influences and impacts on transportation assets and operations (including failure type and potential limits on operations). This included consideration of weather-related impacts on transport operations, including airports. Management of risk and uncertainty continues as a major focus in adaptation planning for transportation when considering evaluation methods to be employed. The main method for such evaluation in transportation has been BCA, although as discussed previously alternative methods are also available. These methods require some revision and extension for decision-making under uncertainty, especially for climate change impacts. The final discussion in this chapter considered some of the alternative approaches for decision-making under uncertainty, including ROA and RDM.

Appendix A: a primer for Multicriteria Analysis and the Analytic Hierarchy Process

MCA methods have achieved some popularity in decision-making, especially in situations where there are multiple stakeholders and multiple objectives to be fulfilled—and some of these objectives may be in conflict. While conventional economic assessment tools such as BCA can be applied in these situations, the end point for these tools is a trade-off between monetary values representing the different costs and benefits associated with an option. In a politically charged environment, it may not be possible to achieve consensus between stakeholders for the required trade-offs. In addition, it is not always possible to estimate reliable monetary values for some costs and benefits. Some of these may be subjective (e.g., 'feelings of safety') if not intangible; some may be readily quantifiable in physical terms (if not monetary ones), but other may only be capable of qualitative assessment (e.g., 'feelings of satisfaction', expressed as values on a semantic scale). Transparency of the evaluation process may also be an issue. MCA methods have been proposed as an alternative approach that allows the inclusion of qualitative and subjective measures as well as quantitative and objective ones. MCA may thus find some resonance in the political process.

Three principles may be applied to provide an overview of MCA:

1. Decomposition
2. Prioritisation
3. Synthesis

In decomposition, a complex problem is broken down into a hierarchy of interrelated decisions elements:

- Decision elements are chained from top to bottom
- The overall goal to be achieved is placed at the end of the chain

- The different specific objectives to be considered, and hopefully satisfied if not optimised, as part of the overall goal are placed in the level beneath the overall goal
- Broad decision elements (i.e., the criteria and priorities) form the next level in the chain. Note that there may be subcriteria associated with any one the criteria
- The bottom level of the chain contains the detailed elements—the decision alternatives, or options—to be considered and from which a problem solution will be selected.

Fig. 5A.1 shows such a decomposition chain, representing the alternatives for a climate change adaptation policy (overall goal). There are five objectives to be included: transport, environment, climate, society and the economy. Each of these objectives includes a number of criteria. For example, in this example, 'transport' includes the criteria of travel time, congestion and reliability, amongst others. The transport objectives also have three subcriteria: the transportation modes of private car, rail and active transport (walking and cycling). There are *n* alternatives to be considered, each evaluated for its potential performance on all of the objectives and criteria. These alternatives form the bottom layer of the chain. The analysis seeks to determine the 'best' or 'most suitable' of these alternatives.

Prioritisation involves the determination of the relative importance, i.e., the weights, of the decision elements. Synthesis is the computation of the individual scores for each alternative (option) for each criterion and the determination of the overall score (merit) of the option.

Use of criterion weights

The basic MCA methods use 'Simple Additive Weights (SAW)' in which the total merit of an option is determined by a weighted sum of the option's scores for a number of criteria. This requires the adoption of specific weights for each criteria, and this may be done in a number of ways—perhaps most simply by a consensus amongst the players involved in selecting the appropriate alternative, although there are more rigorous methods, such as the AHP (Saaty, 1980). The issues of determining criterion weights and applying these to transportation problem are widely discussed elsewhere (e.g., Klungboonkrong and Taylor, 1997, Tsamboulas et al., 1999, Quinet, 2000, Sayers et al., 2003, Aldian and Taylor, 2003, Marcharis and Bernardini, 2015 and Barbosa et al., 2017). Velasquez and Hester (2013) provided a review of the use of MCA methods across a range of infrastructure-related problems.

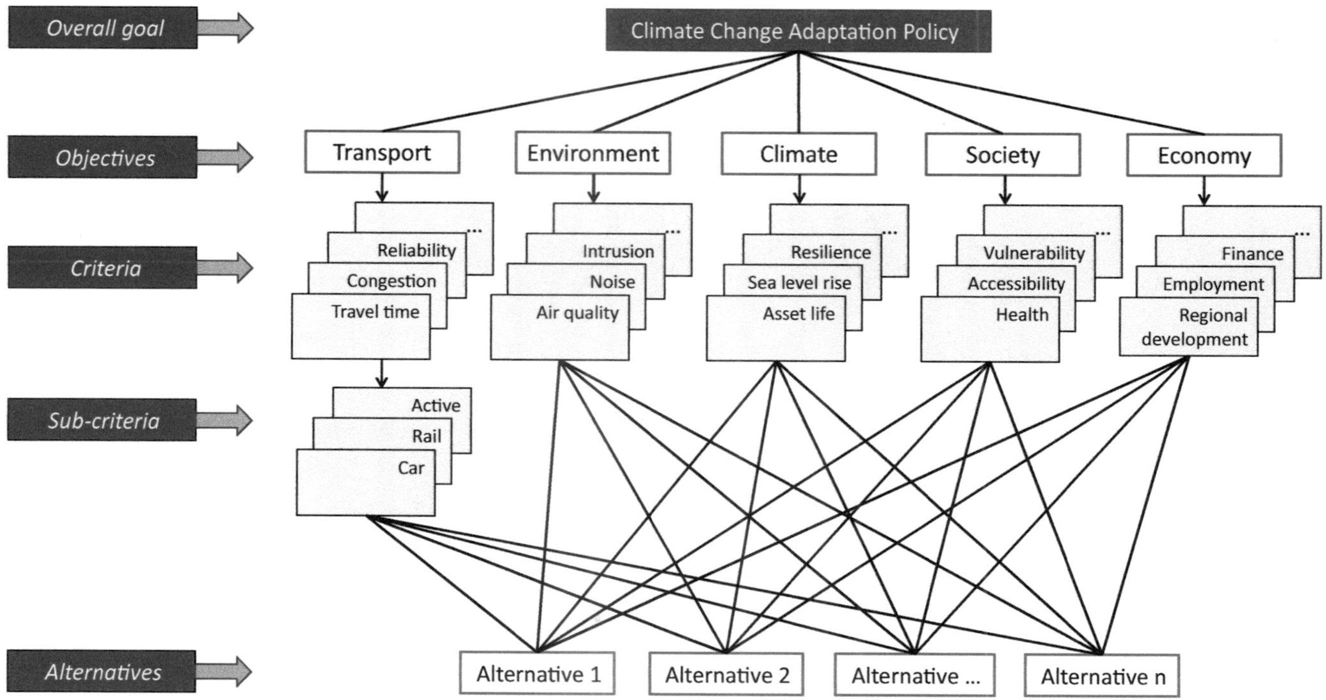

FIGURE 5A.1 the decomposition chain for a complex problem to be addressed using Multicriteria Analysis.

Given a set of criteria k, $k = 1, \ldots, m$ with weights w_k and (normalised[4]) merit scores x_{jk} $0 \leq x_{jk} \leq 1$for alternative j under criterion k, then the overall merit score of alternative j is

$$S_j = \sum_{k=1}^{m} x_{jk} w_k \tag{5A.1}$$

where $k = 1, \ldots, m$.

$$\sum_{k=1}^{m} w_k = 1 \tag{5A.2}$$

and $0 \leq w_k \leq 1$ for all k. The computed values of S_j may be used to compare and rank the alternatives, and examination of the individual criteria scores x_{jk} may be undertaken to assess the degree to which each alternative contributes to meeting the objective criteria.

Normalisation of the merit scores x_{jk} is generally used because the units of measurement of each criterion may be different (e.g., tonnes of CO_2-equivalents per annum, a score on a 1–5 semantic scale, kilometres of sealed road, annual average daily traffic volumes, etc). If $y_{jk}$is the actual (raw) score alternative j under criterion k, then the equivalent normalised score is

$$x_{jk} = \frac{\max\{y_k\} - y_{jk}}{\max\{y_k\} - \min\{y_k\}} \tag{5A.3}$$

where $\max\{y_k\}$ and $\min\{y_k\}$ are the maximum and minimum raw scores for criterion k. These maxima and minima may be absolute values (e.g., the minimum score on a 1–5 semantic scale is '1', while the maximum score is '5') or they may be relative values, determined from the range of raw scores recorded in the assessment. Some criteria will have logical minimum or maximum scores, e.g., many factors will only have positive values, so a minimum value of zero would apply.

In the discussion of the determination of criterion weights using the AHP, it is convenient to rewrite Eq. (5A.1) in matrix form, i.e., as

$$\underline{S} = \underline{XW} \tag{5A.4}$$

in which

$$\underline{S} = \begin{bmatrix} S_1 \\ S_2 \\ \cdots \\ S_n \end{bmatrix}$$ is the column vector of score for the alternatives,

4. Normalised scores are in the range $0 \leq x_{jk} \leq 1$, so that the score for each criterion is readily comparable with those of the other criteria—part of the process of transparency.

$$\underline{X} = \begin{bmatrix} x_{11} & x_{12} & \dots & x_{1m} \\ x_{21} & x_{22} & \dots & x_{2m} \\ \dots & \dots & \dots & \dots \\ x_{n1} & x_{n2} & \dots & x_{nm} \end{bmatrix}$$ is the 'incidence matrix' of criterion scores for the alternatives

and

$\underline{W^T} = [w_1 w_2 \dots w_m]$ is the (transposed) row vector of criterion weights.

Analytic Hierarchy Process

AHP is a mathematical method that can be used to determine the criterion weights via pairwise comparisons of the relative importance of two criteria (Saaty, 1980). To do this, the stakeholders and decision makers are asked to compare the relative importance of each pair of criteria, one after the other. These judgements are then summarised in the pairwise comparison matrix A, given by

$$\underline{A} = \begin{bmatrix} 1 & w_1/w_2 & \dots & w_1/w_n \\ w_2/w_1 & 1 & \dots & w_2/w_n \\ \dots & \dots & 1 & \dots \\ w_n/w_1 & w_n/w_2 & \dots & 1 \end{bmatrix} = \begin{bmatrix} 1 & a_{12} & \dots & a_{1n} \\ 1/a_{12} & 1 & \dots & a_{2n} \\ \dots & \dots & 1 & \dots \\ 1/a_{1n} & 1/a_{2n} & \dots & 1 \end{bmatrix} \quad (5A.5)$$

Saaty (1980) recommended the use of a nine-point scale for assessing the relative importance or 'intensity' of each pair of criteria, where '1' implies equal importance between two criteria and '9' indicates the absolute importance of one criterion over another. Table 5A.1 shows the relative importance scale and the definition of each intensity value.

TABLE 5A.1 Saaty's scales of relative importance for criterion pairs.

Intensity of importance	Definition
1	Equal importance
3	Weak importance of one over the other
5	Essential or strong importance
7	Demonstrated importance
9	Absolute importance
2, 4, 6, 8	Intermediate values between the two adjacent judgements

Matrix A is a square matrix and its maximum eigenvalue (λ_{max}) may be used to compute the criterion weights, using the equation

$$\underline{AW} = \lambda_{max}\underline{W} \tag{5A.6}$$

This method has been widely used in practice. See, for example, Klungboonkrong and Taylor (1998) and Aldian and Taylor (2003).

References

Aldian, A., Taylor, M.A.P., 2003. Fuzzy multicriteria analysis for inter-city travel demand modelling. J. Eastern Asia Soc. Transp. Stud. 5, 1294–1307.

ASCE, 2017. 2017 Infrastructure Report Card. American Society of Civil Engineers. Reston vol. A. https://www.infrastructurereportcard.org/wp-content/uploads/2017/01/Bridges-Final.pdf. (Accessed 19 December 2019).

Austroads, 2018a. Guide to Asset Management – Overview Part 1: Introduction. Austroads, Sydney.

Austroads, 2018b. Guide to Asset Management – Overview Part 6: Defining and Understanding Asset Requirements. Austroads, Sydney.

Austroads, 2018c. Guide to Asset Management – Overview Part 9: Asset Management Information System and Data. Austroads, Sydney.

Balston, J., Li, S., Iankov, I., Kellett, J., Wells, G., 2017. Quantifying the financial impact of climate change on Australian local government roads. Infrastructure 2 (2), 1–16.

Barbosa, S.B., Ferreira, M.G.G., Nickel, E.M., Cruz, J.A., Forcellini, F.A., Garcia, J., Osório de Andrade Guerra, J.B.S., 2017. Multi-criteria analysis model to evaluate transport systems: an application in Florianópolis, Brazil. Transp. Res. A Pol. Pract. 96, 1–13.

Berdica, K., 2002. An introduction to road vulnerability: what has been done, is done and should be done. Transp. Pol. 9 (2), 117–127.

Bhamidipati, S., 2015. Simulation framework for asset management in climate-change adaptation of transportation infrastructure. Transp. Res. Proced. 8, 17–28.

Bowman, E.H., Moskowitz, G.T., 2001. Real options analysis and strategic decision making. Organ. Sci. 12 (6), 772–777.

D'Este, G.M., Taylor, M.A.P., 2003. Network vulnerability: an approach to reliability analysis at the level of national strategic transport networks. In: Iida, Y., Bell, M.G.H. (Eds.), The Network Reliability of Transport. Elsevier: Oxford,), pp. 23–44.

EUROCONTROL, 2014. Adapting Aviation to a Changing Climate: Key Climate Change Risks for Aviation. European Organisation for the Safety of Air Navigation (EUROCONTROL), Brussels. www.eurocontrol.int/resilience.

FHWA, 2007. Asset Management Overview. Report FHWA-IF-08-008. Federal Highways Administration, Department of Transportation, Washington DC. https://www.fhwa.dot.gov/asset/if08008/amo_02.cfm. (Accessed 18 November 2019).

FHWA, 2016. 2015 Status of the Nation's Highways, Bridges and Transit: Conditions and Performance. Federal Highways Administration, Department of Transportation, Washington DC. https://www.fhwa.dot.gov/policy/2015cpr/pdfs/2015cpr.pdf. (Accessed 19 December 2019).

FHWA, 2018. Climate Change and Extreme Weather Vulnerability Assessment Framework. In: Report FHWA-HEP- 18-020, third ed. US Federal Highways Administration, Washington DC.

ISO, 2014. Asset Management: Overview, Principles and Terminology. International Organization for Standardization, Geneva, Switzerland. ISO 55000:2014.

ITF, 2015. Adapting Transport Policy to Climate Change: Carbon Valuation, Risk and Uncertainty. OECD Publishing, Paris. https://doi.org/10.1787/9789282107928-en.

ITF, 2016. Adapting Transport to Climate Change and Extreme Weather: Implications for Infrastructure Owners and Network Managers. ITF Research Reports. OECD Publishing, Paris. https://doi.org/10.1787/9789282108079-en.

Jenelius, E., Mattsson, L.-G., 2012. Road network vulnerability analysis of area-covering disruptions: a grid-based approach with case study. Transp. Res. A Pol. Pract. 46 (5), 746–760.

Jenelius, E., Petersen, T., Mattsson, L.-G., 2006. Importance and exposure in road network vulnerability analysis. Transp. Res. A Pol. Pract. 40 (7), 537–560.

Klungboonkrong, P., Taylor, M.A.P., 1998. A microcomputer-based system for multicriteria environmental impact evaluation of urban road networks. Comput. Environ. Urban Syst. 22 (5), 425–446.

Kwakkel, J.H., Haasnoot, M., Walker, W.E., 2016. Comparing robust decision-making and dynamic adaptive policy pathways for model-based decision support under deep uncertainty. Environ. Model. Software 86, 168–183.

Lempert, R.J., 2019. Robust decision making (RDM). In: Marchau, V.A.W.J., Walker, W.E., Bloemen, P.J.T.M., Popper, S.W. (Eds.), From Theory to Practice: Decision Making under Deep Uncertainty. Springer Nature: Cham, pp. 23–51.

Lock, J.B., Gelling, M.J., 1976. The Tasman bridge disaster – before and after. Aust. Road Res. 6 (2), 9–16.

Lopez, A., 2016. Vulnerability of airports on climate change: an assessment methodology. Transp. Res. Proced. 14, 24–31.

Maracharis, C., Bernardini, A., 2015. Reviewing the use of Multi-Criteria Decision Analysis for the evaluation of transport projects: time for a multi-actor approach. Transp. Pol. 37, 177–186.

Marchau, V.A.W.J., Walker, W.E., Bloemen, P.J.T.M., Popper, S.W. (Eds.), 2019. From Theory to Practice: Decision Making under Deep Uncertainty. Springer Nature: Cham.

Morisugi, H., 2000. Evaluation methodologies for transportation projects in Japan. Transp. Pol. 7, 35–40.

Nellthorp, J., Mackie, P.J., 2000. The UK Roads Review – a hedonic model of decision making. Transp. Pol. 7, 127–138.

Niemeier, D., 1997. Accessibility: an evaluation using social welfare. Transportation 24, 377–396.

OECD, 2018. Cost-benefit Analysis and the Environment: Further Developments and Policy Use. OECD Publishing, Paris. https://doi.org/10.1787/9789264085169-en.

PIARC, 2019. Adaptation Methodologies and Strategies to Increase the Resilience of Roads to Climate Change: A Case Study Approach. World Road Association, Paris. Report 2019R25EN. www.piarc.org.

Primerano, F., Taylor, M.A.P., 2005. An accessibility framework for evaluating transport policies. In: Levinson, D.M., Krizek, K.J. (Eds.), Access to Destinations. Elsevier, Oxford, pp. 325–346.

Quinet, E., 2000. Evaluation methodologies of transportation projects in France. Transp. Pol. 7, 27–34.

Saaty, T.L., 1980. The Analytic Hierarchy Process: Planning, Priority Setting, Resource Allocation. McGraw-Hill, New York).

Salamak, M., Fross, K., 2016. Bridges in urban planning and architectural culture. Proced. Eng. 161, 207–212.

Sayers, A.M., Jessop, A.T., Hills, P.J., 2003. Multi-criteria evaluation of transport options – flexible, transparent and user-friendly? Transp. Pol. 10, 95–105.

Schweikert, A., Chinowsky, P., Kwiatkowski, K., Espinet, X., 2014. The infrastructure planning support system: analysing the impact of climate change on road infrastructure and development. Transp. Pol. 35, 146–153.

Stewart, M., Wang, X., Nguyen, M., 2011. Climate change impacts and risk of concrete infrastructure deterioration. Eng. Struct. 33 (4), 1326–1337.

Stewart, M., Wang, X., Nguyen, M., 2012. Climate change adaptation for corrosion control of concrete infrastructure. Struct. Saf. 35, 29–39.

Taylor, M.A.P., 2008. Critical transport infrastructure in urban areas: impacts of traffic incidents assessed using accessibility-based network vulnerability analysis. Growth Change 39 (4), 593–616.

Taylor, M.A.P., 2017. Vulnerability Analysis for Transportation Networks. Elsevier, New York.

Taylor, M.A.P., Susilawati, 2012. Remoteness and accessibility in the vulnerability analysis of regional road networks. Transp. Res. A Pol. Pract. 46 (5), 761–771.

Taylor, M.A.P., Sekhar, S.V.C., D'Este, G.M., 2006. Application of accessibility based methods for vulnerability analysis of strategic road networks. Network. Spatial Econ. 6 (3), 267–291.

Trojanova, M., 2014. Asset management as integral part of road economy. Procedia Engineering 91, 481–486.

Tsamboulas, D., Yiotis, G.S., Panou, K.D., 1999. Use of multicriteria methods for assessment of transport projects. J. Transport. Eng. 125 (5), 407–414.

Velasquez, M., Hester, P.T., 2013. An analysis of multi-criteria decision making methods. Int. J. Oper. Res. 10 (2), 56–66.

Chapter 6

Coastal issues, including ports and harbours

IPCC (2018) identifies sea level rise as one of the major challenges to be faced in the 21st century. Sea level rise of at least 0.3 m, and perhaps as high as 2.0 m, is almost inevitable over the next 80 years (e.g., Lincke and Hinkel, 2018). Fig. 6.1 indicates the range of forecast rises under five scenarios using Lincke and Hinkel's data. There are thus serious implications for damage to coastal infrastructure, loss of land and displacement of communities. Even if greenhouse gas mitigation measures were to succeed in limiting the temperature increase to 1.5°C (e.g., through Representative Concentration Pathway (RCP) RCP2.6), sea levels will continue to rise many years to come, due to unavoidable emissions already in the system. Note in Fig. 6.1 the overlap of the curves for the RCP scenarios in the first half of the 21st century. Coastal living holds high attraction and has always come with some level of risk from flooding and erosion, but climate change will alter coastlines and requires us to prepare for this new reality.

According to OECD (2019), without adaptation, flood damage under a higher-end sea level rise of perhaps 1.3 m by 2010 (e.g., scenario 95th percentile RCP8.5) would be equivalent to 4% of world GDP, or \$50t (trillion) USD p.a. Implementation of appropriate adaptation measures could reduce this cost by perhaps two orders of magnitude. Such measures do, however, require significant investment, perhaps totalling \$70b by 2100.

Coastal regions often include major cities and transportation hubs – sea ports by definition will be located on the coast or in estuaries close to the coast. Many airports are located in low-lying coastal areas (sometimes including reclaimed land), and some are located on artificial islands built just off the coast. Major industries are located in coastal areas, for instance, agriculture, fisheries and tourism. In consequence major transportation facilities are located to serve the populations and industries. By way of example, at least 80% of Australia's population lives within 50 km of the coast (including all major cities except Canberra) (Cechet et al., 2011) and perhaps 6% of the Australian population resides within 3 km of the shoreline and at elevations less than 5 m above mean sea level (Chen and McAneney, 2006).

A major challenge for adaptation planning for coastal regions is that decisions made in the present time will have long-term implications, stretching

Climate Change Adaptation for Transportation Systems. https://doi.org/10.1016/B978-0-12-816638-3.00006-4

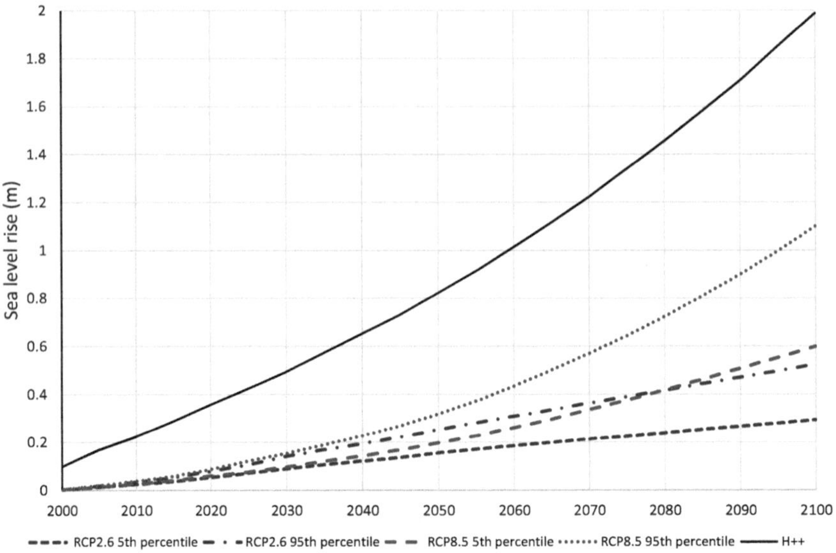

FIGURE 6.1 Forecast climate-induced global mean sea level rise relative to the level of 1986–2005 under the five scenarios studied by Lincke and Hinkel (2018). The five scenarios are: H++, an extreme greenhouse gas emission scenario; 95th percentile RCP8.5; 5th percentile RCP8.5; 95th percentile RCP2.6, and 5th percentile RCP2.6.

into a highly uncertain future. There are three broad strategies for managing risks associated with coastal infrastructure:

- Protection, by reducing the likelihood of hazards. This is done by constructing or maintaining hard defences, such as seawalls, which can be effective in protecting infrastructure assets against extreme events, at least up to the expected level of intensity. If the propensity for higher intensity extreme events increases in the future, then the hard defences may not be able to protect the assets in the long term.
- Accommodation, to reduce the vulnerability of infrastructure assets. This can be done by introducing new design and construction standards which account for sea level rise and more extreme events such as storm surges. This strategy can only be applied to new construction.
- Avoidance, which seeks to reduce exposure to risks of inundation or erosion, perhaps through planned retreat of developments and infrastructure to areas further away from the coast. This strategy, whilst safe, may be expensive and can face strong community opposition.

Each of these strategies has a potential role in coastal adaptation planning. To consider the optimal strategy or combination of strategies first requires an understanding of the various phenomena that may be encountered in coast regions and the identification of the phenomena likely to affect a particular region. Fig. 6.2 shows the major climate change drivers and their potential impacts on the coast. Besides the emission of greenhouse gases, the other drivers from climate change are sea level rise, storm intensity, wind and waves, ocean currents, sea surface temperature, salinisation and precipitation runoff. Each of these drivers can lead to serious impacts on marine environments and coastal structures.

Sea level rise

Of all the climate change drivers affecting coastal regions, sea level rise is perhaps the primary factor as it stands to influence the overall impact of the other drivers. Fig. 6.3 indicates the main contributions to sea level rise and extreme event hazards. The first contributor is global (eustatic) mean sea level rise, which results from an increase in the total volume of water is the seas and oceans of the earth, perhaps due to temperature rises and ice melt. Second is regional sea level rise, due to ocean warming, ocean currents and the climate in general. Coupled with regional net land movements (the geological processes of tectonics and compression), these two factors lead to the net regional mean sea level rise at a given location. There is also variability in sea level at a given location. On top of the net mean sea level, regional variability in sea level stems from the local climate and the sea waves. Tides play a major role in the sea level experienced at any point in time, with a tidal range between low tide and high tide part of the regular gravitational cycle experienced on a daily basis, with extremes in tides (neap and king tides, lowest and highest) experienced as part of the gravitational cycle over the months of a year. Storms then provide the extreme events, through storm surges along a coast which can severely affect the usage of transportation infrastructure in the coastal zone, and indeed damage that infrastructure. The ferocity of storm surges will depend on many factors: the characteristics of the storm itself (its intensity, duration, direction of approach and associated wind speeds and directions) and then the potential combination with other factors, e.g., the coincidence of the particular storm with the occurrence of a king tide. The probability of occurrence of these joint events is small but finite, and this probability will increase if the frequency of storm events is increasing, as may be the case under climate change. There is also a high degree of uncertainty attached to the estimation of future sea level rise. While some of the above factors are well understood and predictable, e.g., tidal range and, to some degree, geological land movements, and some factors are predictable in the short term, e.g., eustatic mean sea level rise and even likely storm surges, predictability in the future is poor for all these factors.

Sea level rise thus implies two important areas of concern for climate change adaptation: (1) beach erosion and inundation of low-lying areas

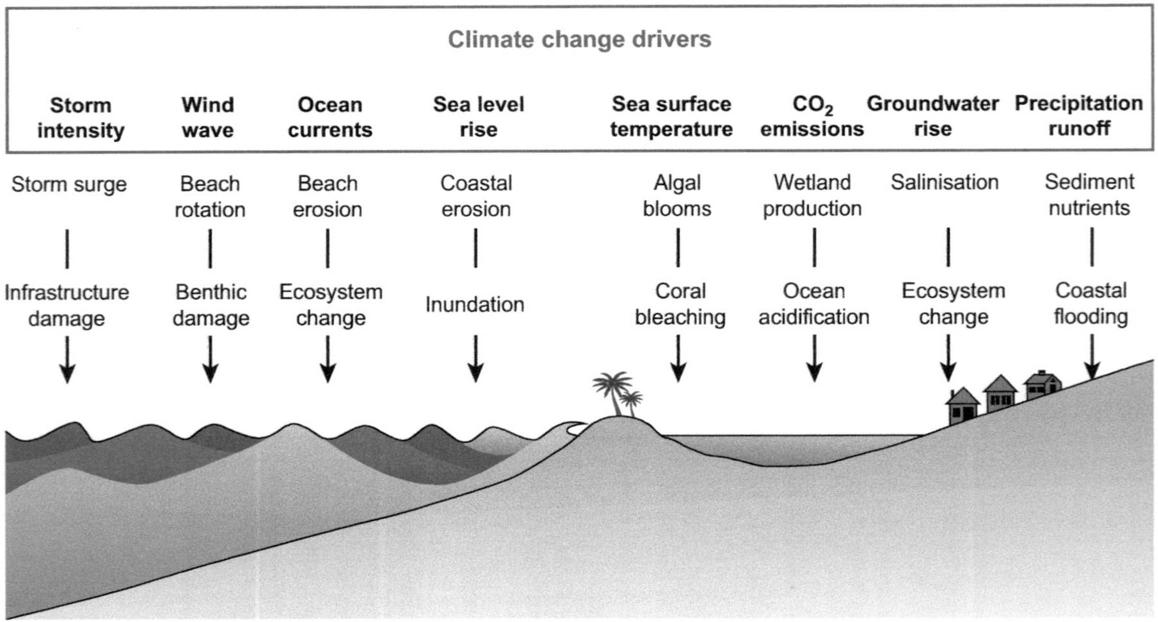

FIGURE 6.2 Climate change drivers, coastal phenomena and impacts. *Derived from DCC, 2009. Climate Change Risks to Australia's Coast: A First Pass National Assessment. Department of Climate Change, Canberra. http://www.environment.gov.au/climate-change and Cechet, R.P., Taylor, P., Griffin, C., Hazelwood, M., 2011. Australia's Coastline: Adapting to Climate Change. Assessing Infrastructure Vulnerability to Rising sea-levels. AusGeo News, Issue 101. Geoscience Australia, Canberra. www.ga.gov.au/ausgeonews.*

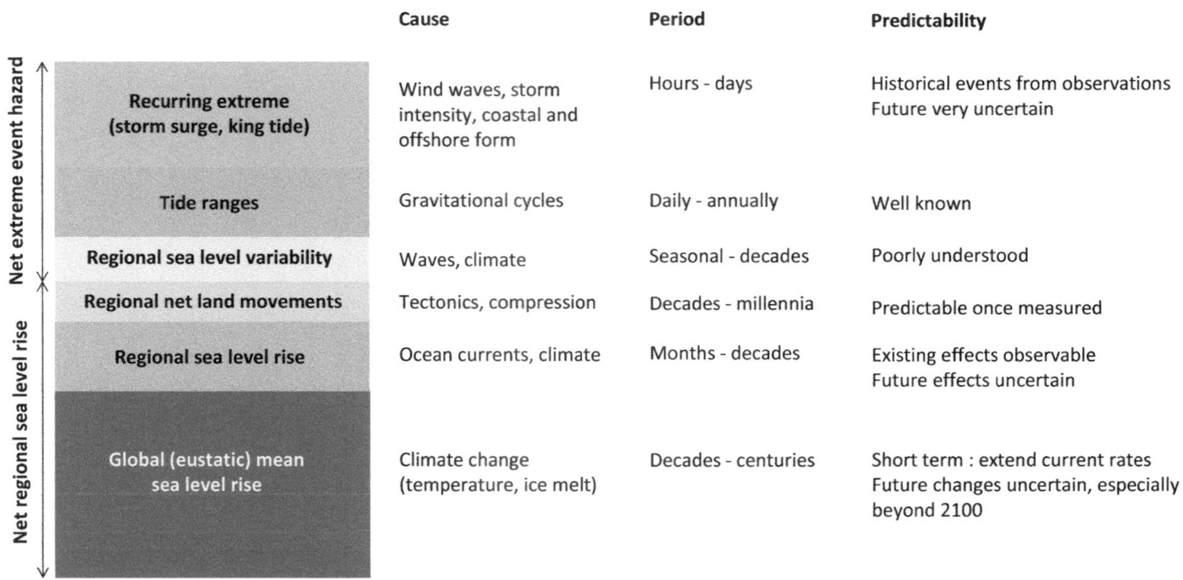

FIGURE 6.3 Contributors to net mean sea level rise and net extreme event hazards for a coastal area. *Derived and modified from DCC, 2009. Climate Change Risks to Australia's Coast: A First Pass National Assessment. Department of Climate Change, Canberra. http://www.environment.gov.au/climate-change.*

directly because of sea level rise and foreshore and land erosion and (2) infrastructure damage due to storm surges exceeding expected (present-day) severity as a consequence of mean sea level rise and extreme storm events (especially if coupled with high tides). This may require strengthening of sea defences, as discussed later in this chapter (see also FHWA, 2014 and Papakonstantinou et al., 2019). In addition, a more subtle impact may arise from rises in groundwater levels and increased salination of existing groundwater. This may reduce the utility of the groundwater for agricultural purposes and may affect the structural behaviour of in-ground or on-ground infrastructure, such as road pavements (Knott et al., 2017). Impacts on the performance of road pavements are discussed in Chapter 6.

Adaptation planning for coastal regions

Adaptation planning for transportation infrastructure in coastal areas may be undertaken using the methods and frameworks described in Chapter 3. The FHWA framework described in that chapter and illustrated in Fig. 3.8 provides a prime example. This framework and its supporting resources form an adaptation planning package that has been applied in several coastal area transportation studies. Table 6.1 summarises the case study applications of the framework in coastal regions. The framework aids agencies in assessing the vulnerability of their transportation infrastructure and systems to climate change and extreme weather. It also provides assistance for the integration of climate adaptation measures in transportation decision-making. The FHWA framework is based on the following seven major steps:

1. Articulate objectives and define study scope
2. Obtain asset data
3. Obtain climate data
4. Assess vulnerability
5. Identify, analyse and prioritise adaptation options
6. Integrate assessment results into decision-making
7. Monitor and review assessments and implementations.

These steps were described in detail in Chapter 3.

An adaptation planning method developed expressly for use in coastal regions is CoastAdapt (Fisk, 2017; CoastAdapt, 2018). This method may be applied to all coastal infrastructure and facilities. CoastAdapt is based on a six-step framework, with internal loops, as shown in Fig. 6.4. The method makes use of the adaptation pathways approach discussed in Chapter 3, to identify trigger points and turning points. The steps are similar to those in the FHWA framework and involve the consideration and prioritisation of risks and

TABLE 6.1 Case study applications of the FHWA adaptation framework in coastal regions (FHWA, 2009).

Case study	Project description	Illustrative project findings and key outcome
Connecticut DOT (CTDOT)	The CTDOT team conducted a systems-level vulnerability assessment of bridge and culvert structures from inland flooding associated with extreme rainfall events. The assessment included data collection and field review, hydrologic and hydraulic evaluation, vulnerability assessment and hydraulic design criteria evaluation.	The CTDOT team found that most structures were built with excess capacity and will therefore be able to accommodate future increases in precipitation. Moving forward, CTDOT recommended that all new infrastructure be designed using the precipitation data from the NRCC-NRCS 'Precip.net' until the new NOAA Atlas 14 data were available. Before this study, CTDOT was still using TP-40 for their designs, which had not been updated since 1961.
Hillsborough Metropolitan Planning Organisation (MPO), Florida	The Hillsborough MPO team assessed the vulnerability of select surface transportation assets to sea level rise, storm surge, and flooding in order to identify cost-effective risk management strategies for incorporation into short-term and long-range transportation planning.	Hillsborough MPO devoted a chapter within its Long Range Transportation Plan (LRTP) to discuss the results of this analysis. One of the assets identified as critical in the study was scheduled for reconstruction in the MPO's LRTP and the MPO found that adaptation measures could be incorporated cost-effectively during reconstruction. For example, a \$4.2 m USD investment to mitigate flood risk for Memorial Highway would result in a net benefit of \$2.1–\$8.4 m USD if it experienced a Category 1 storm surge (and higher benefits for stronger storms).
Maine DOT	The Maine DOT team identified transportation assets that are vulnerable to flooding from sea level rise	The analysis found that the majority of damage would be from storm surge, rather than sea level rise. At each site,

Continued

TABLE 6.1 **Case study applications of the FHWA adaptation framework in coastal regions (FHWA, 2009).—cont'd**

Case study	Project description	Illustrative project findings and key outcome
	and storm surge in six coastal towns. The team developed depth-damage functions and adaptation design options at three of the sites and evaluated the costs and benefits of the alternative design structures.	they identified the design option with the lowest total life cycle cost under each sea level rise scenario. In general, smaller structures requiring lower or moderate initial construction costs tended to be more cost-efficient.
Maryland State Highway Administration (SHA)	The Maryland SHA team developed a three-tiered vulnerability assessment methodology and GIS layers of state-wide water surfaces to analyse vulnerability to sea level rise, storm surge, and flooding in two counties. The team also reviewed design strategies, best management practices, planning standards, and other ways to support the adoption of adaptive management solutions.	The sea level rise mapping results have been integrated into the project screening process. Additionally, Maryland SHA is using the results in their regional planning processes, such as when the Office of Structures staff are doing a bridge replacement, they will see the vulnerability assessment results. SHA subsequently evaluated the vulnerability of drainage structures state-wide using the approach developed in the study.
Massachusetts DOT (MassDOT)	The MassDOT team sought to better understand the vulnerability of the I-93 Central Artery/Tunnel system (CA/T) in Boston to sea level rise and extreme storm events. The team combined a state-of-the-art hydrodynamic flood model with agency-driven knowledge and priorities to assess vulnerabilities and develop adaptation strategies.	The project team used the model to develop a series of projected water surface elevations for hurricanes and north easterly winds. Using a Monte Carlo approach, the team was able to estimate the probability of flooding on a high-resolution grid under current and two future sea level rise scenarios, and to assess flood entry points and pathways, thus identifying potential locations for regional adaptation strategies. In many cases, large upland areas are flooded by a relatively small and distinct entry point (e.g., a low elevation area along the coastline).

TABLE 6.1 Case study applications of the FHWA adaptation framework in coastal regions (FHWA, 2009).—cont'd

Case study	Project description	Illustrative project findings and key outcome
New Jersey DOT/North Jersey Transportation Planning Authority (NJTPA) – Coastal and Central New Jersey	The NJTPA led this interagency partnership to assess the vulnerability of the State's transportation systems. Much of New Jersey's infrastructure is aging and concentrated near major rivers and the coast. The NJ Partnership wanted to understand how to make more strategic capital investments in light of the changing climate. To accomplish this goal, the project team conducted a Geographic Information System (GIS)-based climate vulnerability assessment on transportation assets in a Coastal Study Area along the Atlantic Ocean and in a Central Study Area, which includes six counties across the State that encompass a significant transit corridor.	The assessment found that the 1-in-100 year floodplain will expand under future climate conditions, with the greatest expansion occurring under the most severe scenario. This could be significant by 2050 and highly disruptive by 2100, with over 19 miles of critical roadway at risk of inundation. NJ TRANSIT indicated that temperatures higher than 35°C will increase the risk of rail buckling and that catenaries may sag or experience pulley failures during extreme heat. The Partnership study developed a series of matrices to identify potential adaptation strategies that could be implemented at the planning, design, and operations phases of transportation decision making. The matrices also indicate whether impacts are expected to occur more or less frequently in the absence of adaptation.
Oahu MPO, Hawaii	Oahu MPO facilitated a workshop to identify and prioritise transportation assets that may be vulnerable to climate impacts. The study focused on five high-priority sites with existing vulnerability to extreme weather and climate variability. Oahu MPO developed a 'triage' approach that could be	The study identified Honolulu Harbor, Honolulu International Airport, and Farrington Highway on the Waianae Coast as the three transportation asset groups with the highest integrated risk due to climate change. Overall, the project team found that warmer temperatures and increased wind speeds will not pose a

Continued

TABLE 6.1 Case study applications of the FHWA adaptation framework in coastal regions (FHWA, 2009).—cont'd

Case study	Project description	Illustrative project findings and key outcome
	applied both within the State and across Pacific island nations. Prior to the workshop Oahu MPO consulted climate scientists to develop a baseline understanding of the current climate change impacts affecting the islands. Oahu MPO also consulted with lead planners and engineers to gather knowledge on Oahu's highways, harbors, and airports.	large risk to transportation assets. The climate impacts of greatest concern are sea level rise, storm surge, and intense rainfall.
Oregon DOT (ODOT)	The ODOT team engaged maintenance and technical staff and utilised asset data to assess the vulnerability of highway infrastructure in two coastal counties to extreme weather events and higher sea levels. Based on the results of the vulnerability assessment, the pilot conducted further analysis of specific adaptation sites, options, and benefits and costs for five priority storm and landslide hazard areas. Options analysed ranged from 'do nothing' to options for increased operations and maintenance and options with significant construction and engineering requirements.	Nearly all the designated 'Lifeline Routes' in the study area, which are essential for emergency response and economic connectivity, were found to be vulnerable to projected climate impacts. ODOT developed a list of adaptation options for highly vulnerable sites. However, they found that implementing adaptation strategies would not be cost-effective at the two sites for which they performed cost-benefit analyses, due to availability of detour routes and low traffic volumes, and other factors. This suggests adaptation may be more appropriate at a corridor-level in Oregon. ODOT also identified many parallels between adaptation planning work and seismic resilience planning work, and is looking for ways to enhance that collaboration.

TABLE 6.1 Case study applications of the FHWA adaptation framework in coastal regions (FHWA, 2009).—cont'd

Case study	Project description	Illustrative project findings and key outcome
San Francisco Bay area MTC (Metropolitan Transportation Commission)	The MTC team refined its first vulnerability assessment (2010–11 FHWA pilot program) with additional sea level rise mapping and hydraulic analysis. Using the revised vulnerability data, the project team developed a comprehensive suite of adaptation strategies for three focus areas, and through a systematic evaluation process, they selected five adaptation strategies for further development: living levees (in two locations), an offshore breakwater, a drainage study, and mainstreaming climate change risk into transportation agencies planning processes.	The policy/research and physical adaptation strategies developed as part of this pilot all include information on the process and partners needed for implementation, preliminary scopes/ conceptual designs (including cost estimates), potential barriers, and a summary of impacts of implementation. This information helped to inform regional and State policy and investment decisions, and the overall process served as a framework for similar projects in the region.
Virginia DOT – Hampton Roads	Hampton Roads, Virginia, is a low-lying, coastal metropolitan region that serves as the site for multiple military installations, including the largest naval base on the East Coast. This study used an existing decision support model to evaluate how the transportation priorities of the region might be influenced by a variety of climate change, economic, regulatory, travel-demand, wear-and-tear, environmental, and technology scenarios.	This study found that the most important scenario for priority-setting was a combination of sea level rise and storm surge with increased traffic demand. This scenario significantly disrupted existing priorities for projects, assets and policies. Prioritisation of planned projects was most sensitive to the climate-change-only scenario. The decision support model exists as an Excel workbook tool that guides users through the process of identifying assets, selecting criteria, building a base case, and developing climate and climate-plus scenarios.

Derived from Appendix C of FHWA, 2009. Vulnerability Assessment and Adaptation Framework, third ed. Federal Highways Administration, Washington DC. https://www.fhwa.dot.gov/environment/sustainability/resilience/adaptation_framework/chap00.cfm.

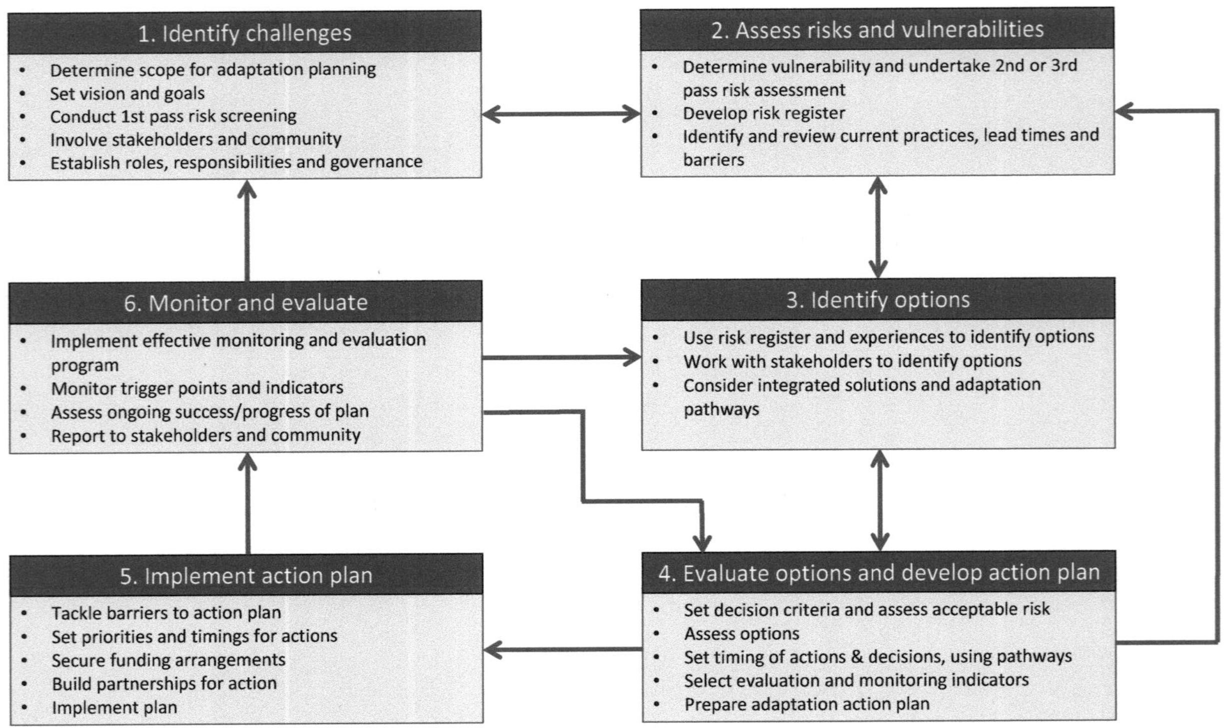

FIGURE 6.4 The six steps of the CoastAdapt risk-based framework for developing climate change adaptation plans for coastal infrastructure and facilities. *Derived from CoastAdapt, 2018. How to Conduct a Climate Change Risk Assessment. https://coastadapt.com.au/how-to-pages/how-to-conduct-a-climate-change-risk-assessment. (Accessed 29 February 2020).*

vulnerabilities. The framework may also be applied at three levels of screening: first pass, second pass and third pass. The six steps in the Coast-Adapt framework are as follows:

1. Identify challenges: This initial step provides the basis for the analysis to follow. It is used to determine the scope of the required adaptation plan, within the goals and objectives of the organisation responsible for the plan. An initial, broad (first pass) risk screening for the issue under consideration is performed in this step. The step also requires the planner to seek out and involve relevant stakeholders and communities affected by the challenges at hand. The roles of the agency, stakeholders and community, their responsibilities and the governance structure to be used are determined in this step.
2. Assess risks and vulnerabilities: On the basis that Step 1 indicates the need for further investigation, Step 2 is used to explore and assess risks. This may be done using second- or third-pass risk assessment procedures. The consequence is the development of a register of the risks. These risks are then placed in context by a review of the current practices in use (if any) to deal with the risks and to identify potential lead times before actions could be implemented as well as potential barriers to such implementations. The findings from Step 2 could lead to feedback into Step 1, e.g., to revise the scope of the investigation.
3. Identify options: The risk register developed in Step 2, coupled with experiences garnered from within the organisation and from others, is used to identify potential options for utilisation in the adaptation plan. Stakeholder input may also be used to refine and extend the set of options. Adaptation pathways including integrated solutions to the problem at hand may then be developed for further consideration. Step 3 may also lead to a review of the risk register developed in Step 2.
4. Evaluate options and develop an action plan: First in this step is the determination of decision criteria to be applied and assessment of acceptable levels of risk. With this information available, the options identified in Step 3 may be assessed and timelines established for the actions and decisions in the adaptation pathways for the preferred options. Indicators for use in evaluation and monitoring are selected, leading to the preparation of an adaptation action plan. The findings of Step 4 may also lead to reviews of the outputs from Steps 2 and 3.
5. Implement the adaptation plan: Step 5 first requires actions to deal with potential barriers to the plan and the allocation of the required resources for the plan. This will involve the determination of priorities within the plan and the resulting timing of the individual actions in it.
6. Monitor and evaluate the plan in operation: In this step the ongoing progress of the plan and its successes or otherwise of its implementation are examined and reported. Monitoring is essential, not only to judge the success of the specific plan but also to provide experience and new

knowledge for use in future plans. Thus Step 6 feeds back into Step 1 as part of an ongoing cycle of adaptation planning and also informs future work in Steps 3 and 4.

The three-level risk assessment process included in CoastAdapt is intended to support the different goals, data and resource availability of different organisations which may be involved in adaptation planning. CoastAdapt includes a database of tools and information as well as guidance on risk assessment procedures for use at each of the three levels, which are

- First-pass risk assessment, which guides a user in conducting a desktop study and screen climate-related exposure using readily available datasets. It can also provide guidance on the need for more detailed (second- or third-level) assessment.
- Second-pass risk assessment uses the risk-based approach including national data, available local information and expert knowledge. It assists the user in identifying how climate change may compound existing risks or create new risks and will indicate if a third-level assessment may be required.
- Third-pass risk assessment is a detailed assessment process to allow a user to more deeply investigate short-listed (high priority) risks and to prioritise strategies and actions to mitigate those risks.

The risks to coastal transportation infrastructure are most likely to emerge from sea level rise, as a gradual impact over extended time periods, and storm surges and flooding from extreme weather events such as storms, hurricanes and cyclones. The latter are well-known causes of infrastructure damage along a coast, but their effects are likely to be exacerbated by climate change through influences on the frequency and intensity of the extreme weather events.

Storms, surges and flooding

While sea level rise is the primary manifestation of climate change in a coastal zone, the major cause of infrastructure damage and flooding will come from storms and resulting storm surges. A storm surge is an increase in coastal water levels well above the normal (expected) high tide and is caused by the combined actions of severe winds and low atmospheric pressure resulting from the storm (and at its extremes during a hurricane). Should the storm surge be combined with daily variations in the tide, then the resultant water level is termed the storm tide. The height of the storm tide will increase as the storm pushes the water up against the coastline. Fig. 6.5 provides a schematic diagram of a storm tide with surge and wave runup onto the beach/foreshore/coastal defences in place. A storm tide level exceeding the highest astronomical tide (as in Fig. 6.5) is likely to cause inundation and flooding in coastal areas. If the wave runup is sufficiently high so that waves may break over any defensive barrier (e.g., seawall or revetment) then flooding may occur behind that barrier.

A number of factors can influence storm tide height and any inland propagation of flooding. These factors include storm intensity, storm size

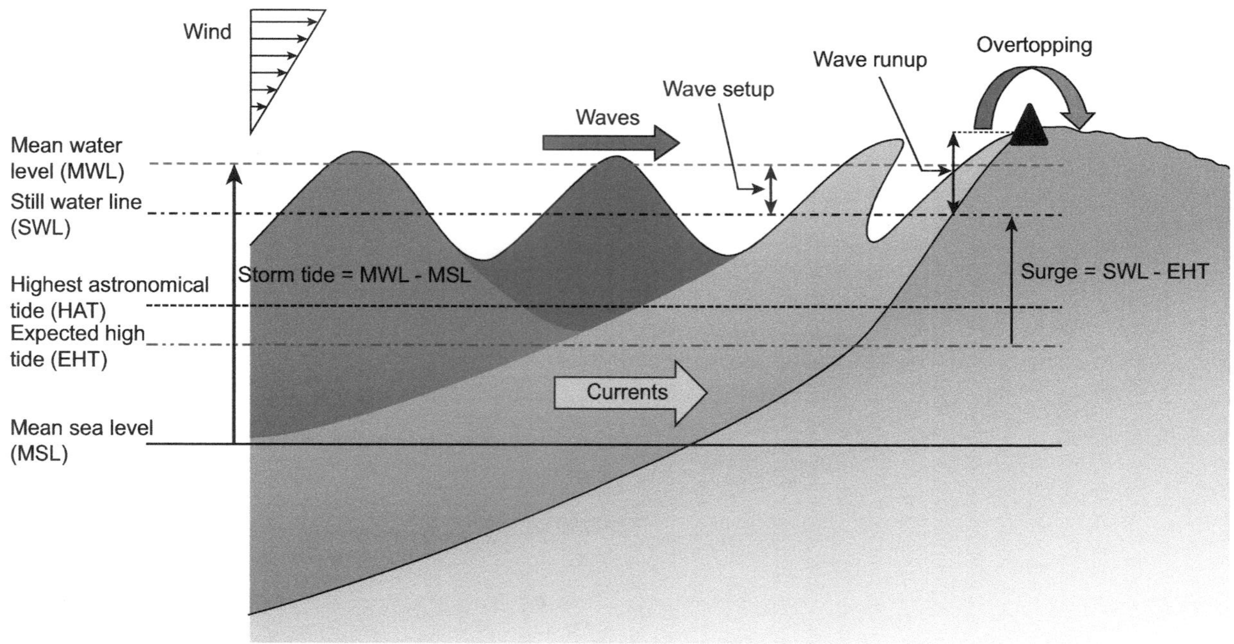

FIGURE 6.5 Water components in a storm tide, including overtopping. *As derived from DES, 2018. A Guide to 'Good Practice' Storm Tide Inundation Mapping and Modelling. Department of Environment and Science, Queensland Government, Brisbane. https://www.publications.qld.gov.au/dataset/19c20822-f29e-494c-880a-113ccd13a04b/resource/93336e30-e1fd-4a1e-89e8-b4056692e26c/fs_download/storm-tide-inundation-guidelines.pdf. (Accessed 19 February 2020).*

(physical diameter), storm speed, the angle of approach of the storm, the stage of the tide and coastal geometry (which includes coastal shelf width and slope). Higher intensity storms generate higher storm surges and storm surges can also increase with increasing storm diameter. High approach speeds lead to faster build up of surges and then greater impact because of higher energy levels. As a general rule, storms approaching perpendicular to the coast generate higher surges, but local factors such as narrow inlets and bays may influence surge height. Wide and gently sloping continental shelves also amplify storm surges, as the friction between the sea water and the ocean floor over the shallower shelf region slows the wind-generated surge. This causes the surge wave length to decrease and the wave height to increase. Topography may also play a role: a headland may either amplify or attenuate a storm surge depending on the wind direction. Enclosed waterways such as bays, estuaries, harbours and inlets may also experience surge amplification as the surge is funnelled into the smaller, shallower area. A more complete discussion of the factors affecting storm surges and resultant inundation is given in DES (2018).

Thus storm tides in the nearshore are results from the combination of

- Water level elevation due to low barometric pressure and strong onshore winds associated with the storm,
- The position in the astronomical tide cycle at the coast location at the time of storm approach and
- Wave setup (see Fig. 6.5) due to increased wave energy pushing water towards the shore on sloping beaches.

Wave action, elevated water levels and wave runup attack sand dunes and foreshore structures, potentially causing erosion and structural damage.

According to Gordon and Cox (2018), the vulnerability of a structure to wave attack depends on the ratio of the water depth to wave height at the structure. In deep water, waves surge on to the structure, progressively dispersing energy. Damage to the structure may occur over time, as in the case of an offshore light house (e.g., see Nancollas, 2018), much like a fatigue failure. A structure in shallow water may fare differently. Waves plunge on to the structure dissipating their energy in a narrow zone around the mean water level – a 'depth-limited wave attack'. The plunging breaker delivers a far more intense attack on the structure. The focus of this attack moves up and down the face of the structure with the tide, storm surge and wave setup. In the worst case, the 'design wave' – the highest energy storm wave expected to occur in the region containing the structure – just breaks as a plunger on the structure at the time of maximum water level.

Flooding inland of the foreshore region may occur under some conditions. Even if storm tide levels do not exceed the height of coastal barriers, it is still possible for localised inundation to occur due to wave runup and wave overtopping. As the height of the storm tide increases, wave runup lessens in significance as water overtops the coastal barrier and follows flow paths inland. Wave setup is important at this stage as it defines the water levels required to overtop dunes. Further increases in storm tide height reduce the importance of wave setup as the flooding hazard is then due to water speed, overland wave propagation and wind pushing the water further inland. In areas of tidal waterways, the storm tide may propagate up the estuary to flood low-lying areas behind coastal defences that may otherwise have offered protection. Wave setup only influences storm tide levels relatively close to the coast (i.e., within the beach and foreshore zones).

Coastal erosion is a natural phenomenon of beaches. As environmental conditions change, so the beach profile may change as sand is moved onshore or offshore. Many beaches never achieve a stable profile as conditions continually change, e.g., through an annual cycle of shifting winds and currents. Some beaches may experience ongoing erosion which is manifest as long-term shoreline recession. This is known as long-term erosion. In addition, short-term erosion may occur because of extreme weather events such as severe storms or hurricanes. This erosion may take place over a number of days and alter the beach profile as sand is swept offshore. After the event, normal beach processes usually resume and the normal sand transport processes return the sand to the beach, although this may take many months or even years. Indeed, the effects of severe storm systems such as hurricanes can, in some cases, last for decades and so become relatively permanent features of the beachfront. Projected sea level rise is likely to result in more severe coastal erosion during extreme events, and eroded coastlines will result in permanent loss of land to the sea. Coastal infrastructure close to the shoreline may then be placed at risk from the erosion.

Increases in mean sea level rise and in storm intensity from climate change will exacerbate the potential for coastal erosion, structural damage, inundation and flooding resulting from storm surges. The choice of flood mitigation measures is complex, for there is evidence that a given flood mitigation measure (e.g., tidal or high embankment water level) may exacerbate an alternative flooding measure (e.g., beach overtopping), as discussed by Gallien et al., (2014). Under a climate change adaptation regime where new measures may be sought, careful analysis and planning will be required. The use of models to estimate likely sea level rise, beach erosion and storm surge impacts is therefore essential.

Modelling

There are many models of coastal phenomena related to extreme weather events and climate change. These models range from simple linear equations (e.g., for the long-term extent of beach erosion) to complex hydrodynamic models of inundation and flooding for a given locality. This section provides a brief overview of coastal models and some guidance about the applications of the different models to particular circumstances. The models described do not provide an exhaustive set, and the discussions on modelling details are limited. The interested reader should seek further information and advice on coastal modelling, e.g., as provided in FHWA (2014), Gallien et al., (2014), Hansen (2016) and DES (2018).

For sea level rise, FHWA (2014) cited a simple but flexible model for estimation of future sea level rise at a given location. The model has two components: (1) the change in eustatic sea level and (2) the local relative change in sea level. These two components describe the net regional sea level rise as defined in Fig. 6.3, for the local relative change in sea level is assessed from tide gauge data and so includes both regional sea level rise and regional net land movements. The change in eustatic sea level rise Δ_{ESL} at time t is given by

$$\Delta_{ESL}(t) = at + bt^2 \tag{6.1}$$

where a is the existing linear sea level rise (mm/y) and b is the sea level rise acceleration rate (mm/y^2). FHWA (2014) suggests that a value of $a = 1.7$ mm/y is generally accepted. The value of b will vary depending on the particular climate scenario under investigation. Table 6.2 shows the values of b corresponding to the five climate change scenarios RCP2.6 (5th percentile), RCP2.6 (95th percentile), RCP8.5 (5th percentile), RCP8.5 (95th percentile) and H++ used by Lincke and Hinkel (2018) and shown in Fig. 6.1.

If $\Delta L(x,t)$ is the estimated local relative change in sea level at location x and at time t, then the projected change in sea level at that location ($\Delta SL(x,t)$) is

$$\Delta SL(x,t) = \Delta_{ESL}(t) + \Delta L(x,t) \tag{6.2}$$

FHWA (2014) suggests that $\Delta L(x,t)$ can be calculated by subtracting 1.7 (mm/y) from the local sea level change as measured by a tide gauge. This assumes that the future local sea level change rate will be similar to the existing rate, i.e., any acceleration of sea level rise will be due to the eustatic component in Eq. (6.2). This is a starting assumption and could be varied given the advice of the relevant Geological Survey agency for the region if it is believed that the regional net land movement rate is changing.

TABLE 6.2 Sea level rise acceleration term (b, mm/y^2) in Eq. (6.1) for the five climate change scenarios used by Lincke and Hinkel (2018) and shown in Fig. 6.1.

Climate change scenario: Acceleration term b (mm/y^2)				
RCP2.6 (5th percentile)	RCP2.6 (95th percentile)	RCP8.5 (5th percentile)	RCP8.5 (95th percentile)	H++
1.3	3.5	4.2	9.1	16.9

As discussed above, beach and sand dune (foreshore) erosion is a natural phenomenon that can result in land loss, which may threaten infrastructure, facilities and buildings located near the shoreline. The likely area to be affected by erosion over a given planning period *n* (years) is the 'erosion prone area', and the width of this area (i.e., the distance perpendicular to the shoreline of the erosion prone area) is of concern for planning and management purposes. This width (W_e) will be subject to both long-term and short-term erosion. A simple assessment formula for estimating W_e for sandy coasts exposed to moderate to high wave energy was proposed by DEHP (2013). This formula allows for long-term erosion, short-term erosion due to an extreme event and erosion due to sea level rise. The DEHP formula is

$$W_e = (1+\theta)(nr + c + s) + d \tag{6.3}$$

In this formula, *n* is the planning period, in years, *r* is the rate of long-term erosion (m/y), estimated as discussed below, *c* is the short-term erosion from the design storm/hurricane (m), *s* is erosion due to sea level rise (m), *d* is a dune scarp component (m), intended to allow for slumping of the erosion scarp, and θ is a factor of safety − DEHP (2013) recommends $\theta = 0.4$.

A typical planning period (*n*) of 100 years was suggested by DEHP (2013), on the basis that the primary issue to be addressed in considerations of beach erosion is the placement of new urban development, i.e., permanent development that cannot easily be relocated.

Long-term erosion is expected to occur over decades − but needs to be considered separately from erosion due to sea level rise. The rate of long-term erosion (*r*) can be estimated by one of the two methods: (1) extrapolation of past trends from geological records or from surveys and aerial photography or (2) by considering the annual quantity of sand removed from the beach. Fig. 6.6 shows a simple beach profile response to long-term erosion and displays the amount of erosion (sand loss) over a year. Two height dimensions are indicated in this figure: h_1, the height of the frontal beach ridge above the low

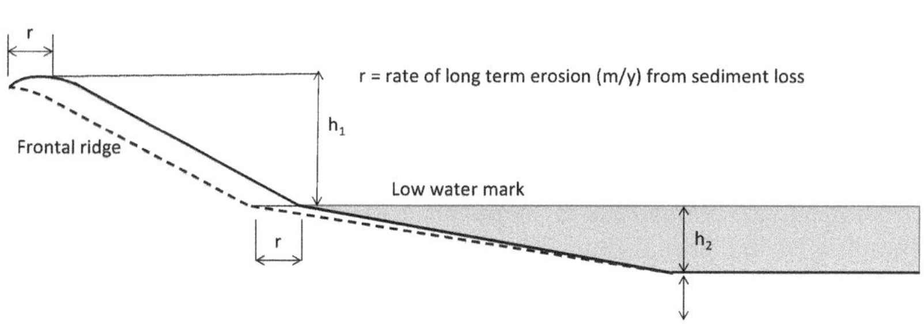

FIGURE 6.6 Schematic diagram showing simple beach profile response to long-term erosion, indicating the annual amount of erosion (*r*).

water mark, and h_2, the depth of closure (distance between the low water mark and the most landward point seaward of which there is no significant change in bottom elevation and no significant net sediment exchange between nearshore and offshore). If Q_e ($m^3/m/y$) is the erosion quantity in cubic metres per metre of beach p.a., then, using DEHP (2013),

$$r = \frac{2Q_e}{2h_1 + h_2} \tag{6.4}$$

DEHP (2013) suggested that the term c (short-term erosion component) in Eq. (6.3) can be determined using the following procedure:

1. Assess the acceptable risk for assets under threat from a severe storm and thus define the design storm for the region
2. Select the relevant parameters for the design storm
3. Estimate the horizontal recession of the beach associated with this storm event.

The 1 in 100 storm event is often considered to represent an acceptable risk. The extent of coastal erosion to be expected under a design storm will also be affected by other factors, such as the storm tide level and the significant wave height. The former should be based on a chosen probability of occurrence, with DEHP (2013) suggesting an average recurrence interval of 1 in 100 years. The latter — significant wave height — for a moderate storm could use the 1 in 20 year value. For wave-dominated coastlines where extreme storm tide levels can be relatively small, the significant wave height and the duration of the storm are likely to be the major factors affecting short-term erosion.

Erosion due to sea level rise must also be accounted for. This can be done by assuming a supposed value of sea level rise over the planning period and then estimating shoreline response to that rise in sea level. DEHP (2013) suggested use of the 'Bruun Rule', which is based on the concept that an equilibrium beach profile is maintained during sea level rise, but is translated upwards and landwards. Under this rule, the original beach profile and nearshore shallow water conditions are maintained. This is a useful starting assumption.

Dune scarp slumping is included in Eq. (6.4) through the factor *d*. The short-term erosion component (*c*) indicates the shoreline recession as far as the limit of wave runup, at least when the frontal beach ridge is not overtopped. The dune scarp component is included in Eq. (6.3) to allow for the possible slumping of the frontal dune beyond this sunup level — and possible undermining and collapse of structures located on the dune.

Eq. (6.4) is a simplified model of beach erosion. It is useful because it identifies the component factors to be considered in beach erosion and indicates the data items required in the estimations. More refined models are needed, and FHWA (2014) discussed some of these, e.g., EDUNE (Kriebel, 1986; Kriebel and Dean, 1985) and SBEACH (Larson and Kraus, 1989; Larson et al., 1990).

Inundation of areas close to the shoreline due to extreme weather events such as storms is an important consideration in the design, construction and management of transportation infrastructure assets in coastal zones. As discussed above and detailed in DES (2018), a storm tide in the nearshore area results from three basic processes:

- Elevated water levels as a consequence of reduced barometric pressure and strong onshore winds from the storm, hurricane or cyclone,
- The stage of the astronomical tides on the coast and
- Wave setup due to increased wave energy pushing water on to the shore of a sloping beach.

If these processes combine to produce water levels exceeding the local coastal barriers (e.g., sand dunes), then inland flooding is possible. The occurrence and extent of coastal inundation will depend on many factors applying in the particular area, including the relative height of the water. Even if the storm tide does not exceed the height of the coastal barriers some inundation may still occur, due to local wave runup and wave overtopping of coastal structures Wave runup becomes less significant as the storm tide increases, as overtopping throw water onto inland flow paths – producing fast flowing water. Wave setup is the factor that defines these overtopping water levels. If the storm tide increases further, then wave setup loses significance and the inundation may be fuelled by water velocities, overland wave propagation and wind pressure pushing the water further inland. In tidal waterways, e.g., estuaries, the storm tide (less the wave setup) can propagate upstream to flood low-lying areas behind coastal barriers, denying the protection that the coastal barriers would otherwise have provided. Wave setup really only influences storm tide levels close to the coast itself (i.e., in the surf zone).

Inundation models thus have to include and represent a large number of natural and physical processes relating to shallow water flows over low-lying topography. The processes are complex and require significant input data for accurate representations. There are many models available, at differing degrees of complexity and representation. Table 6.3 lists a number of models as identified by FHWA (2014) for different application, including

- Beach, dune and coastal erosion
- Hydrodynamic modelling of flood and inundation from extreme weather events

TABLE 6.3 Numerical models for coastal engineering applications identified by FHWA (2014).

	Model type					
Model	**Erosion**	**Hydrodynamic**	**Morphology**	**Storm surge**	**Waves**	**References**
ADCIRC		✓		✓		Luettich et al., (1992), Dietrich et al., (2011)
CSHORE			✓		✓	Johnson et al., (2012)
CHAMPS			✓		✓	FEMA (2007)
CH3D		✓				Sheng (1990), Johnson et al., (1991)
CMS		✓	✓		✓	Buttolph et al., (2006)
DELFT3D		✓	✓		✓	Vatvani et al., (2012)
EDUNE	✓					Kriebel (1986), Kriebel and Dean (1985)
ET-SURGE				✓		Glahn et al., (2009), Kim et al., (1996)
FVCOM		✓				Chen et al., (2006)
MIKE21		✓	✓		✓	Savioli et al., (2003)
SBEACH	✓		✓			Larson and Kraus (1989), Larson et al., (1990)
SLOSH				✓		Glahn et al., (2009)
STWAVE					✓	Smith et al., (2001)
SWAN					✓	Booij et al., (1999), Ris et al., 1999)
WAM					✓	Group (1988)
XBEACH		✓	✓		✓	Roelvink et al., (2009)

- Morphological models indicating potential changes to the form and structure of a coastal zone subject to extreme weather events[1]
- Storm surges and storm tides
- Wave modelling.

Inundation models may be classified in terms of their dimensional representation of water flows. This dimensionality relates to the consideration of water flow as linear or area-wide, with assumptions about the vertical distributions of water velocity and pressure. All of the models require a digital elevation model (DEM) of the study area to define the topography of the coastal zone and its hinterland. There are then four levels:

- 0D modelling, which uses the DEM, probably in a Geographic Information System (GIS) (or other mapping tools), to estimate the land surface that would be flooded due to a predicted storm tide water level. Any DEM value lower that this level is assumed to fill with water. The common name for this analysis is the 'bathtub' method. This method does not consider water flow at all, rather the inundation is assumed to occur instantaneously to the storm tide water level. Therefore, it does not predict flow velocities, inundation flow pathways or inundation times. It is a widely used and relatively simple approach. DES (2018) suggested that the bathtub approach can lead to overestimation of the areas of inundation because real-world water flows will be influenced by man-made or topographical features.
- 1D models, which model water flows in rivers or along defined pathways. Water flows in one direction only, with the river or channel represented by a connected set of lines, each line with its own geometry. 1D models are strictly for river flooding or situations where overland flows are constrained to predetermined flow paths.
- 2D models consider the area-wide flow of water, based on a grid or mesh representation of the topography of the area. The 2D models work best in situations where horizontal dimensions dominate over the vertical dimension (i.e., shallow water depths), for their underlying assumption is that water velocity and pressure at any point can be represented by the average velocity and pressure (in the vertical plane) for the specific depth of water. Hydrodynamic 2D models accommodate flow in two horizontal directions through the open boundaries in the topography. Overland surge and wave processes can be included by coupling a hydrodynamic model with a shallow wave model. The 2D models have become commonly used

1. Morphology is the study of the form and structure and the changes of form and structure of the earth's surface. Geomorphology is (1) that branch of physical geography dealing with the form of the Earth, the general configuration of its surface and the distribution of the land, water, etc., or (2) the investigation of the history of geological changes through the interpretation of topographical forms.

to investigate the impacts of storm tide events, including wind waves, on coastal communities and infrastructure.

- 3D models are similar in scope to the 2D models but allow for water velocity and pressure at any point to vary according to water depth. They thus simulate water movements both horizontally and vertically within the body of water. The 3D models are particularly suited to modelling the complex interaction of wave, tide and surge processes with the underlying bathymetry of the coastal zone.[2] A further feature of the 3D models is that they can also be used to model flows around structures, including bridge scour.

The data requirements, computational effort and expertise for inundation modelling increase with increase dimensionality, with the 3D models requiring the highest levels of these resources. FHWA (2014) defined three general 'levels of effort' for vulnerability assessment of coastal transportation infrastructure to extreme coastal events and climate change. The degree of uncertainty in model results decreases as the level of effort increases, while the amount of detail and degree of complexity increase commensurately. FHWA's three levels of effort are as follows:

1. Use of existing data and resources, such as existing inundation or tsunami hazard maps, or the use of the bathtub method, to determine the potential exposure of infrastructure under selected climate change scenarios and sensitivity to depth-limited wave or wave runup processes
2. Original modelling of inundation resulting from storm surge and wave fields for specified storm and climate change scenarios
3. Modelling using a probabilistic risk framework to consider storm surge, sea levels, currents and waves under a range of climate change scenarios with assigned probabilities.

A guide to the selection of suitable models was provided by DES (2018). This guide is summarised by the flow chart shown in Fig. 6.7. The steps in the chart consider the availability of data for the study area, the resources available for the study (time, money and expertise), the nature of the coastline, topography and bathymetry of the study area, possible riverine flooding and the amount of fetch available to generate overland wind waves.[3]

2. Bathymetry is the study of underwater depth of lake, sea or ocean floors, i.e., the underwater equivalent of land topography.
3. Fetch is the area of lake, sea or ocean surface over which the wind blows in an essentially constant direction, thus generating waves. The term is also a synonym for fetch length, which is the horizontal distance over which wave-generating winds blow.

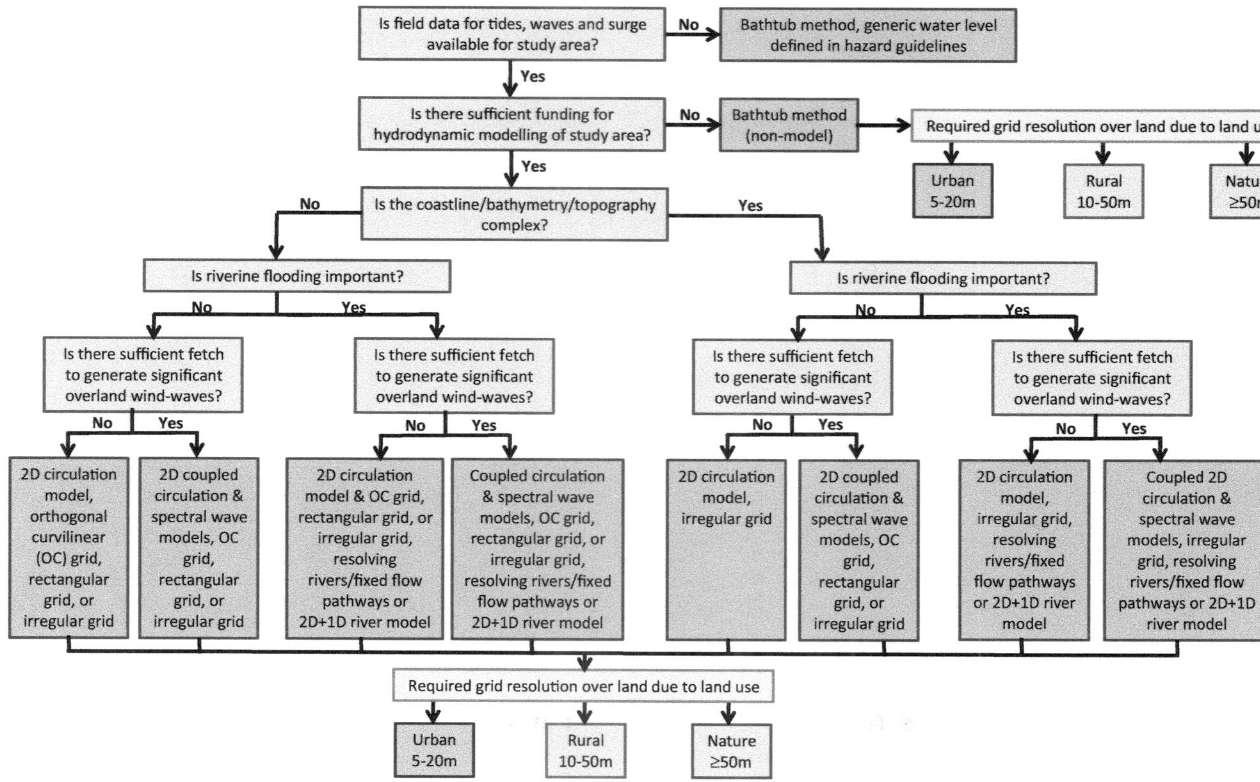

FIGURE 6.7 Inundation model selection guide summary. *As derived from DES, 2018. A Guide to 'Good Practice' Storm Tide Inundation Mapping and Modelling. Department of Environment and Science, Queensland Government, Brisbane. https://www.publications.qld.gov.au/dataset/19c20822-f29e-494c-880a-113ccd13a04b/resource/93336e30-e1fd-4a1e-89e8-b4056692e26c/fs_download/storm-tide-inundation-guidelines.pdf. (Accessed 19 February 2020).*

FIGURE 6.8 The Highway One/NZ Rail major transportation corridor in the South Island of New Zealand near Kaikoura, showing the Pacific Ocean on the left, the winding roadway and a rail tunnel through the edge of the escarpment on the right.

Coastal transportation infrastructure

Transportation infrastructure in coastal zones is subject to the impacts of storms, extreme weather and storm surges. Under climate change scenarios including sea level rise and increases in the frequency and intensity of extreme weather events, the infrastructure will face increased risks. Adaptation to face such risks is then particularly important, especially when a major transportation corridor is located in a coastal zone. Fig. 6.8 shows a striking example of this situation: the case of the major transportation corridor in the South Island of New Zealand, where the major highway (Highway One) and railway links from the South Island to the North Island (via the ferry terminal at Picton) run through a narrow coastal strip near Kaikoura. The coastal strip is less than 100 m wide, with the Pacific Ocean on one side and a steep escarpment on the other. The photograph in Fig. 6.8 shows the winding roadway and a tunnel entrance for the railway, all located in a very narrow coastal zone. The infrastructure in this area could be severely affected by an extreme weather event, leading to a loss of connectivity between the major city (Christchurch) of the South Island and the North Island of New Zealand.

Fisk (2017) produced a summary tabulation of the risks to transportation infrastructure from climate change, with the risks being the following:

- For sea level rise: increased areas exposed to erosion, storm tides and inundation

- For extreme weather events (including hurricanes, cyclones and storms): increased erosion, storm surges, storm tides and flash flooding; increases in high winds and increased thunderstorm activity and lightning strikes.

Table 6.4 lists these climate change factors and risks along with their potential impacts on road and rail transportation, airports and sea ports.

The New Zealand Transport Agency has produced a set of guidelines for the assessment of coastal effects on transportation infrastructure (NZTA, 2017). A feature of these guidelines is that the agency not only identifies the potential impacts of climate change factors on transportation assets but also the potential effects of those assets on the coastal environment in which the assets are located. Thus, for instance, while inundation due to a storm tide may reduce the availability of road features (such as a bridge or culvert) to traffic and may degrade the asset, the bridge or culvert may then itself cause wave deflections into neighbouring areas or produce changes in water flow causing further erosion and inundation in those areas. Table 6.5 shows the broad climate change impacts identified by NZTA (2017), while Table 6.6 provides further detail of the impacts for specific types of transportation assets.

Table 6.6 identifies four asset components unique to coastal areas: causeways, groynes, revetments and seawalls. These components provide physical protection against sea processes such as waves and surges and in the case of the causeway may also provide the transportation linkage between two land masses. They may be grouped as 'coastal defence works'. Seawalls are rigid structures while revetments and groynes are more flexible, being constructed of rock or concrete piles, ideally with specially designed rock or block size distributions. Gordon and Cox (2018) examined the utility of coastal defence works under climate change and concluded that conventional seawalls are not readily adaptable and may be prone to catastrophic failures when subject to wave energies and storm surges exceeding their design limits. Revetments on the other hand are more flexible structures and therefore more readily adaptable.

FHWA (2014) also examined coastal damage mechanisms and the sensitivity of transportation assets to climate change, sea level rise, storms and extreme weather events. The following damage mechanisms were identified:

- Roadway damage by wave attack
- Roadway and railway damage by coastal 'weir flow'
- Roadway damage by erosion and shoreline recession
- Bridge deck damage by surges
- Structural damage by wave setup and wave runup
- Tunnel and roadway damage by overtopping and damage by tsunamis.

Subsequently, Knott et al., (2017) identified rises in groundwater levels in coastal zones as a further mechanism threatening damage to road pavements.

TABLE 6.4 Climate change risks and potential impacts to coastal transportation infrastructure.

		Potential impact on			
Climate change factor	**Risk**	**Road assets and operations**	**Rail assets and operations**	**Airport assets and operations**	**Seaport assets and operations**
Sea level rise	Increased areas exposed to erosion, storm tide and inundation	Inundation of low-lying roads causing increased delays, costs and damage Salt water intrusion onto roads Increased groundwater levels damaging road pavements Additional costs to protect and restore coastal roads from future erosion events	Inundation of low-lying rail tracks and infrastructure (yards, depots) causing increased delays, costs and damage Saltwater intrusion onto railways and facilities Increased groundwater levels damaging or weakening rail track formations Additional costs to protect and restore coastal rail from future erosion events	Inundation of low-lying facilities, including more permanent inundation of runways, taxiways and aprons Saltwater intrusion onto runways, taxiways and other facilities Increased groundwater levels damaging runway and taxiway pavements Additional costs to protect airport infrastructure from future erosion events	Exposure of structures to increased wave action and corrosive effects of saltwater Reduction in clearance between ships and booms affecting loading and unloading Changes to vessel clearance beneath overhead obstacles such as bridges and power lines Impacts on rail and road access and supply chains affecting port operations

Hurricanes, cyclones, storms and extreme weather events	Increased erosion, storm surge, storm tide and flash flooding events	Increased risk of erosion, storm tide, storm surge and flood damage to road infrastructure Degradation and failure of tunnel and bridge structures in coastal zone Delays and closure of roads leading to network severance and potential community isolation Increased maintenance and repair of damaged roadways Increased impacts on road drainage systems including silting and blockages of culverts Landslides, slope failures and embankment instability causing safety risks, damage and delays Reduced driver safety and slow movement during extreme weather, causing delays	Increased risk of erosion, storm tide, storm surge and flood damage to rail infrastructure Degradation and failure of tunnel and bridge structures in coastal zone Delays, service cancellations and reduced reliability due to inundation of track, drainage structures and infrastructure Increased likelihood of power outages Increased maintenance and repair of damaged railways Landslides, slope failures and embankment	Increased risk of erosion, storm tide, storm surge and flood damage to runways, taxiways, aprons and ground transportation access Suspension of operations with flow-on effects for passengers and supply chains Increased likelihood of power outages due to flooding of electrical facilities Increased impacts on airport drainage systems	Increased risk of erosion and wave damage to wharves and other portside facilities including container yards and bulk storage facilities Suspension of operations with flow-on effects for supply chains Increased likelihood of power outages due to flooding of electrical facilities Increased maintenance and repair costs, including emergency dredging following extreme events Increase impacts on port drainage

Continued

TABLE 6.4 Climate change risks and potential impacts to coastal transportation infrastructure.—cont'd

		Potential impact on			
Climate change factor	**Risk**	**Road assets and operations**	**Rail assets and operations**	**Airport assets and operations**	**Seaport assets and operations**
			instability causing safety risks, damage and delays Reduced traction and slow movement during extreme weather, causing delays, service cancellations and reduced reliability		systems Inundation, loss or escape of stockpiled cargoes and/or hazardous materials leading to adverse environmental impacts
	Increase in high winds	Unsafe driving conditions in exposed areas Debris blown onto roadway causing safety risks, damage and delays Damage to road furniture and signals	Wind damage to overhead catenary structures Increased likelihood of power outages affecting services Debris blown	Curtailment of operations or restrictions on runway operating modes leading to reduction in runway capacity and flight movements Suspension of ground handling operations due to safety concerns	Damage to cargo loading infrastructure and equipment such as cranes and gantries Stoppage of work when cranes, gantries and

			onto catenary, track or rolling stock causing safety risks, damage and delays Damage to signage and signals		other port infrastructure cannot be used above specified wind speeds Limited or no maritime navigation due to unsafe conditions, with flow-on effects on supply chains
	Increased thunderstorm activity and lightning strikes	Unsafe driving conditions Damage to roadways, bridges and other infrastructure from direct lightning strikes	Delays, cancellations and reduced service reliability due to direct lightning strikes on rail infrastructure and indirect strikes on electrical and communications equipment	Temporary suspension of operations Damage to electrical and communications equipment from direct and indirect lightning strikes, including airport lighting systems Damage to runways, taxiways and aprons from direct lightning strikes	Temporary suspension of operations Damage to electrical and communications equipment from lightning strikes

Derived and extended from Fisk, G.W., 2017. Climate Risks and Adaptation Pathways for Coastal Transport Infrastructure. Guidelines for Planning and Adaptive responses. National Climate Change Adaptation Research Facility, Gold Coast. www.nccarf.edu.au.

TABLE 6.5 Broad-scale climate change and environmental impacts for transportation assets located in a coastal zone as identified by NZTA (2017).

Impact on transportation assets in coastal zone	Effect of transportation asset on coastal environment
Inundation by storm tide reducing asset (bridge/culvert/road) availability for safe and efficient traffic operations	Wave deflection to neighbouring areas or changes in water flow causing erosion and inundation
Saturation and erosion of embankments/abutment/footings soils, leading to structural failure (including impacts of storm tides and wave action)	Increased deposition or erosion in channels around culverts and bridges, reducing hydraulic capacity
Chemical degradation of surfaces (paint/steel/wood) leading to more frequent maintenance or replacement	Habitat and biodiversity modification as a result of deposition/erosion changes in chemical characteristics and water movement
Instability and loss of formed areas associated with asset (e.g., landscaping, walls)	Environmental quality impacts, e.g., for water, beaches, mud flats and mangroves
Increased structural stress and degradation of engineering assets	

TABLE 6.6 Climate change and environmental impacts for specific transportation assets located in a coastal zone.

Transportation asset	Impact on transportation asset in coastal zone	Effect of transportation asset on coastal environment
Bridge	Salt water corrosion Structural damage from wave or wind energy Bridge scour due to coastal processes including waves, tides and storm surges	Heavy metal and oil pollution from surface runoff and windborne dust Damage to marine habitat Adverse effects on coastal ecology Modification of natural water flow pattern
Causeway	Inundation from storm surges and sea level rise Structural damage from wave energy	Heavy metal and oil pollution from surface runoff and windborne dust Adverse effects on coastal ecology Modification of natural water flow pattern

TABLE 6.6 Climate change and environmental impacts for specific transportation assets located in a coastal zone.—cont'd

Transportation asset	Impact on transportation asset in coastal zone	Effect of transportation asset on coastal environment
Crash barrier	Salt water corrosion Damage by shoreline erosion	Loss of natural landscape Adverse effects on visual quality and amenity of locality
Groyne	Structural damage from wave energy	Inhibit interaction between coastal marine and terrestrial systems
Lighting	Salt water corrosion Structural damage from wave or wind energy Damage by shoreline erosion	Light pollution – some marine life forms are vulnerable to light
Noise barrier	Salt water corrosion Structural damage from wave or wind energy	Loss of natural landscape Adverse effects on visual quality and amenity of locality
Pavement	Salt water corrosion Damage by shoreline erosion Inundation from storm surges and sea level rise Damage to pavement base and subbase from groundwater rise Sea spray	Heavy metal and oil pollution from surface runoff and windborne dust Adverse effects on coastal ecology and habitat
Pavement marking	Salt water corrosion	Adverse effects on coastal ecology due to contaminant discharges (e.g., dye chemicals)
Retaining wall	Salt water corrosion Structural damage from wave energy	Loss of natural landscape Adverse effects on visual quality and amenity of locality
Revetment	Structural damage from wave energy	Inhibit interaction between coastal marine and terrestrial systems Damage to or loss of marine habitat Adverse effects on coastal ecology
Roadway	Inundation from storm surges and sea level rise Damage by shoreline erosion	Heavy metal and oil pollution from surface runoff and windborne dust Adverse effects on coastal ecology

Continued

TABLE 6.6 Climate change and environmental impacts for specific transportation assets located in a coastal zone.—cont'd

Transportation asset	Impact on transportation asset in coastal zone	Effect of transportation asset on coastal environment
Seawall	Salt water corrosion Structural damage from wave energy	Inhibit interaction between coastal marine and terrestrial systems Damage to or loss of marine habitat Adverse effects on coastal ecology
Signage	Salt water corrosion Structural damage from wave or wind energy Damage by shoreline erosion	Loss of natural landscape Adverse effects on visual quality and amenity of locality
Tunnel	Inundation from storm surges and sea level rise	Heavy metal and oil pollution from surface runoff and windborne dust Damage to or loss of coastal flora and fauna

As derived and modified from NZTA, 2017. Coastal Effects Assessment Guideline for Transportation Infrastructure. Issue 004. New Zealand Transport Agency, Wellington, www.nzta.govt.nz.

The study by these authors is described in more detail in the case studies cited in Chapter 6.

One major transportation system and associated assets located on a coast or major water is the ports and harbours used for sea transportation. Implications for climate change adaptation for ports and harbours are the next subject for discussion in this chapter.

Ports and harbours

All low-lying coastal infrastructures are at risk from sea level rise. Ports and harbours by their very nature and location at the sea front or in estuaries close to the sea are especially exposed to sea level rise, storm surges and inundation and flooding. Port operations also require good access for land-based transportation, for the delivery and removal of goods. Ports are therefore vulnerable to potential damage to the infrastructure that provides land access. Ports are trade-dependent facilities and so port performance depends largely on regional and international trade patterns. If climate change affects those patterns, then the demand for services provided by a port may also change. Global supply chains may also be affected if port operations are compromised, e.g., by climate-induced effects.

Ports are thus major transportation hubs consisting of many components and utilise multiple service providers. Climate hazards may affect different port service providers and actors in different ways, so port vulnerability needs to be assessed in a multidimensional framework (Becker et al., 2013). Fig. 6.9, derived from PFI (2017), presents a view of port assets and operations and the land-side and marine-side influences that may affect port operations. Port operations and the infrastructure that supports these may be grouped into six categories:

- Goods handling and storage, the basic function of the port
- Built infrastructure, being the infrastructure, equipment and vehicles that enable the goods handling and storage and connect the port to the land-based transportation systems and networks
- Social performance, relating to the occupational health, welfare and safety of personnel directly or indirectly involved in port operations
- Environmental performance, concerned with the prevention of possible pollution or environmental damage emanating from port operations, including the handling of bulk hazardous materials (e.g., oil)
- Navigation, dredging and berthing, which concern safe and efficient ship movements into and at the port
- Insurance and finance, concerned with asset protection and maintenance – for both goods and the port infrastructure.

On the land side, the port is a focal point in multiple supply chains for industry and commerce. It requires efficient long-term land transport access, power supply and water supply. On the marine side, the port is subject to

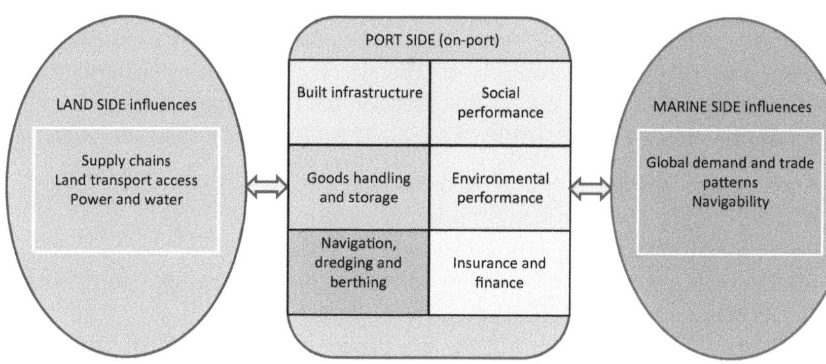

FIGURE 6.9 The influences on port assets and operations that are potentially at risk from climate change and extreme weather events. *Derived from PFI, 2017. Building Port Resilience to Climate Change – Some Practical Tools. Port Finance International. http://www.portfinanceinternational.com/categories/outlook-forecast/item/2561-building-port-resilience-to-climate-change-%5f-some-practical-tools. (Accessed 7 June 2018).*

global demands and trade patterns and requires maintenance of good navigability to allow vessels to enter and leave the port easily.

Climate change and extreme weather events may have both short-term and long-term impacts on port operations. Stenek et al., (2011) identified the following set of major risks to climate change faced by ports:

- Ports have long life times and thus stand to face considerable climate change
- Being located on coasts, rivers or lakes, they are often exposed to many climate hazards, including sea level rise, storm surges, extreme winds and waves, inundation and riverine flooding
- Shipping movements into and out of a port may be affected by adverse climatic conditions, causing delays to port operations and potential disruptions to supply chains
- Ports are vulnerable to the economic impacts of climate change, especially through impacts on global demands
- Ports often tranship goods that are climate sensitive – in both demand and supply – such as agricultural produce and fuels
- Inland movement of goods from ports depends on transportation infrastructure, managed by other organisations and agencies and which is itself vulnerable to climate change
- Ports are vulnerable to disruptions in utilities such as water and power. Water supply and power supply are themselves vulnerable to climate change, so decreased reliability of these utilities stemming from climate change is then a risk to the port.

Fig. 6.10 summarises the risks to port operations and services discussed by Stenek et al., (2011).

In terms of transportation, particular aspects of port operations at risk from climate hazards thus include navigation, berthing, goods handling and storage, vehicle movement and vehicle storage. Climate change is likely to impact each of these port subsystems similarly to the ways it will impact (land) transportation more generally – and as discussed in the following Chapters 6 and 7. For example, citing ITF (2016):

- Asphalt surfaces are prone to heat damage
- Rail tracks are prone to buckling under extreme heat
- Port superstructures are exposed to wind damage
- Embankments and abutments may be eroded by wave action, storm surges and flooding
- Electrical power and other utilities are prone to damage or disruption from flooding, high winds and extreme heat.

In addition, port operations may need to be suspended during storms, high winds or heat waves. Concrete materials may be subject to accelerated rates of carbonation or chloride-induced corrosion (Scott et al., 2013). Adaptation

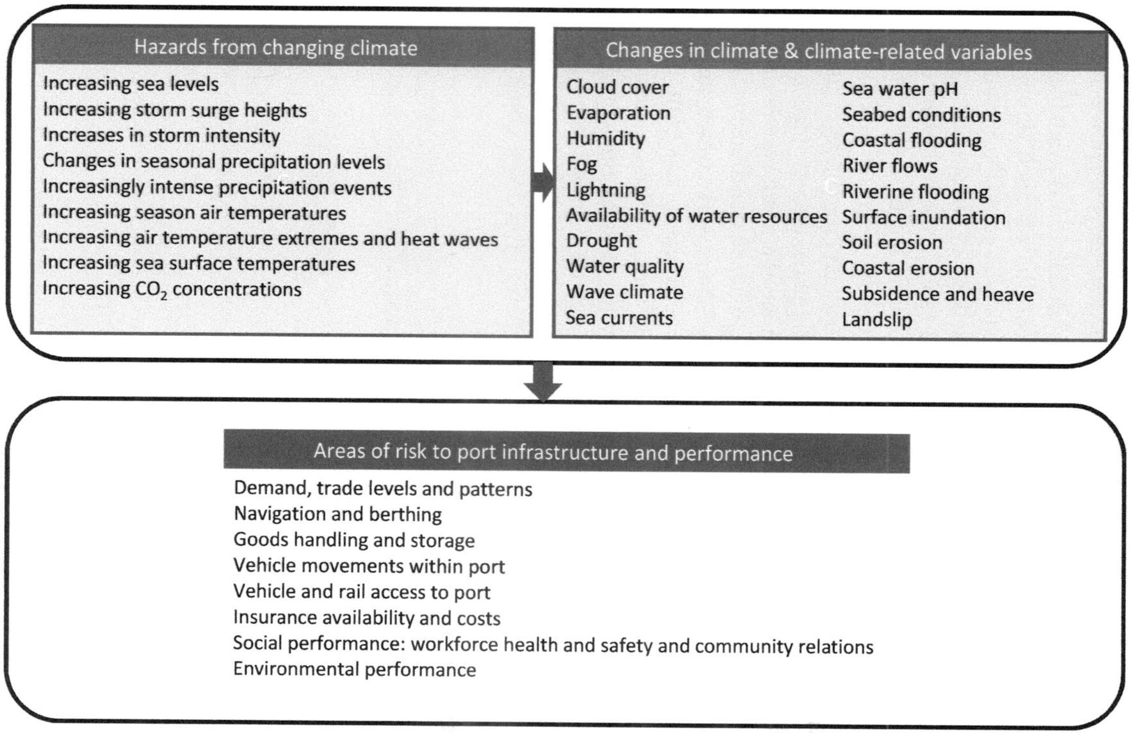

FIGURE 6.10 Climate change hazards and consequent changes in climate-related variables and the corresponding risks to port operations and services. *After Stenek, V., Amado, J.-C., Connell, R., Palin, O., Wright, S., Pope, B., Hunter, J., McGregor, J., Morgan, W., Stanley, B., Washington, R., Liverman, D., Sherwin, H., Kapelus, P., Andrade, C., Pabón, J.-D., 2011. Climate Risks and Business Ports. Terminal Marítimo Muelles El Bosque Cartagena, Columbia. International Finance Corporation. World Bank Group, Washington DC.*

plans and measures are thus required. PFI (2017) outlined a basic process for adaptation of ports to climate change impacts, for both

1. Existing port assets, where the broad strategies are protect, accommodate or retreat and
2. New port assets, where the strategies would avoid, accommodate or accept.

Fig. 6.11 summarises these strategies and the broad actions available under each of them. For existing ports, protection may be obtained through the installation or reinforcement of hard structure such as seawalls, breakwaters and groynes. Complete retreat implying abandonment of the port may not be realistic, but might rather involve sacrificing an asset at the end of its design life, and its replacement by another asset in a different location. New assets in new (greenfield) locations can be viewed differently, with the avoid option including modification of the land surface to allow (say) for sea level rise, but where new assets are intended as in-fill at existing ports, then avoidance is not possible and so accommodation and acceptance are the available options.

Scott et al., (2013) proposed a climate change adaptation framework specifically designed for ports. Fig. 6.12 shows this framework, which involves six major phases with multiple tasks in each. The framework is built around the notion that any port will develop, possess and use a port risk management system (PRMS), and so adaptation planning and its considerations of climate change risks and infrastructure vulnerabilities to those risks will be incorporated into the PRMS. In addition, the framework includes both 'top-down' and 'bottom-up' communications and information flows. Top-down components

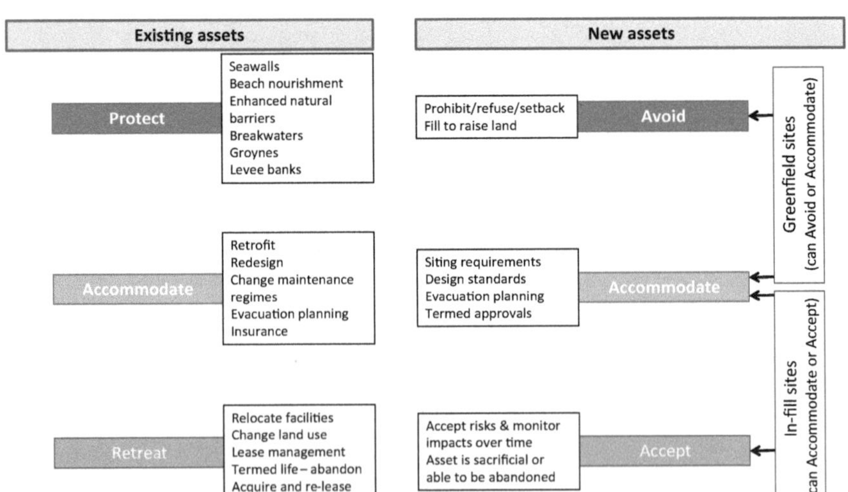

FIGURE 6.11 Resilience and adaptation options for existing and new port assets as proposed by PFI (2017).

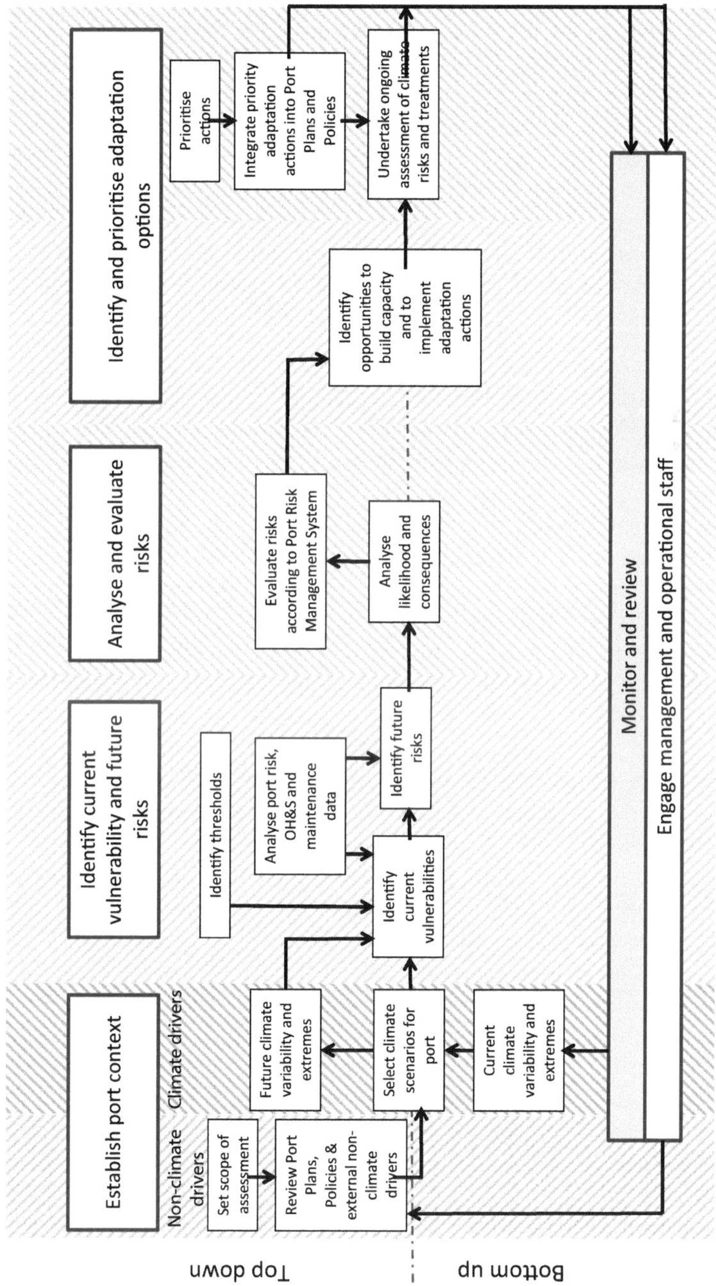

FIGURE 6.12 Port adaptation framework based on that proposed by Scott et al., (2013).

involve the sitting of adaptation plans and actions within the scope of strategies, policies and plans under which the port authority operates. Bottom-up components involve the input and interpretation of information relating to port operations and climate hazards provided by port personnel. Monitoring and review and the engagement of management and operational staff are two of the major phases in the framework, and both apply to the bottom-up components of the framework. These two phases also provide the ongoing feedback that lead to the framework representing an ongoing process — a necessity in an environment, such as climate change, wrought with uncertainties that will only be fully resolved over time.

The six phases in the framework of Fig. 6.12, along with their associated tasks, are as follows:

1. The establishment of the appropriate context for the particular port. This involves consideration of nonclimate planning and management drivers by first determining the proper scope of the risk assessment and the review of the plans, policies and objectives under which the port seeks to operate. Climate drivers are also considered, stemming from review of the current climate variability and weather extremes affecting the port. This information allows the port planner to select relevant future climate scenarios for the port and estimate the future climate variability and weather extremes associated with each of the scenarios.
2. The identification of current vulnerability to climate factors and the risks associated with projected future climate under the selected scenarios. This requires specification of threshold values (e.g., wind speeds, wave heights, precipitation intensities) that would affect port operations and place infrastructure assets and personnel at risk. Port risk assessment can be made using the information provided by the PRMS about port operations and vulnerabilities under historical weather events.
3. Analysis and evaluation of risks. Given the identified future risks and assessment of their likelihood, consequences can be undertaken and the results of the analysis evaluated using the PRMS. Identification and prioritisation of adaptation options: In this phase the planner seeks to identify the opportunities to build adaptation capacity for the port, including the human resources, assets and infrastructure to manage the expected impacts of climate change. This includes executive risk and climate awareness training specifically targeting executive level management at ports; training on how to adapt organisational management systems to incorporate climate considerations; climate risk management training; general climate risk awareness training for management, administrative and frontline staff, and working with specialist port personnel to help them identify and find appropriate climate information, interpret and analyse the data.
4. The identification and prioritisation of adaptation options. This involves the use of assessment tools such as benefit—cost analysis and multicriteria

analysis, as described in Chapters 3 and 4, to evaluate and rank feasible options and select the preferred options. These options then need to be integrated into the port's plans and policies.

5. Monitoring and review of implemented adaptation plans and actions. This provides a growing level of corporate knowledge and expertise about the risks applying to the port, the degree of success of the implementations and, over time, the actual course of climate change occurring at the port. This information is fed back to inform the ongoing adaptation process.
6. Engagement of managerial and operation staff. This essential phase is ongoing throughout the adaptation process, not only to facilitate the ongoing implementation of plans and actions but also to foster ownership of these and provide for the bottom-up inputs that are a vital part of the framework itself.

A number of port-related case studies have been reported in recent years. These include

- the development of a comprehensive climate change adaptation plan for the Port of Felixstowe, UK (FDRC, 2015),
- the simulation of container port operations under the impact of extreme weather events (Chhethri et al., 2016), using Port Botany, Australia, as the case study and
- planning of the optimal installation of levee banks in San Francisco Bay as protection against sea level rise (Papakonstantinou et al., 2019).

Summary

Coastal regions stand out as a primary area of concern for the impacts of climate change and the needs for adaptation of transportation assets and infrastructure. Thus Chapter 6 focused on these regions. Sea level rise and its implications are the underlying issues with respect to climate change, manifest particularly in the increasing effects of storms, surges and flooding, and resultant coastal damage. Damage includes specific threats to network components located in close proximity to the coast. Thus the transportation facilities and structures in these areas, and their components and the materials they are constructed from, are of interest. Susceptibility to corrosion and water damage for these structures is well known, but a changing climate may lead to new requirements to guard against these, both in intensity and in coverage. Ports and harbours are of necessity located in coastal areas, as are many airports, so the infrastructure requirements and potential climate impacts on these were discussed, including citation of some recent case studies.

References

Becker, A., Acciaro, M., Asariotis, R., Carera, E., Cretegny, L., Crist, P., Esteban, M., Mather, A., Messner, S., Naruse, S., Ng, A.K.Y., Rahmstorf, S., Savonis, M., Song, D., Stenek, V., Velegrakis, A.F., 2013. A note on climate change adaptation for seaports: a challenge for global ports, a challenge for global society. Clim. Change 120 (4), 683–695.

Booij, N., Ris, R.C., Holthuijsen, L.H., 1999. A third-generation wave model for coastal regions. I-model description and validation. J. Geophys. Res. 104 (C4), 7649–7666.

Buttolph, A.M., Reed, C.W., Kraus, N.C., Ono, N., Larson, M., Camenen, B., Hanson, H., Wamsley, T., Zundel, A.K., 2006. Two-Dimensional Depth-Averaged Circulation Model CMS-M2D: Version 3.0, Report 2, Sediment Transport and Morphology Change. Technical Report ERDC/CHL-TR-06-9. Engineer Research and Development Center, Vicksburg, MS.

Cechet, R.P., Taylor, P., Griffin, C., Hazelwood, M., 2011. Australia's Coastline: Adapting to Climate Change. Assessing Infrastructure Vulnerability to Rising sea-levels. AusGeo News, Issue 101. Geoscience Australia, Canberra. www.ga.gov.au/ausgeonews.

Chen, K., McAneney, J., 2006. High resolution estimates of Australia's coastal population. Geophys. Res. Lett. 33, L16601. https://doi.org/10.1029/2006GL026981.

Chen, C., Beardsley, R.C., Cowles, G., 2006. An unstructured grid, finite-volume coastal ocean model (FVCOM) system. Oceanography 19 (1), 78–89.

Chhetri, P., Jayatilleke, G.B., Gekara, V.O., Manzoni, A., Corbitt, B., 2016. Container terminal operations simulator (CTOS) – simulating the impact of extreme weather events on port operation. Eur. J. Transp. Infrastruct. Res. 16 (1), 195–213.

CoastAdapt, 2018. How to Conduct a Climate Change Risk Assessment. https://coastadapt.com.au/how-to-pages/how-to-conduct-a-climate-change-risk-assessment. (Accessed 29 February 2020).

DCC, 2009. Climate Change Risks to Australia's Coast: A First Pass National Assessment. Department of Climate Change, Canberra. http://www.environment.gov.au/climate-change.

DEHP, 2013. Coastal hazard technical guide: determining coastal hazard areas. In: Report to Queensland Department of Environment and Heritage Protection, Brisbane. https://www.ehp.qld.gov.au.

DES, 2018. A Guide to 'Good Practice' Storm Tide Inundation Mapping and Modelling. Department of Environment and Science, Queensland Government, Brisbane. https://www.publications.qld.gov.au/dataset/19c20822-f29e-494c-880a-113ccd13a04b/resource/93336e30-e1fd-4a1e-89e8-b4056692e26c/fs_download/storm-tide-inundation-guidelines.pdf. (Accessed 19 February 2020).

Dietrich, J.C., Zijlema, M., Westerink, J.J., Holthuijsen, L.H., Dawson, C., Luettich Jr., R.A., Stone, G.W., 2011. Modeling hurricane waves and storm surge using integrally-coupled, scalable computations. Coast. Eng. 58 (1), 45–65.

FDRC, 2015. The Port of Felixstowe: Climate Change Adaptation Report. Felixstowe Dock and Railway Company, Felixstowe. https://assets.publishing.service.gov.uk/government/uploads/system/uploads/attachment_data/file/530910/climate-adrep-port-felixstowe.pdf. (Accessed 15 March 2018).

FEMA, 2007. CHAMP: Coastal Flood Hazard Analysis Modeling Program, version 2.0. http://www.fema.gov/national-flood-insurance-program-flood-hazard-mapping/coastal-hazardanalysis-modeling-program.

FHWA, 2014. Highways in the coastal environment: assessing extreme events. Hydraulic Engineering Circular No 25 – Volume 2. Federal Highways Administration, Washington DC report FHWA-NHI-14-006. https://www.fhwa.dot.gov/engineering/hydraulics/pubs/nhi14006/nhi14006.pdf.

FHWA, 2009. Vulnerability Assessment and Adaptation Framework, third ed. Federal Highways Administration, Washington DC https://www.fhwa.dot.gov/environment/sustainability/resilience/adaptation_framework/chap00.cfm.

Fisk, G.W., 2017. Climate Risks and Adaptation Pathways for Coastal Transport Infrastructure. Guidelines for Planning and Adaptive Responses. National Climate Change Adaptation Research Facility, Gold Coast. www.nccarf.edu.au.

Gallien, T.W., Sanders, B.F., Flick, R.E., 2014. Urban coastal flood prediction: integrating wave overtopping, flood defenses and drainage. Coast. Eng. 91, 18–28.

Glahn, B., Taylor, A., Kurkowski, N., Shaffer, W.A., 2009. The role of the SLOSH model in national weather service storm surge forecasting. Natl. Weather Digest 35 (1), 3–14.

Gordon, A.D., Cox, R.J., 2018. Adaptive coastal defence works. Proceedings NCCARF 2018 Conference, Melbourne, 8–10 May. National Climate Change Adaptation Research Facility. Griffith University, Brisbane. http://climateadaptation2018.com.au/conference-papers.

Group, T.W., 1988. The WAM model – a third generation ocean wave prediction model. J. Phys. Oceanogr. 18 (12), 1775–1810.

Hansen, J.E., 2016. The Use of Modelling Tools to Assess Local Scale Inundation and Erosion Risk. CoastAdapt, National Climate Change Adaptation Research Facility, Gold Coast. https://coastadapt.com.au/use-modelling-tools-assess-local-scale-inundation-and-erosion-risk. (Accessed 19 February 2020).

IPCC, 2018. Global Warming of 1.5°C. Special Report 15, UN International Committee on Climate Change. www.ipcc.ch/report/sr15/.

ITF, 2016. Adapting transport to climate change and extreme weather: implications for infrastructure owners and network managers, ITF Research Reports. OECD Publishing, Paris. https://doi.org/10.1787/9789282108079-en.

Johnson, B.H., Heath, R.E., Hsieh, H.H., Kim, K.W., Butler, H.L., 1991. Development and Verification of A Three-Dimensional Numerical Hydrodynamic, Salinity and Temperature Model of Chesapeake Bay; Volume I, Main Text and Appendix D. US Army Engineer Waterways Experiment Station, Vicksburg, MS. Technical Report HL-91-7.

Johnson, B.D., Kobayashi, N., Gravens, M.B., 2012. Cross-shore Numerical Model CSHORE for Waves, Currents, Sediment Transport and Beach Profile Evolution. Final Report ERDC/CHL-12-22. US Army Engineer Waterways Experiment Station, Vicksburg, MS.

Kim, S.C., Chen, J., Shaffer, W.A., January 1996. An operational forecast model for extratropical storm surges along the US east coast. In: Preprints, Conference on Oceanic and Atmospheric Prediction. American Meteorology Society, Atlanta, GA, pp. 281–286.

Knott, J.F., Elshaer, M., Daniel, J.S., Jacobs, J.M., Kirshen, P., 2017. Assessing the effects of rising groundwater from sea level rise on the service life of pavements in coastal road infrastructure. Transp. Res. Rec. 2639, 1–10.

Kriebel, D.L., 1986. Verification study of a dune erosion model. Shore Beach 54 (3), 13–21.

Kriebel, D.L., Dean, R.G., 1985. Numerical simulation of time-dependent beach and dune erosion. Coast. Eng. 9 (3), 221–245.

Larson, M., Kraus, N.C., 1989. SBEACH: Numerical Model for Simulating Storm-Induced Beach Change. Report 1. Empirical Foundation and Model Development. Coastal Engineering Research Center, Vicksburg, MS. Technical Report CERC-TR-89-9.

Larson, M., Kraus, N.C., Byrnes, M.R., 1990. SBEACH: Numerical Model for Simulating Storm-Induced Beach Change. Report 2. Numerical Formulation and Model Tests. Coastal Engineering Research Center, Vicksburg, MS. Technical Report CERC-TR-89-9.

Lincke, D., Hinkel, J., 2018. Economically robust protection against 21st century sea-level rise. Glob. Environ. Change 51, 67–73.

Luettich Jr., R.A., Westerink, J.J., Scheffner, N.W., 1992. ADCIRC: An Advanced Three-Dimensional Circulation Model for Shelves, Coasts and Estuaries. Report 1. Theory and Methodology of ADCIRC-2DDI and ADCIRC-3DL. Coastal Engineering Research Center, Vicksburg, MS. Technical Report CERC-DRP-92-6.

Nancollas, T., 2018. Seashaken Houses: A Lighthouse History from Eddystone to Fastnet. Particular Books, London).

NZTA, 2017. Coastal Effects Assessment Guideline for Transportation Infrastructure. Issue 004. New Zealand Transport Agency, Wellington. www.nzta.govt.nz.

OECD, 2019. Responding to Rising Seas: OECD Country Approaches to Tackling Coastal risks. Policy Highlights. Organisation for Economic Cooperation and Development, Paris.

Papakonstantinou, I., Lee, J., Madanat, S.M., 2019. Optimal levee installation planning for highway infrastructure protection against sea level rise. Transp. Res. D Transp. Environ. 77, 378–389.

PFI, 2017. Building Port Resilience to Climate Change – Some Practical Tools. Port Finance International. http://www.portfinanceinternational.com/categories/outlook-forecast/item/2561-building-port-resilience-to-climate-change-%5F-some-practical-tools. (Accessed 7 June 2018).

Ris, R.C., Holthuijsen, L.H., Booij, N., 1999. A third-generation wave model for coastal regions: 2. verification. J. Geophys. Res. 104 (C4), 7667–7681.

Roelvink, D., Reniers, A., van Dongeren, A., van Thiel de Vries, J., McCall, R., Lescinski, J., 2009. Modelling storm impacts on beaches, dunes and barrier islands. Coast. Eng. 56 (11), 1133–1152.

Savioli, J., Pedersen, C., Szylkarski, S., Kerper, D., 2003. Modelling the threat of tropical cyclone storm tide to the Burdekin Shire, Queensland Australia. In: Kench, P.S., Hume, T.M. (Eds.), Coasts & Ports 2003 Australasian Conference : Proceedings of the 16th Australasian Coastal and Ocean Engineering Conference, the 9th Australasian Port and Harbour Conference and the Annual New Zealand Coastal Society Conference. Barton, ACT. Institution of Engineers, Australia, pp. 285–292.

Scott, H., McEvoy, D., Chhetri, P., Basic, F., Mullett, J., 2013. Climate Change Adaptation Guidelines for Ports. Enhancing the Resilience of Seaports to a Changing Climate Report Series. National Climate Change Adaptation Research Facility, Gold Coast. www.nccarf.edu.au.

Sheng, Y.P., 1990. Evolution of a three-dimensional curvilinear-grid hydrodynamic model for estuaries, lakes and coastal waters: CH3D. In: Estuarine and Coastal Modeling. American Society of Civil Engineers, NY, pp. 40–49.

Smith, J.M., Sherlock, A.R., Resio, D.T., 2001. STWAVE: Steady-State Wave Model User's Manual for STWAVE, Version 3.0. Special Report CHL SR-01-1. US Army Engineer Research and Development Center, Vicksburg, MS.

Stenek, V., Amado, J.-C., Connell, R., Palin, O., Wright, S., Pope, B., Hunter, J., McGregor, J., Morgan, W., Stanley, B., Washington, R., Liverman, D., Sherwin, H., Kapelus, P., Andrade, C., Pabón, J.-D., 2011. Climate Risks and Business Ports. Terminal Marítimo Muelles El Bosque Cartagena, Columbia. International Finance Corporation. World Bank Group, Washington DC.

Vatvani, D., Zweers, N., van Ormondt, M., Smale, A., de Vries, H., Makin, V., 2012. Storm surge and wave simulations in the gulf of Mexico using a consistent drag relation for atmospheric and storm surge models. Nat. Hazards Earth Syst. Sci. 1, 2399–2410.

Chapter 7

Road transportation systems

This chapter considers road transportation, with a particular focus on road pavements. The road network is a vital and valuable asset, and in many places provides the basic conduit for people movement, goods transport and even communications. As indicated earlier in this book, road network infrastructure also supports other infrastructure systems, such as water, power, wastewater and telecommunications. This may be done directly, when multiple infrastructure systems share a specific asset such as a bridge, or indirectly, such as when the road network provides the means by which maintenance and inspection crews can gain access to other infrastructure systems. In rural and regional areas, the road network may indeed provide the only available transportation system for business and social activities, with outlying communities completely dependent on it. In urban areas, there will be alternatives for mobility, such as public transit, but the road network still provides access to all properties.

The road network is a valuable asset, perhaps the most valuable asset in public hands in any society. The US Bureau of Transportation Statistics estimated that the US road network had an asset value of $3.483 trillion in 2016 (BTS, 2018). This network included 76,334 km of major highways, more than 3.7 million km of other sealed roads, and about 3.0 million km of unsealed roads for a total road length exceeding 6.5 million km. Australia, occupying about the same geographical area as the continental United States but with only one 13th of the population, had 874,142 km of roads (2945 km of major highway, 378,240 km of other sealed roads and 492,958 km of unsealed roads) in 2015 (BITRE, 2017). The asset value of the Australian road network was then about $160 billion, and it was the largest public asset in the nation (Austroads, 2018), worth about $6800 per head of population (the equivalent per capita value for the United States was about $10,500).

The bulk of the road network comprises road pavement. Earlier chapters of this book have considered climate change impacts on major transportation

Climate Change Adaptation for Transportation Systems. https://doi.org/10.1016/B978-0-12-816638-3.00007-6

infrastructure facilities, such as tunnels and bridges, that are common to all land-based transportation systems. This chapter considers the mundane but vital asset of road pavement. Pavements come in many forms — flexible and rigid pavements, sealed and unsealed pavements — but all share a common goal; to provide for safe, efficient and continuous traffic operations under a wide range of environmental conditions.

The following sections of this chapter consider the basic structure of roads and the place of the road pavement in that structure. The importance of structural integrity of the pavement so that it can carry the expected traffic loads is explored, and the contribution of the road pavement to safe and efficient traffic operations is discussed. The potential damage to pavements and traffic performance from water penetration into the pavement is highlighted, and this may be used to examine the potential climate change impacts on pavement performance. Modelling of road pavement performance is an important facet in pavement design and in the monitoring of traffic performance. The introduction of a specific climate variable — the Thornthwaite Moisture Index (TMI) — into this modelling is described as a convenient and powerful way to explicitly include climate impacts in the study of pavement performance. This chapter includes a detailed case study investigation of pavement performance for a road traversing a wide range of climates and under a number of different climate change scenarios, using the TMI to represent the present and future climates. It also reviews some other case study investigations of climate change impacts on road pavements.

Roads and pavements

A useful starting point for consideration of road pavements is to look at the basic composition of a modern road. Fig. 7.1 provides a schematic view of a simple road cross section, showing the roadway situated in natural landscape. This is a road in a rural area, but its main features are the same as roads in urban areas and as those of freeways and highways. In Fig. 7.1, the natural surface of the road slopes from left to right, so that the left-hand part of the road cross section is in cut (below the natural surface level), while the right-hand part lies on a compacted fill embankment. The roadway fits into the overall formation width of the road, which itself lies in the right of way (road reserve). This contains all of the earthworks associated with the road, so that the whole road structure is separate from the abutting properties. A road pavement is classified in one of two ways: flexible or rigid. This depends on the materials used in the pavement. A flexible pavement is composed of unbound granular materials, possibly stabilised (e.g., through the injection of cement into the material) and/or asphalt.[1] A rigid pavement is constructed

1. Asphalt, sometimes known as bituminous concrete, may be used in all layers of the pavement or may just be used as the wearing course.

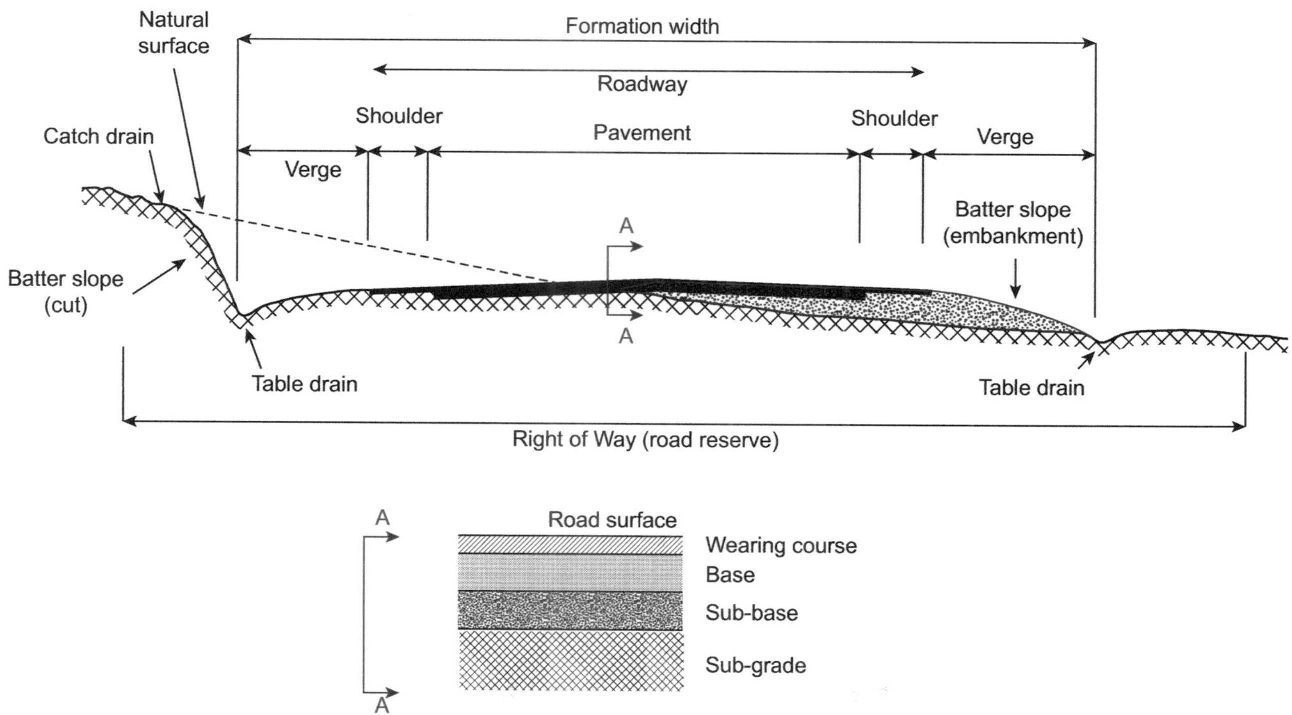

FIGURE 7.1 Cross section for a simple rural road, showing the roadway (pavement and shoulders), formation width and drainage provisions all located in the road reserve. The cross section contains a section A-A showing the pavement structure (wearing course, base, subbase and subgrade).

using concrete pavement with expansion joints and steel reinforcement. All pavement structures other than those categorised as rigid pavements are termed as flexible, including unbound pavements with thin bituminous surfaces and bound pavements. They are designed and generally constructed in continuous form without formal joints. Mechanistic design methods using elastic layer modelling are now widely used for pavements incorporating a bound layer or full depth asphalt pavement (Austroads, 2005; AASHTO, 2015). This approach is based on the stiffness (modulus) properties of continuous layers. Older empirically based methods are still used in the case of unbound granular pavement with a thin bituminous seal (Austroads, 2005). The empirically based method relies strongly on laboratory test results for the materials to be used in the pavement. Austroads (2005) describes a rigid pavement as consisting of a relatively high strength concrete base (generally 30 MPa or more) and one of a range of subbase materials (lean mix concrete, cement-stabilised crushed rock, unbound granular material). Concrete base formats may be jointed unreinforced, jointed reinforced, continuously reinforced and steel fibre reinforced. Most rigid pavements have jointing systems sealed against moisture. In the case of continuously reinforced concrete pavements, there are longitudinal joints, but no regular transverse joints for shrinkage and thermal strains.

There are important details to note in Fig. 7.1. The first of these is the provisions made for drainage. A catch drain at the top of the cut is there to prevent runoff from the abutting property travelling down the cut slope and potentially on to the roadway. Table drains on either side of the roadway are intended to remove runoff from the roadway, so that no water residue should be present on the pavement. These drains would be part of a drainage system, probably including culverts at some points along the road, for the removal of water runoff. Water penetration into the pavement structure would lead to potential damage and degradation of the pavement. Water caught on the road surface could reduce the adhesive traction between vehicle tyres and the road surface, leading to safety hazards through reduced braking ability and perhaps skidding. Should any such water freeze and hence turn to ice on the roadway, these hazards would increase substantially.

The second detail from Fig. 7.1 is section A-A through the road pavement, indicating the pavement structure and its components. These components are for a flexible pavement and from bottom to top

- The subgrade, usually formed from the (compacted) natural material on which the road is constructed but sometimes – especially for roads bearing very heavy traffic loads – composed of selected imported material
- The subbase, which for a flexible pavement is a load carrying course of lower quality to the material in the base above it. The choice of this

material (and hence the existence of a separate subbase) depends on the economics of the road construction and the anticipated lower stress levels than those expected nearer the pavement surface. The subbase is designed to provide adequate support for the base and reduce the stresses and strains applied to the subgrade. The subbase may also act as a barrier to reduce the pumping of subgrade fines through joints or cracks into the base and wearing course of a pavement resulting from traffic loads or groundwater pressure

- The base, which is the main 'load carrying' course within the pavement. The base course may be bound, e.g., comprise bituminous concrete and thus be of similar type if of different material composition such as aggregate size to the wearing course, or be unbound[2]
- The wearing course, which is intended to withstand the prevailing load and environmental impacts (e.g., moisture and dust) and provide a safe and functional riding surface with reduced moisture spray and noise, and protect the underlying pavement courses (base, subbase and subgrade) from moisture penetration. Three common types of wearing courses are sprayed (chip) seals, asphalt (bituminous concrete) and concrete.

In the case of a rigid road pavement, a similar structure would exist. The wearing course is either concrete or a bituminous concrete layer placed on top of the base. The thickness of the concrete base will vary according to the type of shoulder and the joint and reinforcement details employed. Many road agencies (e.g., Austroads (2005)) recommend the inclusion of a bound or lean mix concrete subbase to provide uniform support under the base, enhance load transfer across joints and assist in the control of shrinkage and swelling of reactive subgrade soils (when these exist).

Pavement integrity

Road pavements have a finite life; indeed they are designed to eventually wear out. The general failure mode for a pavement is fatigue failure, due to the imposition and removal of heavy loads on the pavement (i.e., the loads are applied cyclically). These loads are primarily due to heavy goods vehicles. Each load occurs with the transmission of the wheel load from the tyres of a

2. An unbound base course comprises materials which are granular or mechanically stabilised or treated with binders to improve properties other than strength (e.g., plasticity). An unbound base course behaves as if its component parts were not bound together although significant mechanical interlock can occur. In the majority of cases, an unbound granular base course is provided under a sprayed seal surface. Stabilisation of the base material is used to improve the quality of the base. The most common stabiliser used with unbound granular materials is cement. In rural applications, a sprayed seal surfacing is generally applied over the stabilised base.

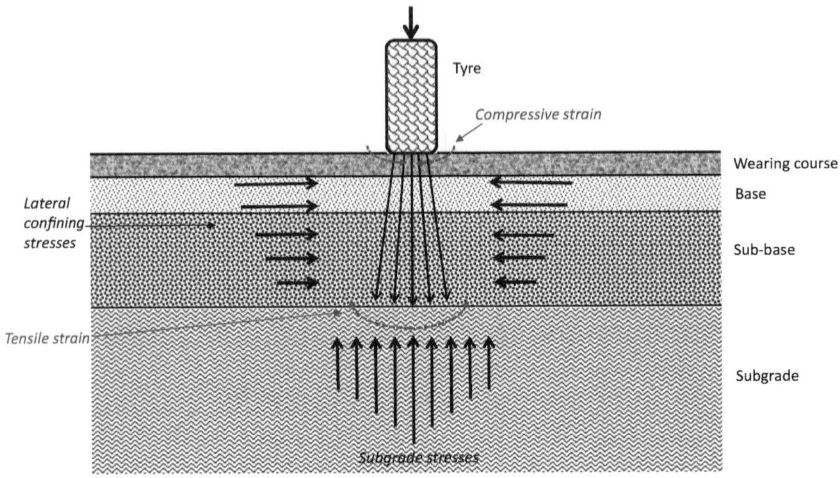

FIGURE 7.2 Transmission of vehicle load to a flexible road pavement and the distributions of stresses and strains associated with that load.

vehicle into the pavement, as indicated in Fig. 7.2. The cumulative number of (standard) axle loads applied to the pavement is the design load.[3]

Fig. 7.2 indicates the dispersion of the wheel load into the pavement and the vertical and horizontal stresses generated in the pavement to support the load and thus maintain an equilibrium of forces. Compressive strains occur in the top section of the pavement, with tensile strains towards the bottom. The strength of the materials in the base, subbase and subgrade – and hence the ability of the pavement to generate and maintain the required levels of stress to cope with the traffic load – depends to a large degree on the moisture content in the materials. An optimum moisture content will have been applied in the design and initial construction of the pavement. Water penetration into the pavement structure – from above, below or laterally – during the operational life of the pavement will have a detrimental effect on pavement performance. Such penetration and the change of moisture content in the pavement layers stands to be a significant potential impact from climate change. In addition, the frequency of occurrence and severity of storms and flash flooding may lead to

3. A rule of thumb commonly applied for the impact of an axle load on a pavement is the 'fourth power rule', which indicates that the relative damage caused to the pavement is proportional to the individual axle load raised to the fourth power (i.e., a quartic relationship between load and impact). This rule emphasises the damaging role of the most heavily laden axles on the pavement (and is perhaps more important as a concept than as a definite mathematical relationship between axle load and pavement damage). Pavement design includes the (cumulative) number of 'equivalent standard axles' (ESA) applied to the pavement over time, where one ESA is taken as a dual-wheeled (4-tyre) axle transmitting a load of 80 kiloNewton (KN) on to the road pavement surface. See Austroads (2008) for more details.

washouts (e.g., at culverts along the road, or other locations where volumes of water may accumulate).

Road pavements have expected service lives of the order of 15–30 years, depending on the traffic loads experienced (i.e., cumulative number of Equivalent Standard Axles (ESA)), the maintenance regime used and environmental conditions. The pavement will be in its best condition just after construction, and will deteriorate thereafter. Pavement condition can be assessed in terms of riding quality, roughness and the incidence of cracking, potholing and undulation. One scientific measure of pavement quality, the International Roughness Index (IRI), is used later in this chapter in mathematical modelling of pavement condition over time. Fig. 7.3 provides a generalised schematic picture of pavement performance over time.

This figure shows the deterioration of the pavement over time, which will lead to increase road operating costs for traffic. At some stage, the pavement will require major rehabilitation (e.g., resurfacing, refurbishment or even reconstruction) which will extend its service life, although the rehabilitated pavement would probably never be quite as good as its initial state. There are different levels at which intervention to refurbish the pavement could be undertaken, with an optimum level such that the costs of refurbishment are balanced by the prevention of further increases in vehicle operating costs. If the road is left without the required level of restoration, it will eventually

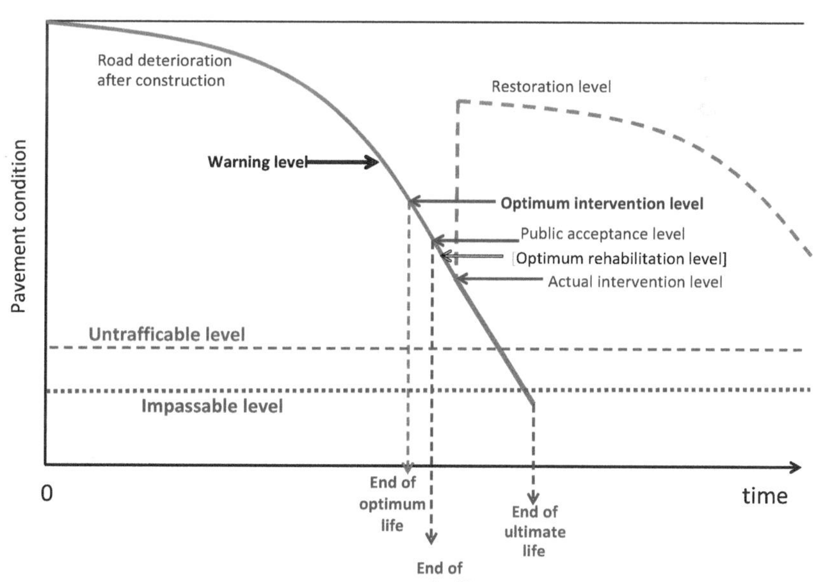

FIGURE 7.3 Schematic view of road pavement performance over time, showing different levels of acceptable and unacceptable performance and the impact of pavement restoration through resurfacing, refurbishment or reconstruction.

become untrafficable and ultimately impassable. Policy decisions are needed about the design standards for construction, maintenance and restoration of the road, and these decisions may even include abandoning the road in some circumstances. Climate change impacts stand to have strong implications in the policy decisions.

Traffic operations

Safe and efficient traffic operations are the main service function to be provided by the road and its pavement. As indicated above, deteriorating pavement condition leads to increased vehicle operating costs. These costs include travel time, riding comfort, vehicle maintenance and service expenses, and fuel costs. Pavement deterioration will be seen as increased roughness, undulations, rutting, cracking, heaving, potholing and bleeding. Bleeding occurs when – generally under thermal stresses – the bitumen binder in the base and/or wearing course separates from the aggregates and percolates to the road surface. The result may be that the slipperiness of the road surface will increase – meaning a reduction in the skid resistance of the road. A more slippery road surface may also result from the polishing of the aggregate in the wearing course.

Herein is a major safety problem. Road traffic operates through the adhesion between vehicle tyres and the road surface. This is vital for both vehicle braking and for cornering. The friction coefficients between the tyres and the road provide the necessary restorative forces to enable vehicles to stop safely and to negotiate bends in the road. Of course, these friction coefficients are also affected by the presence of water – and, more seriously, ice – on the road. A basic design parameter in the geometric design of roads is the Stopping Sight Distance (SSD), which applies to both vertical and horizontal road alignments – how far over the crest of a hill, or how far around the next bend, can the driver see. Fig. 7.4 displays this sight distance concept for vertical and horizontal alignments.

SSD is the minimum sight distance ahead of a vehicle, travelling at the road design speed *V*, such that the vehicle can stop safely to avoid a collision with a fixed object lying on the road. SSD has two components:

1. The distance travelled by the vehicle during a reaction time (t_R), which is the time required for the driver to see the object and begin to apply the brakes. The vehicle continues to travel at speed V during the reaction time. Typical values of t_R are 2–3 s
2. The distance required in braking to bring the vehicle to rest from speed *V*.

A simple kinematic equation then defines the SSD:

$$SSD = t_R V + \frac{V^2}{2 f_L g} \tag{7.1}$$

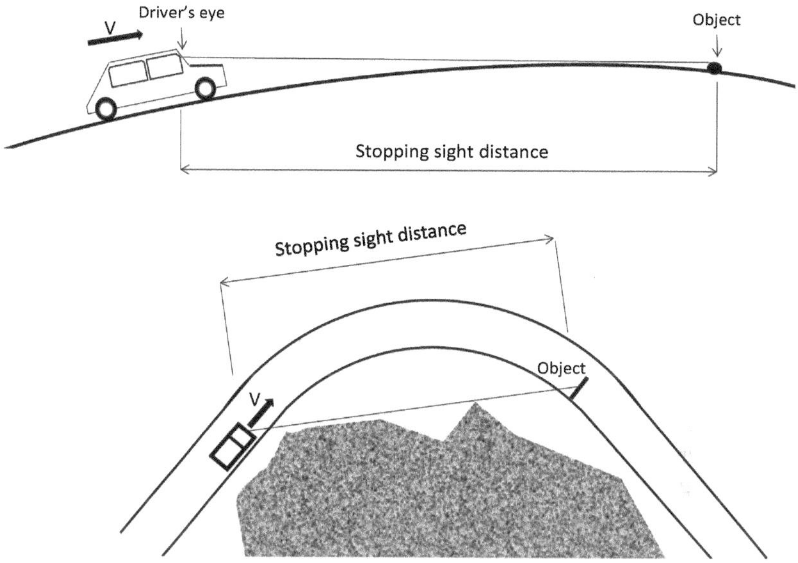

FIGURE 7.4 Representations of stopping sight distance for vertical and horizontal road alignments.

In Eq. (7.1)[4] $f_L g$ is the average rate of deceleration during braking, g is gravitational acceleration, and f_L is the coefficient of longitudinal friction for the road surface. Typical values of f_L are in the range 0.28–0.35, with values in the lower part of the range used for higher values of V. Any factor leading to increased slipperiness of the road surface will lower the coefficient of friction, thus increasing SSD and leading to more hazardous driving conditions. See AASHTO (2018) and Austroads (2017) amongst other references on geometric design for more discussion on SSD.

Another facet of road performance involving adhesion between tyre and pavement is cornering, and this also requires a friction coefficient, f_s, which is the coefficient of sideways friction. A vehicle travelling around a circular horizontal curve (radius R) at speed V is subject to a horizontal centrifugal force WV^2/Rg, where W is the weight of the vehicle. This force tends to cause the vehicle to slide outwards on the curve (i.e., to continue travelling along the tangent to the curve at that point). To successfully negotiate the curve this force needs to be matched by an equal and opposite force directed horizontally towards the centre of the curve. Fig. 7.5 shows the forces at work on the

4. Gravity may also affect SSD. For vehicles climbing a grade, gravitational force will act to decrease SSD, while on descent it will increase SSD. For a grade of $G\%$, where a positive G is for an upgrade and a negative G is for a downgrade, Eq. (7.1) may be rewritten as $SSD = t_R V + \frac{V^2}{2(f_L + 0.01G)g}$.

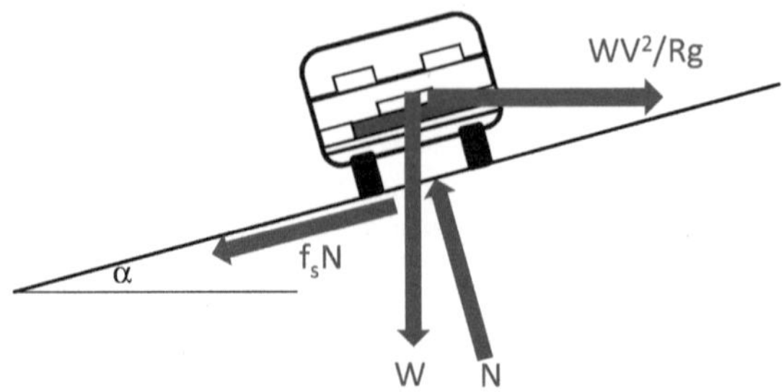

FIGURE 7.5 Forces acting on a vehicle negotiating a circular curve of radius R at constant speed V.

vehicle in this situation. The required balancing force has two components: the vector component of the vehicle weight acting down the slope of the curve (angle α, with $E = \tan(\alpha)$ being the superelevation of the curve) and the sideways friction force f_sN, where N is the normal force to the road surface, given by $N = W\cos(\alpha)$. See Fig. 7.5. A little algebra (e.g., see Underwood (1995)) shows that, for equilibrium of forces and therefore safe cornering,

$$\frac{V^2}{Rg} = E + f_s \tag{7.2}$$

Typical values for f_s lie in the range 0.1–0.2 (AASHTO, 2018; Austroads, 2017; Underwood, 1995). While superelevation E can play a major role is ensuring safe cornering, the impact of sideways friction is substantial and any reduction in the friction coefficient due to increased slipperiness of the road surface will be hazardous to traffic operations. There are also limits to the value of superelevation that can be used on a road (unlike a specialised facility such as a velodrome) because the stability of vehicles with high centres of gravity (e.g., heavy goods vehicle with high loads) could be endangered at high values of E.

Representing climate

Moisture levels, precipitation and higher temperatures emerge as the main climate factors likely to adversely impact road pavements. Flooding, landslides, rockfalls and avalanches may also damage pavements. These weather-related events also lead to significant disruptions in traffic operations through road blockages, delays and detours.

Given that road pavements will wear out over time – see Fig. 7.3 – maintenance and refurbishment programs are required to keep them in suitable condition for traffic operations. Internationally, as indicated by ITF (2016), climate change impacts may have different effects on pavement life cycles and necessary maintenance regimes in different places. Thus, local climate trends and effects need to be studied.

In particular, flexible pavements may be affected by changes in temperatures in a number of ways. Temperature changes include

- Higher average daily temperatures and warmer summer days
- Increases in the frequency of and duration of heatwaves
- Increases in the number of freeze–thaw cycles.

Increases in maximum pavement temperatures and duration of heatwaves will increase the potential for asphalt deterioration through increased rutting and bleeding. Higher levels of ultraviolet radiation may lead to faster ageing – increased brittleness – of asphalt, so that wearing courses would become more susceptible to cracking, potentially leading to increased water penetration into lower pavement layers. Prolonged hot, dry conditions and droughts may also lead to subgrade shrinkage and loss of bearing capacity. Rigid pavements are liable to heat warping, curling from thermal stresses and transverse cracking when subject to higher temperatures. While concrete slabs are largely resistant to moisture intrusion, moister base layers may expand leading to dislocation and severe cracking of the slab.

There is a further human factor to consider under increased temperatures. The scheduling of construction and maintenance activities may be adversely affected by warmer weather and heatwave extreme temperatures. Heat stress reduces the labour capacity for outdoor work (ITF, 2016) in daytime, so that more expensive nighttime maintenance operations may become more necessary. Warmer winter temperatures may allow for more scheduling of work in the winter months, but this may also be more subject to increased periods of rainfall.

The likely impacts of warmer winters and less extreme cold temperatures are mixed (ITF, 2016). In general terms, warmer average temperatures in winter may reduce the incidence and depth of winter frost, and possibly then the incidence of frost heave. This would decrease pavement fatigue and local failures (pot holes). Less de-icing activity might then be possible. However, in some places, warmer winters may contribute to increased levels of freeze–thaw cycling as temperatures linger around freezing point for longer. This would lead to increased frost heave damage to pavements. As thaw-saturated soils tend to lose bearing capacity, there may be less opportunity for the use of thawing roads with changes in the freeze–thaw cycling. In the most northerly latitudes warmer temperatures, both winter and summer, may lead to deeper permafrost melting with consequent increases in heaving and pavement damage.

Increased moisture levels also badly affect road pavements. Surface water, and ice, can significantly reduce vehicle manoeuvrability and stability through reduced road–tyre adhesion. Water intrusion into base and subbase pavement layers reduces pavement integrity and can lead to accelerated pavement failure. Road drainage systems are designed to remove surface water or prevent it reaching the roadway. Increased levels of precipitation may require enhanced

FIGURE 7.6 Pavement destruction on R M Williams Way, at Yanyarrie Creek north of Carrieton, mid-North South Australia, following flash flood on 20 January 2007 [Attribution: Creative Commons Attribution 4.0 International (CC BY 4.0), Government of South Australia, January 2007 flood images, sourced on 8 May 2007, www.transport.sa.gov.au/quicklinks/jan_2007_flood_images/3.jpg].

drainage capacity and improved maintenance to ensure drainage capacity is maintained. Inundation of pavements leads to water penetration and closures of roads with adverse effects on traffic operations. Flash flooding may not only overload drainage systems but may also lead to washouts, requiring significant reconstruction and accompanying long duration road closures (e.g., see Fig. 7.6). Increased incidence of flash flooding may require reconstruction of drainage facilities and flood protection works to new standards. Storm surges in coastal regions will stand to have similar effects. Prolonged submersion of roadways will decrease earthwork slope stability and increase water damage to pavement structures. Unpaved roads – noting that these are a substantial part of the road networks of countries such as the United States and Australia, see introduction to this chapter – are especially vulnerable to increases in average precipitation levels and extreme rainfall events. These roads may then need extensive increases in maintenance costs or substantial upgrading (e.g., paved surfacing). Upgrading may not be otherwise economically justified, and so decisions will be required about the future of such roads – can degraded access and loss of viability for affected communities be unavoidable?

Thus, two major climate factors emerge for consideration of road pavement design, construction and maintenance. These are temperature and precipitation(/rainfall), and the distributions of these over time in a given locality are of concern. One approach, which accounts for these factors through a composite index and can include climate change scenarios at the local level, is the use of the TMI.

Thornthwaite Moisture Index (TMI)

Thornthwaite (1948) introduced a new index, now known as the TMI, to describe climate types which could be calculated using actual data from the region under investigation, primarily as an aid in agricultural science for determining the types of crops most suitable for that region. TMI describes the aridity or humidity of the soil and climate of a region and is calculated from the collective effects of precipitation, evapotranspiration, soil water storage, moisture deficit and runoff. Thornthwaite found that the actual evaporation and transpiration is not what must be compared with precipitation in order to obtain a moisture index, but, rather, the potential evapotranspiration, which he identified as a principal climate factor. However, it represented a theoretical construct that would be possible only under ideal soil moisture and vegetation conditions, and was thus difficult to determine. He then went on to describe indices for humidity (I_h) and aridity (I_a) to define water surplus or deficit in terms of the water need or potential evapotranspiration. Thornthwaite theorised that since water surplus and water deficiency occur at different seasons in most places, both must enter into a moisture index. He defined TMI as a mathematical function M as

$$M = I_h - I_a = \frac{100\alpha - 60\beta}{\gamma} \tag{7.3}$$

where α is water surplus, β is water deficiency, and γ is water need or potential evapotranspiration. A further simplification of the index was given by Gentilli (1972), which relates the Thornthwaite index to 'effective annual rainfall' (P_e).

$$M(t) \approx 1.25P_e(t) - 60 \tag{7.4}$$

$$P_e(t) = \sum_{m=1}^{12} P_{em}(t) \tag{7.5}$$

$$P_{em}(t) = 1.65 \frac{P_{Tm}(t)}{(T_m(t) + 12.2)^{1.1111}} \tag{7.6}$$

where $P_{Tm}(t)$ is monthly total rainfall, $P_{em}(t)$ is the effective monthly rainfall, and $T_m(t)$ is mean monthly temperature, in the months m of year t. This approximation for the TMI is of practical use because it relates the index directly to specific, observable (or predictable) climate variables. As TMI is representative of climatic conditions based on actual data it has application to the design and maintenance of infrastructure. Taylor and Philp (2016) provided a comprehensive review of the use of TMI in the design or maintenance of infrastructure with an emphasis on transportation infrastructure.

Pavement degradation model using the Thornthwaite Moisture Index

Austroads (2010a) developed a mathematical model of road pavement degradation that includes climate variables and the potential impact of climate change, expressed in terms of the TMI. The Austroads model is cast at the level of network and program planning rather than as a pavement design tool, which makes it suitable for applications across a region. Taylor and Philp (2015) extended the model for use in climate change studies, including alternative climate change scenarios, for road pavements. A case study application is given later in this chapter, and the full nomenclature for the pavement degradation model is given in Table 7.1.

In the model, overall pavement degradation is expressed in terms of the IRI, $R(t)$ (m/km) at time t, where $R(t)$ is given by

$$R(t) = R_0 + \Delta R(t) \tag{7.7}$$

in which R_0 is the initial roughness index of the pavement and $\Delta R(t)$ is the change in roughness over time t. The road will be considered to have reached the end of its service life when $R(t) \geq R_{max}$. Thus, determination of $t_{\max}$, where

$$R(t_{\max}) = R_{\max} \tag{7.8}$$

will indicate the time of failure of the pavement.

The overall roughness of a sealed pavement is made up of considerations of rutting and surface cracking, which are affected by traffic load and climate, and this can be assessed in terms of changes in IRI. The model proposed by Austroads (2010a) was

$$\Delta R(t) = 196.74Z(t) + 0.016c(t) + 0.25r(t) + 0.972E(t) \tag{7.9}$$

where $Z(t)$ represents the cumulative traffic load on the pavement, $c(t)$ is the percentage of cumulative cracking (% total lane area, 0%–100%) by year t, $r(t)$ is the cumulative rutting deterioration for a sealed granular pavement by year t (which includes a factor for maintenance expenditure – see below), and $E(t)$ is an environmental/climate term. $E(t)$ is given by Eq. (7.10):

$$E(t) = \lambda(t)R_0 t \tag{7.10}$$

where

$$\lambda(t) = 0.0197 + 0.00000155M(t) \tag{7.11}$$

and $M(t)$ is the value of the TMI in year t.

TABLE 7.1 Nomenclature for the Austroads model of pavement degradation (Austroads, 2010a).

a_j	Coefficient in cumulative cracking deterioration equation: $j=1$, granular sealed pavement, $a_1=0.234$; $j=2$, asphalt pavement, $a_2=0.682$
b_j	Coefficient for estimating field layer thickness (FLTs) of bitumen binder: $j=1$, single seal, $b_1=0.6$; $j=2$, double seal, $b_2=0.9$
c(t)	Cumulative cracking (% total lane area, 0%–100%) by year *t*
δc(t)	Incremental cracking (% total lane area, 0%–100%) in year *t*
d	Days
D_0	Maximum falling weight deflectometer (FWD) deflection from pavement test (mm)
E(t)	Environmental/climate term in cumulative roughness deterioration equation, up to year *t*
δE(t)	Incremental environmental/climate term in roughness deterioration equation, for year *t*
F	Risk factor in ARRB seal life equation (1 = very low, 10 = very high)
Ih	Index of humidity
Ia	Index of aridity
M(t)	Thornthwaite Moisture Index for climate pavement conditions in year *t*
N	Pavement design life (years)
$P_e(t)$	Effective annual rainfall (mm) in year *t*
$P_{Tm}(t)$	Total monthly rainfall (mm) in month *m* of year *t*
$P_{em}(t)$	Effective monthly rainfall (mm) in month *m* of year *t*
Q(t)	Cumulative traffic load per lane in Mega-ESA (millions of equivalent standard axles), to the end of year *t*
r_{max}	Mean maximum vertical deformation from original surface profile (mm)
r(t)	Cumulative rutting deterioration for sealed granular pavements by year *t*
δr(t)	Incremental rutting deterioration for sealed granular pavements in year *t*
R	International Roughness Index (IRI), in m/km
R_0	international Roughness Index at $t=0$
R_{max}	Maximum value of IRI for a road considered to be in serviceable condition
δR(t)	Incremental deterioration in IRI for a sealed granular pavement, in year *t*
ΔR(t)	Cumulative deterioration in IRI for a sealed granular pavement, after *t* years
S(t)	Modified structural number for pavement/subgrade strength at year *t*

Continued

TABLE 7.1 Nomenclature for the Austroads model of pavement degradation (Austroads, 2010a).—cont'd

S_0	Modified structural number for pavement/subgrade strength at year $t=0$ [default value 4.5]
t	Time since construction or last rehabilitation (years)
t_c	Cracking age (elapsed time from commencement of cracking, in years): $t_c = t - \tau_c$ if $t > \tau_c$ otherwise $t_c = 0$
$T_m(t)$	Mean monthly temperature (°C) in month m of year t
T_{min}	Average annual minimum temperature
T_{max}	Average annual maximum temperature
$\overline{u}(t)$	Annualised pavement maintenance expenditure ($/lane-km/year) by year t
$v_j(t)$	$v_j(t) = \frac{1}{[1+(S_0-0.0000758c(t)b_j\varnothing)]^5}$
$w_j(t)$	$w_j(t) = \left(\frac{a_j t_c(t)}{8-0.04M(t)}\right)^{3.5}$
$y(t)$	$y(t) = 0.594Q(t) - 0.000102\overline{u}(t) + \frac{0.022(100+M(t))}{S_0}$
$Z(t)$	Traffic load term in cumulative roughness deterioration equation
$\delta Z(t)$	Change in traffic load term in incremental roughness deterioration equation, in year t
$\lambda(t)$	Environmental coefficient, which varies in response to changes in the thornthwaite Moisture Index $M(t)$
τ_c	Seal life (years)
$\varnothing$	Nominal maximum size of seal aggregate (mm)

As extended by Taylor, M.A.P., Philp, M.L., 2015. Investigating the impact of maintenance regimes on the design life of road pavements in a changing climate and the implications for transport policy Transp. Pol. 41, 117–135.

The impacts of traffic load on pavement condition are represented by the term $Z(t)$ in Eq. (7.9). This term exists in two alternative forms, $Z_1(t)$ and $Z_2(t)$, depending on the seal type for the road pavement. It is given by

$$Z_j(t) = v_j(t)Q(t)\exp[\lambda(t)t] \tag{7.12}$$

in which

$$v_j(t) = \frac{1}{[1+(S_0 - 0.0000758c(t)b_j\varnothing)]^5} \tag{7.13}$$

where $j=1$ for single seal, $b_1 = 0.6$; $j=2$ for double seals, $b_2 = 0.9$, and $\varnothing$ is the nominal maximum size of seal aggregate (mm), and the initial modified structural number (MSN) (S_0) for the pavement can be estimated from the observed MSN at time t,

$$S_0 = \frac{1.1068S(t)}{2 - \exp\left[0.0023M(t) + 0.185\left(\frac{t}{N}\right)\right]} \tag{7.14}$$

$$S(t) = 3.2D_0^{-0.63} \tag{7.15}$$

which is an estimate of the MSN for the pavement at time t, based on the result (D_0, mm) of a falling weight deflectometer test (see NCHRP, 2006) – assuming that such test results can be obtained. It is also possible (and perhaps inevitable in scenario planning) to use a default value for S_0, and Austroads (2010a) suggested a default value of $S_0 = 4.5$. $Q(t)$ is the cumulative traffic load on the pavement, expressed as the number of ESA imposed on the pavement, and measured in mega-ESA. Taylor and Philp (2015) described a suitable method for the estimation of $Q(t)$ on rural roads in Australia.

Cumulative rutting deformation $r(t)$ up to time t for the road pavement is given by

$$r(t) = (t - 1)^{0.617}y(t) \tag{7.16}$$

where

$$y(t) = 0.594Q(t) - 0.000102\overline{u}(t) + \frac{0.022(100 + M(t))}{S_0} \tag{7.17}$$

and $\overline{u}(t)$ is the annualised pavement maintenance expenditure ($/lane-km/year) by year t. Typical values for maintenance costs are given in Austroads (2010a).

Cumulative cracking deterioration ($c(t)$) (as a percentage of pavement surface area) is given by

$$c(t) = 100\left[1 - \frac{2}{1 + \exp\{w_j(t)\}}\right] \tag{7.18}$$

where

$$w_j(t) = \left(\frac{a_j t_c(t)}{8 - 0.04M(t)}\right)^{3.5} \tag{7.19}$$

in which $j = 1$ is for a sealed granular pavement for which $a_1 = 0.234$, and $j = 2$ is for an asphalt pavement with $a_2 = 0.682$. Cracking age t_c, the elapsed time from the commencement of cracking, is given by

$$t_c(t) = t - \tau_c \quad \text{if } t > \tau_c, \text{ otherwise } t_c(t) = 0 \tag{7.20}$$

in which seal life τ_c, before the onset of cracking, is given by Oliver's equation (Austroads, 2010a), which is

$$\tau_c = \left[\frac{0.158T_{\min} - 0.107F + 0.84}{0.0249(T_{\min} + T_{\max}) - 0.216d + 0.000381\varnothing^2}\right]^2 \tag{7.20a}$$

Note that the temperature variables T_{min} and T_{max} in Eq. (7.20) are average annual values up to a particular point in time, and so can be varied in response to changes in climate. The factor d in the equation is the result (in days) of the ARRB Durability Test (Austroads, 2010a), and usually has a value in the range 8–10. The factor F is a risk factor, ranging in value from 1 (low risk) to 10 (high risk). Typical values are in the range 6–8, with the factor being higher for higher traffic loads.

In an environment where traffic loads and climatic factors (and maintenance regimes) may vary over time, then the pavement degradation model needs to be written in terms of incremental (year by year) effects. The Austroads model, as above, only considered changes in annual traffic load. A more general incremental model is needed, so that the effects of variation in other factors, such as road maintenance expenditures and climate change, can be included. On the basis of the Austroads incremental model, Taylor and Philp (2015) proposed the following expression for the IRI ($R(t)$) at time t years after initial construction or rehabilitation of the pavement:

$$R(t) \approx R_0 + \sum_{i=1}^{t} \delta R(i) \tag{7.21}$$

The requirement is then to define $R(t)$ in terms of the annual incremental changes in the variables in Eq. (7.3), and so produce a model based on the incremental changes over each year. The starting point is to consider the incremental change in IRI ($\delta R(t)$) between year $t-1$ and year t. This is

$$\delta R(t) = \Delta R(t) - \Delta R(t-1) \tag{7.22}$$

and, following the form of Eq. (7.9), $\delta R(t)$ can then be written as

$$\delta R(t) = 196.74\delta Z(t) + 0.016\delta c(t) + 0.25\delta r(t) + 0.972\delta E(t) \tag{7.23}$$

where

$$\delta Z(t) = Q(t)v(t)\exp[\lambda(t)t] - Q(t-1)v(t-1)\exp[\lambda(t-1)(t-1)] \tag{7.24}$$

$$\delta c(t) = 200\left\{\frac{\exp[w(t)] - \exp[w(t-1)]}{(1+\exp[w(t)])(1+\exp[w(t-1)])}\right\} \tag{7.25}$$

$$\delta r(t) = (t-1)^{0.617}y(t) - (t-2)^{0.574}y(t-1) \tag{7.26}$$

$$\delta E(t) = R_0(\lambda(t)t - \lambda(t-1)(t-1)) \tag{7.27}$$

Solution of Eq. (7.8) using Eqs (7.22)–(7.27) provides a model of pavement life dependent on changes in traffic, maintenance and environmental variables over time.

Use of the model, especially for climate change scenario studies, requires knowledge of and future scenarios for TMI. For the case of Australia, a database of TMI values for the period 1960–2007 together with predictions of

TMI until 2100 was developed by CSIRO[5] for Austroads as a climate forecasting tool for Australia. The tool provides historical data, and climate predictions, for any location in Australia (Austroads, 2010b).

Case studies

A set of case studies on pavement performance under different climate change scenarios is presented as examples of current practice in the examination of climate impacts on road pavement performance. The first of these case studies involves the use of the pavement degradation (IRI) model described above, for a road corridor through the Australian state of South Australia. The other case studies exemplify recent studies in the United States, and the consideration of the potential impacts of sea level rise on pavements in coastal regions.

South Australia, N–S transect

Taylor and Philp (2015) undertook a case study analysis of the potential impacts of climate change on road condition, applying the pavement degradation model to establish a baseline inventory as a reference for future research on adaptation in South Australia. The main roads lying along a road corridor designated as a north–south transect line were selected for the study. The north–south transect line is shown in Fig. 7.7. It is located in the Mid North/Adelaide Hills region of South Australia and stretches from Hawker (138° 25′ E, 31° 53′ S) at the northern end to Goolwa (138° 47′ E, 35° 30′ S) at the southern end, a road distance of about 460 km. These two towns as well as some other major towns along the route are shown in Fig. 7.7. In terms of the TMI, climate conditions along the transect (in 2000) varied from (type v) semiarid in the north to (type iii) temperate in the south. The climate types are those defined in Australian Standard AS2870 (Standards Australia, 2011), as shown in Table 7.2. Fig. 7.7 also shows the predominant land uses along the road corridor, which start as pastoral in the northern reaches, then moves to agricultural and finishes in the coastal region at Goolwa. This case study provides a test of the effects of forecast climate changes on road degradation and indicates the needs for policy direction in terms of road asset maintenance programs under different climate change scenarios.

Taylor and Philp (2015) examined past, current and future climatic conditions along the transect (for the time period from 1990 to 2049). The historical data cover the period 1990–2007. The model included three climate change scenarios for the period 2007–49: low, average and high climate change scenarios. Fig. 7.8 summarises the climate model outputs for the transect. It shows the TMI values for 1990, 2000, 2007, 2028 and 2049.

---

5. CSIRO is the Commonwealth Scientific and Industrial Research Organisation, the Australian federal government's primary scientific research agency.

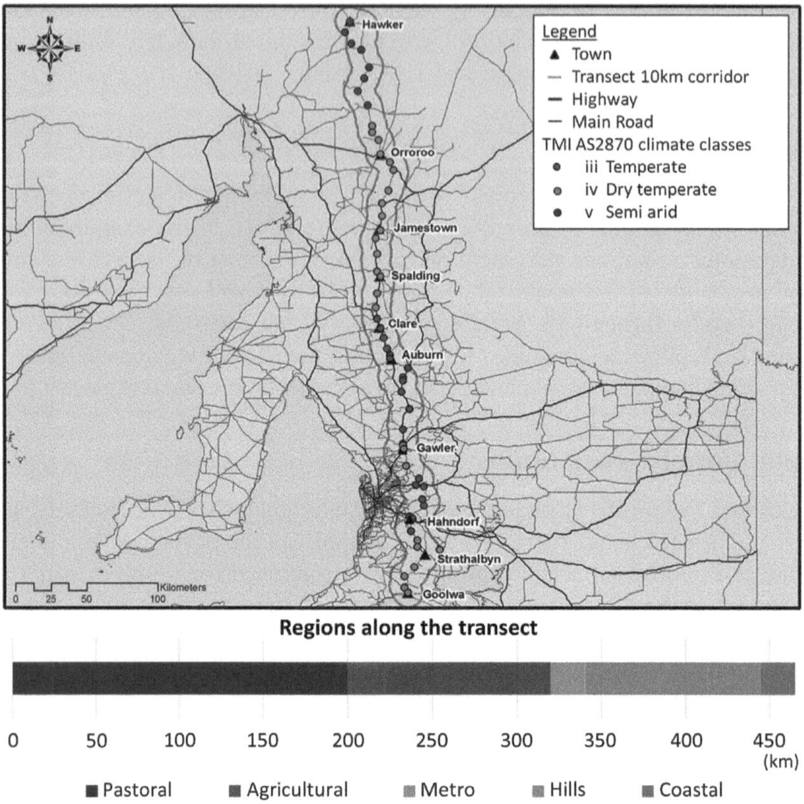

FIGURE 7.7 The north–south transect in regional South Australia, showing main towns and regional land use types (chainage starts at 0 km at Hawker, northern end of the transect). *Reproduced with permission from Taylor, M.A.P., Philp, M.L., 2015. Investigating the impact of maintenance regimes on the design life of road pavements in a changing climate and the implications for transport policy Transp. Pol. 41, 117–135, Fig. 1, p.121.*

TABLE 7.2 Australian climatic types adapted from the Australian Standard AS2870 climate classes (Standards Australia, 2011).

Climatic types for Australia		TMI value range
i	Alpine/coastal	$M > 40$
ii	Wet temperate	$10 < M \leq 40$
iii	Temperate	$-5 < M \leq 10$
iv	Dry temperate	$-25 < M \leq -5$
v	Semiarid	$-40 < M \leq -25$
vi	Arid	$M \leq -40$

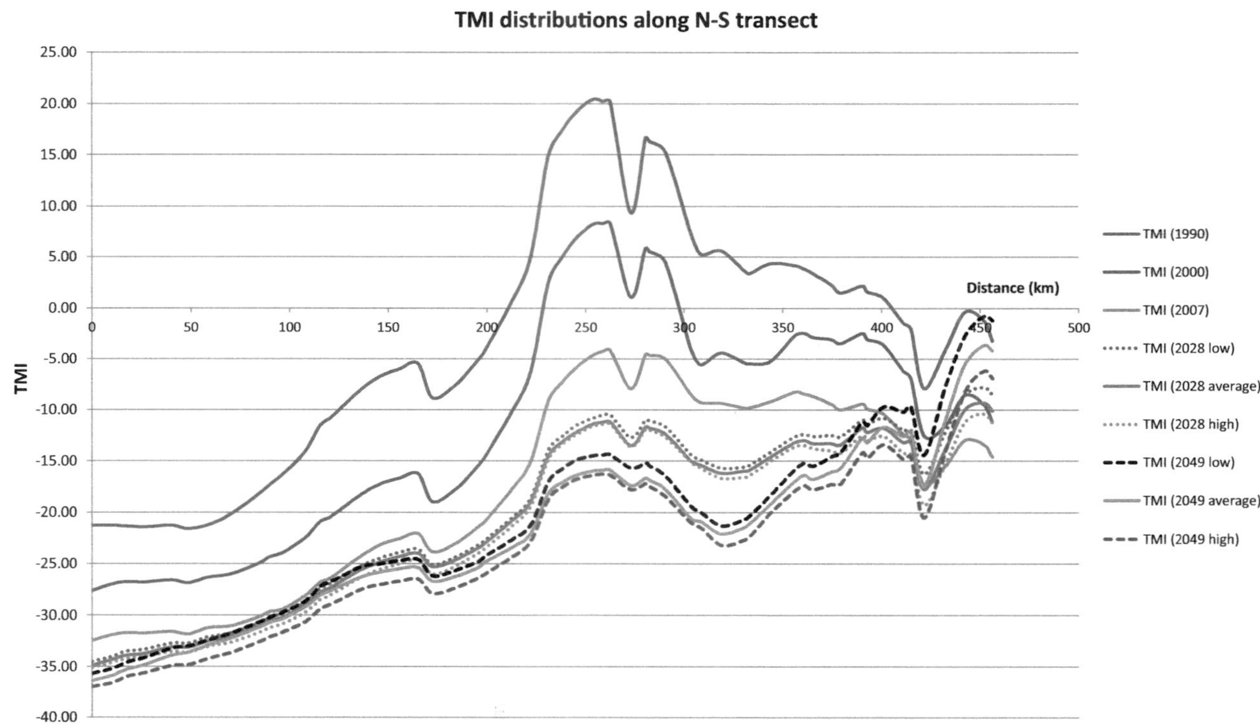

FIGURE 7.8 Historical and projected TMI values along the transect. Shows historical data for 1990, 2000 and 2007, and forecast climate scenarios (low, average and high) for 2029 and 2049. Low and high scenarios are shown as dashed lines. *Modified and reproduced with permission from Taylor, M.A.P., Philp, M.L., 2015. Investigating the impact of maintenance regimes on the design life of road pavements in a changing climate and the implications for transport policy Transp. Pol. 41, 117–135, Fig. 3, p.121.*

TABLE 7.3 Past and estimated future Thornthwaite Moisture Index values for towns along the transect.

Thornthwaite moisture index (*M*) values							
		Historical			2049 forecasts		
Town	Chainage (km)	1990	2000	2007	Low	Average	High
Hawker	0.0	−21.28	−27.61	−32.20	−35.7	−36.4	−37.0
Orroroo	108.0	−14.05	−22.47	−27.93	−28.6	−29.2	−30.6
Jamestown	165.1	−5.48	−16.26	−21.93	−24.6	−25.4	−26.5
Spalding	1996.	−4.00	−14.40	−20.68	−24.2	−24.8	−25.9
Clare	238.6	17.48	5.07	−6.70	−15.7	−17.1	−17.5
Auburn	262.4	20.23	8.34	−4.16	−14.4	−15.9	−16.4
Riverton	282.6	16.30	5.51	−4.64	−15.5	−16.9	−17.5
Strathalbyn	421.6	−7.90	−12.53	−17.32	−14.4	−17.5	−20.5
Goolwa	456.2	−3.20	−11.21	−14.60	−1.2	−4.2	−6.9

Reproduced with permission from Taylor, M.A.P., Philp, M.L., 2015. Investigating the impact of maintenance regimes on the design life of road pavements in a changing climate and the implications for transport policy Transp. Pol. 41, 117–135, Table 2, p.122.

The historical data up to 2007 show clear indication of a changing climate, basically a drying and warming of climatic conditions along the transect seen as decreasing values of the index from 1990 to 2007. The 2029 and 2049 values are forecast for each of the three climate scenarios and as such are seen as two bands each of three curves.

The general trend of the forecasts is for a decrease in the Thornthwaite index (indicating a drier climate) along the transect, except at the southern end where the forecasts are for slight increases in the index. Decreasing values of the index should lead to a potential reduction in pavement degradation in the model defined by Eq. (7.21), depending also on traffic volume forecasts. Table 7.3 shows past and estimated future TMI values for towns along the transect. This trend for decreasing TMI values occurs along the transect except for its southern end, from about chainage 400 km (see Fig. 7.8). The difference in trend in the southern region corresponds with the coastal zone, at the end of the transect.

The road route along the transect is two-lane two-way rural road with a spray sealed granular road pavement, and as such represents the large majority of the Australian regional road network. This is the road type for which the pavement degradation model was expressly developed. Traffic volume along the transect is relatively light over most of its length, reflecting the sparse population density of much of the region it serves, especially in the north.

The pavement degradation modelling used the three future climate scenarios (low, average and high) along with a fourth scenario in which the TMI was kept constant at its value in the year 2000. This base case was used to enable comparisons with the other climate scenarios, and represented the situation of no climate change over the period 2000–49.

Maintenance regimes

Three maintenance regimes were selected for the study, with unit costs (in AUD) taken from the data supplied in Austroads (2010a). These were

- maintenance regime A, which involved minimal maintenance of the road, on a 'patch and repair as needed' basis, which was costed at $100/lane-km p.a.
- maintenance regime B, which represented a systematic annual maintenance program without major reconstruction, and was costed at between $500 and $1000/lane-km p.a. depending on traffic load on the road section (measured in MESA p.a., i.e., mega-ESA, so that the annual cost was $500/lane-km if MESA < 0.1, $700 for $0.1 <$ MESA ≤ 1, and $1000/lane-km for MESA > 1)
- maintenance regime C, which used the systematic annual maintenance of regime B but also included resealing/reconstruction of the road section at years 16 and 32 of the study period, i.e., in calendar years 2016 and 2032 from the starting year 2000, whether or not the IRI (R) of the section had exceeded the set critical value of $R_{max} = 5.33$ m/km. The cost of this regime varied between $3600 and $4200/lane-km p.a., depending on the MESA traffic load.

Thus, maintenance regime A represented a minimal amount of maintenance over the life of the road and may be regarded as a poor regime, while regime C represented a high standard (and expensive) maintenance program. Regime B fell in between, at what might be considered a general minimum acceptable level of maintenance although, as the modelling analysis later suggested, it was not too different in performance to that of regime A. The representative costs of maintenance for each regime were taken from the values cited in Austroads (2010a).

Modelling results

The pavement degradation model described above provides estimates of the IRI ($R(t)$) at time t in terms of traffic load, physical/structural, maintenance and environmental/climatic variables. Traffic load in cumulative MESA was estimated for each road section along the transect, using data provided by the South Australian transport department (and the department's estimate of a 2%

annual compound growth in heavy vehicle traffic in the region). Fig. 7.9 shows this distribution of total traffic load over the 50 years from 2000 to 2049. Traffic load is lightest in the northern reaches of the transect and increases towards the south (and the more populated regions). There are local maxima around the population centres along the transect.

The computed roughness index was used in two ways in the analysis for the transect. First was the year in which $R(t)$ first exceeded the critical value R_{max}. Second was the value of the roughness index at year 50, i.e., $R(50)$. Together these two results provide some insights into the potential impacts of climate change on pavement performance, and on the possible impacts on maintenance programs under different climate change scenarios. Given the different climatic conditions along the transect, the analysis was conducted along its entire length. The analysis accounted for the four alternative climate scenarios (base case (i.e., static TMI), and low, average and high climate change scenarios) and the three maintenance regimes (A, B and C, as described above).

The modelled pavement life along the full transect for the Base climate scenario under each maintenance regime is shown in Fig. 7.10, in which pavement life is represented by the year in which $R \geq R_{max}$ (and $R_{max} = 5.33$ m/km). Note that the modelling period was 50 years, so that any points lying above that value indicate that R had not exceeded R_{max} during that period – this occurred for some low traffic volume locations along the transect under maintenance regime C. Fig. 7.10 suggests only small differences in pavement life between maintenance regimes A and B, and much more substantial differences for regime C for the Base case, as expected. The effects of the climate change scenarios may be seen in Fig. 7.11, which shows the differences in pavement life between each climate change scenario and the base scenario under each of the three maintenance regimes. Table 7.4 summarises the model outputs for pavement life. It shows computed pavement life under the base scenario and the differences in life under the climate change scenarios, for each maintenance regime, in the vicinity of the towns and settlements along the transect.

All of the climate change scenarios show increased pavement lives, except at the southern end of the transect where the forecast wetter climate leads to a small decrease in life, especially under the high cost maintenance regime (C) – an interesting result. This regime also has a different general shape of the pavement life curve for the transect than those for regimes A and B. Increases in life of between 0.5 and 1.3 years are apparent along most of the transect under each maintenance regime.

The modelling results indicate some general findings:

- as expected, higher levels of maintenance provide for better pavement performance
- climate change can have significant effects on pavement performance, with the direction of the performance depending on the trends in the TMI –

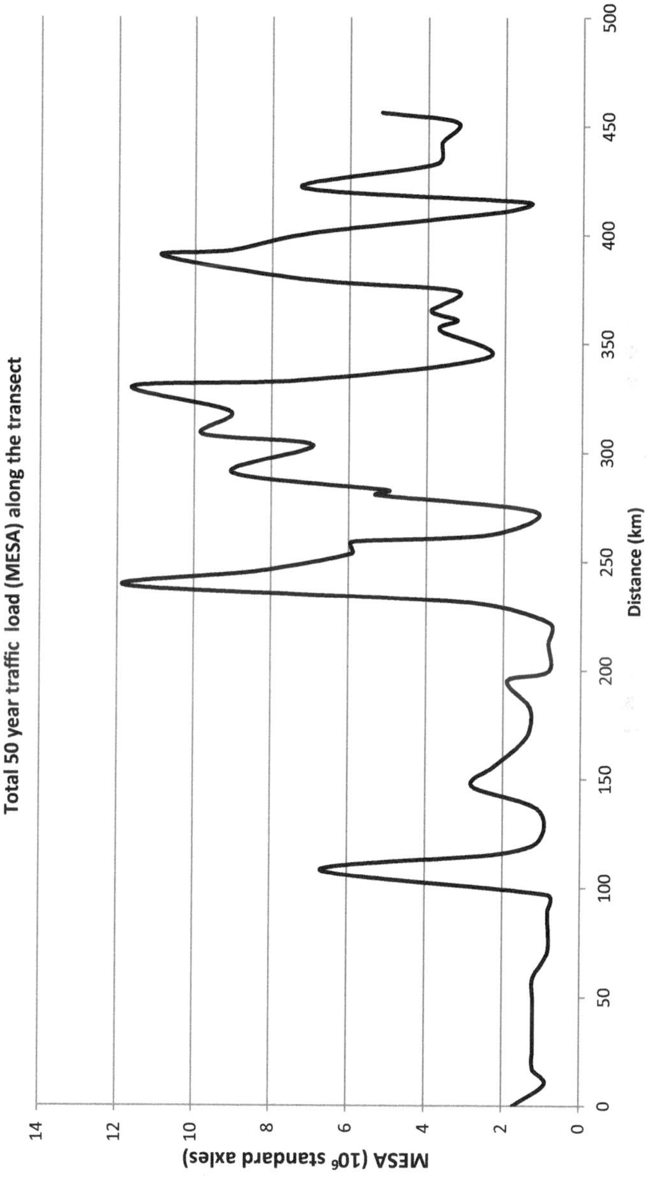

FIGURE 7.9 Distribution of total cumulative traffic load along the transect, in MESA.

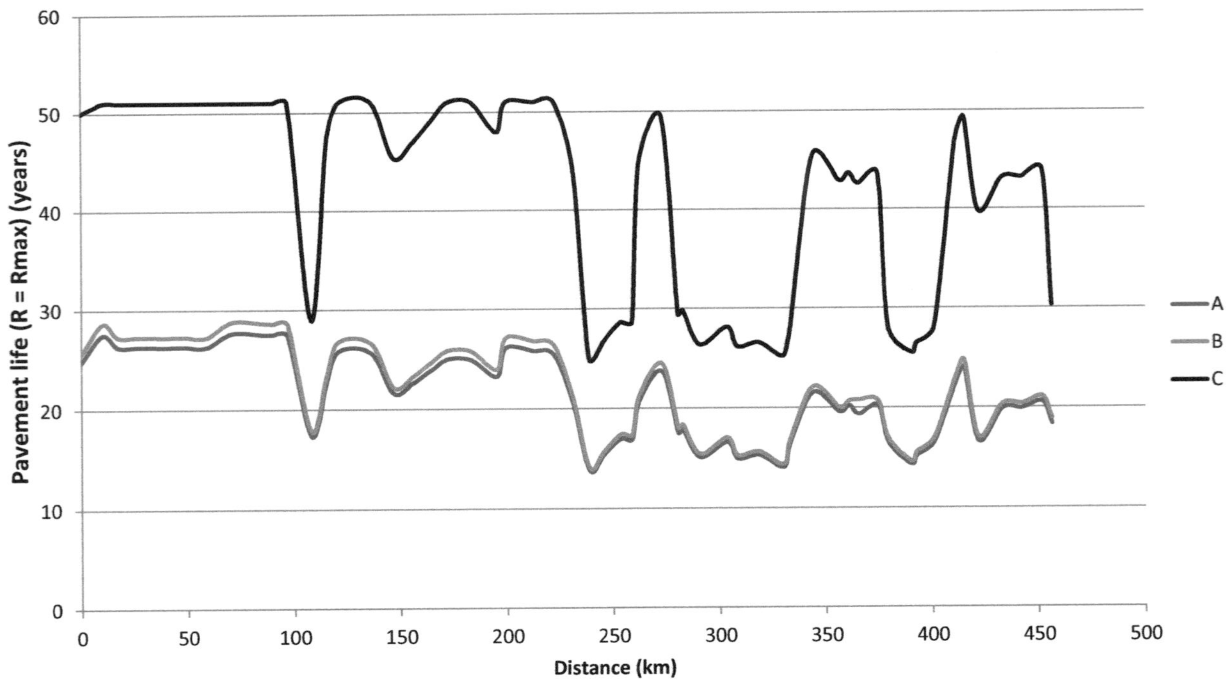

FIGURE 7.10 Base scenario pavement life (year in which $R \geq R_{max}$) by maintenance regime (A, B and C). *Reproduced with permission from Taylor, M.A.P., Philp, M.L., 2015. Investigating the impact of maintenance regimes on the design life of road pavements in a changing climate and the implications for transport policy Transp. Pol. 41, 117–135, Fig. 10, p.128.*

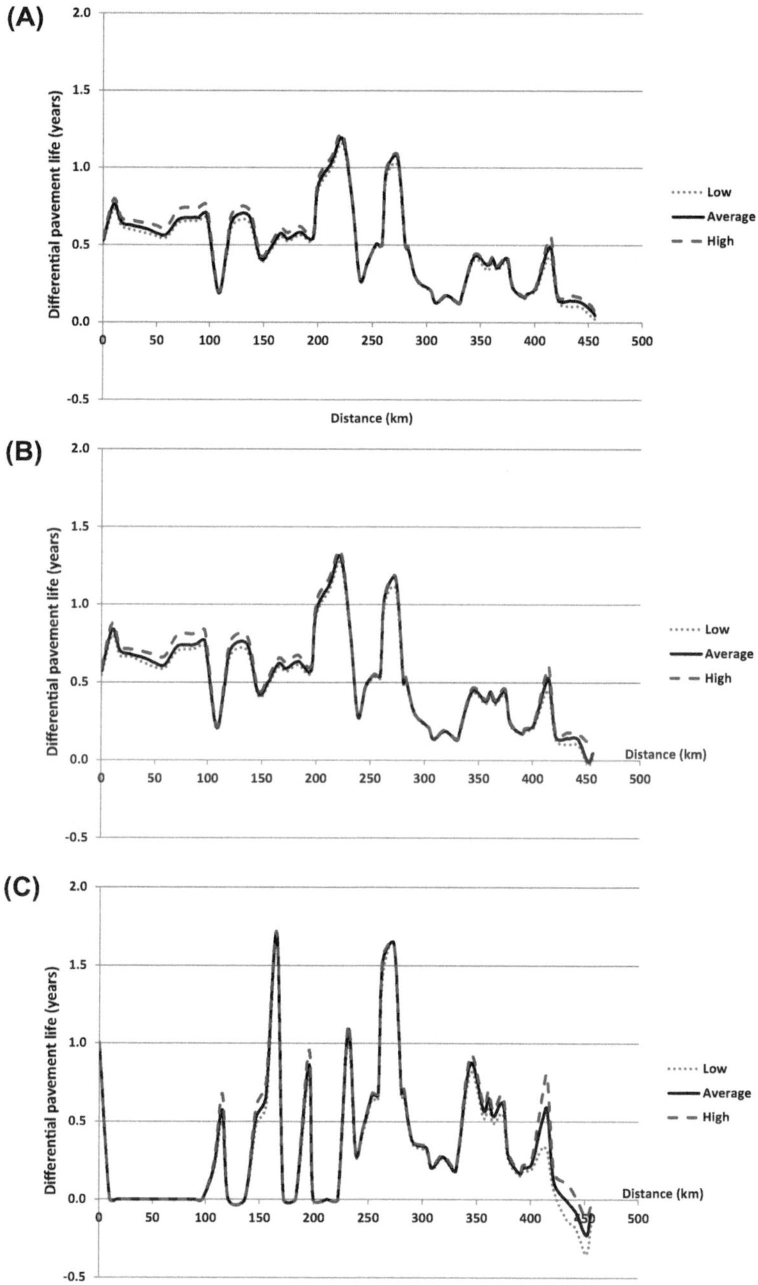

FIGURE 7.11 Differences in pavement life under climate scenarios and three maintenance regimes (A = top, B = middle and C = bottom). *Modified and reproduced with permission from Taylor, M.A.P., Philp, M.L., 2015. Investigating the impact of maintenance regimes on the design life of road pavements in a changing climate and the implications for transport policy Transp. Pol. 41, 117–135, Fig. 11, p.129.*

TABLE 7.4 Sample results for pavement life on N–S transect: year in which $R \geq R_{max}$ for towns and settlements along the transect – shows year for Base climate scenario and differences for other climate scenarios for each maintenance regime.

		Maintenance regime A				Maintenance regime B				Maintenance regime C			
		Base	Differential life (y)			Base	Differential life (y)			Base	Differential life (y)		
Location	Dist (km)	(y)	Low	Ave	High	(y)	Low	Ave	High	(y)	Low	Ave	High
Hawker	0.0	24.81	0.50	0.52	0.54	25.62	0.55	0.57	0.59	50.00	1.00	1.00	1.00
Cradock	26.8	26.31	0.60	0.63	0.66	27.29	0.67	0.68	0.71	51.00	0.00	0.00	0.00
Carrieton	70.7	27.65	0.64	0.66	0.73	28.79	0.70	0.73	0.80	51.00	0.00	0.00	0.00
Orroroo	108.0	17.35	0.19	0.20	0.20	17.81	0.20	0.21	0.22	28.94	0.20	0.21	0.24
Black rock	121.1	25.85	0.63	0.66	0.71	26.80	0.68	0.72	0.77	51.00	0.00	0.00	0.00
Mannanarie	146.8	21.61	0.40	0.41	0.43	22.19	0.41	0.43	0.45	45.36	0.48	0.53	0.60
Jamestown	165.1	24.02	0.55	0.57	0.61	24.80	0.60	0.62	0.65	49.29	1.71	1.71	1.71
Bundaleer north	172.2	25.01	0.53	0.54	0.58	25.88	0.57	0.59	0.63	51.00	0.00	0.00	0.00
Spalding	199.6	26.12	0.85	0.87	0.92	27.12	0.93	0.95	1.01	51.00	0.00	0.00	0.00
Clare	238.6	13.84	0.27	0.28	0.28	14.12	0.28	0.28	0.28	25.01	0.28	0.29	0.30
Sevenhill	245.4	15.38	0.38	0.39	0.39	15.67	0.46	0.47	0.47	26.73	0.44	0.46	0.46
Watervale	253.7	16.95	0.50	0.51	0.51	17.39	0.54	0.55	0.55	28.65	0.65	0.67	0.68
Auburn	262.4	20.85	0.94	0.97	0.98	21.40	1.00	1.03	1.04	44.87	1.42	1.52	1.55

Saddleworth	273.1	23.69	1.01	1.06	1.08	24.47	1.10	1.16	1.17	49.37	1.63	1.63	1.63
Riverton	282.6	17.82	0.48	0.49	0.50	18.34	0.51	0.53	0.53	29.80	0.67	0.70	0.72
Gawler	333.2	16.48	0.19	0.19	0.20	16.90	0.20	0.20	0.21	27.97	0.29	0.30	0.32
Gumeracha	365.4	19.33	0.34	0.35	0.36	20.78	0.36	0.37	0.39	42.59	0.49	0.53	0.57
Lobethal	374.4	20.21	0.39	0.41	0.43	20.71	0.42	0.44	0.46	43.66	0.55	0.61	0.67
Woodside	379.4	16.49	0.22	0.23	0.24	16.91	0.23	0.24	0.24	27.97	0.26	0.28	0.31
Hahndorf	392.8	15.24	0.18	0.18	0.19	15.59	0.19	0.20	0.20	26.52	0.18	0.20	0.22
Macclesfield	410.9	22.46	0.41	0.46	0.50	23.12	0.42	0.47	0.52	46.94	0.34	0.51	0.68
Strathalbyn	421.6	16.65	0.13	0.15	0.17	17.08	0.13	0.15	0.17	39.82	0.06	0.11	0.17
Currency creek	451.8	20.57	0.04	0.08	0.11	21.09	−0.03	−0.01	0.11	43.97	−0.35	−0.23	−0.12
Goolwa	456.2	18.34	0.02	0.05	0.07	18.88	0.02	0.05	0.07	30.26	−0.16	−0.09	−0.03

Base year = 51.00 means that R at that location had not exceeded R_{max} in the 50-year modelling period.

drier climate (lower *M* values) leading to slight improvement in performance, wetter climate (higher *M* values) leading to slight deterioration in performance
- these changes occur across a range of traffic loads and maintenance regimes, as found by analysis along the case study corridor of the north–south transect in regional South Australia.

On the basis of these results, there is a strong case for considering the potential impacts of climate change in road network planning and management. The climate change scenarios only represent anticipated changes in average climate conditions. The impacts of extreme weather events are also important, and to date the available climate change forecasts do not include quantitative indications of the potential trends in the occurrence and severity of extreme weather events. What is suggested is that, for the case study corridor and especially at its northern end, a drier climate is likely to lead to increased occurrence of thunderstorms and the potential for washouts at culverts and bridges, which also have impacts on maintenance and management of the roads in question (e.g., see Fig. 7.6, which is from the northern section of the transect). The impact of extreme weather is another area requiring substantial future research.

Summary of case study findings

The Taylor and Philp (2015) case study represented a first step towards developing quantitative approaches to inform future policy determination. Based on recent research from highway engineering concerning potential climate impacts on road pavements, and aided by the availability of an appropriate climate forecasting tool, they developed and applied a scenario planning model for road pavement performance that accounted for the effects of traffic load, environment and climate, and maintenance regime. This model may be used to consider alternative strategies and plans for the management of road infrastructure, at least in terms of road pavement degradation and performance. Its key climate/environment parameter is the TMI, a climate factor that has found widespread use in agriculture and in infrastructure engineering. As such it provided a useful initial contribution to the consideration of climate change adaptation in road network planning.

The analysis in the case study indicated that different directions and levels of change were expected at different locations. The general trend was for a drier and warmer climate, reflected in decreasing values of TMI. In the model, such changes in TMI would lead to improved pavement performance, all other factors being equal, and the model indicated potential improvements in the order of 0.5–1.5 years in operational life for road pavements under those conditions. At one end of the corridor, however, the climate change forecasts indicated increases in TMI, suggesting a wetter future climate, and under these conditions pavement performance would be expected to be worse. Different maintenance regimes could affect the outcomes, suggesting that authoritative information on likely local climate change will be an imperative for policy and program determination.

That said, there are other serious concerns that the proposed model did not address. There is more to the state of a road section than the evolving state of its pavement. As discussed in previous chapters of this book, other components of infrastructure, such as bridges and culverts, must also be accounted for. In terms of climatic conditions, severe weather events such as thunderstorms and resultant flash flooding can have major impacts on such infrastructure elements. This is a particular factor for low traffic volume rural roads, where economic considerations may have led to the installation of lower standard components such as culverts, with perhaps small diameter pipes and an above surface floodway. This is the case in, for instance, the northern section of the case study corridor where there is some history of washouts resulting from culvert failure under extreme rain storm events (see Fig. 7.6). The consequence of a washout is failure of the road network and disruption of regional transport for some period of time until repairs can be made. The likely occurrence of this phenomenon has been considered in the existing road design and presumably deemed as acceptable risk, especially in areas of low population density. Climate change may well upset this balance, as the frequency and intensity of extreme weather events may change. Increased occurrence of washouts would imply reappraisal of risk and hence of road construction standards. The current climate forecast models focus on average conditions, not variations in weather and consequent extreme events. Given that thunderstorm activity and localised flash flooding tend to be more pronounced under the drier (e.g., arid and semiarid) climate classes, climatic shifts towards these conditions may well cause significant problems for road asset managers. This situation is further exacerbated when the drier climate conditions start to reach more heavily populated areas, as is the forecast situation for the case study corridor. Further research is definitely needed to relate extreme event probabilities to changing climate conditions.

The focus of the impacts of climate change in urban areas may leave the rural population in a vulnerable situation if climate change effects on the transport networks in these areas are not considered. The case study conducted as a part of this investigation found some beneficial results under the generally warmer, drier climate predicted for parts of rural South Australia. Where there may be run on benefits from the increased design life of roads under this scenario, it is still unknown what the cost of extreme events will be in these areas. Alternatively, for areas where there is a wetter climate forecast in the future, the reduced design life and higher level of maintenance required could cause further road funding issues, especially if compounded by increasing extreme weather events. The lack of practical secondary routes in rural areas may isolate the local communities if the primary road network is compromised. Policy-makers and governments need to readjust their focus in relation to climate change and transport as the effects are widely spread, and impact areas beyond the urban environment.

Recent US studies

Three recent case studies on the impacts of climate change on road pavement performance are

1. Gudipudi, Underwood and Zalghout (2017), who used climate projections for five different regions across the United States to examine the potential impacts on the structural performance of road pavements on the Interstate Highway System
2. Quao et al. (2015), who investigated the impacts of climate change on the long-term performance of road pavements, focussing on potential new requirements for pavement maintenance
3. Knott et al. (2017), who considered the potential effects of rising groundwater from sea level rise on the service life of pavements in coastal areas.

Each of these studies is summarised below.

Pavement structural performance

The study by Gudipudi et al. (2017) involved the modelling of pavement performance at five selected sites on the Interstate Highway System across the United States. Modelling of pavement performance was performed using the AASHTOWare Pavement Design ME software package (AASHTO, 2015), for the selected pavement locations over a 20-year period (spanning 2040–60). Climate data for each location over this time period were estimated using a set of three well-known climate models with model outputs downscaled to the local conditions at each site. Two climate scenarios were used for the estimations, the IPCC representative concentration pathways RCP 4.5 and RCP 8.5.[6] RCP 8.5 corresponds to a high greenhouse gas emission scenarios (and is the upper limit of the RCPs), while RCP 4.5 is a scenario assuming radiative forcing stabilises by 2100. The former RCP essentially assumes little or no abatement of emissions, while the latter assumes the adoption of policies leading to emissions reduction by the middle of the 21st century (and is now widely viewed as the likely best achievable outcome). Existing climate conditions were used as the baseline for comparisons.

The five test sites were chosen to give a useful geographic spread across the continental United States and because calibrated AASHTOWare Pavement ME models existed for the sites. The sites were located in Arizona, Indiana, Maine, Montana and Virginia. The 20-year analysis period was chosen to

6. See Chapter 1 for a discussion of the RCPs.

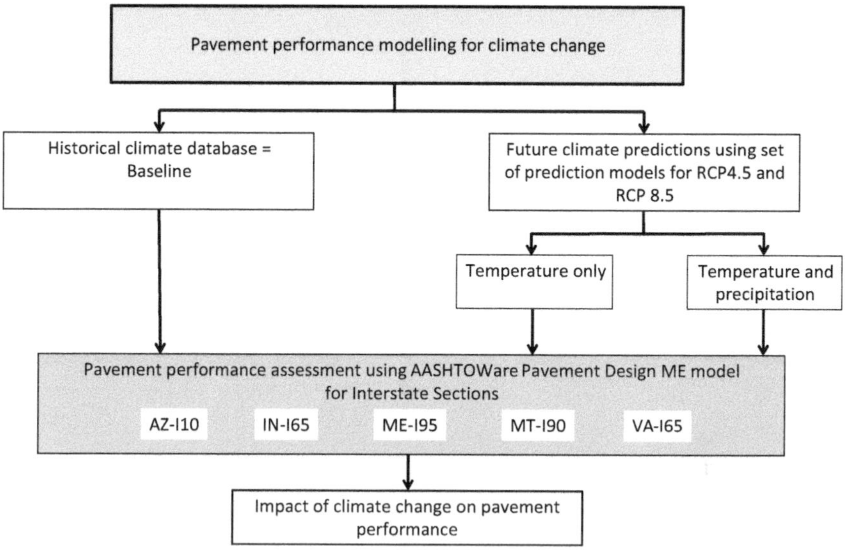

FIGURE 7.12 The Gudipudi–Underwood–Zalghout framework for assessing impacts of climate change on pavement performance. *Derived from Gudipudi, P.P., Underwood, B.S., Zalghout, A., 2017. Impact of climate change on pavement structural performance in the United States. Transp. Res. D Transp. Environ. 57, 172–184.*

match the generally accepted pavement life span. The AASHTOWare Pavement ME model explicitly identifies material selection and local climate parameters, making it suitable for the proposed study. Two parallel approaches to climate inputs into the ME model were used: (1) temperature estimations only and (2) temperature and precipitation estimations. These considerations yielded a set of 16 different future cases, and each of these was modelled for each of the chosen sites. The framework in Fig. 7.12 outlines the adopted modelling strategy.

As shown in Fig. 7.12, two strands were used in the modelling. The first strand used the historical climate data record as inputs to the pavement models and thus provide a performance baseline. The second strand used each climate prediction model to assess performance under the two climate scenarios, first with temperature data only, then with temperature and precipitation data. All of the model outputs were treated as statistically random variables for pavement performance at each test site, and therefore able to be analysed using statistical methods. A summary of the study results is shown in Fig. 7.13. This figure comprises a set of 'box and whisker' plots showing percentage differences in fatigue cracking, asphalt rutting and total rutting. Each box and whiskers plot is constructed as follows:

- The top and bottom sides of the box are the 75th and 25th percentiles of the results, so that the box indicates the spread of the middle 50% of the data

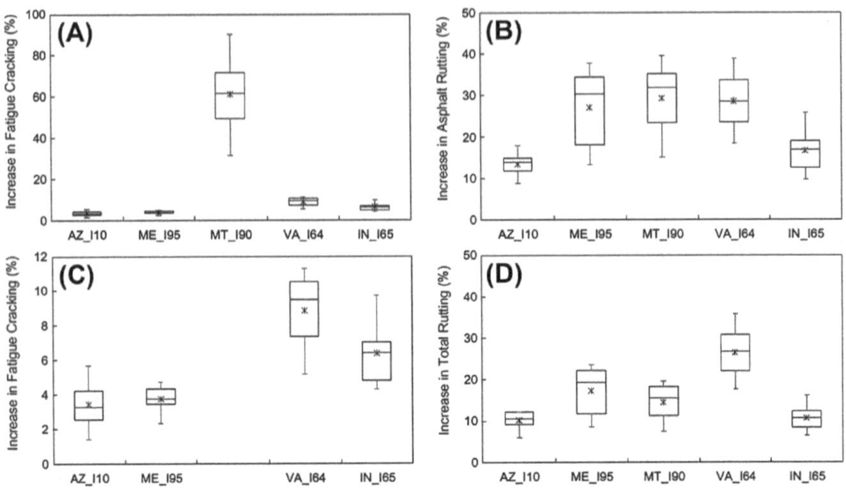

FIGURE 7.13 Percentage differences in modelled pavement performance for climate models using predicted temperature and precipitation across the five test sites: (A) fatigue cracking at all sites, (B) asphalt layer cracking, (C) fatigue cracking at four sites and (D) total rutting. *Reproduced with permission from Gudipudi, P.P., Underwood, B.S., Zalghout, A., 2017. Impact of climate change on pavement structural performance in the United States. Transp. Res. D Transp. Environ. 57, 172–184, Fig. 7, p.181.*

- The horizontal line in the box is the median (50th percentile)
- The 'x' is the mean value
- The extremities of the whiskers show the minimum and maximum values in the data.

The figure shows difference in modelled fatigue cracking, asphalt layer rutting and total rutting at each site, between the climate change impact and the baseline. There are two plots for fatigue cracking, due to the substantial difference of percentage increase between the Montana site and the other four sites[7] . Temperature differences were found to dominate the model results. The authors were then able to extrapolate their results to consider nationwide potential impacts on pavement cracking and rutting from future climate change. These results are shown in the two maps of Fig. 7.14, which show the projected distributions in fatigue cracking and rutting across the United States. It can be seen that the most severe impacts are likely to occur in the more northerly states.

Gudipudi et al. (2017) concluded that there could be substantial impacts on road pavement infrastructure from climate change, and that future analysis and

7. The authors note that this difference in percentage resulted because the actual baseline cracking at the Montana site was small in magnitude, so that the climate change results yielded larger percentage differences, but not actual differences.

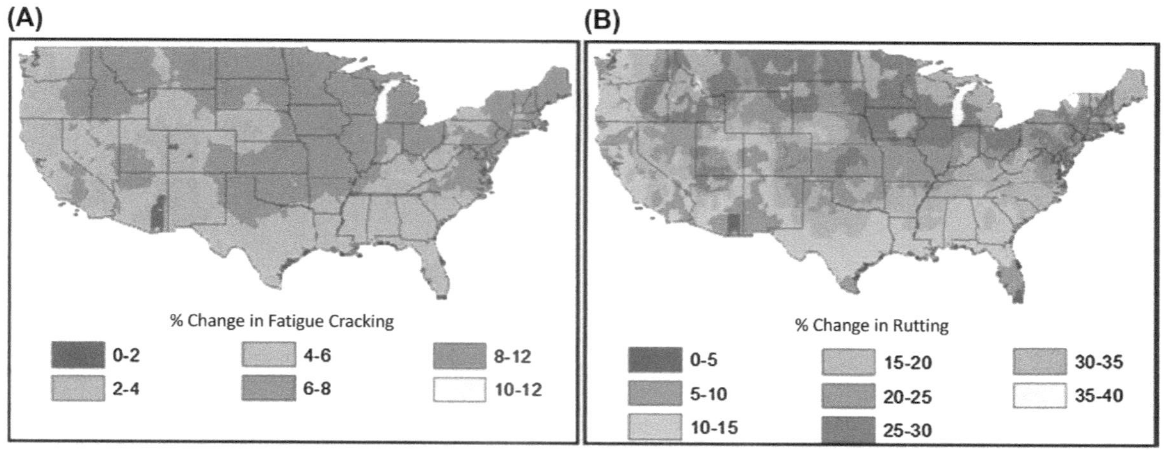

FIGURE 7.14 Projected national impacts on pavement performance of climate change projections for 2040–60, in terms of (A) fatigue cracking and (B) rutting. *Reproduced with permission from Gudipudi, P.P., Underwood, B.S., Zalghout, A., 2017. Impact of climate change on pavement structural performance in the United States. Transp. Res. D Transp. Environ. 57, 172–184, Fig. 6, p.180.*

design of road pavements structures should carefully consider deviations in temperatures from historical norms. Continued reliance on static climate records may lead to more frequent maintenance and rehabilitation requirements, with greater costs as a result.

Pavement maintenance strategies

Quao et al. (2015) considered the potential requirements for changes to pavement maintenance strategies resulting from climate change. They used a flexible pavement test site in Virginia and the anticipated climate change scenario at that site to predict pavement performance using the AASHTOWare Pavement ME model (i.e., the same model as used by Gudipudi et al. (2017)), for both the current climatic conditions and projected future conditions. The case study site was thought to be representative of a large number of locations in the United States. In consequence the authors concluded that

- In the absence of maintenance, road user costs will increase under climate change, although the increases may not be significant
- Climate change may have significant impacts on road maintenance planning under scenarios involving only minimum maintenance, generally by triggering the needs for maintenance treatments 8%–16% earlier than would be expected under static climate conditions
- Optimised frequent maintenance strategies can be devised to mitigate the impacts of climate change. This may mean some treatments being scheduled in advance of current practice, or sometimes delayed.

Sea level rise and rising groundwater

Most interest in sea level rise is concerned with the potential surface water flooding and damage to structure through storm surges (see Chapter 5). Another aspect of sea level rise is the expected rise in groundwater levels, and this may have significant impacts on road pavements in coastal areas. Knott et al. (2017) used a New Hampshire case study as a preliminary investigation of this topic. They used a regional groundwater flow model for coastal areas in New Hampshire to identify road sections where rising groundwater would move into the subbase and base materials of the roads during the design lives of the respective pavements. Modelling of the pavement structures was undertaken using the multilayer elastic methods of AASHTO (2015). This modelling was used to examine the magnitude of fatigue and rutting life reduction expected under different scenarios of sea level rise. All of the sites studied experienced reductions in pavement service life; the magnitude and timing of the reductions depended on the current depth of the groundwater, the pavement structure and the nature of the subgrade.

Those roads in zones of predicted groundwater rise with current water tables near the top of the subgrade would experience the greatest reductions in service life (and indeed some of these would face future surface inundation from the sea level rise). Roads with existing groundwater levels more than 3 m beneath the surface were not likely to experience adverse effects from rising groundwater before the end of the 21st century. Those roads that were affected were likely to see reductions in service life of 5%–17% if groundwater rose into the subgrade, increasing to 50% reductions when groundwater moved into the subbase and base layers of the pavement. The main contribution of the study to future pavement design and maintenance practice was the use of groundwater information available from hydrogeological studies, such as the regional groundwater flow model. Adoption of such interdisciplinary approaches provides a means to reduce the future costs of premature pavement failure in affected regions and provides guidance for targeted adaption planning for coastal zones.

Extreme weather

Extreme weather events can affect road infrastructure and cause major disruptions to traffic operations. Many of the scenarios for climate change suggest that adverse weather conditions, including extreme events, are likely to occur more frequently, be more extreme and be of longer duration. The geographic spread of events such as floods, wild fires and hurricanes is also likely to widen. This stands to lead to increased levels of traffic disruptions in time and space. These disruptions will occur directly as a result of extreme weather, such as snow and blizzards, dense fog, thunderstorms and hail, and floods. There will also be more disruptions due to indirect impacts of the weather events, such as roadway inundation, landslides and rockfalls leading to blocked and collapsed roadways and damaged roadsides, and more traffic incidents and crashes due to poor visibility and slippery roads. Fig. 7.15 indicates the linkages between potential impacts on the road network, extreme weather and climate change. Transportations systems are vital for society and the economy, so that other impacts on road networks also exist: from changes in society – socioeconomic developments leading to new travel demands – and changes in technology, leading to changes in the form and operations of transportation modes.

The impacts on road networks and traffic operations fall into two main categories: impacts on supply (the states of the road system available for use) and demand (the levels of traffic demand and the temporal distributions of the demand). Following on from Snelder and Calvert (2016), who provided a comprehensive review of the impacts of extreme weather events on road transport operations, the main impacts on road network operations are

- For network supply:
  - reduced capacity, resulting from incidents and lane closures
  - reduced travel speeds and increased travel time and delays
  - reduced network connectivity, when roads are blocked due to flooding, fire or infrastructure failures

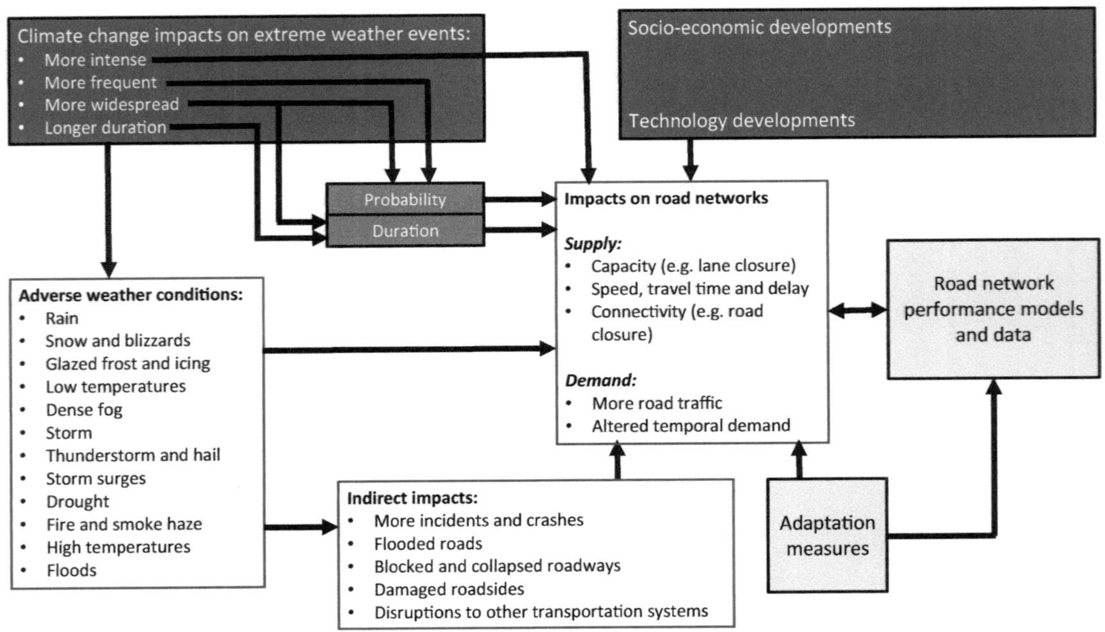

FIGURE 7.15 Relationships between extreme weather and road network performance. *Revised and extended from Snelder, M., Calvert, S., 2016. Quantifying the impact of adverse weather conditions on road network performance. Eur. J. Transp. Infrastruct. Res. 16 (1), 128–149l.*

- For network demand:
  - increased levels of traffic on unaffected parts of the network, as travellers seek alternative destinations
  - altered patterns of temporal demand as travellers adjust their schedules.

Snelder and Calvert (2016) also considered the availability of methods to quantify the impacts of extreme weather conditions, and the implementation of adaptation measures to alleviate potential impacts. The needs for refinement of existing traffic network models and the development of new models expressly to consider traffic redistribution under adverse weather were principal findings from their study. Other researchers are also considering these developments. In the case of flooding, for example,

- Pregnalato et al. (2017) proposed a relationship between the depth of standing water and vehicle travel speed for inclusion in existing traffic network models, to capture the effects on travel times of partially flooded roadways
- Kalantari et al. (2017)introduced a new model for quantifying and mapping the probability of flooding at critical locations in road networks
- Bil et al. (2015) formulated a method for evaluating road network damage caused by flooding, including estimations of the likely levels of damage to individual communities in an affected region.

The impacts of extreme weather events on transportation networks is an area ripe for further research, as is discussed in Chapter 10.

Summary

This chapter first discussed the importance of road networks as regional, state and national assets. It then considered road pavement structures and pavement design methods, including consideration of temperature impacts and water penetration. Mathematical modelling of road pavement performance was described and used to indicate how climate change factors could be incorporated in performance evaluation and therefore influence both design methods and maintenance regimes for road systems. Temperature and rainfall are the main climate factors included in the performance models. A climate variable representing temperature and rainfall — the TMI — has been shown to provide a useful representation of climate in the performance assessment of road pavements. Other factors related to extreme weather events (e.g., storms, flooding, landslides and washouts) also have to be considered. Besides their detrimental effects on road infrastructure, these weather events may also lead to restrictions on traffic operations, for periods of hours to weeks, depending on the level and extent of damage. Road agencies and operators then have to have plans and procedures to deal with these disruptions.

References

AASHTO, 2015. Mechanistic-empirical Pavement Design Guide: A Manual of Practice, second ed. American Association of State Highway and Transportation Officials, Washington DC.

AASHTO, 2018. Policy on Geometric Design of Highways and Streets, seventh ed. American Association of State Highway and Transportation Officials, Washington DC.

Austroads, 2005. Guide to Pavement Technology. Part 1: Introduction to Pavement Technology. Austroads Report AGPT01/05. Austroads, Sydney.

Austroads, 2008. Guide to Pavement Technology. Part 2: Pavement Structural Design. Austroads Report AGPT02/08. Austroads, Sydney.

Austroads, 2010a. Predicting Structural Deterioration of Pavements at a Network Level – Interim Models. Austroads Report AP-T159/10.

Austroads, 2010b. Impact of Climate Change on Road Performance: Updating Climate Information for Australia. Austroads, Sydney. Austroads Report AP–R358/10.

Austroads, 2017. Guide to Road Design Part 3: Geometric Design, third ed.2. Austroads Report AGRD03-16. Austroads Sydney.

Austroads, 2018. About Austroads. Austroads, Sydney. https://austroads.com.au/about-austroads.

Bil, M., Vodak, R., Kubecek, J., Bilova, M., Sedonik, J., 2015. Evaluating road network damage caused by natural disasters in the Czech Republic between 1997 and 2010. Transp. Res. A Pol. Pract. 91, 90–103.

BITRE, 2017. Growth in the Australian Road System. Information Sheet 92. Bureau of Infrastructure, Transport and Regional Economics. Canberra ACT. www.bitre.gov.au.

BTS, 2018. TET Chapter 8 – Value of and Investment in Transportation Infrastructure and Other Assets. Bureau of Transportation Statistics, US Department of Transportation, Washington DC. https://www.bts.gov/sites/bts.dot.gov/files/u796/TET%202018%20Chapter%208.pdf.

Gentilli, J., 1972. Australian Climate Patterns. Thomas Nelson, Melbourne.

Gudipudi, P.P., Underwood, B.S., Zalghout, A., 2017. Impact of climate change on pavement structural performance in the United States. Transp. Res. D Transp. Environ. 57, 172–184.

ITF, 2016. Adapting Transport to Climate Change and Extreme Weather: Implications for Infrastructure Owners and Network Managers. ITF Research Reports. OECD Publishing, Paris. https://doi.org/10.1787/9789282108079-en.

Kalantari, Z., Cavalli, M., cantone, C., Crema, S., Destouni, G., 2017. Flood probability quantification for road infrastructure: data-driven spatial-statistical approach and case study applications. Sci. Total Environ. 581–582, 386–398.

Knott, J.F., Elshaer, M., Danieal, J.S., Jacobs, J.M., Kirshen, P., 2017. Assessing the effects of rising groundwater from sea level rise on the service life of pavements in coastal road infrastructure. Transp. Res. Rec. 2639, 1–10.

NCHRP, 2006. Falling Weight Deflectometer Usage: A Synthesis of Highway Practice. In: National Cooperative Highway Research Program Report, vol. 381. Transportation Research Board, Washington DC.

Pregnalato, M., Ford, A., Wilkinson, S.M., Dawson, R.J., 2017. The impact of flooding on road transport: a depth-disruption function. Transp. Res. D Transp Environ. 55, 67–81.

Quao, Y., Dawson, A.R., Parry, T., Flintsch, G.W., 2015. Evaluating the effects of climate change on road maintenance intervention strategies and life-cycle costs. Transp. Res. D Transp Environ. 41, 492–503.

Snelder, M., Calvert, S., 2016. Quantifying the impact of adverse weather conditions on road network performance. Eur. J. Transp. Infrastruct. Res. 16 (1), 128–149.

Standards Australia, 2011. Residential Slabs and Footings. Standards Australia, Sydney. Australian Standard AS2870-2011.

Taylor, M.A.P., Philp, M.L., 2015. Investigating the impact of maintenance regimes on the design life of road pavements in a changing climate and the implications for transport policy. Transp. Pol. 41, 117–135.

Taylor, M.A.P., Philp, M., 2016. Beyond agriculture: a review of the Thornthwaite Moisture Index with respect to road pavements and other infrastructure applications. Int. J. Sustain. Transp. 10 (6), 528–540.

Thornthwaite, C.W., 1948. An approach toward a rational classification of climate. Geogr. Rev. 38, 55–94.

Underwood, R.T., 1995. Road Engineering Practice. MacMillan, Melbourne.

Chapter 8

Rail transportation systems

Railways are major transportation systems that perform important and vital transport tasks. They provide for bulk goods movement over long distances, form the backbone of urban transit systems in many cities and in some areas provide for long distance passenger transport, often at high speed. Specialised railway systems support industry and move commodities such as coal and mineral ores. Railway infrastructure has long life times. However, much of the existing basic rail infrastructure in many countries is old, possibly dating back to the 19th century. This infrastructure includes bridges, tunnels, cuttings and embankments. The older infrastructure was designed for trains only capable of operating on slight gradients and hence includes rail alignments with extensive cuts and embankments to provide a level track profile. Maintenance has become a major issue in many countries, with a lack of proper comprehensive maintenance now recognised in many places (e.g., ASCE, 2017). The quality of older earthworks is uncertain, and the works were designed and constructed using methods considered primitive by modern standards. This implies susceptibility to failure, especially under climate change, evolving hydrologic regimes and greater frequency and intensity of extreme weather events. Railway earthworks are similar to those employed in road networks and thus share many of the vulnerabilities described in Chapter 7. Changes in precipitation and humidity, inundation, storm surges and water penetration can all have serious impacts on rail infrastructure, as for roads. Maintenance systems may be affected similarity, with increased summer temperatures possibly restricting the time available for track maintenance and these may not be compensated for in winter months, which may be milder but wetter.

There are further issues specific to rail transportation too, and these are explored in this chapter. Largely these relate to the specific forms of propulsion and guidance under which rail vehicles (rolling stock) operate. One major concern is rail buckling under high temperatures, which may either restrict travel speeds—leading to delays and service disruptions—or even service cancellation. More generally, damage to earthworks and other components can reduce the bearing capacity of tracks, which also leads to reduced travel speeds and ultimately failure of track structures, which then require costly repairs and service degradation. While modern high-speed rail lines are built to higher design standards and may expressly include recognition of climate change in their design parameters, they are still potentially vulnerable to changes

Climate Change Adaptation for Transportation Systems. https://doi.org/10.1016/B978-0-12-816638-3.00008-8

in precipitation. Overhead components (e.g., overhead wires (or 'catenary') and pantographs for electric rail systems) and signalling systems are also at risk.

Railway systems comprise two main components: the trackway infrastructure, which includes the rails, ballast and track base as well as bridges, viaducts, tunnels, drainage, culverts, sidings, stations, marshalling yards and depots and signal and control systems, and rolling stock, i.e., the rail vehicles (locomotives, wagons and carriages) that operate on the trackway. The rolling stock will be specific to a given rail line, and the interaction between rolling stock and track is quite different to that between road vehicles and roads. The difference may be explained in terms of the following four factors (Vuchic, 2007):

1. Support, the vertical contact between the vehicle and the riding surface. For rail systems, this is generally steel wheels on steel rail[1].
2. Guidance, which covers the lateral movement of vehicles. While road vehicles are steered around corners and use tyre/pavement adhesion for this (see Chapter 7), rail vehicles are guided by flanges and the curved shape of the wheel surface. In fact a particular feature of rail technology is that the wheel–rail assembly provides both support and guidance.
3. Propulsion, the energy source and method of traction. For modern rail systems diesel engines and electric motors are the common forms for propulsion. The use of electricity as the energy source requires the use of continuous overhead wires and cables (or in some cases a 'third rail' embedded in the track structure, such as in some urban rail systems).
4. Control, which covers the methods adopted for regulating the traversal of one or all vehicles in the rail system. For rail, with long deceleration distances, the longitudinal spacing of vehicles on a given track is crucial, especially on single track corridors where trains may be operating in each direction. Strict control measures are required to ensure that vehicles are kept separate at all times. Overtaking is only possible at designated sidings or passing loops or at stations with multiple connected tracks.

As described in the next section, consideration of these four factors provides the basis for the component structure of a rail transportation system.

Railway systems are valuable assets, which may be in either public or private sector hands. BTS (2018) estimated the net value of the US rail system as $397 billion. The United States has the world's largest rail network with about 225,000 km of track and over 100,000 bridges (ASCE, 2017). The system contains two categories: intercity passenger rail operated by Amtrak and private freight railroads. Passenger rail is concentrated on the east coast

1. Some urban transit (metro) systems use rubber tyred rolling stock, e.g., some lines on the Paris metro, and on several other metro systems around the world

and the upper Midwest (Chinowksy et al., 2019). The freight railroads may be seen in three classes based on distance traversed and earnings (ASCE, 2017): 7 large Class I railroads, 21 regional Class II railroads and 547 short line Class III railroads.

By way of comparison:

- France has about 32,000 km of rail track, valued at about $31 billion. Passenger travel dominates, largely through the very fast train (TGV) intercity system (SNCF, 2018).
- The United Kingdom has about 28,000 km of rail track, valued at about $83.3 billion (Network Rail, 2018).
- Australia has some 36,000 km of trail track, valued at $3.2 billion. While the network is transcontinental, coverage is sparse. Freight transport dominates the long distance travel (ARTC, 2018).
- China has about 112,000 km of railways (Liu et al., 2018).

In addition, the rail track infrastructure in France, the UK and Australia is managed in the public sector, while train services may be operated by a mixture of public and private operators (France) or by private operators (UK and Australia). One planning and management issue common to many railway systems is a lack of funding and resources for adequate maintenance of existing infrastructure assets. Climate change may only exacerbate this issue.

Adapting railway infrastructure to climate change is a substantial challenge (ARA, 2014). Rail infrastructure is vast, is ageing and has an extremely long useful life, and decisions made now will have impact on whether or not future generations will be granted the same level of mobility and supply chain efficiencies as currently experienced. Future proofing rail infrastructure requires time and resources, which may not be readily available under current planning and management regimes. UITP (2016) argued that climate change is likely to have significant impact on rail operations, through the gradual changes in climate that could affect the durability and functionality of rail infrastructure—such as increases in temperature and sea level rise—and through increased intensity, severity and frequency of extreme weather events. Increased climate hazards along with increased demand for mobility will lead to increased levels of disruption in rail services. Fig. 8.1 provides an initial summary of the weather events that may affect rail transportation, the problems stemming from these events, likely component failures in the rail system, and the potential impacts of those failures. This figure uses the seven component subsystems identified by UITP (2016) as forming the basic parts of a rail transportation system; these components and the relationships between them are described more fully in the next section of this chapter. Stipanovic et al. (2013) present a similar diagrammatic view of events, problems, failures and impacts, directed specifically to the railway system in the Netherlands.

Rail infrastructure failures can lead to cascading impacts on service delivery, starting with delays to individual trains that spread into timetable

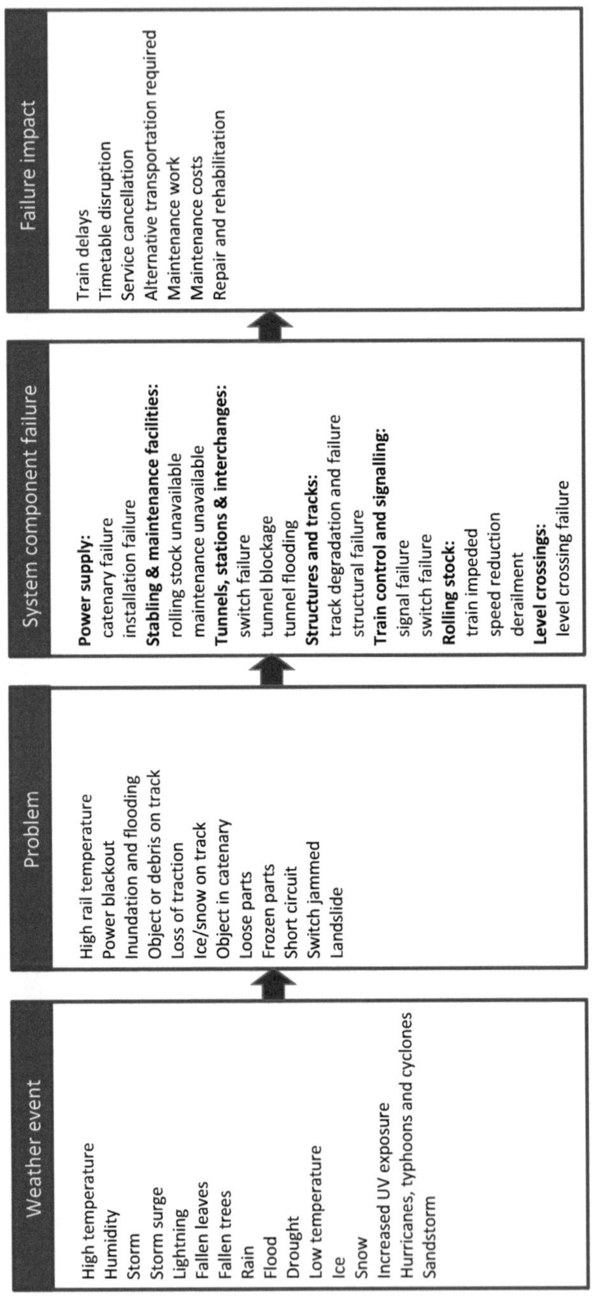

FIGURE 8.1 Broad impacts of extreme weather events on rail transportation, using the seven rail subsystems identified by UITP (2016).

disruptions and eventually service cancellations. Blocked, unusable or degraded track sections and train control and signal system failures will lead directly to these impacts. Failures in power supplies (for electrified services) and reductions in capabilities for infrastructure maintenance will also have significant impacts. Quinn et al. (2017) introduced the 'Rail Adapt' vision for rail transportation, which is 'A transport system in which the world's railways have acquired the flexibility to intelligently adjust to climate change, thereby providing their economies and societies with reliable and cost-efficient transportation services.' (Quinn et al., 2017, p.2).

They further specified that a climate adapted rail system should exhibit the following characteristics:

1. Operated by organisations which are themselves adaptive, embedding the capacity for adaptation in all of their functions, not merely in asset management
2. Study and understand the range of current and future weather conditions which will affect the rail system, with management and operational plans in place to enable the organisation to respond effectively to weather challenges both at present and in future times
3. Comprehend how climate change may affect the range of operating conditions over time and evolve its operational and management plans to keep pace with or anticipate the changes in the climate affecting the system
4. Adapt to climate change as part of 'business as usual' so that the costs of adaptation have only marginal effects on financial performance.

To achieve these characteristics, Quinn et al. (2017) recommended that strategic planning for railway systems take on board two main criteria:

1. Resilience, the ability of a rail organisation to provide services effectively and sustainably as the climate changes. This includes elements of robustness—the ability to resist disruption; redundancy—the ability to use backup facilities to provide service during disruption; and recovery—the ability to quickly return to service after disruption.
2. Adaptation, the process of making changes to the delivery of services so that they are resilient to disruption now and in the future. This includes both physical changes to infrastructure and organisational changes that facilitate intelligent adjustments to service provision, foresight of problems and learning from experience.

The Rail Adapt framework proposed by Quinn et al. (2017) is based on the integration of adaptation into 'business as usual' for rail systems. Fig. 8.2 presents the framework.

The Rail Adapt framework has two main parts. The first is an adaptation strategy. The second is an implementation plan. The objectives of the rail organisation drive the adaptation strategy, which involves identification of hazards, system vulnerabilities and potential consequences. These tasks are

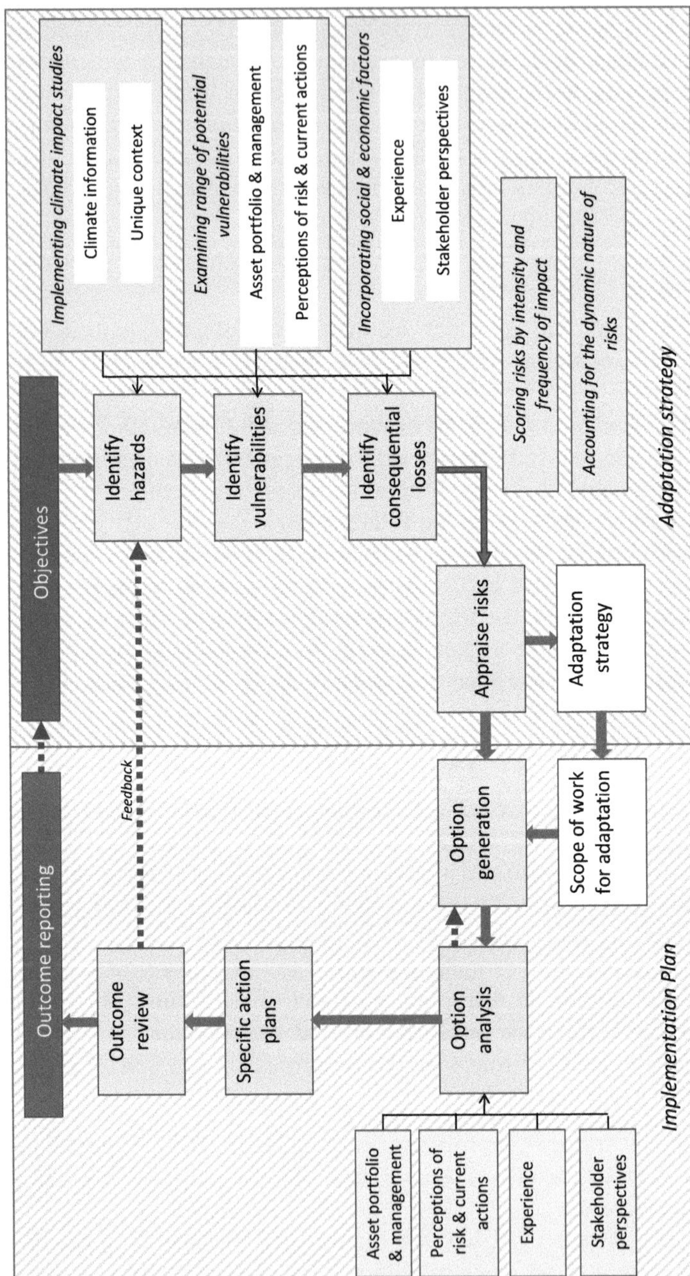

FIGURE 8.2 The Rail Adapt framework proposed by Quinn et al. (2017) as a climate change adaptation strategy for railway systems.

informed by considerations of the range of potential vulnerabilities in the rail system, the outputs of climate impact studies for the region served by the railway and the social and economic factors impinging on the rail system. Inputs to the latter two of these considerations come from the management of the assets available, perceptions of risk and current actions by the organisation, the expertise and experience of the organisation and the perspectives of its stakeholders. The climate impact studies are based on thorough knowledge of existing climatic conditions for the region and forecasts of its future climate. Risk appraisal completes the adaptation strategy. This appraisal accounts for the dynamic nature of the risks identified and their intensities and frequencies of impact. Given the available resources for the organisation, the implementation plan can be instigated. The first stage of the plan is the generation of alternative options, which are then analysed—again making use of the organisation's asset management, perceptions of risk and experience, along with stakeholder inputs. An iterative process between option generation and analysis results, from which a set of specific action plans can be developed and implemented. The outcomes of the action plans provide new feedback for future hazard identification, and the broader view of the outcomes may influence the ongoing objectives of the organisation. The framework thus defines an ongoing adaptation system, which involves learning and knowledge development on climate impacts over time.

Quin et al. (2017) suggested that this framework could be applied to any rail organisation.

Rail system components

Railways are complex transportation systems, and climate and weather factors may affect them in a variety of ways. To come to terms with the complexity inherent in rail, there is value in considering the set of subsystems that together form a railway transportation system. UITP (2016) proposed the following set of subsystems to this end. These subsystems have already been seen in Fig. 8.1. The seven subsystems are the following:

1. Power supply, which for an electric rail system is commonly based on overhead cables (catenary) to which the train connects via a pantograph. The catenary is subject to excessive temperatures, wind, ice, snow and possibly falling debris (e.g., trees) amongst other factors. Loss of power means that a train cannot proceed. Diesel powered locomotives are less affected, as long as adequate fuel supplies are available.
2. Stabling and maintenance facilities, including the depots, sidings, marshalling yards and storage facilities, which are all subject to the prevailing weather conditions in a region.
3. Tunnels, stations and interchanges, which provide for track progression through hills and mountains or in underground systems in urban areas and

allow for passenger access to and egress from trains and to and from other transportation modes. Flooding is a particular issue for tunnels and underground facilities and may also be subject to blockages, restricting services.

4. Structure and track, which includes bridges, viaducts and culverts, as well as earthworks. Rail track is the basic and essential element of any rail system.
5. Train control and signalling: efficient, fail-safe control systems are essential for all rail operations, and in modern systems include direct communications between a train control centre and individual trains as well as conventional signal installations along the rail line. Any failure in the control system may lead to service shutdown, at least on affected lines, with potential cascading effects to other parts of the system because of train delays and lack of availability of rolling stock.
6. Rolling stock, which are the rail vehicles—locomotives, carriages and wagons—that form the trains using the system.
7. Level crossings, as the places where road networks intersect at grade with rail lines. These are points of hazard for all transportation operations and strict and efficient operation of crossing facilities (e.g., boom gates and flashing signals) is essential. While major rail lines may have grade separation between road and rail, there are still very many level crossings present on rail systems, and these points of interaction with other transportation modes need to be properly identified and treated.

Fig. 8.3 provides a schematic view of these subsystems as would be seen on a basic rail transportation system. Elements of these systems were considered by Pant et al. (2016) in terms of different assets which were necessary for rail operations and could be vulnerable to a range of impacts, including extreme weather and climate change. Table 8.1 shows the asset elements identified by Pant et al. (2016) and the UITP subsystems to which the elements belong.

In addition, the rail transportation system involves a number of interdependencies with other infrastructure systems. These interdependencies were also explored by Pant et al. (2016). Railway systems exhibit all of the four types of infrastructure interdependencies discussed in Chapter 3. Besides geographical interdependency, when different infrastructure systems share a common infrastructure asset, such as a bridge,

- Physical interdependencies exist in many cases, such as when an electrified rail system is used to supply coal to the power station that generates the electricity. A case study on this particular interdependency was reported by Wood (2019) as part of the 'Tomorrow's Railway and Climate Change Adaptation' (TRACCA) project (Dora, 2011).

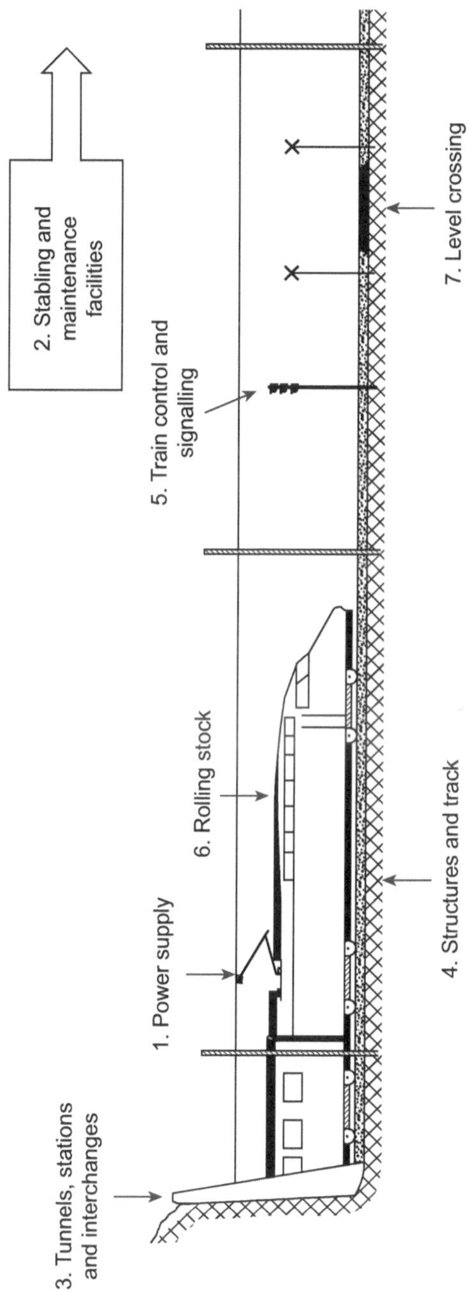

FIGURE 8.3 Schematic representation of the seven UITP (2016) subsystems which together form a rail transportation system.

TABLE 8.1 Component elements of rail transportation identified by Pant et al. (2016) and the UITP subsystems to which they belong.

		UITP sub-system						
Component	Element	Power supply	Stabling and maintenance	Tunnels, stations and interchanges	Structure and track	Train control and signalling	Rolling stock	Level crossings
Local electrification	Electrification switching	✓						
	Local electrification substation	✓						
Signalling system	Supply point					✓		
	Signal centre/route					✓		
	Control/relay room					✓		
	Signal box					✓		
Lighting	Yards and maintenance		✓					
	Walkways			✓				
	Tunnels			✓				
	Bridge/navigation				✓			
Traction	Grid supply substation	✓						
	Overhead cables	✓			✓		✓	

Heating and cooling	Pumps		✓	✓				
	Points heating		✓	✓		✓		
Monitoring	Electrical control room	✓	✓					
	Remote monitoring			✓		✓	✓	
	Level crossing control							✓
	Telecommunications		✓	✓			✓	

- Cyber interdependency, when the operating state of the rail system depends on the transmission of information, e.g., for train control and monitoring, through a telecommunications system.
- Logical interdependency, due to connections between rail and road transportation through freight hubs and service scheduling (e.g., for multimodal urban public transport).

Rail systems present unique vulnerabilities to the track structure, overhead components and signalling elements. The next section considers these vulnerabilities.

Rail infrastructure

The 'structures and track' subsystem forms the bulk of the infrastructure in a rail network. Rail track structure consists of a pair of rails, laid on sleepers (ties), and with joints between each rail section. Modern track provision uses continuous welded rail, which means that individual rail sections may be up to 200–250 m long. This provides for good riding quality but, as will be discussed, is a new potential hazard under increasing temperatures associated with climate change. The track structure is laid on a bed of ballast (gravel or crushed rock) or on concrete slabs (e.g., at stations or in metro systems). The ballast may be in one or more layers. Fig. 8.4 provides a basic profile of a single track railway. The service life of rail track components is relatively long; for instance, ITF (2016) cites the following service lives for rails, sleepers, points and ballast:

- Timber sleepers, 35 years
- Concrete sleepers, 55 years
- Continuously welded rail (CWR), 70 years
- Bolt joint tails, 60 years
- Ballast, more than 60 years.

There are two ramifications from these service lives: (1) much of the existing rail infrastructure may already be quite old (given the limitations on rail maintenance observed in recent years, e.g., ITF, 2016; Bai et al., 2017; Chinowsky et al., 2019), and (2) even newly installed rail track is most likely

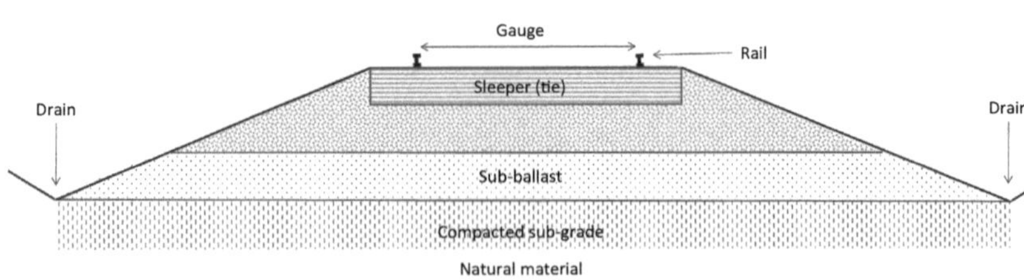

FIGURE 8.4 Simple representation of a rail track, showing rails, sleepers (ties) and ballast.

to be affected by mid- to long-term changes in climate. This in conjunction with the long service lives of rail earthworks is a pointer to the particular vulnerability of rail systems to climate change.

Rails have particular vulnerabilities, especially for CWR. Expansion due to extreme temperatures or a wide range of temperatures at a given location can lead to rail buckling. The rail structure exemplified by Fig. 8.4 is designed to carry heavy vertical loads, but it is less capable with regard to lateral loads. Thermal expansion of the rails due to temperatures well above the installation temperature for the rail[2] induces compressive stresses in the rail which can lead to lateral movement of the rail: buckling. Rail susceptibility to buckling is a function of the level of thermal-induced compressive strength, weakened track and ballast conditions, and the dynamic loadings applied to the rails by passing trains. While the rail buckling problem has been known for a long time and design measures to prevent or mitigate buckling are in common use, climate change with increased temperatures and perhaps more occasions of extreme temperatures introduces new levels of risk into track management. Cognition of likely future increases in expected temperatures should mean the adoption of progressively higher Rail Neutral Temperature (RNT) for future track installation and replacement of existing tracks, with growing attention also to the potential longitudinal, lateral and vertical movements of the rails. Periods of high temperature and wide (diurnal) temperature ranges may require track monitoring and the possible adjustment of train loads and speeds. This may then have an impact on rail service provision and on network capacity (ITF, 2016). Fig. 8.5, from Yang and Bradford (2018), shows an example of rail buckling.

Volpe (undated) identified three major factors influencing rail track buckling. These are the following:

1. The rail longitudinal force (RLF), which is related to the difference between the actual temperature of the rail and the rail neutral temperature (RNT), the temperature at which the rail is 'stress-free'. The initial value of RNT is the temperature at which the rail was installed; however, RNT is likely to decrease over time due to a variety of factors including longitudinal movement of the rail over time, lateral shifts on curves, vertical settlement of the track and maintenance activities. This is the major factor influencing buckling, as the compressive force in the rail is a direct cause of buckling. Even under a stable climate, this influence is likely to increase over time; a warming climate will exacerbate this influence.
2. Track lateral resistance (TLR) is the reaction force of by the ballast to the rail-sleeper structure, and this provides the primary restraint against buckling. TLR is highly variable and is influenced by many factors, including track construction and maintenance procedures. A rail track with

2. This temperature is known as the RNT.

FIGURE 8.5 Example of buckled railway track. *From US Department of Transportation 2015, 1, p.108.*

decreased TLR subject to a high RLF is susceptible to buckling. TLR is a complex force including both static and dynamic components. Analytical predictions of buckling require a detailed knowledge of the TLR for a given location.

3. Track lateral alignment (TLA) is also important, for defects in the lateral alignment increase the potential for track buckling. Specific locations with large alignment defects are the most likely locations for the initiation of vbuckling.

Yang and Bradford (2018) developed a finite element model of the derailment vulnerability of trains passing over a buckled track. This model considered the effects of train speed, buckle amplitude, buckle shape, rail size and TLR on the propensity for derailment. They concluded that train speed and amplitude of buckle played significant roles in derailments. Rail size and track maintenance work were found to be secondary factors on the derailment propensity for the same size buckling amplitude because they could increase the buckling length. Buckling amplitude is strongly affected by RLF, TLR and TLA.

Temperature may be taken to be the primary environmental/climate factor affecting rail buckling (Nemry and Demirel, 2012; Chinowsky et al., 2019). On the assumption that RNT is the temperature for which the rail is intended to operate stress-free, then the rail would function optimally at this temperature. Chinowksy et al. (2019) used this assumption to develop a probabilistic model of rail buckling based on European research (e.g., Esveld, 1998 and

Nemry and Demeril, 2012). They then used this model to investigate rail network performance in the United States under different climate scenarios and adaptation approaches for the study period 2016–99. This study is reported as a case study later in this chapter, but it is useful to look at the relationship between rail temperature (T) and buckling probability (P_b) at this point in the discussion. The starting point is the design value for RNT, which is generally taken as three quarters of the expected maximum temperature for the region ($T_{\max}$), i.e., if T_N is the RNT, then

$$T_N = \frac{3}{4} T_{\max} \tag{8.1}$$

The actual temperature of the track (T) is required for the analysis. This temperature will be higher than the ambient air temperature (T_a), and the installation of temperature sensors on the track is now being proposed (Chinowksy et al., 2019). However, sensor installation is expensive and track length is great, so that sensor-based information may not be readily available until sometime in the future. Consequently, the following relation between air temperature and assumed rail temperature has been employed:

$$T = \frac{3}{2} T_a \tag{8.2}$$

Eq. (8.2) can be readily employed to estimate trail track temperatures at a given location under alternative climate scenarios, where T_a is taken to be the projected average maximum temperature in summer (Chinowksy et al., 2019).

The operational consequence of increased likelihood of rail buckling is the reduction of travel speeds for trains on the affected rail section. Three important temperature values may be identified:

1. The maximum track temperature at which there is no risk of buckling ($T_{b,\min}$),
2. The temperature at which buckling will definitely occur (i.e., for which $P_b = 1$), designated as $T_{b,\max}$ and
3. For temperatures $T_{b,\min} < T < T_{b,\max}$, there will be a finite probability that buckling will occur, i.e., $0 < P_b\ (T) < 1$. To ensure track safety, T_m is the maximum allowable track temperature, above the RNT, that is considered safe.

Esveld (1998) indicated that T_m should be taken as the temperature at 50% of buckling energy, given by

$$T_m = T_{b,\min} + \frac{1}{4}\left(T_{b,\max} - T_{b,\min}\right) \tag{8.3}$$

Then the buckling probability can be calculated using a relationship between buckling energy and rail temperature. At temperature $T_{b,\max}$, the *additional* energy required to buckle the track is zero. At temperature $T_{b,\min}$,

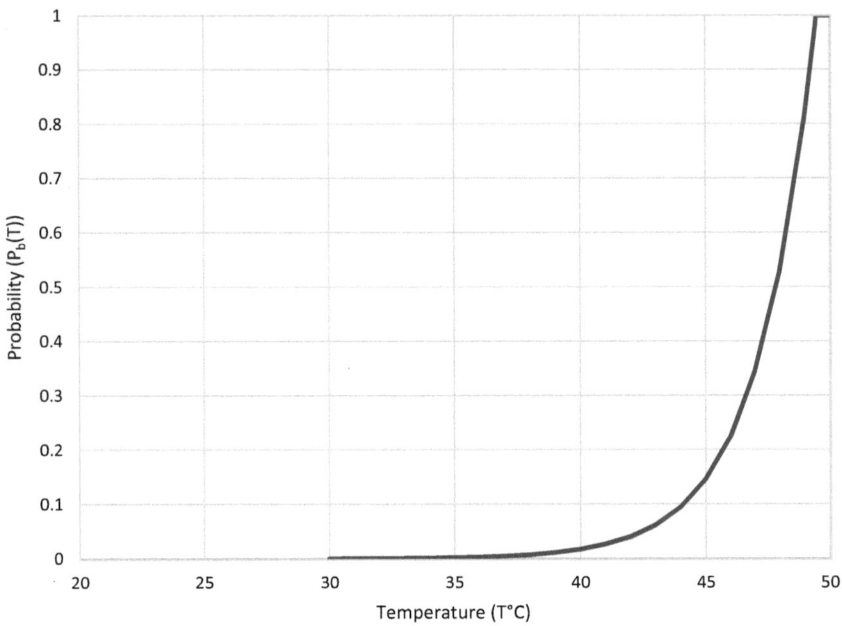

FIGURE 8.6 Buckling probability P_B as a function of temperature (T), using the relationship given by Chinowsky et al. (2019).

the maximum amount of additional energy is required to buckle the track, and for temperatures $T_{b,\min} < T < T_{b,\max}$, the amount of additional energy required for buckling decreases exponentially. Consequently, there will be an exponential relationship between buckling probability and temperature. Chinowsky et al. (2019) used the following relationship for buckling probability, for $30 < T < 50$ where T is °C:

$$P_b = 6 \times 10^{-10} \exp(0.4291T) \tag{8.4}$$

This relationship is illustrated in Fig. 8.6.

Chinowsky et al. (2019) used Eq. (8.6) to compute the reduced speed ($V_r(T)$) to avoid buckling using the Kish–Samavedam equation (Kish and Samavedan, 2013), which is

$$V_r(T) = V_{\max}\sqrt{1 - \frac{P_b(T)}{P_b(T_m)}} \tag{8.5}$$

where $V_{\max}$ is the permissible maximum speed on the rail line section. Some interpretation and judgement of the use of this equation is necessary under extreme temperature scenarios, for the equation may indicate reduced speeds of the order of 16 km/h (10 mph) which is far below common practice. Chinowsky et al. (2019) suggested a minimum value for reduced speed of

64 km/h (40 mph) would in line with common practice. Eqs (8.1)–(8.6) represent a risk-based approach to train speed reduction in an environment where temperature-induced rail buckling is possible. The use of this mathematical model along with estimations of potential impacts on rail services in the United States is described in the case studies section of this chapter.

Overhead cable structures—the catenary—in electrified rail systems also pose a significant vulnerability to climate change which is unique to rail transportation. Changes in winter precipitation regimes may lead to increased winter rainfall in conditions near freezing. The icing that may potentially occur as a result can damage the overhead cables, leading to delays and service disruptions. Increases in the frequency and severity of storms and extreme winds may also contribute to service disruption and delay through falling trees and other debris landing on the catenary. Increased proactive maintenance involving management of trackside vegetation may thus be necessary.

As for road infrastructure, railway infrastructure such as earthworks, tunnels and bridges is vulnerable to extreme weather and associated events. Flooding is a major cause of service disruption and can cause damage to infrastructure. Given that the lateral resistance of rail track structures is comparatively low when exposed to extreme precipitation and the hydraulic forces inherent in flood events, and rail track is particularly vulnerable to erosion and subsidence, rail infrastructure may experience significant adverse impacts from increased extreme weather events under climate change.

One specific existing rail track problem that may be impacted by climate change so that it requires new treatments is that of track components at bridge transition zones or approach areas, where sudden changes in track stiffness between the subgrade and the bridge may lead to high impact dynamic loads and vibration. This issue was recently investigated by Setsobhonkul et al. (2017). Three issues can arise in transition zones:

1. An abrupt change in vertical stiffness of the track may lead to an abrupt change in elevation of the wheel, due to uneven track deflection between the subgrade and the (bridge) slab,
2. Ballasted track located on ground formation (and at-grade track) will tend to settle more than ballasted track on a structure (e.g., a slab) and
3. Settlement of at-grade track is highly variable due to geotechnical issues such as deficient compaction, poor drainage, erosion and low strength soils.

Current design practices include two main options for transition zones: (1) equalisation of the stiffness and rail deflection of the ballasted and slab tracks, such as the use of softer elastic materials to reduce the stiffness of the on-slab track to match that of the on-ballast track, and (2) gradually increase the stiffness of the ballasted track in the transition zone to match that of the on-slab track. Transition zones are a maintenance priority as ballast can deteriorate more rapidly in the zone, leading to differential settlement.

A number of techniques to provide gradual changes in track stiffness or reduce the stiffness of track on a bridge are in use, including the following:

- Ballast bonding (ballast glue method), which reduces ballast settlement and increases ballast stiffness by applying adhesive material to bond ballast gravel pieces together. The 'glue' is applied at different densities between groups of (usually four) sleepers in the transition zone, with the sleeper group immediately adjacent to the bridge receiving the highest density of adhesive material
- Embankment treatments, in which the embankment structure under the ballast in the transition zone is modified using selected backfill materials that are heavily compacted
- Rail pads, which are relatively soft elastic materials used to support the rail and reduce track stiffness over the bridge
- Soft baseplates. The baseplate is constructed from rubber and steel components and is used to form a rail fastening system so that the rails are fitted to the bridge slab via the baseplate. This reduces the stiffness of the on-slab rail
- Underballast mats are designed to reduce dynamic loads by moderating the stiffer portions of the track, especially for ballasted tracks on bridges and viaducts. The mat is an elastic material installed between the ballast and the underlying slab structure
- Undersleeper pads, which are resilient materials installed between the ballast and the sleepers in the transition zone. The pads generally contain two types of material: one to provide additional stiffness and the other for environmental protection.

The choice of appropriate treatments for transition zones depends on a number of factors, including climatic conditions, with temperature, precipitation and flooding prominent amongst these. Setsobhonkul et al. (2017) conducted a series of experiments to ascertain the performance of the above treatments under different conditions—existing conditions, high temperatures, low temperatures and flash flooding—and considered the life cycle costs of the treatments (and how these costs varied under the different climate conditions). Their results are summarised in Table 8.2. Overall, while soft baseplates and rail pads performed best under existing conditions for both bridges and viaducts, other treatments were preferable under changed climatic conditions. Under high temperatures, ballast bonding performed best, and this treatment was also suitable for long-span bridges under flash flooding and low temperatures (and indeed for existing conditions). Embankment treatments were best under low temperatures and satisfactory under existing conditions. These results suggest that design and maintenance practices for transition zones may need to change in adapting to climate changes.

TABLE 8.2 Recommendations for rail transition zone treatments for long span bridges and viaducts (short span bridges) on the basis of service performance and cost, as indicated by Setsobhonkul et al. (2017).

	Climate scenario							
	Existing conditions		High temperatures		Low temperatures		Flash flooding	
Transition zone treatment	Long-span	Viaduct	Long-span	Viaduct	Long-span	Viaduct	Long-span	Viaduct
Ballast bonding	②		①	①	②		②	
Embankment treatment	②				①	①		
Rail pad	①	①						
Soft baseplate	①	①					①	①
Underballast mat						②		
Undersleeper pad								②

Rail operations

Consideration of rail operations requires some background in the nature of rail traffic flow. Rail traffic flow is granular in nature—consisting of large flow units (trains) with headways (time separations) dictated by stringent operating rules. In the main, these rules require that no two trains should occupy the same section (track, junction or platform) at the same time. In general terms, the capacity at any location in a railway system is then the maximum number of trains that can occupy that location over a time period τ, where τ is commonly taken to be an extended period of time such as an hour or, quite frequently, a day. If $\overline{h}$ is the required average headway between trains, then the capacity (maximum number of trains) MT is given by

$$MT = \frac{\tau}{\overline{h}} \tag{8.6}$$

The average headway needs to be defined according to the particular component of the railway system under consideration:

- For rail lines, the average headway would be the average time gap between the front of a moving train to the front of the next moving train, as measured by an observer standing at the side of the track
- For rail tracks at stations, the average headway is the time gap between two successive occupations of the track, irrespective of whether the trains stop or not
- At junction nodes, the average headway is the time gap between two successive trains, departing from the same starting or finishing points in their paths.

Calculation of capacity using Eq. (8.6) is further complicated by the facts that train arrivals are often stochastic and that there may be irregular (not on time) trains that have different impacts on each component of a railway system.

The main idea behind railway capacity analysis is therefore to identify present and future bottlenecks in the railway system. Two aspects reflect all criteria that can be defined with respect to the capacity of railway infrastructure:

1. Operational feasibility—indicates whether a given traffic scenario can be performed on the infrastructure while satisfying a certain predefined quality of service criteria (in terms of punctuality, reliability, delay sensitivity and stability).
2. Planning flexibility—refers to the range of traffic scenarios that are feasible on the same infrastructure.

The evaluation of the capacity of railway systems is of key importance for the management of rail infrastructure. In formal terms, railway capacity can be defined as the maximum frequency of a certain pattern of train movements for which delays do not propagate unduly. The capacity of a railway system has to be determined using different methods for rail lines and for railway stations.

The starting point for railway capacity study is the 'train graph', a trajectory diagram which shows the position of a train along a rail track over time. Fig. 8.7 shows a set of simple train graphs. The starting point is Fig. 8.7A, which is a train graph showing the movement of one train along a rail track from location O to location S3. This train is travelling at a constant speed, which may be taken as the posted maximum speed (and is given by the slope of the diagonal lines in the trajectory). The train makes two stops along the section, at S1 and S2. Fig. 8.7B shows the same train journey, but at a reduced speed (perhaps as a result of a speed reduction because of an increased potential for rail buckling). The dashed line in this graph is the train journey at the reduced speed. The time difference between the arrival time at S3 for the scheduled journey and for the reduced speed journey is the delay time. There will be a cost associated with this extra travel time, which is the additional cost incurred because of the need to reduce the speed. However, there is more to consider. Fig. 8.7C shows a second train travelling from O to S3 at about the

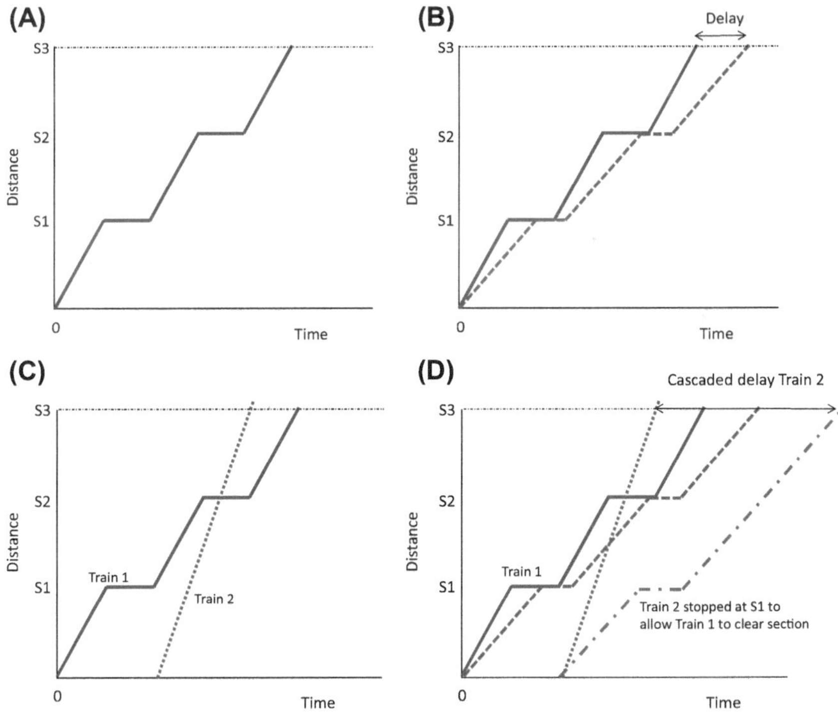

FIGURE 8.7 Simple train graphs showing (A) a single train journey along a track, (B) the same journey at reduced speed (e.g., through temperature-based buckling potential) and hence experiencing delay, (C) two trains on the same track, where Train 2 is an express that passes Train 1 at station S2, and (D) potential for cascading delay under reduced speeds, as Train 2 must wait at S1 (an unscheduled stop) to allow Train 2 to clear the track S1–S2 before it can proceed.

same time as the first train. This train, Train 2, is an express service that makes no stops along the section and can pass Train 1 whilst Train 1 is stationary at S2. This can only happen if all trains are travelling at their posted (maximum) speeds. In Fig. 8.7D, speeds have been reduced to a safe level (because of rail buckling potential) and both trains must adhere to this reduced speed. Now it is no longer possible for Train 2 to pass Train 1 at S2, and in fact Train 2 must now make an unscheduled stop at S1 to allow Train 1 to clear the track section before it can proceed. Train 2 now experiences a large delay, not just due to reduced speed but also due to the necessary rescheduling of services on the track. The delay to Train 2 and possibly other subsequent trains is thus cascading, and the capacity of the rail track will be reduced.

Rail line capacity has two basic dimensions:

- *Traffic capacity of a rail line*, which represents the maximum traffic volume expressed in trains or railcars on the respective line within a certain time frame (day or hour), depending on the existent fixed installations(infrastructure), the type and power of the locomotives, the types of cars and the way the traffic is organised.
- *Transport capacity of a rail line*, which represents the possible volume of freight traffic (or passengers) that can be hauled on a rail line during a year, expressed in million tonnes of freight (or number of passengers). Transport capacity can be further classified as
  - existing capacity
  - potential capacity (designed)
  - required capacity.

Existing capacity is determined taking into account the existing resources of the line (infrastructure, rolling stock, staff, etc.) and the method used to organise train traffic.

The design potential capacity is calculated taking into account the planed resources of the line and the corresponding method of traffic organisation.

Required capacity is calculated as a function of the planned transport volume and has to satisfy the traffic of the planned number of trains of a certain tonnage on the respective line, taking also into account the required reserve of capacity. Opportunity to undertake scheduled maintenance work will also need to be taken into account.

The reserve of traffic capacity is determined for each section of the rail track taking into account general technical and economic considerations, by calculating the difference between the existing traffic capacity of the line and the required traffic capacity. Generally the reserve of capacity has to be

1. for double-track lines, 15%–20% of the maximum designed capacity
2. for single-track lines, 25%–35% of the maximum designed capacity

The traffic capacity can be calculated not only globally for a rail line/section but also locally for stations. The principal elements of the technical installations, which determine the traffic capacity, are the

- number of lines
- length of the lines
- profile of the line
- type of locomotive
- train tonnage
- type of rail cars
- signalling installations
- number of sidings
- maintenance lines
- depot lines
- fuelling installations, etc.

The smallest value of the traffic capacity determined taking into account the stations, depots, and other installations is the 'resultant traffic capacity'. The traffic capacity of each element of the technical installations Z is calculated as a function of the daily or hourly capacity consumed to serve a train, i.e.,

$$Z = \frac{1440 - T_{perm}}{t} \tag{8.7}$$

where T_{perm} is the time the examined installation is occupied with permanent operations (not related to train traffic), in minutes per day and t is the average time in minutes that the installation is occupied by a train. Eq. (8.7) represents the direct method of calculation for traffic capacity and can be used when trying to calculate the capacity of a line. Taking into account the coefficient of utilisation of the capacity K_u, the traffic capacity can be written as

$$Z = \frac{\widehat{Z}}{K_u} \tag{8.8}$$

where $\widehat{Z}$ is the actual number of trains in the train graph and $K_u = \frac{tN'}{1440 - T_{perm}}$.

The traffic capacity can be calculated for both parallel and nonparallel graphs for all the elements of the technical installations. In a parallel train graph (Fig. 8.8A), two successive trains travel at the same speed, keeping a set distance between them. Fig. 8.8B shows a nonparallel graph in which the two trains travel at different speeds. If there is no location where the second train can pass the first, it must wait at a minimum distance behind the first train before it can move again.

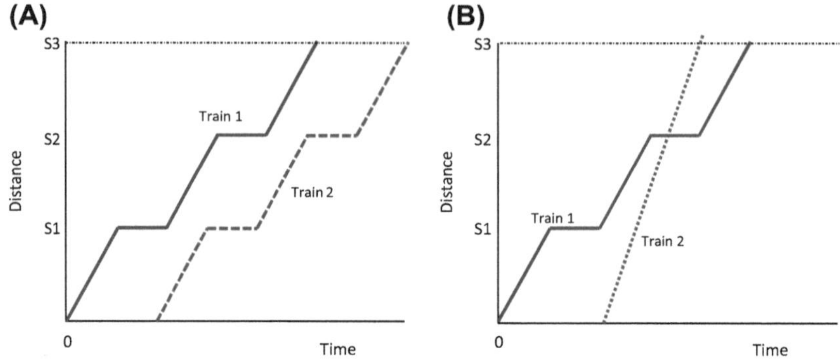

FIGURE 8.8 Parallel and nonparallel train graphs: (A) parallel train graph, with two trains travelling at same speed a set distance apart, and (B) nonparallel train graph with two trains travelling at different speeds (e.g., a local train and an express).

In the parallel graph case the capacity is calculated only for the freight traffic or only for the passenger traffic. In the case of a parallel graph with no interruptions in the movement of the trains, $T_{perm} = 0$ and the traffic capacity Z is

$$Z = \frac{1440 N_T}{T_p} \tag{8.9}$$

where T_p is the period of the graph in minutes and N_T is the number of trains in that period. The traffic capacity of a single track line can then be determined, given that the period of the graph is calculated from

$$T_p = t_1 + t_2 + \sum t_{st} + \sum t_{ss} \tag{8.10}$$

where t_1 and t_2 are the travel times without any stops, in both directions, Σt_{st} is the sum of station intervals and Σt_{ss} is the sum of times spent with the deceleration and acceleration of the train over all of its stops.

In the nonparallel case—Fig. 8.8B, which is the norm—different categories of trains have different speeds so their routes in the graph are not parallel. Although in the nonparallel traffic graph, different categories of trains are represented, in general the traffic capacity is determined in terms of freight trains, taking also into account the time the other trains take in the graph. The time that cannot be used for the traffic of the freight trains is called *reduction time of the freight trains due to the passenger trains*. This time reduction is made up of the following:

1. The time a section of the track is occupied by transiting passenger trains, t_0
2. The time that cannot be used for the traffic of the freight train because the interval between the passenger trains is not a multiple of the time required to fit in a freight train, the supplementary reduction time, t_{sr}.

Then the reduction time for a train (or pair of trains) will be $t_r = t_0 + t_{sr}$ and the traffic capacity for freight trains is

$$N_f = \frac{1440 - t_r N_c}{T_p} \tag{8.11}$$

where N_f is the traffic capacity of freight trains (freight trains or pairs of freight trains) for the studied time period, N_c is the number of pairs of passenger trains and all times are in minutes.

If $\frac{t_r}{T_p} = e_c$, the reduction coefficient of freight trains by passenger trains is then

$$N_f = N - e_c N_c \tag{8.12}$$

where N is the maximum traffic capacity in the case of a parallel graph. For the general case, the traffic capacity is calculated from

$$N_f = N - \sum_{i=1}^{n} e_c^i N_c^i - \left(e_{trc}^f - 1\right) N_{trc}^f - \left(e_1^{mf} - 1\right) N_1^f \tag{8.13}$$

where $\sum_{i=1}^{n} e_c^i N_c^i$ = the sum of the reduction coefficients corresponding to different categories of passenger trains and their number, respectively, the number of freight train pairs eliminated from the graph by the passenger trains e_{trc}^f, e_1^f = the reduction coefficients due to the traffic of other trains (e.g., local freight); N_{trc}^f, N_1^f = the number of other train pairs.

The *transport capacity* C_t of a rail line in each direction is the total volume of freight that can be transported on the line over an extended period, e.g., a year. It is estimated using the equation

$$C_t = \frac{365 N_f Q_g \phi}{10^6 K_n} + C_{trc} + C_{1m} \tag{8.14}$$

where C_t is in million tonnes per annum, N_f is the maximum number of long haul freight trains that can traverse the line in 24 h, Q_g is the gross tonnage of the freight trains, in tonnes, φ is the ratio of the net tonnage to the gross tonnage of the train, K_n is a monthly transport nonuniformity coefficient and C_{trc} and C_{1m} indicate the quantity of freight hauled by other freight trains (local freight, etc.), in million tonnes per annum.

The maximum number of long haul freight trains (N_f), i.e., the traffic capacity, expressed in freight trains (in the case of a double-track line) can be estimated using

$$N_f = N - \sum_{i=1}^{n} e_c^i N_c^i - (e_{trc} - 1) N_{trc} - (e_{1m} - 1) N_{1m} \tag{8.15}$$

where N = the traffic capacity in the case of a parallel graph; $\sum_{i=1}^{n} e_c^i N_c^i$ = the number of long haul freight trains eliminated from the graph by passenger trains (i is the number of categories for passenger trains); e_{tr}, e_{1m} = the reduction coefficient due to the traffic of other trains (local freight, etc.) and N_{trc}, N_{1m} = number of other trains (local freight, etc).

φ is calculated using $\phi = \frac{Q_n}{Q_g}$ where Q_n is the net tonnage per train[3]

The following equation may be used to analyse the transport capacity C_t (M tonne p.a.) as a function of the structure of the freight hauled and the degree of utilisation of the loading capacity of the rail freight cars:

$$C_t = \frac{365 N_f Q_g}{10^6 k_n 1 + \frac{k_t}{k_{ci}}} + C_{trc} + C_{1m} \qquad (8.16)$$

in which k_{ci} is the coefficient of utilisation of the car's loading capacity and k_t is the empty car coefficient, given by $k_{ci} = \frac{q_n}{q}$ and $k_t = \frac{q_t}{q}$ where q is the average loading capacity of the car in tonnes.

If the lengths of rail sidings limit train tonnages, then the transport capacity is calculated as follows:

$$C_t = \frac{365 N_f k_{ci} p_{ml} (L_u - n_1 l_1 - l_p)}{10^6 K_n l_v}$$

In this case, the gross tonnage per train (Q_g, tonnes) is calculated from

$$Q_g = p_{ml}(L_u - n_1 l_1 - l_p) \qquad (8.17)$$

where L_u = length of the siding (usually consider the smallest), in metres; p_{ml} = the car load per metre, in tonnes/m; l_1 = the length of a loco in metres; n_1 = number of locos in the train; l_p = length required for manoeuvring/parking the train (15–30 m).

A more detailed discussion of rail line capacity including the capacity of stations and the determination of level of service is given in Taylor (2017).

Chinowksy et al. (2019) used the concept of temperature-based delays because of speed reductions in the face of increased buckling potential in their study of the potential impacts of climate change on the US rail network. They developed a mathematical model with two main components:

1. The potential increases in buckling failures under reduced speed obligations resulting from higher temperatures associated with climate change. See Eqs (8.1)–(8.5) above for their method for estimating the probability of buckling and the consequent recommended speed reductions.
2. The estimated potential increases in temperature-based delays and the increased costs associate with those delays.

3. Recommended values for φ in the Australian context are (1) for heavy freight (coal, minerals, metal, etc), φ = 0.75–0.9, and (2) for light freight φ = 0.6–0.65. The average value in use on the Australian national railway network is φ = 0.62–0.77.

Delay time was taken as the additional travel time required by a train to complete its journey at a reduced speed compared with the scheduled travel time. Multiplying the delay time by the unit cost of delay (\$/min) then yields the additional cost involved. Chinowsky et al. (2019) used a grid-based approach for their study because of the granularity of available climate projections and reasonable given the macro-level nature of the analysis. In this method, the US rail network was covered by a rectangular grid with the rail track infrastructure and number of trains using each cell of the grid providing the basic input data. The computed impacts were thus averaged over the rail track infrastructure inventory for each grid cell.

The average delay to a train travelling in cell g, $TD(g)$ (min), is given by

$$TD(g) = 60L_g\left(\frac{1}{V_r(g)} - \frac{1}{V_o(g)}\right)\frac{H_{dg}}{H_{og}} \tag{8.18}$$

where $V_r(g)$ = reduced speed in cell g (km/h); $V_O(g)$ = base (posted maximum) speed in cell g (km/h); L_g = length of rail travelled in cell g (km); H_{dg} = hours of speed reduction order in g; H_{Og} = total hours of train operation in g.

The total annual delay to all trains in the grid $D(g,i)$ is then given by the product of $TD(g)$, the average number of trains using the grid cell each day ($N(g,i)$) and the number of incident days per annum ($I_d(g)$) in the grid:

$$D(g) = TD(g)N(g)I_d(g) \tag{8.19}$$

The annual cost of the delays in the grid is $C_d(g)$, given by

$$C_d(g) = c_m D(g) \tag{8.20}$$

where c_m is the unit cost (\$/min) of delay to trains. (If the unit cost of delay were to vary by train type (e.g., passenger, multimodal freight, bulk freight), then the calculations of Eqs (8.19)–(8.20) can be repeated by individual train type, and the total cost is then determined.)

Train scheduling is a vital part of rail operations and is beyond the scope of this book. Interested readers are referred to Howlett and Pudney (1995) and Vuchic (2007) for further details.

Rail maintenance

Track maintenance is an essential activity that has to be fitted into train scheduling as a routine, ongoing activity. Rail defects occur by wear and fatigue because of the passage of trains. Changes in climate may lead to changes in maintenance frequency and intensity, as has been discussed above with regard to rail buckling and the treatment of transition zones. Track maintenance work will require speed restrictions on the affected track section or even temporary closure of the track, depending on the type of work to be conducted. Broadly, track maintenance includes a wider range of activities for preserving the assumed condition of a track and returning degraded track to that condition. Higgins, Ferreira and Lake (1999) identified the main types of track maintenance as

- Rail grinding, to correct rail corrugations, fatigue and metal flow and to reprofile the rail. This is done using grinding machines travelling along the track and equipped with grinding stones—stones oscillating longitudinally or rotating—which abrade the rail surface
- Rail replacement, when degraded rails (due to defects, wear or derailment damage) are replaced by new rails
- Tamping, which involves lifting a number of sleepers (ties) simultaneously to the correct level and inserting tamping tines into the ballast. Tamping is used to correct longitudinal profile, differential cross levels and alignment of track
- Track stabilisation, when the track is vibrated laterally with a vertical load to produce a controlled settlement. Given that tamping and compaction of ballast underneath the sleepers can reduce the lateral resistance of the track, stabilisation can restore the lateral resistance close to its original level
- Ballast injection or 'stoneblowing' is also used to correct longitudinal profile. This process introduces additional gravel stones to the surface of the existing ballast while not disturbing the stable, compacted ballast underneath
- Sleeper (tie) replacement is necessary for almost all types of sleeper defects because remedial actions are generally not possible. Leaving defective sleepers in place can result in a distortion of rail gauge leading to derailments.

An additional maintenance task, as identified by ITF (2016) and of increasing importance in the face of climate change, is trackside vegetation management. This would be required if increases in the incidence of storm storms and high winds are likely, as a preventative measure to reduce the likelihood of network disruptions due to more frequent tree falls and deposit of debris blocking tracks and bring down overhead catenary structures and cables. An increase in the severity and extent of dry conditions and drought would also impact on trackside vegetation, increasing the risk of erosion of or near to the track. Drier conditions may also lead to more frequent wildfires which can damage railway structure and reduce visibility for train operations (another source of speed reduction).

The estimation of rail track service life is a significant task that is required for the safe and efficient operation of railways and for the efficient usage of maintenance and refurbishment resources (Bai et al., 2017). Methods for optimal planning of rail maintenance strategies were outlined by Simson et al. (2000) and Liden (2015).

Climate and weather impacts

As discussed throughout this chapter, rail transportation systems may suffer from a number of climate and weather factors, and these factors may become more important over time with climate change. Rail transportation managers thus need knowledge about the likely impacts of weather and climate change on their systems and how to prioritise and deal with these. For rail, there is not only the direct physical damage to infrastructure possible from extreme weather events but also the potential for cascading problems throughout the network, not just limited to the area experiencing the weather (Liu et al., 2018).

A number of authors and agencies have produced tables and charts to explain the risks associated with different climate and weather factors (e.g., ARA, 2014; Rail Baltica, 2019; UITP, 2016; Quinn et al., 2017; Stipanovic et al., 2013). Each of these summaries of likely weather impacts tends to reflect the climatic conditions in the geographic area of interest to the individual report.

Fig. 8.1 provides a summary of the broad impacts of extreme weather events on rail transportation, using the seven rail component subsystems defined by UITP (2016). Table 8.3 provides a more detailed listing of the expected risks to rail infrastructure and systems from extreme weather. It also uses the UITP subsystem definitions in describing the specific risks. The weather factors and impacts shown in the table are taken from those in UITP (2016), augmented by consideration of other weather events and impacts identified in the other reports just cited.

This table indicates that all component subsystems are at risk from extreme weather events. High temperatures, high winds, extreme precipitation and sea level and groundwater rise all have the potential for severe damage to rail infrastructure and the curtailment of rail services.

Case studies

Four recent case studies provide useful information on current methods for the analysis of climate change adaptation plans for rail transportation. These studies are

- Temperature-induced rail buckling on the US national railway network (Chinowsky et al., 2019)
- Rainfall-induced hazards on the Chinese railway network (Liu et al., 2018)
- High and low temperature impacts on the railway network of the Randstad region of the Netherlands (Stipanovic et al., 2013)
- Interdependency between the railway network and power generation in the north of England (Wood, 2019).

US national rail network

Chinowsky et al. (2019) used the mathematical model described earlier in this chapter to study the likely impacts of climate change on rail operations in the

TABLE 8.3 Extreme weather events and corresponding risks for rail transportation using the component subsystems identified by UITP (2016).

	UITP (2016) rail transportation component subsystem			
Weather factor	**Power supply**	**Stabling and maintenance facilities**	**Tunnels, stations and interchanges**	**Structures and track**
Rain and flood	Substation inundation leading to power outage Flashover of trackside circuit breakers	Damage to rolling stock and equipment in yards	Station and tunnel inundation Reduced accessibility to station/interchange	Wet rail leads to poor adhesion Landslides cause damage to tracks and embankments
High temperatures, drought and increased UV exposure	Overhead catenary loosening causing pantograph crashing Degraded power equipment	Damage to rolling stock and equipment in yards Damage to electrical and electronic equipment	Thermal inertia and cooling issues Damage to electrical and mechanical (E&M) equipment	Rail buckling Points damage Damage to ballast Accelerated wear of sleepers
Wind and storms	Overhead catenary damage by falling trees	Damage to roofs and canopies	Foreign objects block tunnel mouth Damage to roof structure at above ground stations Damage to platform furniture	Tree falls Reduced adhesion Threat to track gauge and clearances
Sandstorm	Overhead catenary damage	Clogging of drains	Accelerated deterioration of ventilation equipment	Threat to track gauge and clearances Reduced visibility of track and signs Unusable track and points

Thunderstorms and lightning	Overvoltage damage Flashover of insulator and substation equipment Failure of lightning arrestor Nuisance tripping of circuit breakers	Damage to electrical and electronic equipment	Lightning strikes E&M equipment damage	Tree falls
Snow, ice, sleet and glazed frost	Overhead catenary damage through ice buildup causing electrical arcing and power surges due to poor electrical contact	Operations shutdown due to jammed switches	Risk of slipping	Slippery rail surface, reduced adhesion Unusable track and points Reduced visibility of signs Avalanche hazards
Sea level rise, groundwater level rise and storm surge	Problems of negative return current Increased corrosion of power equipment	Flooding and inundation of low lying facilities	Tunnel 'floating' Reduced capability of pumping systems	Damage to earthworks and embankments
Blackout	System failure	Electrical maintenance machines inoperable		
Fog		Disruption to shunting operations Disruption to maintenance	Reduced visibility for passengers and staff	Reduced visibility of track and signs
Hurricanes, typhoons, cyclones	Overhead catenary collapse	Damage to rolling stock and equipment in yards	Fire damage to station structure	Damage to track and overhead structures

Continued

TABLE 8.3 Extreme weather events and corresponding risks for rail transportation using the component subsystems identified by UITP (2016).—cont'd

	UITP (2016) rail transportation component subsystem			
Weather factor	**Power supply**	**Stabling and maintenance facilities**	**Tunnels, stations and interchanges**	**Structures and track**
Wildfires	Damage to overhead catenary support structures	Damage to rolling stock and equipment in yards		Fire damage to track structure

	UITP (2016) rail transportation component subsystem		
Weather factor	**Train control and signalling**	**Rolling stock**	**Level crossings**
Rain and flood	Track circuit and equipment damage Safety route cannot be set Potential damage to traffic control centre building	Train damage Failures in electrical parts	Corrosion of framework elements and structures Flooded and invisible track Damage to electrical and electronic components
High temperatures, drought and increased UV exposure	Track circuit and equipment damage	DC motor losses Reliability loss of on-board electronics Reduce on-board comfort Pantograph deformation due to overhead catenary deformation	Accelerated ageing of rubber components Accelerated deterioration of signal foils and lens Overheating of printed circuit boards in equipment cabinets
Wind and storms	Potential damage to traffic control centre building Damage to communication systems	Collisions with flying objects Damage to rolling sock from tree falls Broken glass	Damage to booms and barriers Damage to signs

Sandstorm	Track circuit and equipment damage Deterioration of filters Damage to signalling and safety equipment	Failure of traction engines due to clogging of ventilation systems Accelerated deterioration of filters	Invisible track sections Damage to signs
Thunderstorms and lightning	Overvoltage damage Interference	Overvoltage damage Blown protection fuses lead to loss of traction	Tree falls Overvoltage damage
Snow, ice, sleet and glazed frost	Breakdown of LED optics	Gliding due to snow volume Traction voltage disturbance due to freezing makes vehicles immobile Engine short circuit in powdery snow Reduced reliability of pneumatic components	Destructive effects of water trapped in structures after freezing Invisible track sections Reduced braking capacity Damage to electrical and electronic components
Sea level rise, groundwater level rise and storm surge	Short circuit due to water ingress	Failures in electrical parts leading to vehicle immobility	Invisible track sections
Blackout	System failure	System failure	Signal and boom failure
Fog	Reduced visibility of track and signs Reduced visibility for staff		Reduced visibility
Hurricanes, typhoons, cyclones	Potential damage to traffic control centre building Damage to communication systems		Damage to booms and barriers Damage to signs
Wildfires	Potential damage to traffic control centre building Damage to communication systems	Reduced visibility from smoke leads to service disruption	

United States, using two scenarios of climate change and two alternative strategies for climate change adaptation, with a focus on temperature-induced rail buckling.

The two climate scenarios were RCP4.5 and RCP8.5, where RCP is 'representative concentration pathway' as developed for the IPCC Fifth Assessment Report. These two climate scenarios are the same as those used in the study by Gudipudi et al. (2017) for road pavements, which was described in Chapter 7. RCP8.5 is a scenario of continued high emissions growth in greenhouse gases, while RCP4.5 is a scenario of greenhouse gas mitigation. Both scenarios run from the present to 2100. The two climate change adaptation scenarios were

- A reactive scenario, based on a continuation of the use of established, historical approaches to rail safety and
- A proactive scenario, employing the use of new technology such as rail temperature sensors across the network.

A baseline case assuming static climatic conditions for the period 2016–2100 was also included as a reference. The study results therefore provide a comparison of the estimated costs of the two adaptation strategies. The analysis used five different climate models to estimate average maximum summer temperatures across the USA for the period 2016–2100[4]. The total study period was divided into five eras: 2016–20, 2021–40, 2041–60, 2061–80 and 2081–2100. A summary of the study results is provided in Table 8.4. This table shows the estimated cumulative costs of climate change

TABLE 8.4 Summary results for cumulative estimated costs ($B USD) of climate change impacts on the US rail network for the period 2016–2100 under climate scenarios RCP4.5 and RCP8.5 and the reactive and proactive adaptation strategies, from the study by Chinowsky et al. (2019).

	Reactive adaptation		Proactive adaptation	
	RCP4.5	RCP8.5	RCP4.5	RCP8.5
Baseline	**$73.03B**		**$3.00B**	
Mean of the five climate models	$116.28B	$126.90B	$7.54B	$14.56B
Standard deviation	$7.43B	$8.56B	$2.81B	$7.79B
Standard error of mean	$3.32B	$4.28B	$1.26B	$3.48B

4. Readers should consult Chinowsky et al. (2019) for details of the climate models and the underlying climate data used in the project

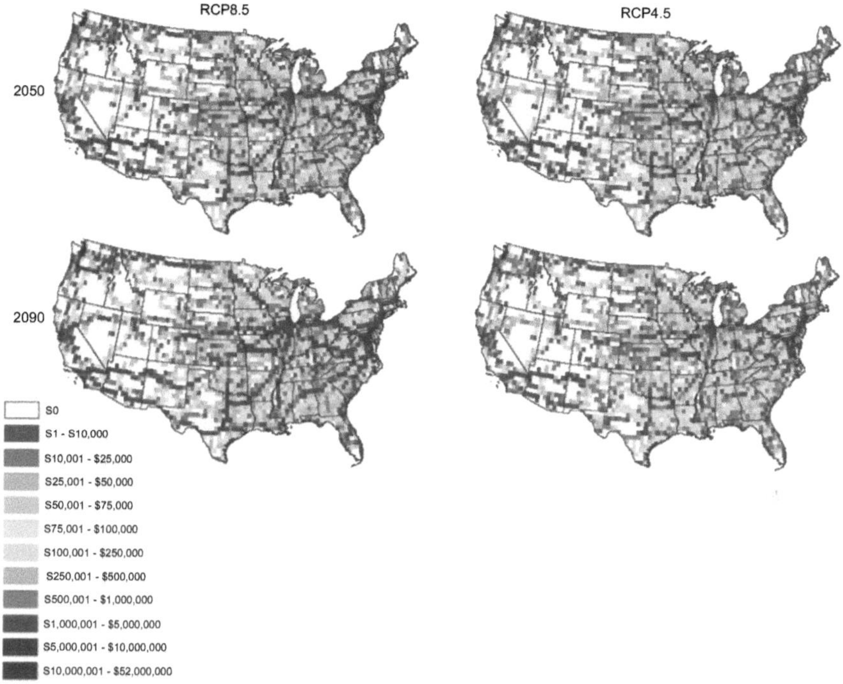

FIGURE 8.9 Average annual costs of climate change on the US rail network (in 2015 USD) for the eras 2041–60, represented by 2050, and 2081–2100, represented by 2090 under climate change scenarios RCP8.5 and RCP4.5. *Reproduced with permission from Chinowsky, P, Helman, J, Gulati, S, Neumann, J, Martinich, J, 2019. Impacts of climate change on operation of the US rail network. Transp. Pol. 75, 183–191, Figure 3, p.189.*

impacts on the US rail system from speed reductions due to rail buckling potential for the period 2016–2100 under the two climate scenarios and the two adaptation strategies.

Two main findings emerge from these results. Firstly, the use of the new technology, proactive adaptation strategy is superior to the continued use of the historical approaches, even despite the high initial cost of sensor installation. Secondly, the high emitting RCP8.5 climate scenario leads to higher costs than under RCP4.5. Fig. 8.9 shows these differences and variations across the United States, in terms of annual average costs, for the two eras containing 2050 (i.e., 2041–60) and 2090 (i.e., 2081–2100) and climate scenarios RCP4.5 and RCP8.5. In all cases the impacts are more profound in the eastern half of the continental USA.

This study indicates the potential vulnerability of the US rail network to projected temperature increases under different climate change scenarios. Under existing strategies regarding rail system management and potential rail buckling, estimated cumulative costs based on train delays could be of the order of \$116B–\$127B. The introduction of new technology-based adaptation plans, in which train speed reductions can be restricted to specific spatial locations rather than be imposed at a broader level, could reduce these costs by at least an order of magnitude. Given that the US rail system is expected to face significant increases in train delays due to rising temperatures over the rest of this century, measures that can alleviate this phenomenon should be strongly considered. More broadly, the methodology adopted by Chinowsky et al. (2019) has a wider range of applications for other climate change impacts, such as the intensity and frequency of precipitation events. Given finer-grained climate forecasts then more detailed studies may also be possible.

Rainfall-induced hazards on Chinese railways

The question of rainfall-based hazards on railway operations was studied by Liu et al. (2018) for the railway network of China. The primary natural hazards affecting the Chinese railway system are rainfall-induced floods, landslides and debris flows. The study involved a risk analysis to identify the vulnerability of different locations across the network, which involved estimating the failure probability of rail infrastructure components in different regions of the network, and the anticipated reductions in network efficiency or capacity loss due to component failure. While the study was not able to use models of future climate change, it developed a modelling framework which could accommodate climate change predictions. This was cited as important because of the belief that rainfall patterns would change in the future and that extreme precipitation events would increase in frequency, duration and intensity. Importantly, the study also allowed for the effects of the ongoing ageing of existing rail infrastructure.

Temperature impacts on railway infrastructure in the Randstad region

The Randstad region of the Netherlands includes the cities of Amsterdam, Rotterdam, The Hague and Utrecht, and contains nearly half of the total population of the country. Stipanovic et al. (2013) undertook a study of the likely impacts of climate change—focussing on minimum and maximum summer and winter temperatures—on the rail network of the region. The starting point of the study was the collation and analysis of data about actual performance of two rail lines in the region—considering weather-related system failures—and the correlation of the performance with regional climate data. Four climate scenarios available for the region were then used to examine the likely future performance of the rail system by considering the probabilities of system failures and the impacts of these on rail operations. Vulnerability risk assessment maps for the region could then be developed and used as decision support in the development of sustainable adaptation strategies for climate change. The general conclusion of the study was that the resilience of infrastructure assets should be increased to allow a move from a current operating strategy reliant on imposing restrictions on train operations—and therefore yielding less reliable performance—to strategies that required fewer restrictions and delivered more reliable performance. This is very much in keeping with the thrust of the Rail Adapt framework (Fig. 8.2) proposed by Quinn et al. (2017).

Interdependency of rail and power generation in the United Kingdom

An example of interdependency between different infrastructure systems was provided by Wood (2019). In this case the two systems were the electricity power generation system and the rail system in the north of England. The specific region was between Leeds and the Port of Immingham on the Humber River. The power generation system in the region is undergoing significant change, with the phasing out of coal-based generation and the introduction of biomass generation (using wood pellets) as a replacement. The biomass system is dependent on the uninterrupted flow of the wood pellets, initially from Immingham. Indeed the biomass traffic is time-critical, unlike coal which is easier to stockpile. Rail is the only effective transportation mode for biomass, given the quantity of fuel required and the need to ensure continuous availability of fuel at the power station. The rail system itself is, however, vulnerable to many factors, including failure in the rail network and interactions with the power system. The impacts of these factors could be worsened by climate change. Consequent measures to increase the reliability of biomass supply have now been introduced, by obtaining wood pellet supplies from other places as well as Immingham, including Liverpool, Hull and Newcastle. In this way, additional redundancy has been put into the system to reduce the overall probability of disruption to the power station's supply chain.

Summary

This chapter considered rail transportation systems. It considered how climate change factors could be incorporated in performance evaluation and therefore influence design methods and maintenance regimes for rail systems, as well as potential impacts of climate change on rail operations. The discussion focuses on the issues facing rail track managers and train operators, largely concerning and rail maintenance systems and railway performance assessment. Extreme temperatures and precipitation events are major climate factors affecting railway performance. Service disruptions can result from these factors, with potentially cascading impacts because of the strict operating rules that are an essential part of railway operations. Rail buckling under high temperatures is a significant problem for many railway systems and is likely to be exacerbated under warmer climates. Case studies are provided as illustrations of current and emerging practice.

Railway systems have some unique properties that require special consideration for climate change adaptation. Rail infrastructure has extremely long service life and is constructed to withstand natural hazards, such as 50-year or 100-year floods. However, as number and intensity of weather-related incidents increase under future climate change, the pressure on rail system capacity will grow, along with the costs of the sector. Many rail systems already face significant cost pressures and there is some evidence in some places of inadequate expenditures on maintenance and refurbishment. Railway system managers need methods, processes and procedures to enable them to adapt their systems to the future operating environments. The frameworks, methods, models and processes outlined in this chapter should assist in this regard.

References

ARA, 2014. Climate Change Adaptation Position Paper: Assessing the Impact on Rail Infrastructure. Australasian Rail Association, Canberra ACT. https://www.ara.net.au/sites/default/files/ClimateChangeAdaptationPositionPaper.pdf. (Accessed 11 July 2018).

ARTC, 2018. 2018 Annual Report. Australian Rail Track Corporation, Adelaide.

ASCE, 2017. 2017 infrastructure report card. American Society of Civil Engineers, Reston VA. https://www.infrastructurereportcard.org/cat-item/rail/. (Accessed 31 January 2020).

Bai, L., Liub, R., Wang, F., Sun, Q., Wang, F., 2017. Estimating railway rail service life: a rail-grid-based approach. Transp. Res. Part A 105, 54–65.

BTS, 2018. TET Chapter 8 – Value of and Investment in Transportation Infrastructure and Other Assets. Bureau of Transportation Statistics, US Department of Transportation, Washington DC. https://www.bts.gov/sites/bts.dot.gov/files/u796/TET%202018%20Chapter%208.pdf.

Chinowsky, P., Helman, J., Gulati, S., Neumann, J., Martinich, J., 2019. Impacts of climate change on operation of the US rail network. Transp. Pol. 75, 183–191.

Dora, J., 2011. Tomorrow's Railway and Climate Change Adaptation. Phase 3 Report: Adapting to Extreme Climate Change. Rail Safety and Standards Board Ltd, London.

Esveld, C., 1998. A New Safety Philosophy for CWR. TU Delft, The Netherlands. http://esveld.com/Download/TUD/safety.pdf. (Accessed 13 February 2020).

Gudipudi, P.P., Underwood, B.S., Zalghout, A., 2017. Impact of climate change on pavement structural performance in the United States. Transp. Res. D 57, 172–184.

Higgins, A., Ferreira, L., Lake, M., 1999. Scheduling rail track maintenance to minimise overall delays. In: Ceder, A. (Ed.), Transportation and Traffic Theory. Pergamon-Elsevier, Oxford, pp. 779–796.

Howlett, P.G., Pudney, P.J., 1995. Energy Efficient Train Control. Springer-Verlag, London.

ITF, 2016. Adapting Transport to Climate Change and Extreme Weather: Implications for Infrastructure Owners and Network Managers. ITF Research Reports, OECD Publishing, Paris. https://doi.org/10.1787/9789282108079-en.

Kish, A., Samavedam, G., 2013. Track Buckling Prevention: Theory, Safety Concepts, and Applications. Federal Railroad Administration, Washington DC. Rep. no. DOT/FRA/ORD-13/16. https://www.semanticscholar.org/paper/Track-Buckling-Prevention%3A-Theory%2C-Safety-Concepts%2C-Kish-Samavedam/f28edcabbf2cc0abb4f9275e0eb22e751418fdc4. (Accessed 12 February 2020).

Liden, T., 2015. Railway infrastructure maintenance – a survey of planning problems and conducted research. Transp. Res. Procedia 10, 574–583.

Liu, K., Wang, M., Cao, Y., Zhu, W., Wu, J., Xiaoyong Yan, X., 2018. A comprehensive risk analysis of transportation networks affected by rainfall-induced multihazards. Risk Anal. https://doi.org/10.1111/risa.12968.

Nemry, F., Demirel, H., 2012. Impacts of Climate Change on Transport: A Focus on Road and Rail Transport Infrastructures. JRC Scientific and Policy Reports. Joint Research Centre, Institute for Prospective Technological Studies, European Commission, Brussels. http://ipts.jrc.ec.europa.eu/activities/energy-and-transport/ettea.cfm. (Accessed 13 February 2020).

Network Rail, 2018. Annual Report and Accounts 2018. Network Rail Ltd, London.

Pant, R., Hall, J.W., Blainey, S.P., 2016. Vulnerability assessment framework for interdependent critical infrastructures: case-study for Great Britain's rail network. Eur. J. Transp. Infrastruct. Res. 16 (1), 174–194.

Quinn, A., Jack, A., Hodgkinson, S., Ferranti, E., Beckford, J., Dora, J., 2017. RAIL ADAPT: Adapting the Railway for the Future. International Union of Railways (UIC), Paris.

Rail Baltica, 2019. Final Report: Study on Climate Change Impact Assessment for the Design, Construction, Maintenance and Operation of Rail Baltica Railway. Rail Baltica, Tartu-Riga-Vilnius. http://www.railbaltica.org/wp-content/uploads/2019/09/CC_final-report.pdf. (Accessed 28 January 2020).

Setsobhonkul, S., Kaewunruen, S., Sussman, J.M., 2017. Lifecycle assessments of railway bridge transitions exposed to extreme climate events. Front. Built Environ. 3 (25) https://doi.org/10.3389/fbuil.2017.00035.

Simson, S., Ferreira, L., Murray, M., 2000. Rail track maintenance planning: an assessment model. Transport. Res. Rec. 1713, 29–35.

SNCF, 2018. SNCF Mobilités Group Annual Financial Report. Société Nationale des Chemins de Fer, Paris.

Stipanovic, I., Ter Maat, H., Hartmann, A., Dewulf, G., 2013. Risk assessment of climate change impacts on railway infrastructure. In: Proc EPOC 2013 Conference, Devil's Thumb Ranch, Colorado, July 9–11, 2013. www.researchgate.net/publication/260565726. (Accessed 25 January 2020).

Taylor, M.A.P., 2017. Vulnerability Analysis for Transportation Networks. Elsevier, New York.

UITP, 2016. Urban Rail, Climate Change and Resilience. International Association of Public Transport, Brussels. www.uitp.org.

Vuchic, V.R., 2007. Urban Transit: Systems and Technology. John Wiley and Sons, Hoboken NJ.

Wood, M., 2019. Rail research into adapting to climate change – tomorrow's railway and climate change adaptation (TRaCCA). In: UNCTAD Ad Hoc Expert Meeting on Climate Change Adaptation for International Transport: Preparing for the Future. https://unctad.org/meetings/en/Presentation/dtltlbpls-AhEM2019_p11_MICHAEL%20WOODS_en.pdf. (Accessed 28 January 2020).

Yang, G., Bradford, M.A., 2018. On train speed reduction in circumstances of thermally-induced railway track buckling. Eng. Fail. Anal. 92, 107–120.

Volpe (undated). Track buckling research. Volpe National Transportation Systems Center, Cambridge MA, https://www.volpe.dot.gov/infrastructure-systems-and-technology/structures-and-dynamics/track-buckling-research. (Accessed 28 January 2020.

Chapter 9

Active transport and urban design

Transportation is a major contributor to global greenhouse gas emissions. IPCC (2014) indicated that the transportation sector contributed approximately 23% of the world's energy-related CO_2e emissions in 2010. The US EPA indicated that transportation was responsible for 29% of these emissions in 2017 (EPA, 2020), while in the EU 27% of emissions came from transportation (EEA, 2020). In addition, transportation is one economic sector that continues to show growth in greenhouse gas emissions. Thus, mitigation is a key concern for transportation policies and transportation agencies. To achieve mitigation of greenhouse gas emissions from transportation, many jurisdictions seek the encouragement of increased usage of active transport modes as a fundamental part of present day transportation policies. In terms of adaptation – the thrust of this book – transportation planners and managers then need to plan, design and operate current and future transportation systems in which there is much greater use of more environmentally friendly transportation modes, such as walking, cycling and public transit, and the commensurate provision and maintenance of infrastructure specifically intended to support these modes. Other concerns, especially in public health, are also focussing transportation policies on provision of new and extended infrastructure for walking and cycling (commonly termed 'active transport'). Urban planners and urban designers are also involved in policies and plans to recast our cities to reinforce the opportunities for active transport.

This chapter thus considers some of the measures available for mitigation of greenhouse gas emission from transportation that can be seen from an adaptation perspective. The starting point for the chapter is to examine the combination of urban land use planning and transportation planning, through land use–transport integration. A discussion of transportation policies for low carbon mobility – and their implications for infrastructure – then follows.

Land use–transport integration

A basic problem for 'new world' cities such as those of North America and Australasia is that these cities are typically composed of low density, dispersed suburbs, which are highly automobile dependent. This is resource and carbon

Climate Change Adaptation for Transportation Systems. https://doi.org/10.1016/B978-0-12-816638-3.00009-X

emission intensive and therefore unsustainable in the long term (Philp and Taylor, 2017). These cities need to transition to a low carbon alternative with more efficient form and function with respect to carbon emissions. A low carbon city must improve the energy efficiency of its buildings and transportation systems and the connections between them. A key aspect of this transition is travel demand, for the level and intensity of the demand depends greatly on the land use system and the land use planning instruments that have been applied. Integration of land use and transportation planning policies and practices directed towards urban sustainability is essential. Transportation systems guide our mobility, that is, our ability to move from one place to another in order to achieve our needs for participation in activities and utilisation of facilities, the locations of which depend on the distribution and intensity of land uses across a region. Transportation provides access to jobs, education and social interactions, for example, all of which are fundamental to human development. Public awareness and perception are two major barriers for the transition to low carbon transport options. Banister (2013) emphasised the need to understand the importance of time and how people want to use time in travel compared to other activities. Aditjandra et al. (2013) suggested residents have to be well informed of the available opportunities for them to pursue sustainable travel choices.

The shape and form of our built environment, along with lifestyle choices, strongly influence the use of the private car in urban areas. Newton and Newman, 2013 addressed this issue in their consideration of the carbon benefits that can accrue from more compact urban forms where public and active transport modes are generally of most benefit. They considered the need for urban design innovation, largely focussing on energy demands in housing and transport and available alternative energy technologies and fuel types. The 'post war' suburbs, i.e., those areas of cities subdivided and developed in the latter half of the 20th century which are heavily car dependent, provide the most challenges in transitioning to a lower carbon future. Thus, Fig. 9.1, which shows a modified and extended version of the Newton–Newman framework, indicates the importance of suburban travel in cities and highlights that this travel is difficult to service using conventional public transportation in low-density developments.

Land use–transport integration offers a planning solution to reduce the needs for travel by providing more options for individuals (e.g., employment, shopping, education and recreation) closer to home. Travel is a derived demand, in that for most purposes it is not undertaken for its own sake. Rather travel is used to access some service or facility, or take part in some activity, at a different spatial location. The decision by an individual to travel is multilayered, involving number of aspects, some of which are related. The basic decision is whether to undertake a journey, with the alternatives including to make a trip

Built Environment Fabric

	Housing	**Transport**
Suburban	• Renewable energy technologies for individual buildings, e.g. solar PV • Precinct scale technologies	• Electric vehicles (Evs), hybrid, hydrogen and autonomous vehicles (AVs) and associated infrastructure • Car, bike and ride sharing • Active transport (walk, cycle) • Micromobility • Smart buses (including EV & AV technologies)
Urban	• Precinct scale zero and low emission energy technologies, e.g. smart grid, co-generation, tri-generation	• Public transport • Active transport (walk, cycle) • Car, bike and ride sharing • Micromobility • EVs, hybrid, hydrogen vehicles, AVs and associated infrastructure

Low/Zero Carbon Technologies

FIGURE 9.1 Extension of the Newton–Newman framework (Newton and Newman, 2013) for low carbon technology interventions in urban and suburban forms of the built environment – focussing on suburban travel and indicating the important role of active transport as part of low carbon mobility for suburban areas.

(some time) today, to delay it until another day, to find an alternative means to satisfy the purpose requiring the travel (e.g., through telecommunications or the Internet) or to find another individual who can travel in your stead or add your requirement to their own activity schedule. Once an individual has decided to undertake travel, the subsequent choices include the destination (where can the activity, service or facility be found, and which is the preferred option if there is more than one alternative), the mode of transport to be used to go to the destination, the time of day when the trip is to be made and the specific route to be taken to reach the destination by the chosen mode.

A number of these choices can be connected, for instance, the need to go to a specific destination may then dictate the alternative set of modes that can be used to reach the destination within a specified time period. The choices will also be affected by considerations of the monetary and total costs of the journey (e.g., including travel time, distance, costs of fares and tolls, fuel prices, costs at the destination, such as car parking charges), expected levels of traffic congestion and crowding and comfort, safety and security issues amongst others. Travel decisions for regular trips, such as the journey to work, tend to be made at particular times (epoch events) in an individual's life, and then adhered to in the longer term unless some significant change in the travel environment occurs (or is perceived to have occurred, for some changes happen gradually). Epoch events include such things as moving home, changing jobs, changing family situation (leaving home, marriage, parenthood, separation and divorce, etc). When changes do occur, they may be seen in terms of the following set of options, arranged in (probable) order of ease:

- Change in trip timing, so that the start time of a (regular) trip, such as the journey to work, is altered (e.g., a trip starts earlier in the day perhaps in response to increased delays due to increased traffic congestion)
- Change in route, to the same destination, because of traffic congestion or new transport facilities or services
- Change in destination, where alternatives exist, e.g., travel to a closer shopping centre seen as less desirable but more accessible in the face of increasing congestion
- Change in trip frequency, where the relative difficulty of accessing a particular destination leads to the decision to make the trip to it more or less often (the phenomenon of travelling home for lunch, often seen in rural townships but seldom in a metropolis, would be one example. A second might be travel to a shopping centre for basic purchases such as food)
- Change in vehicle occupancy, when two or more individuals travelling to the same or proximate destinations decide to share vehicles
- Change in transport mode, due to increased costs and inconvenience of the initial choice of mode, e.g., through increasing congestion or changes in travel costs
- Change in origin (e.g., place of residence), perhaps because of serious changes in travel conditions or an epoch event in the life of the individual
- Decisions not to travel or a particular day, but to delay that travel until another day, when it may be rolled up with other activities involving travel

The key concept behind land use–transport integration lies in what may be taken as the basic driver of urban development – accessibility. In the planning context, accessibility is about the effort required for people and enterprises to engage in everyday life. The notion of accessibility in transportation planning can be illustrated through a basic definition: accessibility is 'the ease with which desired destinations may be reached' (Niemeier, 1997). In particular circumstances such as those pertaining to low carbon mobility and the availability and use of alternative transport modes, this broad definition may be refined to explicitly include other relevant factors, such as time dependency which may be an issue in, for instance, assessing accessibility levels for public transport users where the level of service of public transport provision varies widely over hours of the day or days of the week. Thus, Primerano and Taylor (2005) defined accessibility as 'the ease for people to participate in activities from specific locations to a destination using a mode of transport at a specific time'. This is an appropriate definition for use in urban studies where different regions within a metropolis have different levels of access to public transport services. 'Wegener's Wagon Wheel' model (Wegener, 1996) of the urban development process (and the interaction between the land use and transport systems) illustrates the

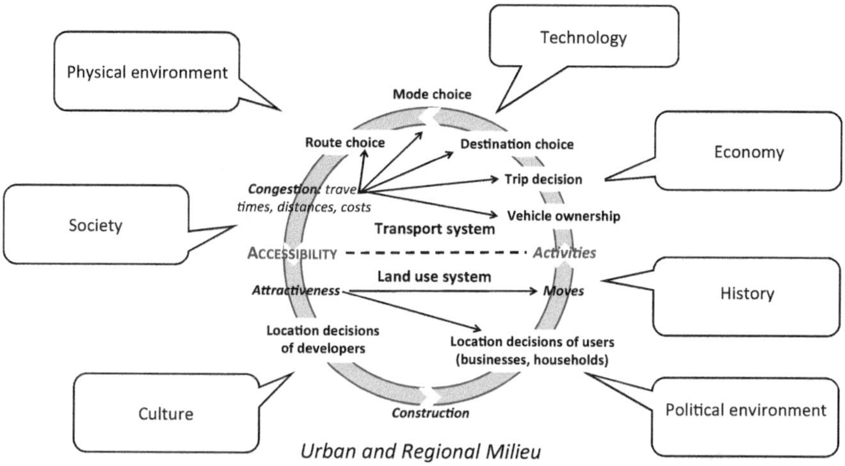

FIGURE 9.2 'Wegener's Wagon Wheel' conceptual model of urban development and the role of accessibility. *Adapted and extended from Wegener, M., 1996. Reduction of CO_2 emissions of transport by reorganisation of urban activities. In: Hayashi, Y., Roy, J.R., (Eds.), Transport, Land-Use and the Environment. Kluwer Academic Publishers, Dordrecht, pp. 103–124.*

primary role of accessibility in the key decisions that underpin urban development and urban activity. Fig. 9.2 shows this model. Urban development – indeed urban evolution – is shown as a continuous process in the figure. The central part of the figure comprises the land use system and the transport system, connected through accessibility and the activities undertaken in the urban area. The wheel includes a number of decisions made by different players and a number of outcomes stemming from those decisions. The outcomes are indicated in italics in Fig. 9.2. The basic outcome is the set of activities. Location decisions of developers and consumers are made on the basis of the relative accessibility of different areas – outcome 'attractiveness' – including their suitability for different activities (services and facilities). The accessibility of a given location is affected by the travel choices of the consumers (when, where and how to travel, and of course a basic decision about private vehicle ownership and use), which lead to the development of congestion and hence the actual (time, distance and cost) separations between localities. These separations affect the accessibility actually experienced by people, hence the ongoing evolution of the system. Choices of location, vehicle ownership and travel depend on (or are influenced by) broader characteristics and influences of the urban area, including its physical environment, history and culture, social and economic environment and available technology. These factors in the urban milieu serve to influence the choices of players in the urban development system, at macro, meso and micro levels. While subject to external shocks (such as geopolitics, energy prices and overall economic conditions, including competition between regions and cities, and climate change) the system is effectively closed and is evolutionary.

Land use−transport integration policies and planning practices may be used to influence location and travel decisions in a city towards achieving goals of sustainability and low carbon mobility, by facilitating use of active transport and public transport and by location of services and facilities close to residences, so that travel distances are reduced for some trip purposes and high capacity public transport is widely available for longer distance travel. Given the likely trade-off between housing type and location, with resulting impacts on demand for transport which are largely met at present by the private car in suburban locations, strategies to reduce urban carbon emissions need to be directed at providing substantial alternatives to that mode, based around greater use of the active modes and public transport. To make this direction feasible requires in-depth consideration of built form, relationships between transport modes and land use development, land use mixes, the location and intensity for services and facilities and the supporting infrastructure, and precinct planning and design including the relationships between neighbouring precincts and between precincts and major activity centres such as the CBD. Integration strategies, policies and plans thus offer a pathway to urban sustainability. Santos et al. (2010) considered a wide range of low carbon transport policy options, which they grouped into three categories:

- *Physical policies*, concerning infrastructure and service provision,
- *Soft policies*, aimed at bringing about behavioural change, and
- *Knowledge policies*, emphasising the role of investment in research and development for future sustainable mobility.

They argued that policy integration was the key and that optimal blending of mutually reinforcing policies was essential – see Taylor (2017) for a more complete discussion of the development of transportation policies and plans, using these ideas, to facilitate low carbon mobility.

Avoid, shift, share, improve

One useful approach to developing policy packages for low carbon mobility is the ‘Avoid-Shift-Share-Improve’ (ASSI) framework (Nakamura et al. 2004; Dia, 2017). ASSI has found wide recognition in Europe and East Asia. The framework provides a blueprint for policy packages aimed at promoting alternative mobility solutions and sustainable transport systems. It involves consideration of policy measures along the four dimensions (*Avoid*, *Shift*, *Share*, *Improve*):

- *Avoid* considering measures and policy instruments that reduce or avoid the need to travel and thus improve the efficiency of the transport system. Planning for land use−transport integration and management of travel demand can reduce the overall need for physical travel activity and, in particular, seek reductions in trip length

- *Shift* policy instruments, which seek to improve trip efficiency, generally through shifts from high energy consuming modes (e.g., the private car) to more environmentally friendly modes such as active transport (walking and cycling) and public transport
- *Share* initiatives enable and promote shifts from automobile ownership and private vehicle use towards car sharing, ride sharing, bicycle sharing (and even vehicle parking space sharing in space-constrained urban centres). The Share dimension of ASSI is a recent phenomenon largely coming from the 'bottom up', through advocacy and actions by individuals, community groups and enterprises
- *Improve*, which considers measures that focus on technology and infrastructure use, especially with regard to vehicles, propulsion systems and energy and fuel efficiency, including the potential of alternative energy sources for transport.

Fig. 9.3 illustrates the ASSI framework, including examples of the strategies for each dimension and the general policy outcomes expected from each dimension. *Avoid* policies should improve system efficiency through reductions in the total amount of travel effort (e.g., measured in person-km of travel, PKT), *Shift* policies should lead to improvements in trip efficiency through reductions in the use of road space and scarce resources such as transport fuels, *Share* policies should encourage both system and trip efficiencies and *Improve* policies may result in better efficiency in travel mode performance as well as trip and system efficiencies.

ASSI policy framework for Low Carbon Mobility (LCM)			
Avoid	**Shift**	**Share**	**Improve**
Strategies			
Reduce or avoid the need for travel e.g. congestion pricing, teleworking, mixed land use	Shift to environmentally friendly modes e.g. road space allocation, transit vehicle priority	Share mobility resources e.g. car sharing, ride sharing, micromobility	Improve energy efficiency and emissions of transport systems e.g. electric vehicles, intelligent transport systems
Outcomes			
System efficiency	Trip efficiency	System and trip efficiency	System, trip and mode efficiency

FIGURE 9.3 The ASSI (Avoid, Shift, Share, Improve) policy framework for low carbon mobility. *Adapted from Dia, H., 2017. Policy principles for low carbon mobility. In: Dia, H., (Ed.), Low Carbon Mobility for Future Cities: Principles and Applications. IET Books, London, pp. 41–63.*

Dia (2017) proposed the following 10 planning principles for the application of the ASSI framework:

1. Plan denser cities
2. Develop transit-oriented cities
3. Optimise road network and its use
4. Implement public transit improvements
5. Encourage walking and cycling
6. Regulate vehicle use
7. Manage car parking
8. Promote cleaner vehicles
9. Stakeholder consultation and communication
10. Pathways to comprehensive deployment

Of these 10 principles, the last one – pathways to comprehensive development – is of direct interest in planning and management for climate change adaptation in a transportation agency. This principle includes the creation of entities responsible for overseeing low carbon mobility initiatives, integrating transportation operations and services into climate change adaptation action plans, developing low carbon mobility plans and monitoring the implementation of the action plans and of transportation system performance. Table 9.1 maps the 10 principles in terms of the ASSI framework.

TABLE 9.1 Dia's 10 key transportation policy principles and the ASSI (Avoid, Shift, Share, Improve) framework.

Policy principle	Avoid	Shift	Share	Improve
Plan denser cities	✓	✓	✓	✓
Develop transit-oriented cities	✓	✓		✓
Optimise road network and its use	✓			✓
Implement public transit improvements		✓		✓
Encourage walking and cycling	✓	✓		
Regulate vehicle use	✓	✓	✓	✓
Manage car parking			✓	✓
Promote cleaner vehicles				✓
Stakeholder consultation and communication		✓	✓	
Pathways to comprehensive deployment	✓	✓	✓	✓

Active transport

The encouragement of active transport – walking and cycling – is an important facet of the drive towards low carbon mobility and has important ramifications for transportation system planners and managers. While the active travel modes have been included in transportation planning for many years, attention to them, and the infrastructure and facilities they need, has not been strong in many jurisdictions. Yet walking, especially, has long been a major transportation mode in terms of use, while cycling offers a significant alternative to other forms of personal transportation, at least for short- to medium-length trips. In addition, there are community health benefits to accrue for increased levels of active transport.

Ogilvie et al. (2004) provided a systematic review of international research on interventions to promote active transport. They found consistent evidence that transport policies increasingly seek to reduce traffic congestion by discouraging car use and encouraging the take-up of active modes. Pucher et al. (2011) used the US National HTS database to examine active transport usage from 2001 to 2009. They found that walking activity was growing, albeit at a slow rate, while cycling levels appeared static. Active travel was declining for women, children and the elderly. Plaut (2005) also considered non-motorised commuting in the United States, using published journey to work data. She found that higher-income people had a greater propensity to work at home, but were less likely to walk or cycle, although university graduates exhibited higher use of the active modes. There were also regional differences. At the intraurban level, central city and inner-suburban residents were more likely to use the active modes, while, nationally, Californian residents were less likely to do so. Negron-Poblete et al. (2014) noted that pedestrian activity did not depend on distance alone, but was also affected by the presence of obstacles to movement resulting from car-related planning and design decisions, a particular concern for the elderly.

Policies and initiatives to increase active transport usage are generally predicated on two grounds: (1) improved environmental sustainability and (2) enhanced health outcomes. For the latter, walking and cycling may be undertaken expressly for the purpose of recreation and exercise, but this activity is also undertaken for utilitarian transport purposes. This can include access to public transport or for local trips to specific destinations. Some researchers have considered the ability of active transport, either for recreation/exercise or for transport, to meet health supportive targets for physical activity. International data provide strong evidence for the population level health benefits of active travel (Pucher et al., 2010). Tudor-Locke et al. (2005) used Australian Bureau of Statistics (ABS) Time Use Survey data to consider representative patterns of walking for transport and exercise. They found that although walking for transport was often undertaken in multiple brief episodes, the accumulated durations approximated the desired levels of recommended activity in public health guidelines. Cole et al. (2006) also considered walking activity with respect to these guidelines. They found that walking for transport was less likely to meet the guidelines when compared to walking for recreation and exercise. There were also socio-demographic differences. Men over 60 years were less likely to walk for transport, while men 45–59 years were more likely to walk for recreation and exercise. Women were more likely to meet the public health guidelines than men. Wasfi et al. (2013) studied daily walking activity in Montreal. They confirmed the important role of public transport in supporting active transport, indicating that suburban rail users could achieve much of the recommended activity for health benefits by commuting to work or school.

Morency et al. (2011) used Montreal Household Travel Survey (HTS) data to study walking distances to public transport and assess the actual level of physical activity undertaken. They first estimated pedestrian access distances to transit stations using actual travel behaviour and pedestrian network path calculations. These distances were then converted to numbers of steps, with an average public transport return trip involving some 2500 steps, or 25% of the recommended daily quantity of physical activity. This study suggested that socio-demographic factors should be considered in studies of active transport. Cole et al. (2006) found that gender and age factors featured in observed levels of walking activity. In this regard, children's travel behaviour, especially the journey to school, has become a major topic of research. This behaviour is strongly linked to health concerns for children and learned habits taken into adulthood (Mackett, 2012). The 'walking school bus' (Mackett, 2012) was suggested as a viable alternative for distances under 2 km. Mackie (2010) studied children cycling to school in New Zealand and found strong latent demands. Approximately 20% of students wanted to cycle to school, although only about half of those actually did so. The main barriers were the traffic environment and lack of cycling infrastructure, which reinforced parental concerns about their child's safety.

The above review suggests a paucity of comprehensive data on active transport. Some of the above studies used special purpose surveys to provide data on particular aspects of walking and cycling behaviour, while some used HTS data for this purpose. None of the studies cited provide an overall picture of the extent of active transport in a given city. HTS data using activity travel have particular value in this regard. These allow a full picture of respondents' daily travel and activity patterns to be established and provide mechanisms for the expansion of the survey sample data to represent the full population. This permits determination of total active transport usage in relation to socio-demographic and spatial characteristics. An examination of why and when active travel is undertaken, either for its own purposes or as part of more complex journeys, is possible with HTS data. Analysis of the travel diary information held in the VISTA HTS database for Melbourne, Australia, by Taylor and Thompson (2019) produced metrics of total active travel for

Melbourne, thus offering a baseline for future studies of potential changes in active travel in response to planning policies and plans. Two outputs from this analysis are of direct interest here. The first is the current role of walking and cycling in the total travel demand for metropolitan Melbourne. The second is the socio-demographic characteristics of those people undertaking active travel.

Total travel in Melbourne circa 2011 is summarised in Fig. 9.4. This figure shows the percentages of usage of travel modes in the daily travel task for the metropolis. The travel activity is seen in three dimensions: (1) travel decisions, (2) travel effort and (3) travel exposure. Travel decisions are reflected in the number of trips made. Travel effort can be described as distance travelled (person-km of travel, PKT) and travel exposure by travelling time (person-hours of travel, PHT). The travel modes used in VISTA and presented in Fig. 9.4 are

1. Private vehicle driver
2. Private vehicle passenger
3. Motorcycle
4. Walking
5. Cycling
6. Taxi
7. Public transport
8. All other

The dominance of the private car, especially 'vehicle driver' mode, is clear in Fig. 9.4. Vehicle driver accounts for nearly half of trip numbers, over 60%

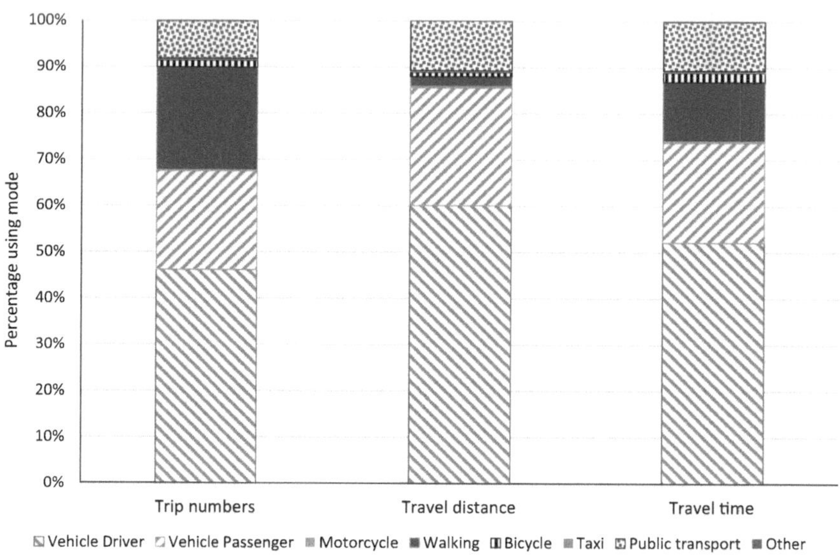

FIGURE 9.4 Percentage usage of transportation modes by trip numbers, distance and travel time for Melbourne (2011).

of travel distance, and just over half of travel time. In terms of trip numbers, walking is the second most common mode (22%), just ahead of vehicle passenger (21%). The latter is nevertheless the second most used mode in terms of distance and time. Walking accounts for 2.0% of travel distance and 12.7% of travel time. Walking distances are much less than those for wheeled modes, but walking is the third highest mode in terms of travel time. Public transport (train, tram, school bus, public bus) accounts for 8.2% of trip numbers, 10.7% of travel distance and 10.6% of travel time. Train is the dominant public transport mode, especially for distance travelled. Bicycle use is small, constituting 1.5% of trip numbers, 1.0% of distance travelled and 2.1% of travel time.

The existing importance of walking as a contributor to the total metropolitan transportation task is apparent. Proper provision of suitable infrastructure and facilities for this travel mode should be of growing concern to transportation planners.

Trip length frequency distributions for walking and cycling in Melbourne, by gender, are shown in Fig. 9.5. The two distributions for walking are effectively and practically identical, whereas the distributions for cycling are quite different. Table 9.2 shows the median, 85th percentile and 90th percentile distances for these trip length frequency distributions. Further results are given in Taylor and Thompson (2019).

In terms of general usage, Taylor and Thompson's analysis of trip length frequencies by mode and socioeconomic characteristics suggest that walking is a universal activity, undertaken by many people at similar activity levels

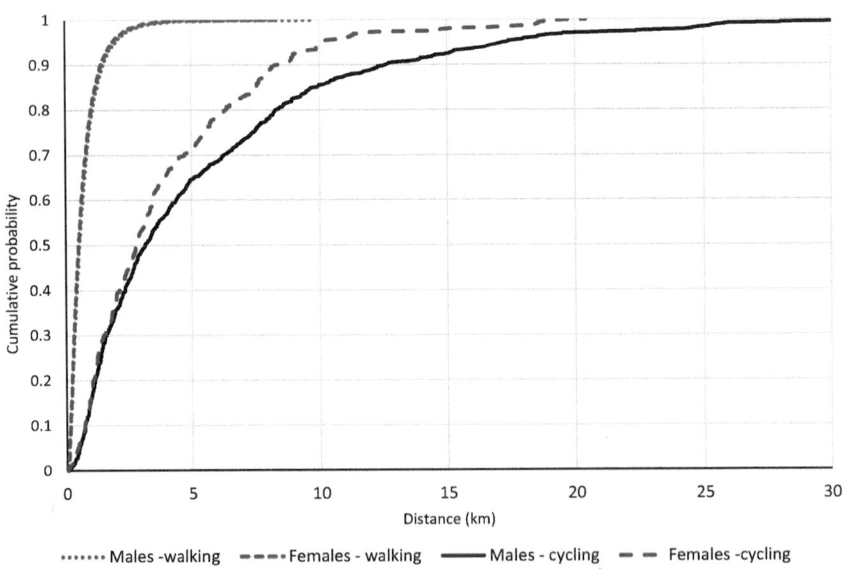

FIGURE 9.5 Trip length frequency distributions (Cumulative distribution functions, CDF) for walking and cycling by gender, Melbourne 2011.

TABLE 9.2 Percentile values for walking and cycling trip length frequency distributions in Melbourne (2011), by gender.

		Percentile distances (km)		
Travel mode	Gender	Median	85th percentile	90th percentile
Walking	Female	0.53	1.21	1.44
	Male	0.56	1.28	1.53
Cycling	Female	2.80	7.48	8.36
	Male	3.15	9.79	12.61

across the community. Cycling, on the other hand, is very much an activity undertaken by a small minority with different rates between diverse groups, especially in terms of age and income, although household bicycle ownership is comparable to household car ownership. As assessed from VISTA, just over 2% of people reported cycle usage for transport, while 22.8% of people reported walking.

A vital component of active transport, especially walking, in providing access to, transfers in, and egress from public transportation services – the so-called 'first mile' and 'last-mile' travel behaviour. Fig. 9.6 shows the

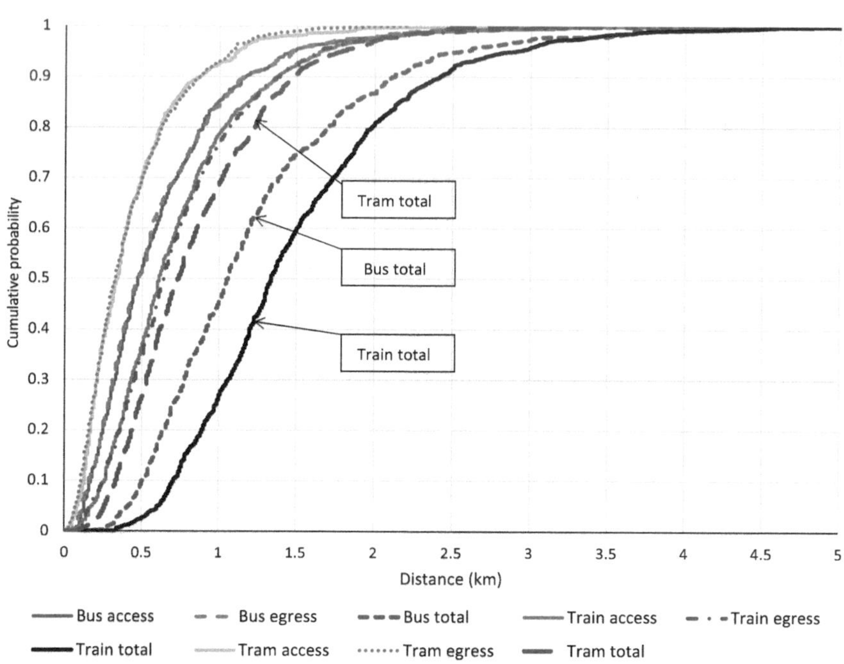

FIGURE 9.6 Cumulative distribution functions (CDFs) for access, egress and total walking distances for public transport trips in Melbourne (2011).

combined set of observed access, egress and total walking distance distributions for travel by the public transport modes of train, tram and bus in Melbourne, whilst Table 9.3 lists some relevant percentile values for these distributions. Melbourne has an extensive tram network serving the central city and inner suburbs, whereas most bus services are in middle and outer suburbs. The metropolis has an extensive radial suburban train network, basically serving the central city. There are two main observations from Fig. 9.6. The first is that the distributions of access and egress distances for each mode are very similar. The second observation is that the distributions of distances for each mode are markedly different from each other. Walking distances for train tend to be longer than those for public bus, which are in turn longer than those for tram. Longer observed walking distances for train services are expected, both from the literature review and because the spacings between railway stations are generally longer than those between bus stops or tram stops – because of the way that the service infrastructure is designed (Vuchic, 2007). The provision of good pedestrian facilities and networks, possibly including weather protection such as rainfall or shade shelters, will become more important under a changing climate.

The provision of networks and facilities to meet increasing usage of the active modes points to the need for land use–transport integration, and for a stronger focus on urban design.

TABLE 9.3 Percentile values for walking access, egress and total distances in public transit trips in Melbourne (2011).

		Percentile distances (km)		
Public transit mode	**Walk**	**Median**	**85th percentile**	**90th percentile**
Tram	Access	0.34	0.71	0.83
	Egress	0.32	0.73	0.88
	Total	0.74	1.32	1.48
Bus	Access	0.47	0.99	1.17
	Egress	0.48	1.02	1.15
	Total	1.06	1.88	2.12
Train	Access	0.61	1.19	1.38
	Egress	0.64	1.20	1.39
	Total	1.34	2.16	2.42

Urban design and low carbon mobility

In urban planning terms, the future for low carbon urban development hinges on increased urban densities and on mixed land uses, as discussed for the ASSI policy framework. Detailed urban design considerations are also important, especially in the planned layouts of precincts and neighbourhoods. For example, Capri et al. (2016) highlighted the potential effects of climate change, with more extreme weather conditions (such as heat and rainstorms) on pedestrian behaviour. They developed a modelling tool to support planning and design of walking networks, by assessing the effects of actions intended to increase resilience with respect to extreme weather conditions as part of a climate change adaptation strategy. They adopted an integrated approach, combining transport and land use planning concepts with elements of outdoor thermal comfort and network accessibility. Walking networks can then be analysed through centrality indexes, including thermal comfort aspects. Tait (2011) focussed on the potential impacts of increasing heat on people's ability to undertake outdoor activities which could then limit the opportunities for participation in active transport. He further proposed that urban design should seek to mitigate the effects of excess heat in public spaces and on walking networks – a subject discussed further by Hiscock et al. (2017).

Guidance on suitable urban planning and design measures is increasingly available. For instance, NCHRP, 2016 provides a comprehensive design guide for low-speed, multimodal roadways in urban and suburban areas. This guide describes a range of acceptable elements, criteria and values for critical dimensions in the design of low-to-intermediate speed (70 km/h and lower design speeds) roadways with mixed road users. It also provides assistance to designers seeking to obtain a balance between operational efficiency, comfort, safety and convenience for all travel modes (motorised and nonmotorised) using low- and intermediate-speed roadways. Doorley et al., 2020 propose a set of planning techniques for the design of optimal infrastructure for cycling networks, while Folkeson et al. (2017) reviewed the state of play in eight Swedish municipalities NCHRP, 2016 concerning the preparedness for climate change adaptation for local transportation infrastructure.

One fundamental problem identified as a significant issue in urban design is the pedestrian barrier or 'community severance' effect sometimes posed by major roads in urban areas. As noted previously, Negron-Poblete et al. (2014) found that the propensity to participate in pedestrian activity did not depend on intended trip distance alone but was also affected by the presence of obstacles to movement resulting from road planning and design decisions, a particular concern for the elderly. More recently, this issue has been studied by Anciaes and Jones (2020), who suggested a new approach for measuring and valuing the barrier effect of different types of roads and for integrating the values into the transportation projects assessment. They developed an index of the size of the barrier effect caused by the different characteristics of roads (number of lanes, presence/width of central reservation (i.e., median strip), traffic density and traffic speed) and pedestrian crossing facilities (type, waiting time and walking time to access them). The index was also related with the estimated willingness to pay to reduce the barrier effect for existing trips, and with the number of new walking trips that could be generated with that reduction.

A comprehensive guide to low carbon urban design principles and practices was provided by Newton and Taylor (2019). The guide provides advice and information on the transition to sustainable urban development in two key environmental domains: resource consumption and greenhouse gas emissions. Its goal is to facilitate an urban development transition that is demonstrably regenerative, low carbon, adaptive and smart and that will underpin the emergence of a green economy that has renewable energy at its core, but is multisectoral in its involvement with new modes of transportation, construction, manufacturing and service industries. This requires urban development that is based on a critical set of planning and design principles and objectives for cities capable of delivering positive environmental outcomes along with cobenefits linked to human health and well-being. It encompasses a new urban design paradigm for city development – and redevelopment – that focusses on people. In terms of low carbon mobility, the guide stresses the need to focus on the following developments:

- More walkable neighbourhood designs
- Reduced areas devoted to automobiles in private property and in the public realm
- Greener streets and verge gardens seamlessly meshed to private green spaces
- Uptake of new transportation modes designed for local area usage, such as mobility services including car sharing and ride sharing, and micromobility

Micromobility travel includes bicycle sharing systems and e-scooters, which have the potential to foster more equitable transportation for all (Gilbert-Stowell, 2020). Grischkat et al. (2014) concluded that the new and emerging mobility services offered significant potential for reductions in greenhouse gas emissions from personal transportation.

Transportation and weather

Transportation system adaptation to climate change also requires transportation planners to consider the potential impacts of climate and weather events on travel behaviour, especially for the active transport modes of walking and cycling. This area is emerging as an important topic for transportation research, to inform future transportation policies and provisions for transportation infrastructure. Precipitation and temperature are two weather parameters of interest. Tait (2011) discussed the impediment of high temperatures on walking, while Ahmed et al. (2010) developed a mathematical model of the impacts of weather on bicycle demand and concluded that about half of the observed variations in bicycle traffic volumes could be explained by changes in weather parameters. Zhao et al. (2019) analysed the impacts of weather and climate conditional changes on walking and cycling in Seattle. They found that while activity for both modes was affected by weather events, cycling was perhaps more severely influenced.

Bocker et al. (2019) undertook an international cross-comparison of weather and daily mobility, using data from a number of cities in North West Europe. They concluded that light, calm, dry and warm atmospheric conditions positively affected cycling and the selection of outdoor leisure destinations in all of the cities studied, while cold and (to a lesser extent) wet and windy weather conditions reduced cycling activity and promoted automobile usage. There were, however, some regional differences in the overall effects of weather on mobility. The authors considered these effects in terms of geographical context, land use and transportation, climate conditions, culture, habits and adaptations in the different cities, and consequently formulated policy advice that could mitigate the exposures of active transport users to adverse weather and make walking and cycling more suitable and adaptable for year round usage.

The impacts of weather events and a changing climate on travel behaviour are important considerations in adaptation planning for transportation agencies.

Summary

This chapter is intended as a primer for transportation planners and system managers on issues related to the prospective increased usage of active transport as a societal response to climate change mitigation. From the perspective of climate change adaptation, transportation agencies, in close collaboration with local government and urban planning agencies, will need to place greater and greater focus on the provision of useful, connected and safe infrastructure and networks for pedestrians and cyclists. Travel behaviour data for Melbourne, Australia, as reported in this chapter, clearly show that walking is already an important transportation mode, yet a review of the international literature shows that this mode is poorly understood and that suitable infrastructure for walking is lacking in many places. As walking activity can be expected to increase, this situation cannot be allowed to continue.

The encouragement of increased usage of active transport modes is a fundamental part of transportation policies for climate change mitigation. The adaptation perspective for active transport is on the provision and maintenance of infrastructure specifically provided for active travel. This infrastructure is most likely to be found in urban areas, and so issues of urban design that encourage – or remove impediments to – active transport are important.

This chapter began by discussing land use—transport integration as a planning philosophy that encourages active travel, by reorganising urban land use distribution to bring destinations closer and thus reduce travel distances, which potentially could ameliorate some of the current pressures on transportation infrastructure. The ASSI – 'avoid, shift, share, improve' – paradigm was described, as an approach to policy development for active travel and the provision and operation of suitable infrastructure, including access to public transport. This chapter concluded by examining the emerging principles for low carbon design of urban precincts and neighbourhoods, and the implications for transportation infrastructure provision that result – including the potential impacts of weather events and climate change on travel behaviour.

References

Aditjandra, P., Mulley, C., Nelson, J.D., 2013. The influence of neighbourhood design on travel behaviour: empirical evidence from North East England. Transport Pol. 26, 54–65.

Ahmed, F., Rose, G., Jacob, C., 2010. Impact of Weather on Commuter Cyclist Behaviour and Implications for Climate Change Adaptation. Papers of the Australasian Transport Research Forum. https://www.australasiantransportresearchforum.org.au/papers/2010. (Accessed 13 March 2020).

Anciaes, P., Jones, P.M., 2020. A comprehensive approach for the appraisal of the barrier effect of roads on pedestrians. Transport. Res. Pol. Pract. 134, 227–250.

Banister, D., 2013. City transport in a post carbon society. In: Givoni, M., Banister, D. (Eds.), Moving towards Low Carbon Mobility. Edward Elgar Publishing, Cheltenham, UK.

Bocker, L., Uteng, T.P., Liu, C., Dijst, M., 2019. Weather and daily mobility in international perspective: a cross-comparison of Dutch, Norwegian and Swedish city regions. Transport. Res. D: Transp. Environ. 77, 491–505.

Capri, S., Ignaccolo, M., Inturri, G., Le Pira, M., 2016. Green walking networks for climate change adaptation. Transport. Res. Transport Environ. 45, 84–95.

Cole, C., et al., 2006. Socio-demographic variations in walking for transport and for recreation or exercise among adult Australians. J. Phys. Activ. Health 3, 164–178.

Dia, H., 2017. Policy principles for low carbon mobility. In: Dia, H. (Ed.), Low Carbon Mobility for Future Cities: Principles and Applications. IET Books, London), pp. 41–63.

Doorley, D, Pakrashi, V, Szeto, W Y, Ghosh, G, 2020. Designing cycle networks to maximize health, environmental, and travel time impacts: an optimization-based approach. Int. J. Sust. Trans. 14 (5), 361–374.

EPA, 2020. Sources of Greenhouse Gas Emissions. US Environmental Protection Agency, Washington, DC. https://www.epa.gov/ghgemissions/sources-greenhouse-gas-emissions. (Accessed 12 March 2020).

EEA, 2020. Greenhouse Gas Emissions from Transport in Europe. European Environment Agency, Copenhagen. https://www.eea.europa.eu/data-and-maps/indicators/transport-emissions-of-greenhouse-gases/transport-emissions-of-greenhouse-gases-12. (Accessed 12 March 2020).

Folkeson, L., Jägerbrand, A.K., Geneli, A., 2017. State of Preparedness for Climate Change Adaptation in Operations and Maintenance of Transport Infrastructure in Eight Swedish municipalities. VTIReport 924A. Swedish National Road and Transport Research Institute (VTI), Linköping, Sweden. www.vti.se.

Gilbert-Stowell, H., 2020. Making micromobility equitable for all. ITEA J. 90 (2), 46–49.

Grischkat, S., Hunecke, M., Böhler, S., Haustein, S., 2014. Potential for the reduction of greenhouse gas emissions through the use of mobility services. Transport Pol. 35, 295–303.

Hiscock, R., Asikainen, A., Tuomisto, J., Jantunen, M., Pärjälä, E., Sabel, C.E., 2017. City scale climate change policies: do they matter for wellbeing? Prevent. Med. Rep. 6, 265–270.

IPCC, 2014. In: Edenhofer, O., Pichs-Madruga, R., Sokona, Y., Farahani, E., Kadner, S., Seyboth, K., Adler, A., Baum, I., Brunner, S., Eickemeier, P., Kriemann, B., Savolainen, J., Schlömer, S., Von Stechow, C., Zwickel, T., Minx, J.C. (Eds.), Climate Change 2014: Mitigation of Climate Change. Contribution of Working Group III to the Fifth Assessment Report of the Intergovernmental Panel on Climate Change. Cambridge University Press, Cambridge, UK and New York, NY.

Mackett, R., 2012. Children's travel behaviour and its health implications. Transport Pol. 26, 66–72.

Mackie, H., 2010. Overcoming barriers to cycling to school: a key to improving transport system performance. Road Transp. Res. 19 (2), 54–61.

Morency, C., Trepanier, M., Demers, M., 2011. Walking to transit: an unexpected source of physical activity. Transport Pol. 18, 800–806.

Nakamura, H., Hayashi, Y., May, A.D. (Eds.), 2004. Urban Transport and the Environment: An International Perspective. Elsevier, Oxford).

NCHRP, 2016. Design Guide for Low-Speed Multimodal Roadways. NCHRP Research Report 880. National Cooperative Highway Research Program, Transportation Research Board, Washington, DC.

Negron-Poblete, P., Séguin, A.-M., Apparicio, P., 2014. Improving walkability for seniors through accessibility to food stores: a study of three areas of Greater Montreal. J. Urban. https://doi.org/10.1080/17549175.2014.990916.

Newton, P W, Newman, P, 2013. The geography of solar photovoltaics (PV) and a new low carbon urban transition theory. Sustainability 5, 2537–2556.

Newton, P.W., Taylor, M.A.P. (Eds.), 2019. Precinct Design Assessment: AGuide to Smart Sustainable Low Carbon Urban Development. Cooperative Research Centre for Low Carbon Living, Sydney. http://builtbetter.org/node/7934. (Accessed 13 March 2020).

Niemeier, D., 1997. Accessibility: an evaluation using social welfare. Transportation 24, 377–396.

Ogilvie, D., Egan, M., Hamilton, V., Petticrew, M., 2004. Promoting walking and cycling as an alternative to using cars: systematic review. Br. Med. J. 329 (763). https://doi.org/10.1136/bmj.38216.714560.55.

Plaut, P.O., 2005. Non-motorized commuting in the US. Transport. Res. Transport Environ. 10, 347–356.

Pucher, J., Buehler, R., Bassett, D.R., Dannenberg, A.L., 2010. Walking and cycling to health: a comparative analysis of city, state, and international data. Am. J. Publ. Health 100 (10), 1986–1992.

Pucher, J., Buehler, R., Merom, D., Bauman, A., 2011. Walking and cycling in the United States, 2001–2009: evidence from the national household travel surveys. Am. J. Publ. Health 101 (S1), S310–S317.

Philp, M., Taylor, M.A.P., 2017. A research agenda for low carbon mobility: issues for new world cities. Int. J. Sust. Trans. 11 (1), 49–58.

Primerano, F., Taylor, M.A.P., 2005. An accessibility framework for evaluating transport policies. In: Levinson, D.M., Krizek, K.J. (Eds.), Access to Destinations. Elsevier, Oxford, pp. 325–346.

Santos, G., Behrendt, H., Teytelboym, A., 2010. Part II: policy instruments for sustainable road transport. Res. Transport. Econ. 28 (1), 46–91.

Tait, P.W., 2011. Active transport and heat. Asia Pac. J. Publ. Health 23 (4), 634–635.

Taylor, M.A.P., 2017. Integrated land-use and transport planning for future cities, and the importance of active transport. In: Dia, H. (Ed.), Low Carbon Mobility for Future Cities: Principles and Applications. IET Books, London), pp. 91–112.

Taylor, M.A.P., Thompson, S.M., 2019. An analysis of active transport in Melbourne: baseline activity for assessment of low carbon mobility interventions. Urban Pol. Res. 37 (1), 62–81.

Tudor-Locke, C., Bittman, M., Merom, D., Bauman, A., 2005. Patterns of walking for transport and exercise: a novel application of time use data. Int. J. Behav. Nutr. Phys. Activ. 2 (5). https://doi.org/10.1186/1479-58682-5.

Vuchic, V.R., 2007. Urban Transit Systems and Technology. John Wiley and Sons, Hoboken NJ.

Wasfi, R.A., Ross, N.A., El-Geneidy, A.M., 2013. Achieving recommended daily physical activity levels through commuting by public transportation: unpacking individual and contextual influences. Health Place 23, 18–25.

Wegener, M., 1996. Reduction of CO2 emissions of transport by reorganisation of urban activities. In: Hayashi, Y., Roy, J.R. (Eds.), Transport, Land-Use and the Environment. Kluwer Academic Publishers, Dordrecht), pp. 103–124.

Zhao, J., Guo, C., Zhang, R., Guo, D., Palmer, M., 2019. Impacts of weather on cycling and walking on twin trails in Seattle. Transport. Res. Transport Environ. 77, 573–588.

Chapter 10

Future directions in research and practice

The subject of this book is climate change adaptation for transportation systems. This subject has been examined using a number of perspectives, starting from general principles and moving to specific approaches for different modes of transportation. The discussion has focused on what is meant by adaptation for the express purposes of the managers of transportation systems. To do so involved consideration of three major themes for climate change adaptation in transportation:

1. The options for changing practice, not merely refining or improving current practice
2. Risk management and the development of adaptation frameworks and pathways, with appropriate decision support tools, and
3. In terms of the natural phenomena affecting transportation systems and themselves affected by climate change, the central role of water, in its many guises, in the degradation and limitation of the performance of transportation facilities, assets and systems. Temperature cannot be ignored either, but water in the wrong place or in the wrong amount is always a problem.

For theme 1, practical examples of the potential need to change design and maintenance practices were seen in Chapter 6, in the provision of coastal defences and transportation infrastructure in coastal zones; in Chapter 7, with the potential impacts of climate change on road pavements and other infrastructure assets (especially bridges); in Chapter 8, with the potential impacts on railways systems maintenance and operations from thermal buckling of rail tracks, and in Chapter 9 with the rising needs to focus more on the provision of suitable, safe infrastructure for the active travel modes of walking and cycling, particularly in urban areas.

Theme 2 – risk management and the development and application of adaptation frameworks and pathways – was dealt with throughout the book. The early chapters (Chapters 1, 4 and 5) described the basis of risk management and the principles adopted in its implementation and use. Chapter 1 provided a set of guiding principles for the planning and implementation of adaptation programs. Chapter 3 considered transportation infrastructure as one

Climate Change Adaptation for Transportation Systems. https://doi.org/10.1016/B978-0-12-816638-3.00010-6

class of infrastructure systems and examined the interdependencies between systems, leading to the identification of critical infrastructure components. Adaptation frameworks and pathways were explored in Chapter 4 and set in the context of a generic systematic approach to planning and decision-making, with practical examples of frameworks for specific areas of transportation described in Chapters 4, 6, 7 and 8. Chapter 5 discussed the information and data resources and the decision support tools available for transportation systems managers, with commentary on the suitability of existing tools, the need to refine or modify those tools, and emerging tools specifically cast at decision-making under uncertainty and with consideration of both short-term and long-term issues – the circumstances at the heart of planning for climate change adaptation.

The role of water as an agent for the degradation or accelerated deterioration of transportation assets was indicated throughout the middle chapters (Chapters 5–8). Sea level rise, storm surges, extreme precipitation events, rising groundwater, water penetration into in-ground structures, scour, flash floods and temporary and long-term inundation were identified as issues for concern in transportation asset management, and issues that are exacerbated by climate change. Corrosion and material degradation are further problems directly affected by water, including water vapour and humidity. Rising temperatures also pose problems, indirectly with sea level rise and directly with degraded performance of road pavements and rail tracks.

Background

To properly consider climate change adaptation first requires some knowledge of the basics of climate science and on the parameters that identify changes in climate. Chapter 2 provided a brief overview of climate system dynamics together with some discussion of observed changes in climate as reported, for example, by the IPCC (2007, 2013, 2014a,b). Weather events such as rainfall, storms, snow, fog, low temperatures and high temperatures have potential impacts on transportation infrastructure and operations. The weather events form one part of climate and their intensity and frequency are of concern, leading to consideration of what may be considered as extreme weather events, e.g., hurricanes, droughts, blizzards and heat waves, which define some of the parameters used in the design and construction of infrastructure assets and in determining the safe operating conditions for use of the infrastructure. Weather-induced events, such as floods, wildfires, landslides and storm surges, can lead to significant disruptions in transportation services and potentially to economic and social disruptions as well. Climate change stands to change the nature, intensity, severity and frequency of these events.

The possible contributions of human activity over time to climate change and to the potential impacts of weather on transportation infrastructure were introduced in Chapter 2. Sea level rise was considered as a major factor affecting coastal and estuarine infrastructure. The importance of these phenomena for transportation network operations was then reviewed. Global climate models were outlined, as an information source for use as inputs in adaptation planning for future climate change affecting transportation. Given the climate models and the capability to downscale from global to regional studies, the Representative Concentration Pathway (RCP) approach was introduced to conclude the chapter. The RCP approach offers climate input data for use in adaptation planning on the basis of climate change scenarios. A number of the case studies described in later chapters of the book (e.g., Knott et al., 2017 and Chinowsky et al., 2019) made use of the RCPs in defining potential scenarios for climate change and the likely resultant impacts on road and rail transportation, respectively.

With this background in hand, the discussion then turned to the relationships between infrastructure systems, the characteristics of transportation infrastructure and the possible impacts of climate change on that infrastructure. Climate stressors relevant to transportation were introduced in Chapter 4. This chapter focused on general methods for adaptation planning in transportation, based on risk management analysis. Detailed methods for analysis and assessment, including a review of relevant decision support tools, were discussed in Chapter 5, along with adaptation planning for airports. Chapters 6–9 of the book considered specific parts of transportation infrastructure, including issues for coastal areas, ports and harbours, road transportation systems, rail transportation systems, the integration of land use and transportation planning and multimodal transportation (including provision for walking and cycling as part of urban design).

Infrastructure systems

Transportation systems belong to the set of distributed infrastructure systems. Their infrastructure components and assets are connected and spread across a region. The physical components of the system form a connected network spanning the region, allowing the movements of people, vehicles and goods. The physical elements are thus subject to the prevailing environmental and climatic conditions of the area. Land-based transportation systems – road and rail – require connected physical assets (i.e., networks) for their operations. Water-based transportation requires some fixed assets besides ports and harbours for operations (e.g., navigable channels, locks and canals). Aviation systems require airport facilities but otherwise no fixed connective assets except – and most importantly – for service and supply by the land-based systems, and thus are also reliant on them. Intermodal interchanges are required whenever people and/or goods move from one transportation mode to another.

The multimodal and hence multinetwork nature of transportation systems is also a pointer to a further feature of those systems. Transportation is inextricably linked to other infrastructure systems (e.g., energy and communications systems). These linkages need to be considered along with transportation systems, and this is best done by considering the interdependencies that can exist between infrastructure systems. Interdependencies exist in a number of forms:

- *Physical interdependency*, involving a physical linkage between the inputs and outputs of two infrastructure systems
- *Cyber interdependency*, when the operating state of an infrastructure system depends on the transmission of information through an information infrastructure such as a telecommunications system
- *Geographic interdependency*, which occurs when a local environmental event, e.g., an extreme weather event, leads to changes in the operating states of a set of infrastructure systems, perhaps because they share a common conduit such as a bridge, and
- *Logical interdependency*, between two infrastructure systems; this occurs when the state of each system depends on the state of the other through a connection or mechanism that is not a physical, cyber or geographic connection.

Transportation systems can have these interdependencies with a range of other infrastructure systems, including power supply, telecommunications, water supply and drainage systems.

A useful way to consider climate change impacts on transportation infrastructure and associated interdependent infrastructure systems was suggested by Tavasszy et al. (2016). This is summarised by the conceptual framework shown in Fig. 10.1 (also shown as Fig. 3.2 in Chapter 3). The framework places the transportation system within the milieu of the society and physical environment in which it exists. It also links transportation to other related or interdependent infrastructure systems. Within the milieu of society, policies and plans are formulated and promulgated. These result in projects and actions to support, manage and extend the infrastructure systems. The framework allows for the impacts of climate change in general and climate-related episodes and events that impinge on the provision and operation of transportation systems. The figure uses the example of sea level rise as a climate change impact, with impacts through storm surge events then affecting transportation. In terms of transportation assets, the storm surge may lead to road inundation or road washout in an affected coastal region. This leads to reduction in network connectivity as affected roads become impassable for some time period, leading to route diversions and possible severance for some communities. Network operations are thus impacted, through increased travel times and perhaps increased traffic congestion in parts of the degraded network. In the longer term, economic losses may accrue through the reduced network performance and severance.

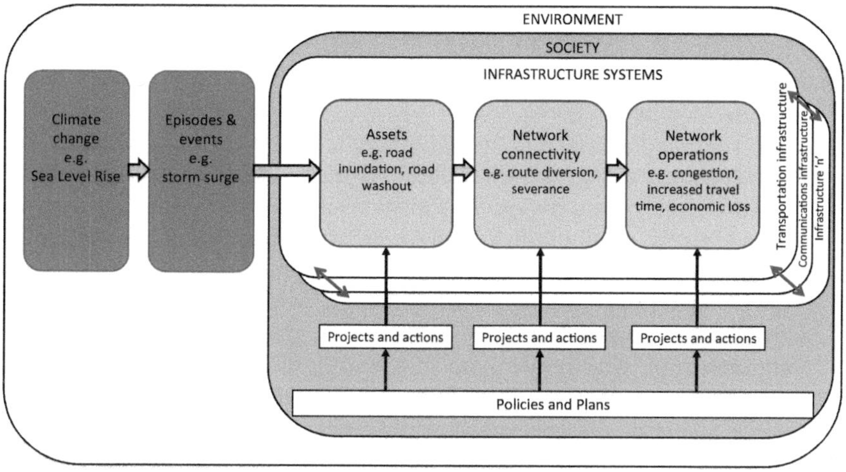

FIGURE 10.1 Conceptual framework for climate change impacts on transportation infrastructure and associated interdependent infrastructure systems. *(adapted from Tavasszy et al. (2016), also shown as Figure 3.2).*

Society, government and responsible agencies need to have policies and plans in place, which lead to actions and projects, e.g., increased coastal protection for those transportation assets located in coastal zones.

Systematic assessments of potential vulnerability of transportation infrastructure to climate impacts, including climate change and extreme weather, are essential in asset management. These assessments need to follow a set framework but be sensitive to local environmental conditions. Key to the systematic assessment is the concept of risk management, which may be applied to considerations of climate change adaptation for transportation, but equally applies to many other aspects of transportation infrastructure management. The four guiding principles developed by ASCE (2009) for the management of critical infrastructure provide the starting point for the development of frameworks for climate change adaptation. These principles are

1. *Quantify, communicate and manage risk*, where risk management is the application of a systematic process for identifying, analysing, planning, monitoring and responding to risk so that critical infrastructure will meet service expectations. Risk may be defined as a product of the probability that an event may occur and the magnitude of consequences that would result from that event
2. *Employ an integrated systems approach,* for critical infrastructure requires planning, funding, design, construction and operation as a system, appropriately integrated with all other interdependent systems.

Critical infrastructure systems must also be resilient and sustainable throughout the system's life cycle. The systems must be properly maintained, operated and modified as necessary to perform effectively under changing conditions
3. *Exercise sound leadership, management and stewardship in decision-making processes*, given that the long-term viability of any critical infrastructure system, irrespective of its resilience and sustainability, will ultimately rely on the human and organisational stewardship applied to the system. Effective organisations can control program outcomes through technical oversight, coordination with related projects and activities, appropriate control and change management and effective communication with project stakeholders. In the absence of sound leadership and management of critical infrastructure, the safety, health and welfare of the public are placed at risk and
4. *Adapt critical infrastructure in response to dynamic conditions and practice,* as critical infrastructure systems generally have long life cycles, spanning decades. These systems are normally designed to meet expected performance levels deemed appropriate at the time of design. However, conditions continually evolve and change, and system managers must adopt change management systems that can effectively address new conditions. These change management systems need to be flexible and robust and must establish discipline in the way critical infrastructure systems are operated, reviewed, maintained and upgraded throughout their life cycle.

The ASCE guiding principles provide the high-level advice on how those responsible for infrastructure systems should fulfil their duties. A clear example of the recognition of those requirements and their application is shown by the US Federal Highways Administration (FHWA) in its framework for assessing the vulnerability of road systems to climate change and extreme weather (FHWA, 2019).

Risk management and adaptation frameworks

For a transportation agency considering the potential impacts of climate change, risk is the potential for unwanted outcomes from events, which include changes in the level, intensity and frequency of climatic conditions and extreme weather events — the climate stressors. The overall measure of risk is given by the product of the likelihood (probability) of an event and its estimated consequence (impact), which is then related to the vulnerability of an asset to that event. In general terms, the assessment of risk for a given event requires the following steps:

- Review assets in terms of their vulnerability to projected climate change
- Assess the likelihood of a particular impact on a given asset arising from a predicted set of climate stressors

- Assess the consequences of the impact (and most properly include not only the immediate transportation consequences but also the wider socioeconomic consequences for the study region)
- Make an integrated assessment of the risk to the asset.

An integrated assessment for those assets seen as vulnerable to climate change can then be undertaken. The 'risk matrix' introduced in Chapter 1 and illustrated in Chapter 4 provides a useful approach for this assessment. Note that those assets deemed as not vulnerable should not be entirely ignored. The assessment process may need to be repeated at intervals in the future, as new data, new experiences and new circumstances arise. Monitoring, review and learning are important tasks in systems planning for climate change adaptation. The integrated risk assessment considers both the likelihood that an asset will undergo a particular impact and the consequence of that impact on the asset and on the communities and region that use the asset. This analysis will yield an overall risk assessment for each asset considered, e.g., in terms of a classification such as

- *Low* – minimal impact on the asset, with minimal oversight required to ensure that the risk remains low
- *Moderate* – the asset may face some disruption and may require alternative management approaches, possibly including additional management surveillance
- *High* – the asset faces an unacceptable level of risk and major disruption is likely. This will entail adoption of alternative management practices and the asset requires priority management surveillance.

Fig. 10.2 (see also Fig. 4.1) shows a schematic interpretation of the risk classification for an asset in terms of its level of likelihood and consequence for a defined weather event.

A range of adaptation frameworks are now available. Those frameworks provided by FHWA (2019) and the International Road Federation (PIARC, 2015) provide good case study applications in the real world. The FHWA framework in particular provides an excellent exemplar because of its evaluated and reported use in a large number of case studies across the United States. The framework includes seven basic steps:

1. Articulate objectives and define study scope
2. Obtain asset data
3. Obtain climate data
4. Assess risk and vulnerability
5. Identify, analyse and prioritise adaptation options
6. Integrate assessment results into decision-making
7. Monitor and review assessments and implementations.

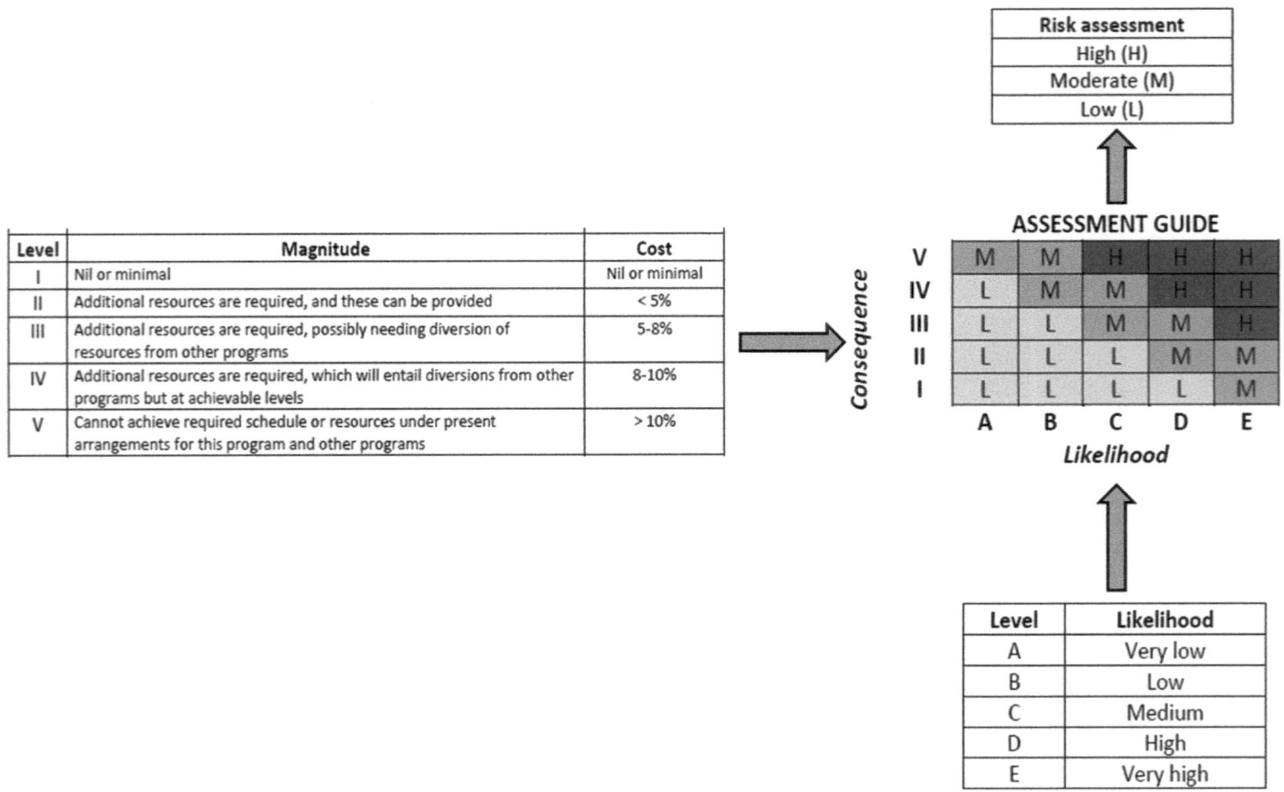

FIGURE 10.2 Use of the risk matrix approach in classifying the levels of risk to transportation assets (see also Figure 4.2).

Fig. 10.3 shows the basics of this framework, emphasising the required continuity in the adaptation planning process. Fig. 10.4 (see also Fig. 4.8) shows the framework in more detail – outlining a number of the tasks in each step – as proposed and applied by the FHWA. In Fig. 10.4 steps 2 and 3 above are considered together in a generalised data collection task. The framework provides a closed system because of the emphasis on monitoring and review. Adaptation planning is an ongoing task involving continual information gathering and learning. The diagram also indicates potential alternatives for assessment and analysis.

Risk management for climate change adaptation requires consideration of climate stressors and their effects on infrastructure. Climate stressors may be manifested through both extreme weather events or through gradual changes in climate (ITF, 2016). The starting point is to remember, from Chapter 2, that climate change will change both average climate variables and the magnitude, frequency and severity of extreme events. The climate stressors for transportation systems include

- Temperature: average, extremes (magnitude and duration), amplitude (daily and seasonal)
- Humidity, for both air and soil
- Precipitation, including rainfall and snowfall: total annual, seasonal (or monthly) variations, extreme intensities

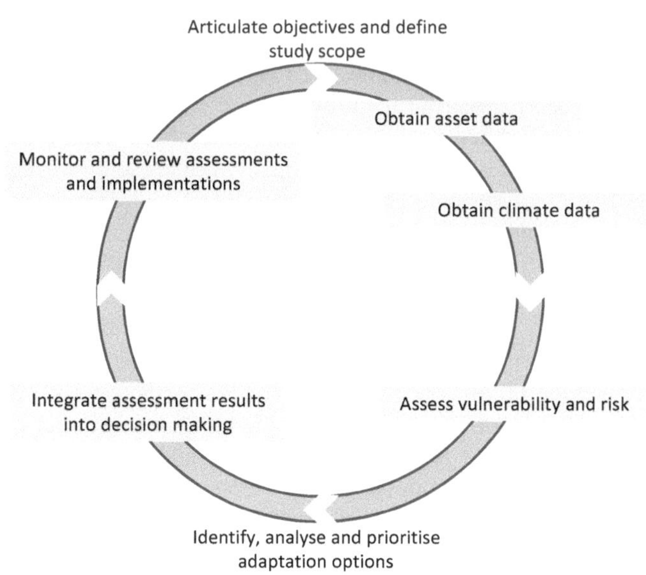

FIGURE 10.3 The basics of the climate change adaptation framework developed by the US Federal Highways Administration, stressing the continuity of the adaptation planning process.

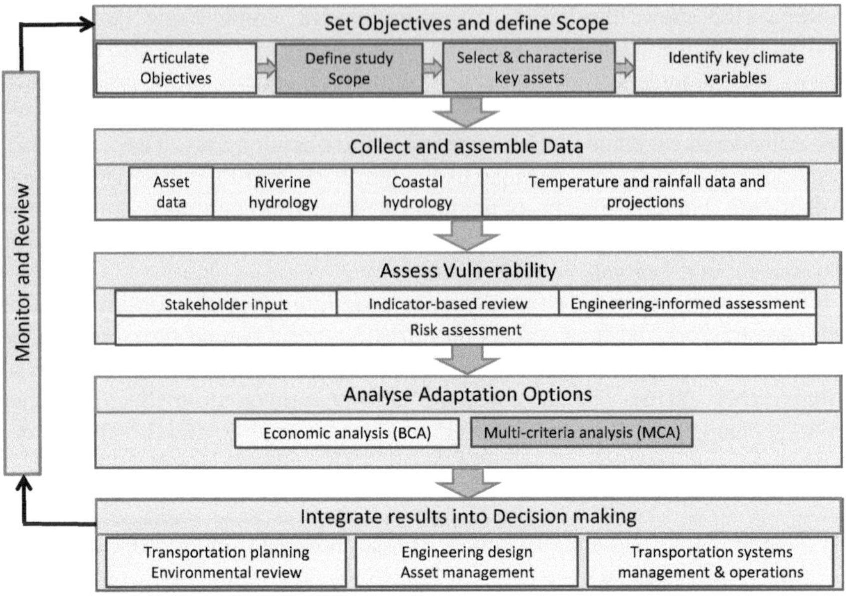

FIGURE 10.4 The climate adaptation assessment framework developed by the US Federal Highways Administration. *(derived from FHWA (2019), see also Figure 4.8).*

- Wind: prevailing direction, average speed, incidence of gusts and gales, incidence and spatial locations of hurricanes and cyclones
- Sea level rise.

All of these climate factors stand to be affected by climate change, probably in the medium to long term. In addition, changes in the incidence and severity of weather-related natural phenomena such as storms and related storm surges, flooding, blizzards, dust storms, wildfires and hurricanes could have severe if not catastrophic effects on transportation infrastructure at any time. By way of example, Fig. 10.5 – derived from ITF (2016) and shown previously as Fig. 5.4– provides an illustration of trends in some of the climate stressors, their impacts on climate and the potential damage to road infrastructure.

One vital aspect of the management of risk and uncertainty in adaptation planning for transportation concerns the evaluation methods to be employed in the assessment of risk. For some time, the main method for similar evaluations in transportation has been benefit–cost analysis, and this technique is well understood and highly developed. However, its application in adaptation planning presents some problems, given the long time spans (the planning horizon) to be accounted for and the high degree of uncertainty about future costs and benefits over that time duration. Conventional benefit–cost analysis may not have the capability to properly account for these concerns, as it tends

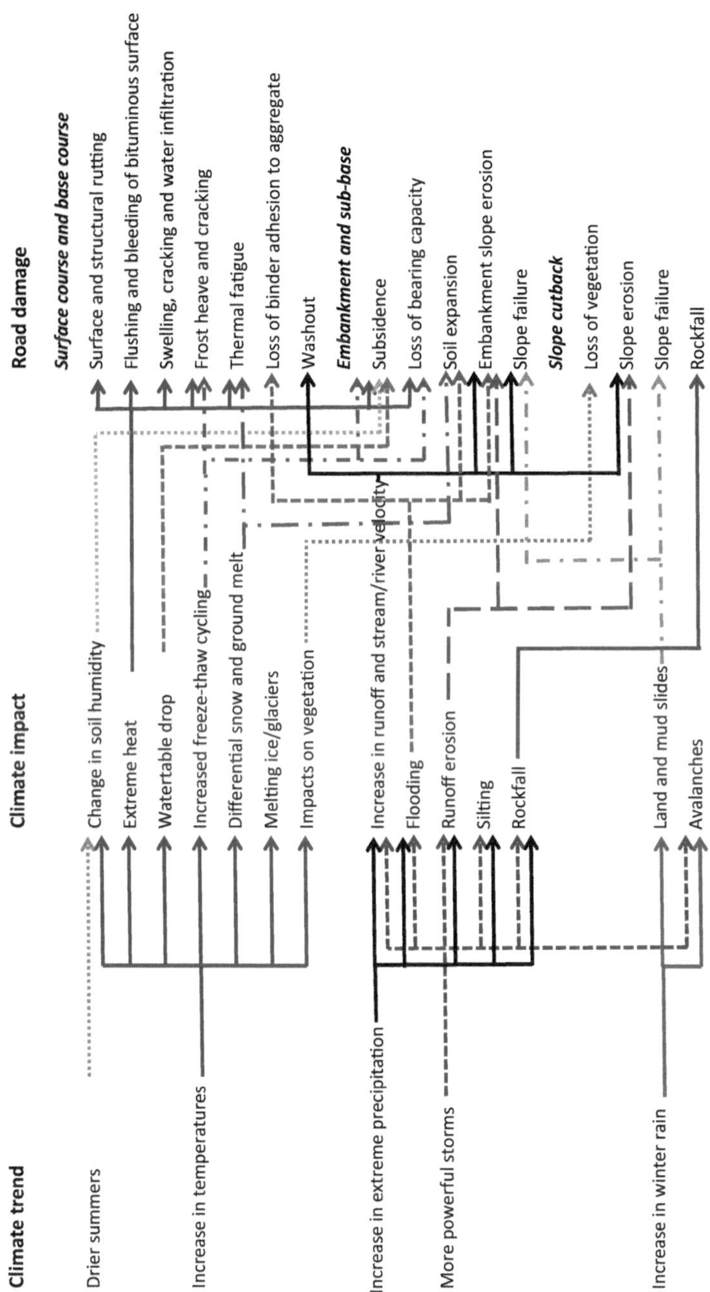

FIGURE 10.5 Indications of climate trends and their impacts on climate and potential damage to road infrastructure. *(adapted from ITF (2016)).*

to place more emphasis on costs and benefits arising in the short to medium term. Other established techniques such as cost-effectiveness analysis and multicriteria analysis may suffer from similar concerns. While multicriteria analysis offers an approach that could focus on longer-term impacts and differing degrees of uncertainty, it may rely on subjective judgements in this regard. Other methods perhaps more suited to decision-making under uncertainty have been promulgated, including real options analysis and robust decision-making. More research and development and practical assessment of the utility of these decision support tools is required. A discussion of the characteristics, strengths, weaknesses and applicability of the decision support tools was given in Chapter 5, and summarised in Table 5.6. In terms of their potential use in climate change adaptation studies in transportation, the following guidance was provided in Chapter 5:

- *Benefit–cost analysis*: this technique values all benefits and costs of all options and estimates the net present values (NPVs) in monetary terms. It is suitable for identification of low- and no-regret options in the near future. It can be used as a decision support tool in iterative climate risk management. It is most useful when (1) climate probabilities are known, (2) climate sensitivity is small compared to overall costs and benefits and (3) good data exist for the major cost and benefit components
- *Cost-effectiveness analysis*: compares costs of options against their effectiveness (monetary or nonmonetary) to rank the options and then uses cost curves for targets and resources. Its suitability is as for benefit–cost analysis, but its use is for applications where benefits are not expressed in monetary terms
- *Multicriteria analysis*: this technique allows consideration of qualitative aspects as well as quantitative data in ranking alternative options. The impact on each individual criterion can also be seen. Its suitability is as for benefit–cost analysis, and it is best used for scoping options to indicate potential poor performance on individual criteria. It can complement other tools and capture qualitative effects
- *Real options analysis*: this technique allows for economic analysis of future options and accounts for the benefits of delaying a decision on a given option, to gather further information over time and maintain flexibility in planning. It is suitable for economic analysis of major asset investment decisions over the medium term and allows analysis of flexibility in the staging of major projects
- *Robust decision-making*: identifies strategies that are robust rather than optimal, by 'stress testing' a number of plausible scenarios for the alternative options. It thus provides for the identification of combinations of strategic (i.e., long-term, scenario-independent) and operational (short-term, scenario-dependent) decisions.

There are new decision support tools emerging, which are specifically designed for climate change adaptation. Schweikert et al. (2014) provides one example: the Infrastructure Planning Support System (IPSS). Kim and Li (2020) provide an example of the use of real options analysis, including specification of the data requirements. The development and use of these new tools is explored further in the section on 'research needs' later in this chapter.

Adaptation for transportation modes

Chapters 6–8 gave attention to specific geographic locations and transportations modes. In terms of geographic location, coastal regions stand out as a primary area of concern for the impacts of climate change and the needs for adaptation of transportation assets and infrastructure. Sea level rise and its implications are the underlying issues with respect to climate change in coastal zones, manifesting particularly in the increasing effects of storms, surges and flooding, and resultant coastal damage. Damage includes specific threats to transportation assets located in close proximity to the coast. Thus, the transportation facilities and structures in these areas, and their components and the materials they are constructed from, are of interest. Susceptibility to corrosion and water damage for these structures is well known, but a changing climate may lead to new requirements to guard against these, both in intensity and in spatial coverage. Ports and harbours are of necessity located in coastal areas, as are many airports, so the infrastructure requirements and potential climate impacts are of direct concern. In addition, damage to coastal infrastructure assets may cause degradation, dislocation and loss of service in transportation networks causing delays and congestion, disruption of supply chains and loss of connectivity for affected communities. Some of these effects may only last for a matter of hours, but others may persist for days, weeks or months.

Road networks are significant regional, state and national assets, providing for basic mobility and accessibility. The major asset component of a road network is road pavement. Chapter 7 described pavement structures and pavement design methods, including consideration of temperature impacts and water penetration. Mathematical modelling of road pavement performance was described and used to indicate how climate change factors could be incorporated in performance evaluation and therefore influence both design methods and maintenance regimes for road systems. Temperature and precipitation are the main climate factors included in the performance models. A significant case study from Australia used a composite climate variable to represent both temperature and precipitation. This variable, the Thornthwaite Moisture Index, has been shown to provide a useful representation of climate in the performance assessment of road pavements. Other studies have used the RCP approach to provide scenarios for climate change, which may then be used to estimate the long-term impacts of climate change on road infrastructure, particularly pavements. Other factors related to extreme weather events (e.g., storms, flooding, landslides and washouts) also have to be considered, along with phenomena such as groundwater rise as a consequence of sea level rise. Besides their detrimental effects on road infrastructure, these events may also lead to restrictions on traffic operations, such as road closure or restrictions on heavy vehicle traffic, for periods of hours to weeks, depending on the level and extent of damage. Road agencies and operators then have to have plans and procedures to deal with these disruptions.

Rail transportation systems also face significant issues from climate change. Chapter 8 considered how climate change factors could be incorporated in performance evaluation and therefore influence design methods and maintenance regimes for rail systems, as well as identifying potential impacts of climate change on rail operations. The discussion focused on the issues facing rail track managers and train operators, largely concerning rail maintenance systems and railway performance assessment. Extreme temperatures and precipitation events are major climate factors affecting railway performance. Service disruptions can be result from these factors, with potentially cascading impacts because of the strict operating rules that are an essential part of railway operations. Rail buckling under high temperatures is a significant problem for many railway systems and is likely to be exacerbated under warmer climates.

Railway systems have some unique properties that require special consideration for climate change adaptation. For example, rail infrastructure has extremely long service life and is constructed to withstand natural hazards, such as 50 year or 100 year floods. However, as the number and intensity of weather-related incidents increase under future climate change, the pressure on rail system capacity will grow, along with the costs of the sector. Many rail systems already face significant cost pressures, and there is some evidence in some places of inadequate expenditures on maintenance and refurbishment. Railway system managers need methods, processes and procedures to enable them to adapt their systems to the future operating environments. Chapter 8 described frameworks, methods, models and processes for railway systems to assist in this regard. The use of the RCP approach for generating climate change scenarios was illustrated by a case study from the United States.

The changing nature of transportation, particularly in urban areas and largely resulting from climate change – and, most pertinently, climate change mitigation policies – was considered in Chapter 9. This chapter provides a primer for transportation planners and system managers on issues related to the prospective increased usage of active transport as a societal response to climate change mitigation. From the perspective of climate change adaptation, transportation agencies, in close collaboration with local government and urban planning agencies, will need to place increasing focus on the provision of useable, connected and safe infrastructure and networks for pedestrians and cyclists. Indeed the encouragement of increased usage of active transport modes is a fundamental part of transportation policies for climate change mitigation. The adaptation perspective for active transport is on the provision and maintenance of infrastructure specifically provided for active travel. This infrastructure is most likely to be found in urban areas, and so issues of urban design that encourage – or remove impediments to – active travel are important. Chapter 9 began by discussing land use transport integration as a planning philosophy that encourages active travel, by reorganising urban land use distribution to bring destinations closer and thus reduce travel distances, which potentially could ameliorate some of the current pressures on transportation infrastructure. The ASSI – 'avoid, shift, share, improve' – paradigm was described in Chapter 9, as an approach to policy development for active travel and the provision and operation of suitable infrastructure, including access to public transit. The chapter concluded by examining the emerging principles for low carbon design of urban precincts and neighbourhoods, and the implications for transportation infrastructure provision that result – including the potential impacts of weather events and climate change on travel behaviour.

Research and development needs

The future task for transportation agencies is to keep their infrastructure and systems climate resilient. This will assist maintaining efficient and safe transportation operations and reduce future costs such as congestion, delays and severance. The potential for service disruptions will also be reduced. On the demand side, ensuring resilience will require travel behaviour changes by the community, as part of wider climate change mitigation initiatives. On the supply side, climate change adaptation is now an essential concern for transportation agencies. Existing infrastructure may require rehabilitation, refurbishment or retrofitting to make it more adaptable. Design methods and maintenance programs will require review and revision. New infrastructure should be planned, designed, constructed, maintained and operated to accommodate the shifts in climate that may occur over the operational lives of the infrastructure assets. Climate-resilient infrastructure should offer improved service reliability, increased asset life and protection for asset returns. Given the uncertainties that still surround potential climate change at the local or regional level, flexible and adaptive approaches are required in the provision and operation of infrastructure. The uncertainties – which in the long term include social and technological change as well as climate change – need to be recognised and accepted, even if they cannot be adequately described. This will provide the means to ensure resilience across a range of future climate scenarios. Policy analysts and decision-makers require access to high-quality information, consistent and expanding databases and suitable analytical techniques to ensure informed planning and decision-making. This access to information needs to be complemented by the development of technical and institutional capacities to manage climate-related risks.

A number of frameworks for climate change adaptation in transportation systems have been identified and described in previous chapters of this book. As indicated in the discussion above, while these frameworks have been developed for different modes of transportation or spatial regions, they are built around a similar core set of connected phases in a closed system procss – the seven steps previously identified as:

1. Articulate objectives and define study scope
2. Obtain asset data
3. Obtain climate data
4. Assess risk and vulnerability
5. Identify, analyse and prioritise adaptation options
6. Integrate assessment results into decision-making
7. Monitor and review assessments and implementations

and illustrated in Fig. 10.3. The identified frameworks described earlier in this book are

- FHWA, see Fig. 10.4 (FHWA, 2019)
- PIARC (2015)
- RoadAdapt (Bles et al., 2016)
- CoastAdapt (2018).
- Ports (Scott et al., 2013)
- RailAdapt (Quinn et al., 2017).

The FHWA framework provides a good exemplar because of the substantial number of reported case studies that have used it (FHWA, 2019). This framework would provide a good starting point for any transportation agency. In addition, agencies need to account for the interdependencies between a transportation system and other infrastructure systems, as indicated in Fig. 10.1 – see also Tavasszy et al. (2016).

The frameworks provide a sound basis for informed adaptation planning, but what is still missing is a properly established analytical methodology designed for use in climate change adaptation studies, which includes environmental and/or climate variables as explicit, required inputs in the models, tools and procedures used in the design and performance assessment of transportation systems, networks and infrastructure. Methods and case studies cited in earlier chapters point towards such a methodology, but much more development, innovation and testing will be required before this is clearly defined. On the basis of the studies reviewed earlier in this book, the structure of a general modelling approach for climate change adaptation in transportation can be defined. Fig. 10.6 presents this structure in conceptual form.

In this structure, the models of asset or system performance take inputs from two separate sources. The first source is the physical and performance data for the object (e.g., infrastructure asset, network or subnetwork) to be modelled, which would include the design loads (including travel demand) to

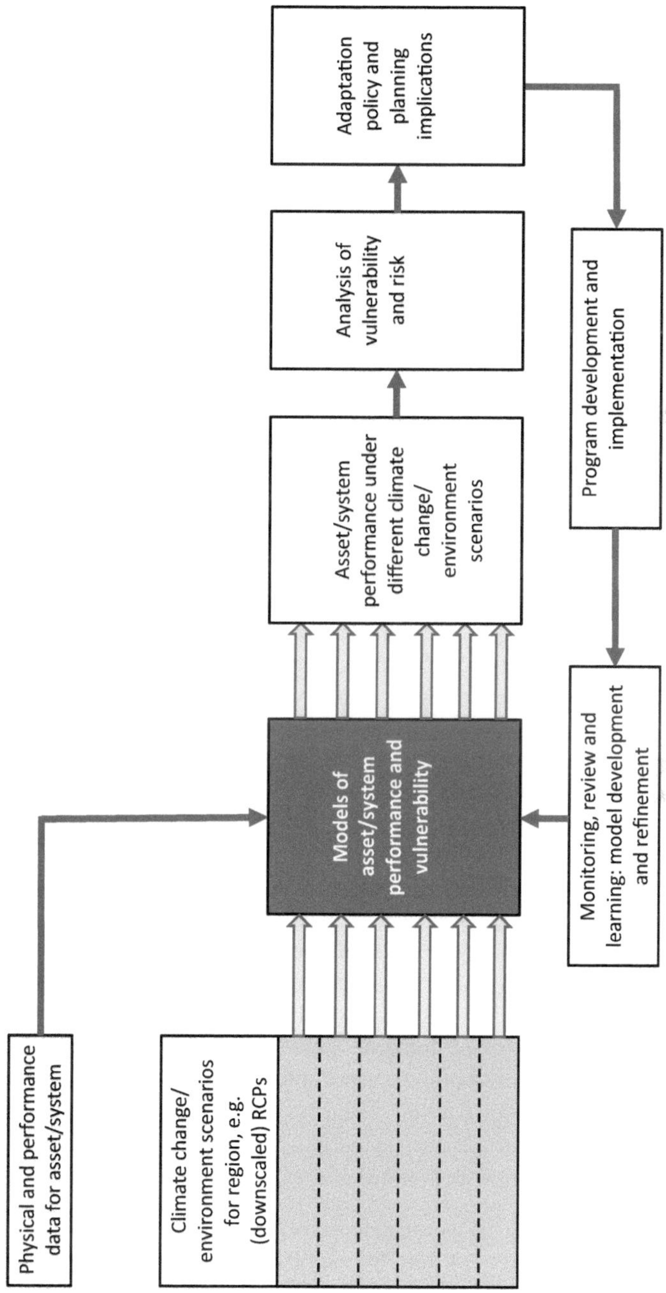

FIGURE 10.6 Concept for a general model structure for the explicit inclusion of environmental and climate factors in performance assessment for transportation infrastructure.

be applied to the object, its physical size and dimensions, component structure, the materials it is composed of and the rules for its operation. The second source is a set of (defined) climate scenarios, downscaled to suit the locality of the object,[1] which could apply over the planned or assumed lifetime of the object. If possible, probabilities of occurrence could be attached to the scenarios, but this is not essential. Suitable scenarios may be found using the RCP approach (e.g., as done by Knott et al. (2017) and Chinowsky et al. (2019)) or using other developed climate scenarios as in Taylor and Philp (2015), who used the set of climate scenarios developed for Australia by Austroads (2010). The choice of suitable climate variables also needs attention. In general, temperature distributions and precipitation patterns are the major climate factors affecting transportation infrastructure. The study by Chinowsky et al. (2019) on rail track buckling was primarily concerned with high temperatures, so that factor alone was enough in that case. For road pavement, both temperature and precipitation are important, and the composite climate factor known as the Thornthwaite Moisture Index provides one approach to represent both temperature and precipitation, as described in Chapter 7 (and in Taylor and Philp (2015)). The performance assessment model in Fig. 10.6 needs to include explicit climate input data. Then the performance of the study object under different climate scenarios can be modelled, and vulnerability and risk for the object assessed and compared over the scenarios. Adaptation policy and planning can then be informed by the results of the analysis, allowing for the development and implementation of appropriate planning and work programs with adaptation components. As emphasised throughout this book, the methodological structure process includes a phase for monitoring, review, learning and model refinement on the basis on experiences gained and observed in earlier cycles of the process.

The impacts of weather on travel behaviour, and especially the impacts of extreme weather events on traffic systems performance (for both road and rail), are an area requiring much further research (Markolf et al., 2019). Given the state of refinement and sophistication of the modern traffic network models, which now have the capability to simulate detailed network movements over time spans from hours to days, the opportunity now exists to explore the potential impacts of weather events, including extreme weather events on traffic movement and on travel demand. This opportunity is enhanced by the arrival of 'big data' for both transportation systems and for weather

1. While downscaling remains a difficult task, improved methods with wider applicability are being developed and promoted, e.g., see Brekke et al. (2013). Transportation agencies should be at the forefront in demanding the development and release of suitable downscaling tools and methods for their regions of concern. Austroads (2010) provides an early example of the use of downscaling methods to provide climate change scenarios for different regions in Australia. Olsen (2015) and Koetse and Rietveld (2012) argue the case for the necessity of downscaled climate forecasts for transportation agencies.

observations – research to integrate data from these disparate sources is now feasible. This issue was explored by Snelder and Calvert (2016), and Fig. 10.7 (previously presented as Fig. 7.15) provides a summary view of the impacts of climate change and extreme weather on the operations of road networks, including both direct impacts (weather-related degradation of operating conditions such as visibility and safe vehicle movement) and indirect impacts such as flooding, road closures and road crashes). Network performance models, including inputs from adaptation plans and measures, can be used to study these impacts and their effects on overall network performance and changes in travel demand.

To use these modelling tools effectively requires substantial research and development. In the first instance, data collection, collation and analysis at a large scale and in many places are needed to provide a thorough understanding of the ways in which weather events affect transportation network performance at present, and to infer how these events may affect network performance in the future. The optimal combination of traffic models/data and weather models/data needs to be ascertained to permit this process. Uncertainty is an issue requiring attention: given the uncertainties inherent in climate scenarios and in the extent to which weather events affect network capacity and travel demand – through both direct and indirect impacts (see Fig. 10.7) – the possible future ranges of network congestion levels and delays due to adverse weather may be very large, which will make it difficult to determine the potential value of adaptation strategies to society. Climate change is a long-term trend so that long-term considerations are paramount in adaptation planning. Given the indications that weather conditions now seen as extreme are likely to become more frequent in the future, be of longer duration and include more extremes than at present experienced, there will be growing needs to make assessments of the costs of extreme weather and the benefits possible from measures to adapt to the new climate. The modelling tools and resources for studies in this topic are now available; the need is for the research effort and support to undertake the studies and translate their results into useful information for use in transportation planning.

At the broader scale of relationships between climate and travel behaviour, Chapter 9 summarised some of the recent research in this field. Much of this research is focused on the use of active transportation modes. The reported studies tend to be individual case studies from a single city or region, sometimes with comparisons between cities (e.g., Bocker et al., 2019). The next stage should be research studies that build on the case studies and seek to set general principles and relationships that can be used by transportation planners more widely.

The transportation performance models discussed above are a necessary but not sufficient component in the general adaptation modelling methodology outlined in Fig. 10.6. These models provide detailed quantitative inputs for use in decision-making, but these inputs need to be applied in the context of the

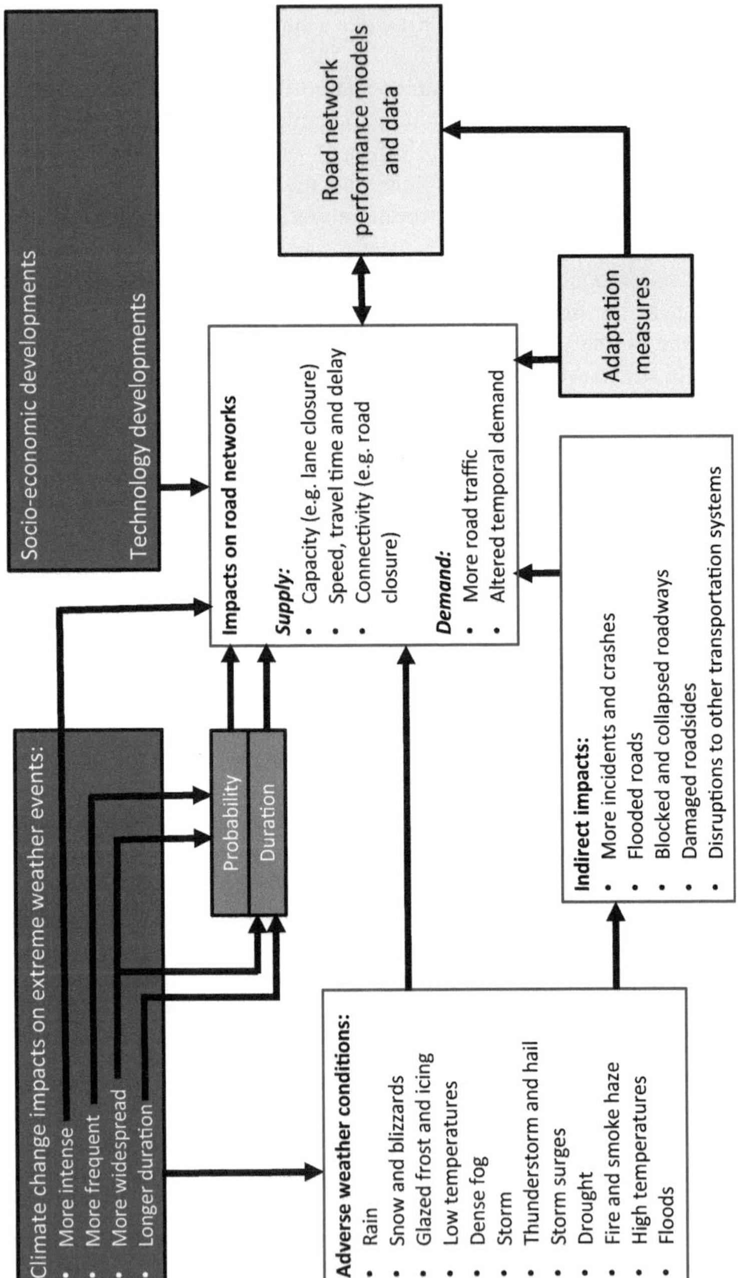

FIGURE 10.7 Relationships between extreme weather and road network performance. *(revised and extended from Snelder and Calvert (2016)).*

decision support tools discussed in Chapters 4 and 5 and summarised previously in this chapter. Ongoing research and experimentation is required with the decision support tools for their realistic use in adaptation planning. One indicator for the way forward is the recent work of Kim and Li (2020). This study used real options analysis to compare two options for a transportation corridor in the remote Northwest Territories of Canada. Historically river barges have been used for transportation along part of the corridor, but climate change is reducing the river navigation season for the barges, requiring increasing usage of air transportation as a replacement, driving increases in freight costs as a result. An alternative option is to construct an all-weather road along the corridor and so shift to road transportation. The issues considered by Kim and Li (2020) were thus the economic comparison of the two alternative transportation plans, and the optimal timing (if any) for the new road construction. The study took historical data for the period 1997–2017 and then forecast corridor performance for the 24 years (2018–41). The three-stage real options analysis approach adopted by Kim and Li is shown in Fig. 10.8.

Stage 1 involves the estimation of uncertain variable inputs. These are the forecasts of future 'open season days' (OSD), the number of days per annum available for river barge operations and the 'volatility' of the OSD (i.e., the variance of those days) under future climate scenarios. OSD numbers are estimated using a stochastic process simulated using geometric Brownian motion, details of which are given in Kim and Li (2020). Stage 2 of the process collates the expected benefits and costs of the two alternative options, including estimation of the expected costs of airlift as replacement for barge transportation. The output of this stage is the expected NPVs for the alternatives. Stage 3 uses the volatility in OSD along with the results of Stage 2 in a binomial lattice (decision tree) model to examine alternative timings for the road construction, and the effects of these timings on the NPV. The stage also yields probabilities for the results for the potential deferments of the road construction. Kim and Li (2020) described the modelling components involved in the analysis. The study concluded that the explicit incorporation of climate uncertainty into cost–benefit analyses through application of the real options approach led to significant changes in project NPV. The proposed framework (Fig. 10.8) could support flexible infrastructure decision-making by accounting for uncertain climate impacts. The key results of the study were that the decision to continue barging grew riskier (i.e., more expensive) from 1997 to 2017 and that this trend will continue for the next two decades. Stage 3 of the modelling process indicated that the road construction project should best be deferred for 9 years (i.e., until 2028). With the consideration of climate uncertainty, the benefit–cost ratio of the road construction project increased significantly towards feasibility at that time, and the option to delay construction allowed for this feasibility to be considered.

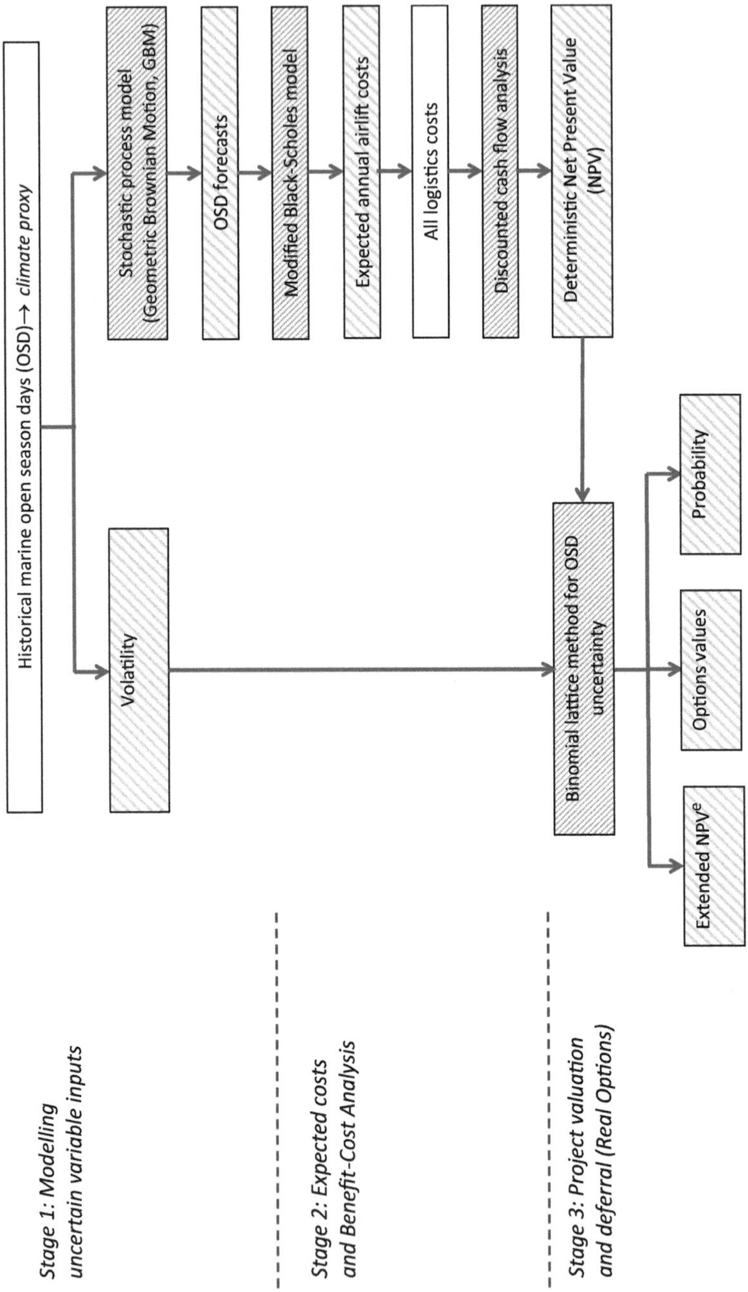

FIGURE 10.8 Real options modelling framework for the study by Kim and Li (2020).

The Kim-Li study provides a possible blueprint for other economic analyses of transportation infrastructure projects that seek to explore and account for the possible impacts of climate change.

The IPSS developed and used by Schweikert et al. (2014) is a decision support intended for use by transportation agencies to provide an holistic, long-term approach to the planning and management of transportation infrastructure and was explicitly designed to include climate change, along with considerations of environment and social impact as well as economic analysis. It incorporates quantitative and qualitative methods to product economic results, along with estimates of greenhouse gas emissions, travel time and cost savings and an indicator of the social impact of road construction. It was developed to offer an alternative to the traditional economic approaches (i.e., benefit—cost analysis and cost-effectiveness analysis) for road infrastructure projects, that

- Allows for the full realisation of development potential for road infrastructure, especially for developing countries and regions where social welfare an overall economic development is a primary concern and
- Accounts for climate change in long-term planning, and so reduces future vulnerability and risks of future costs and damage.

IPSS has found widespread application in both the developed world (e.g., the United States and Japan) and in the developing world (throughout Asia and Africa). Its emphasis is on an holistic systems approach to infrastructure decision-making for both short-term and long-term planning. As such, it provides another prototype for decision-making tools applicable under climate change and the accompanying uncertainties.

Moving forward

OECD (2018) offered a succinct argument for the necessity to include climate change adaptation in all considerations of infrastructure asset management and the planning and design of future infrastructure:

'New infrastructure assets should be prioritised, planned, designed, built and operated to account for the climate changes that may occur over their lifetimes. Existing infrastructure may need to be retrofitted, or managed differently, given climate change. Lastly, additional infrastructure, such as sea walls, will need to be constructed to address the physical impacts of climate change. This additional infrastructure can include traditional infrastructure, such as hard defences and other engineered solutions, as well as natural infrastructure, such as wetlands and other nature-based solutions' (OECD, 2018, Executive Summary).

This book attempts to add the detail for the necessity of considering climate change adaption in transportation and to offer a general review of existing and emerging methods for adaptation planning in transportation.

It is presented as a consolidated introduction to climate change adaptation for transportation professionals and is designed for a wide but interested audience comprising practitioners, policy analysts and policy makers, academics, researchers and above all the students, from whom will come the generations of professionals whose careers will be deeply involved in climate change adaptation. The author wishes those people all the success and good fortune that they will need in that work. We will depend on them.

References

ASCE, 2009. Guiding Principles for the Nation's Critical Infrastructure. American Society of Civil Engineers, Reston, VA. www.pubs.asce.org.

Austroads, 2010. Impact of Climate Change on Road Performance: Updating Climate Information for Australia. Austroads Report AP–R358/10. Austroads, Sydney.

Bles, T., Bessembinder, J., Chevreuil, M., Danielsson, P., Falemo, S., Venmans, A., Ennesser, Y., Lofroth, H., 2016. Climate change risl assessments and adaptation for roads – results of the ROADADAPT project. Transp. Res. Proced. 14, 58–67.

Bocker, L., Uteng, T.P., Liu, C., Dijst, M., 2019. Weather and daily mobility in international perspective: a cross-comparison of Dutch, Norwegian and Swedish city regions. Transp. Res. D: Transp. Environ. 77, 491–505.

Brekke, L., Thrasher, B.L., Maurer, E.P., Pruitt, T., 2013. Downscaled CMIP3 and CMIP5 Climate Projections: Release of Downscaled Cmip5 Climate Projections, Comparison with Preceding Information, and Summary of User Needs. http://gdo-dcp.ucllnl.org/downscaled_cmip_projections/. (Accessed 27 January 2020).

Chinowsky, P., Helman, J., Gulati, S., Neumann, J., Martinich, J., 2019. Impacts of climate change on operation of the US rail network. Transport Pol. 75, 183–191.

CoastAdapt, 2018. How to Conduct a Climate Change Risk Assessment. https://coastadapt.com.au/how-to-pages/how-to-conduct-a-climate-change-risk-assessment. (Accessed 29 February 2020).

FHWA, 2019. Vulnerability Assessment and Adaptation Framework, third ed. Federal Highways Administration, Washington DC https://www.fhwa.dot.gov/environment/sustainability/resilience/adaptation_framework/chap00.cfm.

IPCC, 2007. In: Solomon, S., Qin, D., Manning, M., Chen, Z., Marquis, M., Averyt, K.B., Tignor, M., Miller, H.L. (Eds.), Climate Change 2007: The Physical Science Basis. Contribution of Working Group I to the Fourth Assessment Report of the Intergovernmental Panel on Climate Change. Cambridge University Press, Cambridge, UK and New York, NY.

IPCC, 2013. Summary for policymakers. In: Stocker, T.F., Qin, D., Plattner, G.-K., Tignor, M., Allen, S.K., Boschung, J., Nauels, A., Xia, Y., Bex, V., Midgley, P.M. (Eds.), Climate Change 2013: The Physical Science Basis. Contribution of Working Group I to the Fifth Assessment Report of the Intergovernmental Panel on Climate Change. Cambridge University Press, Cambridge, UK and New York, NY.

IPCC, 2014a. In: Edenhofer, O., Pichs-Madruga, R., Sokona, Y., Farahani, E., Kadner, S., Seyboth, K., Adler, A., Baum, I., Brunner, S., Eickemeier, P., Kriemann, B., Savolainen, J., Schlömer, S., Von Stechow, C., Zwickel, T., Minx, J.C. (Eds.), Climate Change 2014: Mitigation of Climate Change. Contribution of Working Group III to the Fifth Assessment Report of the Intergovernmental Panel on Climate Change. Cambridge University Press, Cambridge, UK and New York, NY.

IPCC, 2014b. In: Field, C.B., Barros, V.R., Dokken, D.J., Mach, K.J., Mastrandrea, M.D., Bilir, T.E., Chatterjee, M., Ebi, K.L., Estrada, Y.O., Genova, R.C., Girma, B., Kissel, E.S., Levy, A.N., MacCracken, S., Mastrandrea, P.R., White, L.L. (Eds.), Climate Change 2014: Impacts, Adaptation, and Vulnerability. Part A: Global and Sectoral Aspects. Contribution of Working Group II to the Fifth Assessment Report of the Intergovernmental Panel on Climate Change. Cambridge University Press, Cambridge, UK and New York, NY.

ITF, 2016. Adapting Transport to Climate Change and Extreme Weather: Implications for Infrastructure Owners and Network Managers, ITF Research Reports. OECD Publishing, Paris. https://doi.org/10.1787/9789282108079-en.

Kim, A.M., Li, H., 2020. Incorporating the impacts of climate change in transportation infrastructure decision models. Transport. Res. Pol. Pract. 134, 271–287.

Knott, J.F., Elshaer, M., Danieal, J.S., Jacobs, J.M., Kirshen, P., 2017. Assessing the effects of rising groundwater from sea level rise on the service life of pavements in coastal road infrastructure. Transp. Res. Rec.: J. Transp. Res. Board 2639, 1–10.

Koetse, M.J., Rietveld, P., 2012. Adaptation to climate change in the transport sector. Transp. Rev. 32 (3), 267–286.

Markolf, S.A., Hoehne, C., Fraser, A., Chester, M.V., 2019. Transportation resilience to climate change and extreme weather events – beyond risk and robustness. Transp. Pol. 74, 174–186.

OECD, 2018. Climate-resilient Infrastructure. OECD Environment Policy Paper No 14. Organisation for Economic Cooperation and Development, Paris. http://www.oecd.org/environment/.

Olsen, J.R. (Ed.), 2015. Adapting Infrastructure and Civil Engineering Practice to a Changing Climate. American Society of Civil Engineers, Reston, VA. www.asce.org/publications.

PIARC, 2015. International climate change adaptation framework for road infrastructure, Report 2015RO3EN, World Road Association/Association Mondiale de la Route (PIARC). www.piarc.org.

Quinn, A., Jack, A., Hodgkinson, S., Ferranti, E., Beckford, J., Dora, J., 2017. RAIL ADAPT: Adapting the Railway for the Future. International Union of Railways (UIC), Paris.

Schweikert, A., Chinowsky, P., Kwiatkowski, K., Espinet, X., 2014. The infrastructure planning support system: analysing the impact of climate change on road infrastructure and development. Transp. Pol. 35, 146–153.

Scott, H., McEvoy, D., Chhetri, P., Basic, F., Mullett, J., 2013. Climate Change Adaptation Guidelines for Ports. Enhancing the Resilience of Seaports to a Changing Climate Report Series. National Climate Change Adaptation Research Facility, Gold Coast. www.nccarf.edu.au.

Snelder, M., Calvert, S., 2016. Quantifying the impact of adverse weather conditions on road network performance. Eur. J. Transp. Infrastruct. Res. 16 (1), 128–149.

Tavasszy, L., Bollinger, A., Dijkema, G.P.J., 2016. Editorial: special issue on climate adaptation of infrastructure networks. Eur. J. Transp. Infrastruct. Res. 16 (1), 95–97. www.tlo.tbm.tudelft.nl/ejtir.

Taylor, M.A.P., Philp, M.L., 2015. Investigating the impact of maintenance regimes on the design life of road pavements in a changing climate and the implications for transport policy. Transp. *Pol.* 41, 117–135.

Index

Note: 'Page numbers followed by "f" indicate figures and "t" indicate tables.'

D

E

F

S

T

U

V

W

FSC
www.fsc.org
MIX
Papier | Fördert gute Waldnutzung
FSC® C083411

Kolibri 360 GmbH
Ferdinand-Jühlke-Straße 7
99095 Erfurt, Deutschland
produktsicherheit@kolibri360.de